The Politics of
Public Budgeting

The Politics of Public Budgeting

Getting and Spending, Borrowing and Balancing

FIFTH EDITION

Irene S. Rubin
Northern Illinois University

CQ PRESS

A Division of Congressional Quarterly Inc.
Washington, D.C.

CQ Press
A Division of Congressional Quarterly Inc.
1255 22nd Street, NW, Suite 400
Washington, DC 20037

Phone: 202-729-1900; toll-free, 1-866-427-7737 (1-866-4CQ-PRESS)
Web: www.cqpress.com

Cover design: Naylor Design

☺ The paper used in this publication exceeds the requirements of the American
National Standard for Information Sciences—Permanence of Paper for Printed
Library Materials, ANSI Z39.48-1992.

Printed and bound in the United States of America

09 08 07 06 05   1 2 3 4 5

Library of Congress Cataloging-in-Publication Data

Rubin, Irene.
   The politics of public budgeting / Irene S. Rubin.-- 5th ed.
     p. cm.
   Includes index.
   ISBN 1-933116-06-4 (alk. paper)
   1. Local budgets—Political aspects—United States. 2. Budget—Political
aspects—United States. I. Title.
   HJ9147.R83 2006
   336.73--dc22

                            2005020863

Contents

List of Tables, Figures, and Minicases   ix
Preface   xi
Acknowledgments   xv

1. The Politics of Public Budgets   1

What Is Budgeting?   3
Governmental Budgeting   6
   Minicase: Highly Constrained Budgeting—Colorado's TABOR
      Amendment   8
   Minicase: City Manager Replies to Scathing Budget Critique   10
   Minicase: The Government Performance and Results Act   21
   Minicase: Doctoring Audit Reports   24
   Minicase: Unfunded Mandates—No Child Left Behind   26
The Meaning of Politics in Public Budgeting   28
Budgetary Decision Making   30
Microbudgeting and Macrobudgeting   33
Summary and Conclusions   36

2. Revenue Politics   37

Raising Taxes   38
   Minicase: Alabama Governor's $1.2 Billion Tax Increase Defeated   39
   Minicase: A Successful Municipal Tax Increase in Dayton, Ohio   41

The Politics of Protection   46
    Minicase: Tax Expenditures and the Battle over Offsets   58
    Minicase: Boeing and Washington State   61
    Minicase: Iowa—How a Tax Incentive Program Was Terminated   64
    Minicase: State Tax Break Prohibitions and Evasion   69
The Politics of Reform   71
Summary and Conclusions   73

3. The Politics of Process   75

Budget Process and the Characteristics of Public Budgeting   76
Macro and Micro Politics   78
    Minicase: Republican Macro-Level Reform Proposals   79
    *Minicase: Micro Politics—Bending the Rules to Win
    Individual Decisions*   83
Designing Process to Achieve Policy and Political Goals   85
    Minicase: How the Governor's Veto Is Used   90
Variation between and among Federal, State, and
    Local Governments   93
Summary and Conclusions   101

4. The Dynamics of Changing Budget Processes   102

Overview   103
    *Minicase: New York State and Pressure to Change the
    Formal Rules*   104
Major Changes in the Federal Budget Process   107
    Minicase: Ad Hoc Scoring Rules   118
Changes in Budget Process at the State Level   120
    Minicase: Maryland's Legislative Budget Power   121
    *Minicase: Nevada—Legislative Access to Agency
    Budget Requests*   125
    *Minicase: The Executive and the Legislature in
    Florida's Budgeting*   126
Changes in Budget Process at the Local Level   131
    Minicase: Florida and Unfunded Mandates   138
Summary and Conclusions   143

5. Expenditures: The Politics of Choice   145

Strategies of Agency Heads or Program Directors   147
    *Minicase: The Department of Housing and Urban Development and
    Boutique Programs*   155

Minicase: The Economic Development Administration Uses
  Defense Funds 158
Top-Down Strategies 159
  Minicase: Federal Trust Funds 162
  Minicase: Calculating the Base in St. Paul, 2005 170
  Minicase: Black Project Failure—The A-12 Navy Fighter
    Plane 176
The Environment Can Affect Spending Priorities 180
  Minicase: The Aviation Trust Fund 181
Analysis: Accountability and Acceptability 183
Summary and Conclusions 184

6. **The Politics of Balancing the Budget** 187

Balance as a Constraint 189
Multiple Actors, Ideologies, and Deficits 190
  Minicase: Balance in the Federal Highway Trust Fund 191
The Environment, Unpredictability, and Deficits 194
Increasing Stress between Payer and Decider 196
The Politics of Deficits: The Federal Level 200
Deficits in the States 209
  Minicase: Wisconsin Confronts Deficits 210
The Politics of Balance in Cities 223
  Minicase: The Politics of Deficits—An Urban Example 225
Summary and Conclusions 228

7. **Budget Execution: The Politics of Adaptation** 230

Tools for Changing the Budget 233
  Minicase: Reprogramming in the Department of Defense 244
Summary and Conclusions 247

8. **Budget Implementation and Control** 249

The Discretion-Abuse-Control Cycle 249
  Minicase: Abuse and Controls at the Department of Defense 253
  Minicase: Massachusetts Overcontrols the Cities, 1875–1933 260
Discretion and Control: The Politics of Finding Waste,
  Fraud, and Abuse 262
  Minicase: Homeland Security Inspector General Not Renewed 263
  Minicase: Tension at the CIA 267
Summary and Conclusions 280

9. **Budgetary Decision Making and Politics** **281**

Real-Time Budgeting 281
A Comparison of the Decision-Making Streams 285
Common Themes 286
Reconceptualizing Reform 294
Avenues for Research 297
Summary and Conclusions 300

Notes 302

Name Index 321

Subject Index 323

List of Tables, Figures, and Minicases

Tables

2.1   Estimated Total Revenue Loss from Tax Expenditures,
        FY 1988–2004   52
2.2   Federal Tax Expenditures as Percentages of Income Tax Receipts,
        FY 1988–2003   53
2.3   Estimated Costs of State Circuit Breaker Programs   66
2.4   States' Losses from Homestead Exemptions   67
6.1   Federal Surpluses and Deficits, 1940–2005   201
7.1   Supplemental Appropriations, Net of Rescissions, 1970s,
        1980s, 1990s   235
7.2   Discretionary Supplemental Spending, 2002–2005   236
8.1   State Inspector General Systems   274

Figure

1.1   Decision Making: Environment, Process, and Strategies   33

Minicases

Highly Constrained Budgeting—Colorado's TABOR Amendment   8
City Manager Replies to Scathing Budget Critique   10
The Government Performance and Results Act   21
Doctoring Audit Reports   24
Unfunded Mandates—No Child Left Behind   26
Alabama Governor's $1.2 Billion Tax Increase Defeated   39

A Successful Municipal Tax Increase in Dayton, Ohio   41
Tax Expenditures and the Battle over Offsets   58
Boeing and Washington State   61
Iowa—How a Tax Incentive Program Was Terminated   64
State Tax Break Prohibitions and Evasion   69
Republican Macro-Level Reform Proposals   79
Micro Politics—Bending the Rules to Win Individual Decisions   83
How the Governor's Veto Is Used   90
New York State and Pressure to Change the Formal Rules   104
Ad Hoc Scoring Rules   118
Maryland's Legislative Budget Power   121
Nevada—Legislative Access to Agency Budget Requests   125
The Executive and the Legislature in Florida's Budgeting   126
Florida and Unfunded Mandates   138
The Department of Housing and Urban Development and
     Boutique Programs   155
The Economic Development Administration Uses Defense Funds   158
Federal Trust Funds   162
Calculating the Base in St. Paul, 2005   170
Black Project Failure—The A-12 Navy Fighter Plane   176
The Aviation Trust Fund   181
Balance in the Federal Highway Trust Fund   191
Wisconsin Confronts Deficits   210
The Politics of Deficits—An Urban Example   225
Reprogramming in the Department of Defense   244
Abuse and Controls at the Department of Defense   253
Massachusetts Overcontrols the Cities, 1875–1933   260
Homeland Security Inspector General Not Renewed   263
Tension at the CIA   267

Preface

Explaining budgeting in the United States is like painting the proverbial moving train. Just when you think you have captured it, it moves on, not only presenting a new set of problems to describe but also upending some prior conclusions. Since the fourth edition of *The Politics of Public Budgeting* was published in 2000 much has changed. At the national level, balanced budgets were replaced within a couple of years by increasing and now massive deficits, aided by the terrorist attacks of 9/11 in New York and near Washington, D.C., and by the wars in Iraq and Afghanistan. What appeared to be a fairly steady trend toward openness and transparency in budgeting has been reversed in favor of more secrecy, budget gimmickry, and obscurantism. The ongoing practice of contracting out has accelerated at the national level and in some states, but budgeting has not caught up with contracts, so large chunks of spending now occur with little transparency or accountability. The budget process at the national level has fallen on hard times, as Congress first ignored the Budget Enforcement Act requirements, after balance was achieved, and then failed to renew the law when it expired in 2002. The erosion of the budget process, combined with the rapid growth of deficits, has renewed interest in the relationship between budget process and budget outcomes.

Some issues remain the same, however. At the federal level, the president and Congress have postponed the worst consequences of current tax cuts, laying booby traps for future elected officials. This tendency to delay the negative consequences of present actions was apparent when the fourth edition was being prepared, as well. The discretion-abuse-control cycle described in prior editions is still very much in evidence, with more states adopting or expanding their inspector general systems, especially in response to scandals. At the same time, the independence of the IGs remains a lively and contentious issue.

As with the prior editions, this book is peppered with real-life cases. Many of the older cases have been dropped or updated and new ones added. For example, there is a case describing the Colorado TABOR amendment, the so-called taxpayer bill of rights, which has limited state revenue and sets a new, lower base during recessions, so that the state cannot easily catch up to prerecession levels even when the economy recovers. The case of the shifting of power between the executive and legislative branches in Florida has been updated. There is a new case that illustrates the impact of contracting on accountability, in which a federal government contractor was allowed to redact elements of an audit report that were unflattering. For those who enjoy following the politics of tax breaks, there is a new case on Washington State and Boeing. The states' response to the federal No Child Left Behind mandate is detailed in one of the cases as well.

This fifth edition, like prior ones, includes federal, state, and local budgeting and where possible casts them in a comparative framework. Unlike prior editions, however, this one emphasizes the intergovernmental relations—the federalism issues—that frame financial policy and budgeting at all levels of government. The federal structure was assumed in prior editions, but many students were unfamiliar with the theory of federalism or how it works in practice; hence this edition is much more explicit about the legal context, the constraints, and the politics of taking the revenue sources of other government entities and attempting to pass on the burden of expensive programs. Moreover, since the last edition, the relationships among federal, state, and local governments have been lively. With the return of deficits at the national level, and as states deal with recession and structural deficits, the issue of unfunded mandates has returned with exclamation points. The federal government has tried to shift expenditures to the states, and the states have tried in some cases to pass along expenses to the local governments or capture the local governments' revenue sources. The National Council of State Legislatures has brought its old unfunded mandates monitor back to life, to estimate and make visible the costs the federal government is imposing on the states. The states have energetically protested the mandates imposed on them by the No Child Left Behind Act. And cities and counties are contending with state tax limits, on the one hand, and unfunded or underfunded mandates on the other. One wonders how local governments will cope with these opposing pressures. Do it, says the state, but we are not giving you the money to do it, and you may not raise taxes to pay for it.

I have been very lucky to have been able to monitor the same issues over time and watch new ones evolve, because the story of public budgeting does not take place in a year or two. The locking and unlocking processes take place over decades and sometimes over generations. The delaying of negative consequences to later years means that the whole story can only be told in retrospect. My hope is that more of the story can now be told and that the explanations are becoming richer and more accurate with each edition. This book is about how processes play out over the long term, the dynamics of cycles, and the tenuous equilibria that are sometimes achieved. Budgeting is, after all, adaptive to the environment, and that means the story is always changing. The best we can hope for is to capture the underlying mechanisms that explain and predict these changes.

Acknowledgments

What an assignment, to think of all the people I owe gratitude to and thank them, in a relatively short space.

One creates many obligations when writing and publishing a book, to those who do their job well and, beyond that, do it with good grace and real friendship.

I am grateful for the continued support and assistance of the wonderful editorial and production team at CQ Press. I am delighted to work with them.

I want to thank my husband for his endless curiosity when I tell him about the examples I have tracked down and how I interpret them, and for his continuing support at keeping my computer running free of viruses and worms and thieves in the night.

Most important, though, I am grateful for the work of dozens of scholars and probably hundreds of practitioners and even more journalists. Key staff members in professional associations also provided data for the book. In particular, I would like to acknowledge Roy Meyers, who kept me up to date on issues of gubernatorial and legislative powers in Maryland; Karen Stanford, who helped me follow budgeting in Florida; and my student, Brian Frederick, who provided research assistance on federal tax expenditures and on state inspectors general.

More generally, I would like to thank all my colleagues in budgeting, whether they are practitioners or academics, who make intellectual dialogue possible; who regularly teach each other and me, as well as their students, and who make real the ideals of an intellectual community.

1. The Politics of Public Budgets

Public budgets describe what governments do by listing how they spend money. A budget links tasks to be performed with the amount of resources necessary to accomplish those tasks, ensuring that money will be available to wage war, provide housing, or maintain streets. Budgets limit expenditures to the revenues available, to ensure balance and prevent overspending. Most of the work in drawing up a budget is technical, such as estimating how much it will cost to feed a thousand shut-ins with a Meals-on-Wheels program or how much revenue a 1 percent tax on retail sales will produce. But public budgets are not merely technical, managerial documents; they are also intrinsically and appropriately political.

- Budgets reflect choices about what government will and will not do. They reflect the general public consensus about what kinds of services governments should provide and what citizens are entitled to as members of society. Should government provide services that the private sector could provide, such as water, electricity, transportation, and housing? Do all citizens have a guarantee of health care, regardless of ability to pay? Are all insured against hunger? Is everyone entitled to some kind of housing?
- Budgets reflect priorities—between police and flood control, day care and defense, the Northeast and the Southwest. The budget process mediates among groups and individuals who want different things from government and determines who gets what. These decisions may influence whether the poor get job training or the police get riot training—either one a response to an increased number of unemployed.

- Budgets reflect the relative proportion of decisions made for local and constituency purposes, and for efficiency, effectiveness, and broader public goals. Budgets reflect the degree of importance that legislators place on satisfying their constituents and the legislators' willingness to listen to interest group demands. For example, the Defense Department may decide to spend more money to keep a military base open because the local economy depends on it, and to spend less money to improve combat readiness.
- Budgets provide a powerful tool of accountability for citizens who want to know how the government is spending their money and whether government has generally followed their preferences. Budgeting links citizen preferences and governmental outcomes; it is a powerful tool for the implementation of democracy.
- Budgets reflect citizens' preferences for different forms and different levels of taxation, as well as the ability of some groups of taxpayers to shift tax burdens to others. The budget indicates the degree to which the government redistributes wealth upward or downward through the tax system.
- At the national level, the budget influences the economy, and so fiscal policy affects the level of employment—how many people are out of work at any time.
- Budgets reflect the relative power of different individuals and organizations to influence outcomes. Budgetary decision making provides a picture of the relative power of budget actors within and between branches of government, as well as of the importance of citizens in general and specific interest groups.

In all these ways, public budgeting is political. But budgeting is not typical of other political processes; it is not just one example among many. It is both an important and a unique arena of politics. It is important because of the specific policy decisions it reflects: decisions about the scope of government, the distribution of wealth, the openness of government to interest groups, and the accountability of government to the public at large. It is unique because these decisions have to take place in the context of budgeting, with its need for balance, its openness to the environment, and its requirement for timely decisions so that government can carry on without interruption.

Public budgets clearly have political implications, but what does it mean to say that key political decisions are made in the context of budgeting? The answer has several parts: First, What is budgeting? Second, What is public budgeting, as opposed to individual or family budgeting or the budgeting of private organizations? Third, What does *political* mean in the context of public budgeting?

What Is Budgeting?

The essence of budgeting is that it allocates scarce resources, implying choices among potential expenditures. Budgeting implies balance, and it requires some kind of decision-making process.

Making Budgetary Choices

All budgeting, whether public or private, individual or organizational, involves choices between possible expenditures. Since no one has unlimited resources, people budget all the time. A child makes a budget (a plan for spending, balancing revenues and expenditures) when she decides to spend money on a marshmallow rabbit rather than a chocolate one, assuming she has money enough for only one rabbit. The air force may choose between two different airplanes to replace current bombers. These examples illustrate the simplest form of budgeting because they involve only one actor, one resource, one time, and two straightforward and comparable choices.

Normally, budgeting does not compare only two reasonably similar items. There may be a nearly unlimited number of choices. Budgeting usually limits the options requiring consideration by grouping together similar things that can be reasonably compared. When I go to the supermarket, I do not compare all the possible things I could buy, not only because I cannot absorb that number of comparisons, but because the comparisons would be meaningless and a waste of time. I do not go to the supermarket and decide to get either a turkey or a bottle of soda pop. I compare main dishes with main dishes, beverages with beverages, desserts with desserts. This gives me a common denominator for comparison. For example, I may look at the main course and ask about the amount of protein for the dollar. I may compare the desserts in terms of the amount of cholesterol or the calories.

There is a tendency, then, to make comparisons within categories where the comparison is meaningful. This is as true for governmental budgeting as it is for shoppers. For example, weapons might be compared with weapons or automobiles with automobiles. They could be compared in terms of speed, reliability, and availability of spare parts, and the one that did the most of what you wanted it to do at the least cost would be the best choice. As long as there is agreement on the goals to be achieved, the choice should be straightforward.

Sometimes budgeting requires comparison of different, seemingly incomparable things. If I do not have enough money to buy a whole, balanced meal, I may have to make choices between main dishes and desserts. How do I compare the satisfaction of a sweet tooth with the nourishment of turkey? Or, in the public sector, how do I compare the benefits of providing shelters for the homeless with buying more helicopters for the navy? I may then move to more general comparisons, such as how clearly the requests were made and the benefits spelled out; who received the benefits last time and whose turn is it this time. Are there any specific contingencies that make one choice more likely than the other? For example, will the country be embarrassed to show our treatment of the homeless in front of a visiting dignitary? Or are disarmament negotiations coming up, in which we need to display strength or make a symbolic gesture of restraint? Comparing dissimilar items may require a list of priorities. It may be possible to do two or more important things if they are sequenced properly.

Budgeting often allocates money, but it can allocate any scarce resource, for example, time. A student may choose between studying for an exam and playing softball and drinking beer afterward. In this example, it is time that is at a premium, not money. It could be medical skills that are in short supply, or expensive equipment, or apartment space, or water.

Government programs often involve a choice of resources and sometimes involve combinations of resources, each of which has different characteristics. For example, some federal farm programs involve direct cash payments plus loans at below-market interest rates, and welfare programs often involve dollar payments plus food stamps, which allow recipients to pay less for food. Federal budgets often assign agencies money, personnel, and sometimes borrowing authority, three different kinds of resources.

Balancing and Borrowing

Budgets have to balance. A plan for expenditures that pays no attention to ensuring that revenues cover expenditures is not a budget. That may sound odd in view of the huge federal deficits we have become used to, but a budget may technically be balanced by borrowing. Balance means only that outgo is matched or exceeded by income. Borrowing means spending more now and paying more in the future, when the debt has to be paid off. It is a balance over time.

To illustrate the nature of budget balance, consider me as shopper again. Suppose I spend all my weekly shopping money before I buy my dessert. I have the option of treating my dollar limit as if it were more flexible, by adding the dimension of time. I can buy the dessert and everything else in the basket, going over my budget, and then eat less at the end of the month. Or I can pay the bill with a credit card, assuming I will have more money in the future with which to pay off the bill when it comes due. The possibility of borrowing against the future is part of most budget choices.

The following brief example illustrates that time is an important dimension of budgeting, whether one is considering formal borrowing or adopting projects now and committing future revenues to pay for them. In the example, a lobbyist for the university is speaking about funding alternatives likely to be used to pay for a project favored by the board of higher education:

> *Lobbyist*: The Board of Higher Education has an initiative that they would like to put forth during the veto session for $2 million for planning funds for this University Center in Lake County. Whether or not they will be successful in putting that forward will depend on if there is a supplemental budget bill for capital items, and if they can get their issue into that [supplemental] budget, which is tricky. I think that if there is no budget opportunity [through the supplemental], they will try to move forward on the Lake County issue [anyway. . . . they are very committed to it. There are $2 million of planning funds. I would expect that they will fund the planning funds and/or the $10 million construction funds out of next year's fiscal year 2000 higher education capital list. If they do not get the planning money [out of this year's supplementals], then they will probably just fund the planning money out of next year's budget and take the other $8 million out the following year. But they are very, very committed to moving forward on this.[1]

Process

Budgeting cannot proceed without some kind of decision process. The process determines who will have a say and at what point in the decision making, and it frames the decisions that have to be made. Budget process typically involves estimates of revenues and limits on expenditures; it structures the comparisons among alternatives, and it regulates the flow of decisions to see that they are made in proper order and in a timely way.

Back to my shopping example: If I shop for the main course first, and spend more money than I intended on it because I found some fresh fish, there will be less money left for purchasing the dessert. Hence, unless I set a firm limit on the amount of money to spend for each segment of the meal, the order in which I do the purchasing counts. Of course, if I get to the end of my shopping and do not have enough money left for dessert, I can put back some of the items already in the cart and squeeze out enough money for dessert.

Governmental budgeting is also concerned with procedures for managing trade-offs between large categories of spending. Budgeters may determine the relative importance of each category first, attaching a dollar level in proportion to the assigned importance, or they may allow purchasing in each area to go on independently, later reworking the choices until the balance between the parts is acceptable.

The order of decisions is important in another sense. I can first determine how much money I am likely to have, and then set that as an absolute limit on expenditures, or I can determine what I must have, what I wish to have, and what I need to set aside for emergencies, and then go out and try to find enough money to cover some or all of those expenditures. Especially in emergencies, such as accidents or illnesses, people are likely to obligate the money first and worry about where it will come from later. Governmental budgeting, too, may concentrate first on revenues and later on expenditures, or first on expenditures and later on income. Like individuals or families, during emergencies such as floods or hurricanes or wars governments will commit the expenditures first and worry about where the money will come from later.

Governmental Budgeting

Public budgeting shares many of the characteristics of budgeting in general but differs from personal and business budgeting in some key ways:

1. In public budgeting there are a variety of participants, who have different priorities and different levels of power over the outcome. In family and business budgeting there may be only one key actor or a few, and they may have similar views of what they want the budget to achieve.

2. Generally speaking, individuals and small business owners spend their own money, not someone else's. In governmental budgeting, elected officials spend citizens' money, not their own. Public officials can force on citizens expenditures they do not want, but citizens can vote the politicians out of office. Consequently, public officials try not to stray too far from what they think the public wants. Because of the variety of budgetary actors and demands, however, there is no single set of demands to follow. To create enough coherence to guide decisions, budget processes in the public sector involve the negotiation of consent among representatives of competing groups and interests.

3. Because elected officials make spending decisions for citizens, accountability is an important part of public budgeting. The budget document helps explain to the public how its money was spent. That document is necessarily public, unlike business budgets, and may be the focus of public controversy if citizens do not like what they see or do not fully understand it.

4. Public budgets are planned well in advance of the beginning of the fiscal year and are intended to last a whole year or even two years. Many changes can occur over that period of time—in the economy, in public opinion, in political coalitions, in the weather. Public budgets need to be able to respond to such events during the year without major policy changes. If the deals that were necessary to prepare the budget come undone during budget implementation, budget actors will lose their trust in the process. Private sector budgets are more flexible: they can be remade from week to week or month to month, and policy changes can be adopted at any time. Private sector budgets are not designed to last unchanged for eighteen months or more. Moreover, private sector budgets are less open to pressures from the outside, from public opinion or frequent changes in elected officials.

5. Public budgets are incredibly constrained compared with those in the private sector. There are often rules about the purposes for which revenue can be spent and the time frame in which it can be spent, as well as requirements for balance and limits on borrowing. Capital projects may require public referendums for approval, and taxation growth may be limited to the inflation rate unless citizens approve higher rates in a referendum. Other levels of government may impose spending requirements or limit the forms of taxation permitted. Past agreements may control spending levels or result in tax sharing with other jurisdictions. Courts may play a role in budgeting, telling jurisdictions what they may tax or how their budget process may or may not change. Rather than one bottom line, which is the business model, government agencies may have multiple bottom lines, each of which must balance. Many elements of public budgeting are beyond the control of those who draw up the budget (see Minicase, page 8).

The minicase concerning the DeKalb budget (see box on page 10) should give the reader a feel for governmental budgeting and some of the ways it differs from personal or business budgeting. One key feature of public budgeting is an ongoing, not always courteous, dialogue between opponents and supporters, because no matter how many interests are served by a budget, some claimants will feel they did not get all they wanted or all that they had in a previous budget. Detractors often make public charges against the budget, and budgeters, equally publicly, defend it. Public budgets represent some compromises between interpretations of the public interest and narrower definitions of individual or group interests, compromises that are always open to interpretation and debate. The very openness of budgeting in a democracy and the constant criticism and

**Minicase: Highly Constrained Budgeting—Colorado's
                     TABOR Amendment**

Beginning in 2001 a recession, or economic slowdown, affected many
states, including Colorado. However, Colorado's problem was compounded by a combination of prior constraints. One constraint, called the
Taxpayers' Bill of Rights, or TABOR, limited the revenue the state could
collect in a year to the previous year's ceiling, plus a factor for population
growth and inflation. A second major constraint, called Amendment 23,
was passed in 2000. Amendment 23 requires the state to increase spending
on K-12 education by the inflation rate plus 1 percent every year through
2010, and by the rate of inflation thereafter. These two laws, when combined with declines in the rate of population growth and in the state's
major growth industries, required deep cuts in services other than K-12
education.

TABOR is a set of constitutional provisions passed in 1992 as a way to
prevent government from growing and to keep tax levels down. It requires
any revenue collected over the legal ceiling to be returned automatically to
the taxpayers. Rather than keeping the size of the government budget stable, however, TABOR has had a notorious ratchet effect: The base on which
maximum allowable tax revenue is calculated drops with recessions, and the
provisions in the constitution make it impossible for the state either to
recover former revenue levels or provide a substantial rainy day fund to
buffer against recession revenue losses. Any new or increased taxes must
be approved by the public in a referendum, and such proposals have been
routinely rejected.

While TABOR cut revenues, Amendment 23 increased expenses, but
only in one, highly popular program—public elementary and secondary
education. With declining revenues and mandated increases in a major portion of the budget, state officials were forced to cut other areas of the budget deeply. What made this vise so difficult to escape is that TABOR had
strong Republican support, and Amendment 23 had strong Democratic
support, and neither party was willing to compromise.

As often happens when budget constraints in the public sector become
extreme and the political process is stalemated with respect to reforming
those constraints, the short-term solution has been to exempt one of the
major budget losers, public higher education, from the constraints. Thus
the state university was made into an enterprise, allowing it to raise tuition
and fees and exempting it from the TABOR limits. This result means, how-

(continued)

ever, that the state system is becoming privatized, with increased tuition and fees that will reduce access to higher education in the state.[1]

1. John C. Ensslin, "Legislative Panel Gives CU New Status to Raise Tuition," *Rocky Mountain News,* August 25, 2004.

frequent misinterpretation or lack of understanding of the issues tempt politicians and budgeteers to try to avoid explaining the constraints they work under. Sometimes, though, they do respond to attacks.

The Dekalb story of charges against, and defenses of, municipal budgeting practices illustrates a number of themes in public budgeting. First, the venue of the debate was the local newspaper. The issues were complex, and the newspaper was trying to explain them to the public, but it was not being an impartial observer or educator. The newspaper editor was being given stories that sounded realistic and were supported by some evidence in the budget, but he did not dig deeper. The result was the kind of muffled communication that is common in public budgeting.

Public officials often think they are giving clear signals on the budget and are puzzled by citizen responses. The budget can be harder to explain than elected officials imagine. Public budgeting is complex and rule bound, whereas political dialogue is simple, simplifying, and sometimes biased. Accountability does not happen by itself; budgets do not wade into crowds and draw around them circles of admiring readers. Budgets have to be interpreted, and someone has to tell a good story to get the readers involved. This is where newspapers come in, but reporters are not necessarily knowledgeable, and newspapers are not necessarily neutral.

Another theme that emerges from the DeKalb minicase is that the former mayor and manager were still playing political roles, albeit indirect ones. Nearly all new administrations have to run against their predecessors. They come into office and find a mess and try to clean it up. If they get started without a process of reckoning, they are likely to be blamed for the financial mistakes of their predecessors who, as in this case, may have run down fund balances and put off expenditures until the next administration. The inherited budget may be boobytrapped in a variety of ways, precisely because time is an element in budgeting, and expenditures can be put off or revenue moved up.

Prior administrations may still be around to find fault, hoping to return to office, and other potential electoral rivals can play a similar role, picking the

Minicase: City Manager Replies to Scathing Budget Critique

DeKalb, Illinois, has a council-manager form of government with an active, policy-oriented mayor. One mayor, who favored business development and expansion, sometimes at the expense of the existing residents and neighborhoods, was defeated by a candidate who advocated balance between new development and existing neighborhoods. Not long after the new mayor and a new manager took office, the local newspaper ran an editorial excoriating the new manager for his fiscal practices. The editorial was filled with innuendo, exaggeration, and outright mistakes.

The newspaper's criticism of the new manager's financial management was a thinly disguised effort to discredit the new administration and its policies of balanced growth. The editorial reflected loyalty to the former mayor and longing for the "good old days." It argued that taxes and fees were growing, that the city was trying to build too large a fund balance (demonstrating unnecessary taxation), and that it was unclear where the increased revenues were going other than into the fund balance. The editorial further charged that the former administration had run a tight ship and that the city was in good financial shape when the new mayor took over, but that now staff were resigning and were not being replaced, reportedly to save money. The implied point was that the new manager and mayor were fouling things up.

The new manager responded with a letter to the editor. In his reply, he pointed out that the previous manager's instructions to the department heads had acknowledged that there was too little reserve in the fund balance to provide the necessary margin of safety and that spending cuts would have to be made during the year to improve the situation. The new manager also noted that before he came on board, the city had hired three new policemen in anticipation of the opening of a new discount mall, which had canceled out. That hiring had been done in the middle of the year, with costs that would balloon in the first full year of the new administration. In other words, the manager had inherited a situation that needed to be fixed. The city finances had not been so fine when he began his term.

As for the revenue increases, property taxes in the town were near long-term averages, but they had to be increased over recent lows because of state-mandated expenditures that the city had no control over. The yield from sales taxes had indeed gone up, but the increases were obligated to the Tax Increment Financing District, a district formed a number of years earlier to fund economic development, and to other units of government through existing intergovernmental agreements. The actual amount of sales

(continued)

tax revenue going into the general fund was decreasing, not increasing, so there was no puzzle about where the increased revenue was going, contrary to what the newspaper editorial had said.

Finally, the editorial had correctly pointed out that the city had increased the fees levied on developers to pay the present and future costs of growth. The new administration's goal was for growth to fund itself, rather than be subsidized by the existing community residents. The manager argued that such policies were common, not only elsewhere in the country, but in the neighboring cities with which DeKalb was competing. This fee policy symbolized the policy difference between the current and previous administrations.

budget apart, making normal decisions look odd, emphasizing projects that have not been completed or that came in over estimated costs. Taxpayer groups may also continually pick apart the budget in highly public situations, from their own somewhat narrow points of view. Politics thus infiltrates budgeting whenever the budget goes public. Budgeteers have to stay alert to the political implications of their actions and the implications of politics for their actions. Keeping governmental finances afloat can be difficult when others are intentionally rocking the boat. There can be great temptation to keep parts of the budget obscure to prevent massive criticism from political opponents.

The attack and defense of the DeKalb budget made clear that there is policy in the budget, not just technical decisions about the timing of debt or the the property tax rate. The editorial was wrong in some of its charges, but it was right in noting the increase in fees for developers. These fees were not just a way of balancing the budget; they reflected a judgment about who should pay for government and who should benefit from public spending. In this case, the former mayor had implemented a policy whereby all residents paid for growth. He claimed that everyone benefited, but it seemed likely that developers and new businesses benefited disproportionately compared with existing residents and businesses. In many cities, growth is highly subsidized, often by citizens who do not benefit directly from it and who might prefer that additional growth not take place. In DeKalb, the citizens were asked in a political campaign precisely whether they wanted to continue to subsidize growth, and they said no, voting to change mayors to change the existing policy. If elected officials drift too far in their policies from what the citizens wish, they are likely to be turned out of office at the next opportunity.

The manager's letter to the editor made clear that public budgeting is constrained—by other levels of government (through prior agreements to earmark tax increases and by state-mandated expenditures) and by competition with surrounding jurisdictions. The manager defended the charging of fees to developers by noting that surrounding towns were doing the same thing, so the community would not lose development by charging a fee.

The point of the minicase is that public officials must not only do the right thing for the community and follow the public will, as best they understand what that is, but also figure out a way to explain and justify their choices. They are engaged in a dialogue in which there are always other arguments, whose advocates represent legitimate interests. Equally important, engaging in this dialogue is a way of getting the public involved and getting across information about budgetary decisions in a way that people can understand.

In sum, public budgeting is necessarily and legitimately different from personal and business budgeting. It is not only that the budget is fought out in public but that it involves a variety of actors with different perspectives and interests. Moreover, those who make the decisions about spending are not the ones who actually pay the bills, and that fact introduces problems of responsiveness of elected officials and accountability to the public. More than personal or business budgets, public budgets are highly constrained, surrounded by rules, and hence somewhat rigid, while at the same time open to, and necessarily influenced by, changes in the environment.

A Variety of Actors

The variety of actors involved in the budget have different and often clashing motivations and goals. On a regular basis bureau chiefs, executive budget officers, and chief executives are involved in the budget process, as are legislators, both on committees and as a whole group. Interest groups may be involved at intervals, sometimes for relatively long stretches of time, sometimes briefly. Sometimes citizens play a direct or indirect role in the budget process. Courts may play a role in budgets at any level of government at unpredictable intervals. When they do play a role in budgetary decisions, what are these actors trying to achieve?

Bureau Chiefs. Many students of budgeting assume that agency heads always want to expand their agencies, that their demands are almost limitless, and that it is up to other budget actors to limit their demands. The reasons given for that desire for expansion include prestige and the acquisition of more subordinates, more space, larger desks, more secretaries, and not incidentally, more salary. The argument presumes that agency heads judge their bureaucratic skills by the extent to which their budget requests are satisfied. Successful bureaucrats bring back the budget. Agency expansion is the measure of success.

Some bureaucrats may indeed be motivated by salaries, but many feel that one of their major rewards is the opportunity to do good for people—to house the homeless, feed the hungry, find jobs for the unemployed, and send out checks to the disabled.[2] For these bureaucrats, efforts to expand agency budgets come from their belief in the programs they work for. The professionalization of the bureaucracy introduces another possible motivation: the desire to put in the best machinery that exists or build the biggest, toughest engineering project or the most complicated weapons.

Not only are the motivations for growth more varied and less selfish than the initial model suggests, but agency heads do not always push for expanded budgets. Sometimes agency heads refuse to expand when given the opportunity,[3] suggesting there are some countervailing values to growth.

One of those countervailing values is agency autonomy. Administrators may prefer to maintain autonomy rather than increase their budget, if it comes down to a choice between the two. A second countervailing value to growth is professionalism, the desire to do a job quickly and right. Administrators may prefer to hire fewer but more qualified employees and refuse to add employees if doing so would not add to the agency's capacity to get things done.[4] A third countervailing value is program loyalty: Expansion may be seen as undesirable if the new mission swamps the existing mission, if it appears contradictory to the existing mission, or if the program requires more money to carry out than is provided, forcing the agency to spend money designated for existing programs on new ones or do a poor job. A fourth countervailing value is belief in the chain of command. Many bureaucrats, if not all, believe that their role is to carry out the policies of the chief executive and the legislature. If that means cutting back budgets, agency heads cut back the agencies. Agency heads may be appointed precisely because they are willing to make cuts in their agencies.[5]

Bureaucrats, then, do not always try to expand their agencies' budgets. They have other, competing goals, which sometimes dominate. Also, their achievements can be measured in other ways than by expanded budgets. They may go for some specific items in the budget, without raising totals, or may try for changes in the wording of legislation. They may strive to obtain a statutory basis for the agency and security of funding. They may take as a goal providing more efficient and effective service, rather than expanded or more expensive service.

The Executive Budget Office. The traditional role of the budget office has been to scrutinize requests coming up from the agencies, to find waste and eliminate it, and to discourage most requests for new money. The executive budget office has been perceived as the naysayer, the protector of the public purse. Most staff members in the budget office are very conscious of the need to balance the budget, to avoid deficits, and to manage cash flow so that there is money on hand to pay bills. Hence they tend to be skeptical of requests for new money.

In recent years, however, there has been a change in the role of the budget office. At the national level under President Ronald Reagan, budgeting became much more top-down, with the director of the Office of Management and Budget (OMB) proposing specific cuts and negotiating them directly with Congress, without much scrutiny of requests coming up from departments or bureaus. OMB became more involved in trying to accomplish the policy goals of the president through the budget.[6] At the state level, too, there has been an evolution of budget staff from an operation concerned mostly with technical goals to one more concerned with political and policy-related goals. When the governor is looking for new spending proposals, these may come from the budget office.

Chief Executive Officers. The role of the chief executive officer (the mayor or city manager, the governor, the president) is highly variable, and hence these executives' goals in the budget process cannot be predicted without knowledge of the individuals. Some chief executives have been expansive, proposing new programs; others have been economy minded, cutting back proposals generated by the legislatures. Some have been efficiency oriented, reorganizing staffs and trying to maintain service levels without increases in taxes or expenditures.

Legislators. Legislators are sometimes depicted as always trying to increase spending,[7] their motivation being reelection, which depends on their ability to provide constituent services and deliver "pork"—jobs and capital projects—to their districts. Norms of reciprocity magnify the effects of these spending demands because legislators are reluctant to cut one another's pork, lest their own be cut in return. As a city council member described this norm of reciprocity, "There is an unwritten rule that if something is in a councilman's district, we'll go along and scratch each other's back." [8]

For some legislators, however, being reelected is not a high priority. They view elected office as a service they perform for the community rather than a career, and while they may be responsive to constituents' needs, they are simply not motivated to start new projects or give public employees a raise in order to get reelected. Also, some legislators feel secure about reelection and hence have no urgent need to deliver pork to increase their chances.[9]

Even assuming the motivation to be reelected, holding down taxes may be as important to reelection as spending on programs and projects. The consequence of tax reduction is usually curtailed expenditures on programs. Legislators are bound to try to balance the budget, which puts some constraints on the desire to spend.

The pressure to provide pork is real, if not universal, but legislators can organize themselves in such a way as to insulate themselves somewhat from this pressure. They can, for example, select more electorally secure representatives for key positions on appropriations committees; they can separate committees that deal extensively with interest groups from those that deal with expenditures; they can set up buffer groups to deal with interest groups; they can structure the budget process so that revenue limits precede and guide spending proposals; they can set aside a limited pool of funds for pork projects.

Moreover, legislators have interests other than providing pork. Some legislators are deeply concerned about solving social problems, designing and funding defense or foreign aid systems, and monitoring the executive branch. The portion of the federal budget spent on pork-type projects has varied over time.[10] "Congressmen are not single-minded seekers of local benefits, struggling feverishly to win every last dollar for their districts. However important the quest for local benefits may be, it is always tempered by other competing concerns."[11] The pull for local benefits depends on the program. Some, such as water projects, are oriented to local payoffs; others, such as entitlement programs for large numbers of people, are not. Programs with local pull account for smaller and smaller proportions of the budget.[12]

Interest Groups. Interest groups, too, have often been singled out as the driving force behind budget increases. They are said to want more benefits for their members and to be undeterred by concerns for overall budget balance or the negative effects of tax increases. Moreover, their power has been depicted as great. Well-funded interest groups reportedly wine and dine legislators and provide campaign money for candidates who agree with their positions.

There is some truth to this picture, but it is oversimplified. Interest groups have other policy goals besides budget levels. In fact, most probably deal with the budget only when a crisis occurs, such as a threat to funding levels. Because they can be counted on to come to the defense of a threatened program, they reduce the flexibility of budget decision makers, who find it difficult to cut programs with strong interest group backing. But many areas of the budget do not have strong interest group backing. For example, foreign aid programs have few domestic constituencies. Agencies may even have negative constituencies, that is, interest groups that want to reduce their funding and terminate their programs. The American Medical Association sought for years to eliminate the Health Planning Program. Often when interest groups are involved, there are many of them, rather than one, and the groups may have conflicting styles or conflicting goals, canceling one another out or absorbing energy in battles among themselves. A coalition of interest groups representing broad geographic areas and a variety of constituencies is likely to be more effective at lobbying. To that end coalitions may form, but some members of the coalition may not go along with measures supported by others, so the range of items that the unified group can lobby for may be narrow. Extensive negotiations and continual efforts are required to get two or more independent groups together for a lobbying effort, and the arrangement can then fall apart. In short, interest groups are often interested in maintaining their autonomy.

Individuals.   Individuals seldom have a direct role in the budget process, but they often have an indirect one. They may vote on referendums to limit revenues, forbid some forms of taxation, or require budgetary balance. They voice their opinions also in public opinion polls, and more informally by calling or writing their elected representatives. Their knowledge of the budget is not usually detailed, but their feelings about the acceptability of taxation are an important part of the constraints on public budgeting. The public's preferences for less-visible taxes and for taxes earmarked for specific, approved expenditures have been an important factor in public budgeting.

The Courts.   The courts play an intermittent role in determining expenditures.[13] They become involved when other actors, often interest groups, bring suit against the government. Suits that affect the budget may involve service levels or the legality of particular forms of taxation. If a particular tax is judged unconstitutional, the result is usually lost revenues. If there is a suit concerning levels of service, a government may be forced to spend more money on that service. There can also be damage suits against governments that affect expenditures. These are usually settled without regard to the government agencies' ability to pay. The result may be forced cuts in other areas of the budget, tax increases, or even bankruptcy. When the courts get involved, they may determine budget priorities. They introduce a kind of rigidity into the budget that says, Do this, or pay this, first.

Typical areas in which courts have become involved and mandated expenditures by state and local governments are prison overcrowding (declared cruel and unusual punishment) and the deinstitutionalization of mentally ill and mentally handicapped patients. In each case the rights of the institutionalized population required more services or more space, often involving expenditures of additional funds. From the perspective of the courts, the priority of rights outweighs immediate concerns for budget balances, autonomy of governmental units, and local priorities.

Not only do these various actors have different and potentially clashing budgetary goals, but they typically have different levels of power. Thus at times the budget office may completely dominate the agencies; at times Congress may differ from the president on budgetary policy and pass its own preferences. The courts may preempt the decision making of the executive and the legislature. Particular interest groups may always be able to obtain tax breaks for themselves. The combination of different preferences and different levels of power has to be orchestrated by the budget process in such a way that agreement is reached and the players stay in the game, continuing to abide by the rules. If some actors feel too powerless over the budget, they may cease to participate or become obstructionist, blocking any agreement or imposing rigid, nonnegotiable solutions. Why participate in negotiations and discussions if the decision will go against you regardless of what you do? If some actors lose on important issues, they may try to influence budget amendments or implementation to favor themselves. Or the actors with less budget power may try to change the budget process so that they have a better chance of influencing the outcomes.

Separation of Payer and Decider

One of the major characteristics of public budgeting is that those who pay the bills are not the ones who make the decisions on how the money is to be spent. The possibility exists that elected officials will spend the money differently than taxpayers wish. This problem and its solution over time are clearly visible at the local level.

In some cities in the later 1800s, the problem was solved by having taxpayer groups elect their own representatives, in some cases requiring property ownership and taxpaying history to qualify as a candidate.[14] At that time nearly all local taxation was based on property taxes. Under the control of these taxpayers, local government spent money on projects that would benefit them, such as markets, ports, roads, and bridges. When the economy turned sour and property owners could not afford to pay for these projects, they stopped paying for them.[15] Over the years, however, as more poor people moved into the cities and voted, with the encouragement of political machines that paid for votes with employment opportunities, the difference between what the wealthy wished to spend tax money on and what elected officials actually spent the money on began to grow. Antitax revolts focused on this gap between taxpayers and "tax eaters," those who consumed public services without paying taxes for them.

During the twentieth century property ownership broadened as immigrants and blue-collar workers bought their own homes. Also, over the last generation taxation at the local level has shifted away from dependence on property taxes and toward sales taxes. The result is that there is not now a class of taxpayers and a class of tax users or consumers of government services. Everyone pays local taxes, including the poor in many cities. The result has been to shift the focus of concern to whether everyone benefits from public taxation or only a few. For those services that benefit only a few, the question arises, Why should everyone have to pay for them? One solution is to charge user fees for services that benefit only or primarily users and not others.

The tension between those who pay and those who benefit occurs at all levels of government, sometimes manifesting itself in similar ways. Revenue from fees has grown substantially at all levels of government in the past twenty years in response to the pressure against paying for anyone else's services. A second approach has been for those who want narrow benefits to form a coalition with others who also want narrow benefits; they tolerate some projects that others want, in exchange for support on their favored projects. Still, there are expenditures in many budgets that benefit one group or interest that are not balanced by benefits to other groups or interests. Such expenditures can be politically contentious.

Sometimes whether there will be political stress depends on perception or presentation, not on the characteristics of the actual program. Taxpayers who earn regular incomes often bridle at paying for welfare for those who do not work, seeing it as an outlay from which they do not and will not benefit. Viewed differently, however, anyone could end up needing unemployment benefits, or even welfare, if the economy performs poorly or downsizing throws older workers out in the cold. If taxpayers see themselves as possible future beneficiaries of a safety net, they may be willing to support it; to the extent that they see such expenditures as only for others and believe that they will never need such services, they are more likely to oppose such programs.

The separation between taxpayer and budgetary decision maker highlights the importance of symbolic politics, that is, the way expenditures are presented and viewed. Expenditures that benefit some narrow group may survive if they are represented as being for the collective good. For example, some economic development policies are justified on the basis that everyone benefits from growth. Alternatively, expenditures may be justified in such terms that opposing them appears callow and inhumane or destructive of collective benefits. Thus federal antipollution mandates may pass because it is politically impossible to oppose "clean air." Education mandates for disabled children may be politically impossible to oppose—who wants to be known for hurting children?[16]

Sometimes it is difficult to make the argument that everyone benefits from an expenditure aimed at a few, or from a tax break that benefits a narrow group. The argument may not be credible. Then the goal may instead be to make the expenditure look small. For example, although the Bush administration presented the war in Iraq as a way of protecting the American people from terrorism, not everyone was convinced of this collective benefit. To minimize opposition, the Bush administration played down the costs of the war in Iraq. The administration put forward the budget proposal for the whole federal government without including any estimate of the cost of the war, preferring instead to ask for a supplemental appropriation—to support the troops—after the budget was passed. Since the costs could be dealt with through a number of supplemental appropriations, each of lower visibility and smaller than the total costs, the real costs of the war and their impact on the deficit were obscured.

Because public demands may not be clearly expressed, because different segments of the public may make different and competing demands, and because public officials themselves may have other priorities, officials may not be able or willing to be bound tightly to public opinion. Nevertheless, if politicians knowingly make decisions that differ from what the public seems to want, there is pressure to present the budget in a way that makes it appear acceptable. That pressure creates a tension between accountability, which requires nearly complete openness, and acceptability, which sometimes involves hiding or distorting information or presenting it in an unclear fashion. This tension is always present in public budgeting.

Because of the separation of payer and decider, the budget document itself becomes an important means of public accountability. How did the public's representatives actually decide to spend taxpayer money? Did they waste it? Did they spend it on defense or police or on social services? The streets are in terrible shape—how much money did they spend on street repair? Citizens do not typically watch the decision making, but they and the press have access to the budget document and can look for the answers. They can hold the government accountable through the budget, to see that what officials promised them was actually delivered. Because some budgetary decisions will not be acceptable to everyone, budgets have not always been clear about the decisions that underlie them.

In recent years there has been pressure to make budgets more readable and more informative. To achieve that budgeters have tried grouping expenditures by program and establishing performance goals and measurements for each program. At the national level, the Government Performance and Results Act of 1993 (GPRA) required that all federal agencies create program plans and performance measures. Agencies have tried to comply, with varying degrees of success. More recently, the administration has added what it calls the PART process, asking each agency to fill out a form explaining its goals and how it plans to achieve them. The goal of "performance budgeting" at all levels of government has been to broaden the notion of accountability from a record of where the money was spent, to how well the money was spent, and to hold public officials accountable for program outcomes and impacts. It is hoped that such clear reporting will help rekindle public respect for government (see Minicase, page 21).

The increased demands for accountability through cost or performance measurement have sometimes been problematic. If particular cost or performance measures make an agency look worse, the agency may want to obscure the results or not use that measure. Performance measurement also assumes a level of funding that is known with reasonable certainty, a condition increasingly difficult to meet. Moreover, there is no clear link between performance measurement and budgeting; that is, it is not clear if a poor performance report warrants additional spending or reduced spending. If they use budgeting to punish poor performance, elected officials may send agencies into a downward spiral of deteriorating management quality.

The movement toward improved accountability, better reporting, and more readable budgets suggests that public officials should be free from prior constraints, and should be allowed to use their training and best judgment, but should be held accountable for their choices after the fact. Accurate reporting of what they have done and the consequences of those decisions is absolutely necessary for this model to work. But if elected officials have made choices that some members of the public disapprove of, officials may be reluctant to report the details of their decisions, lest they open themselves to attack. Political opponents can use performance data to attack an agency or program or administration, and that threat contributes to a desire not to collect possibly damaging data or not to make it public. If public officials have made mistakes, they may be reluctant to reveal them (see Minicase, page 24).

Every budget is selective to some degree about what it will present and how. The art of selective revelation is part of public budgeting. The amount of secrecy in budgets goes up and down with different administrations and requires constant monitoring.

Minicase: The Government Performance and Results Act

The Government Performance and Results Act of 1993 (GPRA) was supposed to be implemented in stages. Agencies were to come up with overall plans, including goals and program impacts, and then with a series of measures for determining what progress they were making, annually and over a period of years, toward the goals. Finally, the plans and measures were to be considered in budgetary decision making.

But agencies have had a difficult time coming up with acceptable plans. The political disagreement over what the goals of some agencies should be is intense. Some agencies have found their goals difficult to measure. Moreover, success is often difficult to attribute to a single agency because many agencies, as well as societal changes, contribute to overall outcomes and impacts. Implementation has been slowed by cutbacks of precisely those personnel who would have been engaged in creating performance plans. And the level of resources that agencies can expect is often unclear. It is difficult to promise a level of service based on uncertain resource levels.

Performance budgeting is often an executive branch activity, changing the budget format in ways that the legislative branch ignores. In the case of GPRA, however, some members of Congress were intensely interested in the reforms, and they were also determined that performance budgeting not shift power away from Congress. Agencies were thus required to consult with their congressional committees before drawing up their agency goals and plans. Key legislators were upset to find in 1997 that the Office of Management and Budget, in the Executive Office of the President, expected to review agency plans before they were submitted to Congress for discussion.[1] To the extent that the plans were jointly arrived at by Congress and the agencies, they could be used as a budgetary standard. Agencies could argue that they needed the resources that were in the plan to achieve the goals agreed on; Congress could argue that programs did not deserve the money because they had failed to achieve appropriate portions of their goals within set time limits.

The performance reports were supposed to elevate the level of discussion between Congress and the agency heads about agency budgets. Congress had nearly stopped examining programs in detail because spending caps had removed much congressional committee discretion. Thus if appropriations subcommittees discovered problems in program implementation, there was not enough flexibility to do much about it. What was given to one agency had to be taken from another. It was easier not to know about prob-

(continued)

lems. But GPRA had the potential to increase congressional control of programs, make agency heads more responsive to congressional direction, and provide a justification for taking resources from one agency and giving them to another.

Interestingly, both the authorizing committees (in charge of designing and monitoring programs) and the appropriations committees (in charge of funding them) have expressed interest in GPRA documents. The authorizing committees are interested in specific plans for improving services and measuring performance and in whether the techniques for achieving the goals hurt or help their constituencies. One subcommittee was concerned, for example, that the administration was trying to reduce the costs of loans by increasing the loan fees beyond the actual program costs. The appropriations subcommittees have been more interested in whether the budget allocations match the goals statements and whether the agencies have clear goals and objectives and performance measures.

Agencies were expected to put their budgets into program formats and integrate those formats with their budget requests. The following testimony from the Office of Personnel Management (OPM) illustrates how one agency framed its budget request in terms of its strategic plan:

> Before considering our request in more detail, it is important to note that, in response to the Government Performance and Results Act, we have included our annual performance plan as an integral part of our budget justification. We have used our strategic goals, and the related series of objectives, as the basis for organizing our performance plan. Some of our objectives relate to overall human resources management concerns; some are limited to specific aspects, such as staffing or compensation. Some are government wide; some are confined to our own agency.
>
> Also, we have included in our budget justification for the first time a crosswalk of annual performance goals and strategic plan goals and objectives, which we have organized by fund and program activity. This presentation clearly links our resource allocations to our strategic plan goals. For example, nearly $60 million and 625 fte's [full-time-equivalent employees] will be directed to activities designed to achieve our goal of providing policy direction and leadership to recruit and retain the federal workforce required for the 21st century.
>
> As I review with you specific aspects of our request, I will touch on the means we will use to achieve specific goals, as well as our strategies for measuring and validating our achievements.[2]

(continued)

Increasingly at the federal level, budgets are being prepared and presented to the Office of Management and Budget and to the appropriations committees and oversight agencies in Congress in program and performance format, with at least some measurable goals.[3]

1. Stephen Barr, "Congress Seeks a Seat at the Table," *Washington Post*, March 7, 1997.
2. Prepared statement of Honorable Janice R. Lachance, director, Office of Personnel Management, before the House Committee on Appropriations Subcommittee on Treasury, Postal Service, and General Government, March 13, 1998.
3. Some of the GPRA material was prepared by Wouter Van Reeth, a visiting scholar from Belgium, in spring 1999.

Openness to the Environment

The need for accountability means that the budget that is passed in public should be the budget that is actually implemented and that the budget should reasonably reflect public desires. But public budgets are open to the environment, which means that they also have to be reasonably flexible and adaptive.

Openness to the environment includes a number of different factors, such as the overall level of resources available (changes in the amount of taxable wealth or in current economic conditions) and a variety of emergencies such as very heavy snowfall, tornadoes, wars, bridge collapses, drought or floods, chemical explosions, terrorist attacks, or water pollution. Public opinion is part of the budgetary environment, and the perception of change in public opinion may bring about changes in budget priorities.

The federal system and the resulting intergovernmental relations are also a key part of the environment for budget actors. The legal sources of revenues, limits on borrowing, strings attached to grants, and mandated costs are but a few of the budgetary implications of the intergovernmental system. The requirement that some grants be spent on particular items or that a recipient match grant amounts may result in a pattern of spending different from what the state or local government would have preferred.

Budgeting is open to the environment not only in the sense of changing revenue levels, emergency demands on spending, and the changing intergovernmental system that frames responsibilities and revenue sources, but also in the sense that decision making itself is public. Committee hearings on the budget are public. Revenue and expenditure proposals are public; they are reported in the

Minicase: Doctoring Audit Reports

Audit reports are essential to after-the-fact accountability. They must be honest and open beyond question. But the temptation to hide wrongdoing or the suggestion of cronyism, ineptitude, laxness of supervision, or outright corruption sometimes leads to delays in releasing audit reports or, as in one recent case, editing out (called "redacting") the suggestive portions.

In 2003, as the government was preparing for war in Iraq, the Defense Department entered into a multibillion dollar, noncompetitive contract with Kellogg, Brown and Root, a subsidiary of Halliburton, a company associated with the vice president. Its purpose was to rebuild Iraqi oil production facilities and to import gasoline for domestic use.

Because the contract was noncompetitive and the company associated with a high-ranking administration figure, it attracted considerable attention and charges of cronyism. The contract had a requirement for an audit, but when the audit was presented, it was given to the contractor to edit: The audit that was released eliminated text that the company thought might be embarrassing, as well as any portions that it disagreed with. The ranking minority member of the House Government Reform Committee, Henry Waxman, D-Calif., obtained a copy of the unedited version and made most of it public for comparison. Perhaps not surprisingly, it was discovered that the company had been overcharging the government for gasoline purchases by hundreds of millions of dollars. The Defense Department knew this and had refused to make the information public.[1]

1. Erik Eckholm, "Now You See It: An audit of KBR," *New York Times,* March 20, 2005.

newspapers and debated in editorials and letters to the editor. The budget as proposed and as adopted is available for public inspection, as are reported comparisons of plans and actual spending. The whole budget process takes place under public scrutiny. Potentially embarrassing mistakes are harder to hide than in the private sector, and that may lead to a kind of caution. Public officials adapt to working in a room with glass walls and no window blinds.

The openness of public budgets to the environment means that budgets have to be adaptable when unexpected events occur. At the national level, supplemental appropriations legislation may help the government deal with emergencies such as wars, hurricanes, or earthquakes. At the state and local levels, there may be contingency accounts to provide for unexpected events. Budget makers aim to build in enough flexibility to manage the problems that arise without changing the underlying policies that have emerged from complex, public negotiations among multiple actors with different points of view.

Constraints

Public budgeting is much more constrained than private sector or family budgeting because public budgeting is not limited only by the amount of revenue involved. For example, the federal government can require state expenditures, preempting states' priorities; similarly, states can mandate local government expenditures. Some state governments tell local governments what format to use for a budget and what information has to be included. States may limit borrowing by local governments or even require that all local borrowing be approved by the state government. The reason for the current emphasis on after-the-fact reporting, rather than prior controls, is that there were so many prior controls that government managers had a difficult time getting anything done. Despite the recent emphasis on after-the-fact reporting, few prior constraints have actually been removed.

One of the constraints in the public sector is the fund structure. Public budgeting is based on "funds," that is, separate accounts for separate purposes. Money can be spent only through those accounts and cannot be freely swapped among accounts. Such transfers normally require justification and explicit permission. Each account or fund must balance; that is, revenue must equal or exceed expenditures. The result is not one bottom line, as in a family or business, but multiple bottom lines. Creating some flexibility within these constraints is a continuing trial.

Some constraints have been placed on budgeting by those who oppose higher taxation. They press for tax limits in statutes and constitutions, which may guide decisions for decades. A second source of constraints is prior history of willfulness. Agency administrators sometimes abuse the discretion they have been granted, inviting tighter controls. If the executive branch makes too many transfers between funds or accounts, in essence changing the budget that was agreed to in public sessions, the legislature may limit the amount of money that the executive can transfer without coming back to the legislature for approval of the changes. A third reason for prior constraints is to facilitate supervision. States cannot easily monitor local budgeting and financial condition if each jurisdiction puts its budget in a different format or includes different information and uses different definitions of balance. Since the states are ultimately responsible for the finances of local governments, they have an interest in keeping local governments financially healthy and identifying those that might be headed for trouble.

Minicase: Unfunded Mandates—No Child Left Behind

Government in the United States is based on a federal system, not a unitary system. That means there is not one central government that creates other units of government that then report to it and have to do its bidding. Instead, there are a number of states, which historically preceded and then created a national (federal) government. The states gave particular, limited powers to the federal government and retained the rest of the responsibilities for themselves. In reality, over the years, the balance between the national government and the states has been continually negotiated. By contrast, the states do have control of, and responsibility for, the local governments within their borders.

One way that the national government is able to influence the states without direct authority over them is to give the states monetary grants with strings or conditions. Sometimes, however, what the states are required to do costs more than the grant amount, resulting in what some call "unfunded mandates," though they might be more accurately called "underfunded mandates." In 2002 Congress, which does not have responsibility for education (that was retained by the states), passed legislation called the No Child Left Behind Act and included it as part of federal financial aid to education for poor children. If states wanted to continue to receive grants to help them educate poor children, they had to comply with the requirements of the new act.

Relying on the powerful symbol that no child's needs should be ignored in the public schools, the federal government required that public schools engage in extensive testing in math and English and that all students, regardless of language skills, developmental difficulties, family income, or ethnic background, be able to pass these examinations. The penalties for failure to bring up lower scores included requirements that school systems hire special tutors for the affected students or allow the students to transfer to other schools that were doing better with slow learners. The program also set minimum standards for teacher training. All of these—the testing, the tutors, the influx of students from poorly performing schools, and the minimum requirements for teachers—were expensive. The cost of the federally mandated program was passed along to the states along with some—but insufficient—increase in grants for disadvantaged students.

State governments were angry, in part because the timing was so bad, as their budgets were already suffering because of a recession, and in part because the federal government had promised in 1995 to stop passing along the costs of federal program requirements to the states (although under-

(continued)

funding was not included in that legislation). The states were also frustrated because the federal government did not, properly speaking, have jurisdiction over education but went ahead with this mandate anyway. Many governors protested, and some threatened not to participate in the program. Twenty-seven state legislatures passed bills protesting the costs, penalties, and federal oversight of education.[1]

The result was a kind of negotiation between the federal government and some forty state agencies, in which the federal Department of Education backed down on or softened some requirements. "States now may defer the test scores of limited-English speakers for one year, a greater number of disabled students are allowed to take alternative tests and rural school districts will have more time to meet federal requirements for teacher qualifications."[2] States are continuing to ask for more flexibility under the act, but additional funds have not been made available. Schools have had to reallocate from one program to another to fund the No Child Left Behind program. Federal requirements took precedence over local priorities. No Child Left Behind illustrates how the intergovernmental system can influence budgeting at the local level.

1. Eric Kelderman, "Feds Quell States' Revolt on No Child Left Behind," online at www.Stateline.org, July 6, 2004.
2. Ibid.

Prior constraints in public budgeting include the fund or account structure and constraints on transfers, tax limits, borrowing limits, requirements that tax increases or general obligation bond issues be approved by referendum, uniform budget formats, and uniform accounting rules. There may be separate rules limiting the number of employees and their rank or requiring the bidding out of contracts or purchases. Reforms in recent years have reduced some of these prior controls—such as separate limits on total spending and on the number of personnel. But each proposal for reducing constraints runs into the reason for the constraint in the first place. Changes may reduce the ability of the state to supervise or of the legislature to control policy. Increased discretion may shift power from the legislative to the executive branches, adding a layer of resistance. Or weakening advance controls may remove some political or policy tool that is still cherished. Thus in 1993 and 1994 the Clinton administration urged greater discretion for executive branch officials, including discretion over staffing levels. Soon thereafter, the administration and Congress proceeded to pass the Workforce Restructuring Act, reducing federal employment levels by some 270,000.

Despite the plea for more agency autonomy, each agency still had an assigned personnel ceiling.

The Meaning of Politics in Public Budgeting

Public budgets have a number of special characteristics that suggest some of the ways in which the budget is political. "Political" is a word with a number of meanings, even when it is narrowed to the context of budgetary decision making. The purpose of this book is to clarify the meaning of politics in the context of budgeting by sorting out some key meanings and showing how they apply to different parts of budgetary decision making.

The literature suggests at least five major ways of viewing politics in the budget: reformism, incrementalist bargaining, interest group determinism, process, and policymaking.

- The first is a *reform orientation,* which argues that politics and budgeting are or should be antithetical, that budgeting should be primarily or exclusively technical, and that comparisons among items should be technical and efficiency based. Politics—in the sense of the opinions and priorities of elected officials and interest groups—is an unwanted intrusion that reduces efficiency and makes decision making less rational. The politics of reform involves a clash of views between professional staff and elected officials over the boundary between technical budget decisions and properly political ones.

- The second perspective is the *incrementalist* view, which sees budgeting as negotiations among a group of routine actors—bureaucrats, budget officers, chief executives, and legislators—who meet each year and bargain to resolution. To the extent that interest groups are included at all in this view, they are conceived of in the pluralist model. The process is open, anyone can play and win, and the overall outcome is good; conflict is held down because everyone wins something and no one wins too much.

- The third view is that *interest groups are dominant* in the budget process. In its extreme form this argument posits that richer and more powerful interest groups determine the budget. Some interests are represented by interest groups, and others either are not, or are represented by weaker interest groups; the outcome does not approximate democracy. There may be big winners and big losers in this model. Conflict is more extensive than in the incrementalist model. This view of politics in budgeting raises the question of whether the interest groups represent nar-

row or broad coalitions, or possibly even class interests. To what extent
do these interest groups represent the oil or banking industries, or the
homeless, and to what extent do they represent business and labor more
broadly?

- The fourth view of politics in the budget is that the budget *process* itself
  is the center and focus of budget politics. Those with particular budget
  goals try to change the budget process to favor their goals. Branches of
  government struggle with one another over budgetary power through the
  budget process; the budget process becomes the means of achieving or
  denying separation and balance between the branches of government.
  The degree of examination of budget requests and the degree to which
  review is technical or political, cursory or detailed, are regulated by the
  budget process. The ability of interest groups to influence the budget, the
  role of the public in budget decisions, the openness of budget decision
  making—all these are part of the politics of process. In this view of politics, the individual actors and their strategies and goals may or may not
  be important, depending on the role assigned to individual actors in the
  budget process, and depending on whether the external environment
  allows any flexibility.
- The fifth view is that the *politics of budgeting centers in policy debates*,
  including debates about the role of the budget. Spending levels, taxing
  policies, and willingness to borrow to sustain spending during recessions
  are all major policy issues that have to be resolved one way or another
  during budget deliberations. Budgets may reflect a policy of moderating
  economic cycles, or they may express a policy of allowing the economy
  to run its course. Each is a policy. Similarly, budgets must allocate funding to particular programs and in the course of doing so decide priorities for federal, state, and local governments. This view of politics in the
  budget emphasizes trade-offs, especially those that occur between major
  areas of the budget, such as social services and defense or police. This
  view also emphasizes the role of the budget office in making policy and
  the format of the budget in encouraging comparisons between programs.

These five views of politics have been developed over time, and as with many
ancient documents, the messages have been written over one another. Surely they
are not all equally true, and certainly they often contradict each other. Parts of
each may still be true, and they may be true of different parts of budgetary decision making, or true of budgetary decision making at different times or at different levels of government.

Budgetary Decision Making

This book explores the kind of politics that occurs in budgetary decision making. What is budgetary decision making like? We have already discovered that public budgeting is open to environmental changes and that it deals with policy conflicts. Policy conflicts can delay particular decisions or prevent them from being made at all; other budget decisions must be independent enough to be made without the missing pieces. They can be corrected later when missing pieces fall into place. Environmental emergencies can reorder priorities and alter targets that have already been determined. As a result, public budgeting must be segmentable and interruptible. The need for segmentation and interruptibility is satisfied by dividing budgeting into separate but linked decision clusters: revenues, process, expenditures, balance, and implementation.

Decision making in each cluster proceeds somewhat separately from, but with reference to decisions made or anticipated in, other decision streams. Decisions on spending are made with an eye on revenue totals, even though revenue estimates may not yet be firm. Decisions in different streams may be made iteratively, with tentative revenue estimates followed by tentative spending estimates, followed in turn by updated revenue estimates and fine-tuning of spending estimates. The order of decision making may vary from year to year. In one year, there may be no change in the definition of balance, so that prior years' definitions frame this year's deliberations. In another year, the definition of balance may change during the deliberations, requiring adjustments in spending or revenue plans. Sometimes the decision making moves faster in one cluster than in another, and decision makers in the cluster that is ahead may have to guess or anticipate what the decisions will be in other clusters and revise later if necessary.

Each cluster attracts a different characteristic set of actors and generates its own typical pattern of politics. Some clusters attract heavy interest group activity, while others have virtually none. Some clusters are marked by intense competition and negotiations and efforts to bind future decisions to restrict open competition. Some are marked by deep ideological splits, while others seem not to be ideological at all. In some a technical perspective prevails, while others are clearly determined by the priorities of elected officials and the public, and still others represent a blend of the two.

The Revenue Cluster

Revenue decisions include technical estimates of how much income will be available for the following year, assuming no change in tax structures, and policy decisions about changes in the level or type of taxation. Will taxes be raised or lowered? Will tax breaks be granted, and if so, to whom, for what purpose? Which tax sources will be emphasized, and which de-emphasized, with what effect on regions, economic classes, or age groups? How visible will the tax burden be? Interest groups are intensely involved in the revenue cluster. The revenue cluster emphasizes the scarcity of resources that is an essential element in budgeting and illustrates the tension between accountability and acceptability that is a characteristic of public budgets. Revenues are also extremely sensitive to the environment because changes in the economy influence revenue levels and because the perception of public opinion influences the public officials' willingness to increase taxes.

The Budget Process

The process cluster concerns how to make budget decisions. Who should participate in the budget deliberations? Should the agency heads have power independent of the central budget office? How influential should interest groups be? How much power should the legislature have? How should the work be divided, and when should particular decisions be made? Normally the legislature takes a key role in establishing budget process, although the chief executive may propose changes. Interest groups play a minor role, if any at all. The politics of process may revolve around individuals or groups trying to maximize their power through rearranging the budget process. This jockeying for power rises to importance when the competing parties represent the executive and legislative branches and try to influence the separation and balance between the branches of government. The politics of process may revolve around the policy issues of the level of spending and the ability of government to balance its budget.

The Expenditure Cluster

The expenditure cluster involves some technical estimates of likely expenditures, such as those for grants that are dependent on formulas and benefit programs whose costs depend on the level of unemployment. But many expenditure decisions are policy relevant—which programs will be funded at what level, who will benefit from public programs and who will not, where and how cuts will be made, and whose interests will be protected. Agency heads are more involved in these decisions than in taxation or process decisions, and interest groups are also often active. The expenditure portion of the budget emphasizes competition for limited resources and the resulting trade-offs—choices between specific sets of alternatives. If we want more money spent on streets, does that translate into less money spent on day care? Does more money spent on hurricane relief translate into less money for defense or for housing for the poor?

The Balance Cluster

The balance cluster concerns the basic budgetary question of whether the budget has to be balanced each year with each year's revenues or whether borrowing is allowed to balance the budget, and if so, how much, for how long, and for what purposes. The politics of balance deals with questions of whether balance should be achieved by increasing revenues, decreasing expenditures, or both, and hence it reflects policies about the desirable scope of government. Sometimes the politics of balance emphasizes definitions, as the group in power seeks to make its deficits look smaller by defining them away. The balance cluster also deals with questions of how deficits should be eliminated once they occur and their amounts are pinned down. At the national level, because deficits may be incurred during recessions in an effort to help the economy recover, the ability to run a deficit is linked to policies favoring or opposing use of the budget to control the economy, and in particular to moderate unemployment. These issues—whether budgets should balance, the proper scope of government and level of taxation, and the role of government in moderating unemployment—are issues that the general public cares about. Citizens may participate in this decision cluster through referendums and opinion polls; broad groups of taxpayers and interest group coalitions representing broad segments of society may be involved in lobbying on this issue. Political parties may even include their policies toward deficits in their election platforms.

Budget Implementation

Finally, there is a cluster of decisions around budget implementation. How close should actual expenditures be to the ones planned in the budget? How can one justify variation from the budget plan? Can the budget be remade after it is approved, during the budget year? The key issues here revolve around the need to implement decisions exactly as made and the need to make changes during the year because of changes in the environment. The potential conflict is usually resolved by treating implementation as technical rather than policy related. Executive branch staff play the major role in implementation, with much smaller and more occasional roles for the legislature. Interest groups play virtually no role in implementation. The allowance for technical changes does open the door to policy changes during the year, but these are normally carefully monitored and may cause open conflict when they occur.

Microbudgeting and Macrobudgeting

The five clusters of decision making outline the nature of the decisions being made, but they tell little about how and why they are made. On the one hand there are a number of budget actors, all of whom have individual motivations, who strategize to get what they want from the budget. The focus on the actors and their strategies is called "microbudgeting." But the actors do not simply bargain with one another or with whomever they meet in the corridor. The actors are assigned budget roles by the budget process, the issues they examine are often framed by the budget process, and the timing and coordination of their decisions are often regulated by the budget process. The budget actors are not totally free to come to budget agreements in any way they choose. Individual actors are bound by environmental constraints. There are choices that they are not free to make because they are against the law, or because the courts have decreed it, or because previous decision makers have bound their hands. The total amount of revenue available is a kind of constraint, as are popular demand for some programs and popular dislike of others. Budgetary decision making has to account not just for budgetary actors but also for budget processes and the environment. This more top-down and systemic perspective on budgeting is called "macrobudgeting." Contemporary budgeting gives some attention to macrobudgeting, as well as microbudgeting.

One way of viewing the determinants of budgetary outcomes is as a causal model, depicted in Figure 1.1. In this schema, the environment, budget processes, and individuals' strategies all affect outcomes. The environment influences budgetary outcomes both directly and indirectly through process and through individual strategies. It influences outcomes directly, without going through either budget process or individual strategies, when it imposes emergencies that reorder priorities. Thus a war or a natural disaster preempts normal budgetary decision making.

The environment influences the budget process in several ways. The level of resources available—both the actual level of wealth and the willingness of the

Figure 1.1 Decision Making: Environment, Process, and Strategies

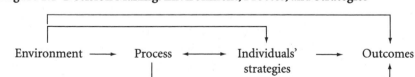

citizens to pay their taxes—influences the degree of centralization of budgeting. When resources are especially scarce and there is apparent need to either cut back according to a given set of policies or make each dollar count toward specific economic goals, there is no room for bottom-up demands that result in compromises and a little bit of gain for everyone regardless of need. When resources are abundant, a more decentralized model of process may hold, with less emphasis on comparing policies and less competition between supporters of different policies.

The environment may influence the format of the budget as well as the degree of centralization of decision making. When revenues are growing, there may be more emphasis on planning and on linking the budget to future community goals, to stimulate public demands for new spending. When there is little new money, the idea of planning may seem superfluous. Changing direction or setting new goals, may seem impossible in the face of declining revenues that make current goals difficult to sustain.

Environment in the sense of the results of prior decisions may also influence process. If there is a huge accumulation of debt and little apparent way to control it, or if the budget has been growing very rapidly for reasons other than war, there may be attempts to change the budget process in an effort to control spending and debt. In contrast, if the environment suggests the need for additional spending, and the current budget process is delivering very slow growth, the process may be changed to make spending decisions quicker and easier.

The environment influences not only the budget process but also the strategies of the budget actors. Clearly, the level of resources available determines whether actors press for new programs and expansion of existing ones, or strive to prevent cuts and protect their revenue sources from encroachment by other programs.

The certainty of funding influences strategies as well. If whatever an agency was promised may never arrive, agency heads are likely to engage in continuous lobbying for their money. Long-term or future agreements will be perceived as worthless; the possibility of toning down conflict by stretching out budget allocation times will disappear. Attention will focus on going after what is available now, whether it is what you want or not, inasmuch as what you really want may never show up and hence is not worth waiting for.

The intergovernmental grant structure is part of the environment that may influence strategies. Because some grant money may seem free, state and local governments may focus their energies on getting grants instead of raising local revenues. Or they may seek to decrease the amount of match required for a grant or increase their authority over how the money can be spent. Intergovernmental grants may make some expenditures relatively cheap, and some cutbacks relatively expensive, and hence frame constraints and choices for state and local budget officials.

The legal environment also influences strategies. For example, if public school teachers want tax raises to fund education and there is a provision in the state constitution forbidding income taxes, the teachers must either campaign for a constitutional revision (a time-consuming and difficult task) or support a tax they know to be more burdensome to the poor. Thus the environment can both frame choices and influence strategies.

In Figure 1.1, the budget process influences strategies, and to a lesser extent outcomes, directly. But there is a double-headed arrow on the link between budget processes and strategies, suggesting that individuals' strategies also influence budget processes.

Budget processes influence strategies in some fairly obvious ways. If the budget structure allows for lengthy, detailed budget hearings, open to the public and interest groups, at which decisions are often made, then various actors are likely to concentrate their efforts on making a good impression at those hearings. If the chief executive prepares the budget, which is subject to only superficial scrutiny and pro forma hearings before being approved by the legislature, anyone who wants to influence the budget—including the legislators themselves—must make their opinions heard earlier in the process, before the final executive proposal is put together. Informal discussion with department heads, or even telephone calls to the budget office, may be the route to influence. If the budget is made two or three times, with only the last time being effective, then strategies may be to play out the first time or two with grandstanding—extreme positions to attract media attention—and to adopt more detailed and moderate positions later when the final decisions are made. The budget process orders the decisions in such a way that some of them are critical and determine or influence those that come afterward. Budget strategies naturally gravitate to those key decisions no matter where they are located.

When budget outcomes contradict some group's preference, the group may try to change the budget process to help it obtain the outcomes it prefers. When coalitions of the dissatisfied can agree on particular changes, fairly substantial changes in process may result. A change in process will bring about a change in outcome if the change in process shifts power from one group of individuals who want to accomplish one goal to another group with different goals.

The final link in the figure is between the strategies of budget actors and outcomes. The effect of different strategies on the outcomes is hard to gauge. It seems obvious, however, that strategies that ignore the process or the environment are doomed to failure. Budget actors have to figure out where the flexibility is before they can influence how that flexibility will be used. Strategies that try to bypass superiors or fool legislators generally do not work; strategies that involve careful documentation of need and appear to save money are generally more successful.[17]

Summary and Conclusions

Public budgeting shares the characteristics of all budgeting. It makes choices between possible expenditures, it has to balance, and it includes a decision-making process. But public budgeting has a number of additional features peculiar to itself, such as its openness to the environment; the variety of actors involved, all of whom come to it with different goals; the separation of taxpayers from budget decision makers; the use of the budget document as a means of public accountability; and numerous constraints.

Public budgeting is both technical and political. Politics takes on some special meanings in the context of budgetary decision making. Budgetary decision making must be flexible, adaptive, and interruptible, which leads to a structure of five semi-independent strands of decision making: revenues, process, expenditures, balance, and implementation. Each such strand generates its own political characteristics.

Budget outcomes are not solely the result of budget actors' negotiating with one another in a free-for-all; outcomes depend on the environment and on the budget process, as well as individual strategies. Individual strategies have to be framed in a broader context than simply perceived self-interest.

Budgeting is not well described as an annual process with little change from year to year. Budgetary decision making changes over time: interest group power waxes and wanes, competition in the budget increases and decreases, and the budget process itself varies over time. Changes in process take place in response to individuals, committees, and branches of government jockeying for power; in response to changes in the environment from rich to lean, or vice versa; in response to changes in the power of interest groups; and in response to scandals or excesses of various kinds.

Chapters 2 to 8 describe the patterns of politics associated with each of the decision streams and the sources and patterns of change over time. The final chapter integrates the decision streams into one model of budgetary decision making and points out the commonalities and differences among the decision streams.

2. Revenue Politics

We . . . seem to be able to defy what is supposed to happen. . . . It was a doctrine of politics that tax increases could not happen in an election year. We have done it quite often in the last years. . . . There is no doubt we can make tough decisions.

—Rep. Barbara Kennelly

In public budgeting the tax payers and the decision makers who determine tax and spending levels are separated. This separation sets up the possibility of some radical disagreements. Citizens would undoubtedly be happier about paying taxes if they could choose the services they wanted and pay only what they felt those services were worth. They might be even happier if they could get others to pay the taxes while they received the services. Individual taxpayers usually do not control the mix of services, however, and thus they may have to pay for some programs they do not want. Moreover, many citizens are convinced that they are paying for waste and mismanagement. Taxpayers also often feel that others are getting away with paying less than they pay. They resent being forced to pay more than their share.

Elected officials have the legal power to raise taxes, but they can easily be turned out of office if they raise taxes beyond the limits that citizens formally or informally set. Angry citizens and activated interest groups can, and sometimes do, revolt against taxes. Some politicians respond to this kind of threat by promising not to raise taxes, no matter what.

Never raising taxes is a difficult position to maintain, however, because expenditures are likely to increase. Even when government does not expand its functions, inflation increases the cost of equipment, such as fire trucks and airplanes, as well as salaries. Revenue sources that do not grow with inflation, such as water and sewer fees, have to be raised periodically to keep up with gradually rising costs. When government does add functions, it has to find new revenues to cover the increased costs. And when general taxes are eroded by special exceptions or other changes in the laws, some provision has to be made either to replace the lost revenues or to decrease the size or scope of government. Changes in the environment, such as termination of grant income, a decline in the economy, or a natural disaster or war, can create the need for more revenues.

The necessity of increasing revenues and the public's reluctance to be taxed, especially for services they do not want, lead to three major characteristics of revenue politics. The first is that when public officials determine that additional revenues are necessary, they go about obtaining support very carefully. They may work out a set of strategies, adapt budget processes specifically for taxation purposes, and choose their timing so that overwhelming environmental pressures seem to require tax increases. The second characteristic of revenue politics is that it develops an underside, a mirror image, a politics of protection from taxation and of tax reductions and exceptions, so that politicians can take credit for tax reductions rather than blame for tax increases. Third, efforts to raise taxes carefully and to protect individuals, interest groups, and regions from taxation lead to a piecemeal, complicated, inconsistent, and inequitable tax structure that periodically needs overhauling. Revenue politics is characterized by periodic efforts at reform.

Raising Taxes

Politicians fear that if they raise taxes, they will be turned out of office, but not all efforts to raise taxes fail. Following are two examples of efforts to increase taxes. One was a flamboyant failure (Alabama), but the other (in Dayton, Ohio) worked quite well (see Minicases, pages 39 and 41). The contrast suggests the care that is necessary to get a tax increase passed.

The failure in Alabama was partly due to traditional high levels of distrust of government and the lack of steps to reduce that distrust. Equally important, the governor did not produce irrefutable evidence of need. Part of the reason for the success of the Dayton tax increase was the care with which the opposition was defused, by making the increases revokable in the future, by widely airing the need, by guaranteeing no waste to those most suspicious of it, and by linking revenues to specific, desired service levels.

Tax increases must be planned carefully. Consideration must be given to the decision-making process, which must be buffered from public and interest group

Minicase: Alabama Governor's $1.2 Billion Tax Increase Defeated

Alabama, like so many other states since the recession of 2001, was experiencing financial stress and a gap between revenues and expenditures. The Republican governor, much to the surprise of his colleagues in the Republican Party, proposed a huge tax overhaul that would produce not only enough to address the revenue gap but also considerable additional revenue and lighten the tax burden on the poor.[1] This proposal for $1.2 billion of tax increases flew in the face of a strong local culture of distrust of government. In September 2003 Alabama voters defeated it by a two-to-one margin.

Government in Alabama has a reputation of being incompetent and corrupt.[2] Given the general level of distrust that formed the backdrop for his tax overhaul proposal, the governor would have had to demonstrate beyond a doubt not only the need for the tax increase, but also that the money would be spent responsibly for those things that the public particularly favored. The actual proposal was worded loosely, with no earmarking, making it possible to spend money for political rather than public priorities. The total to be collected was substantially greater than the estimate of the budget shortfall, which made the public question the need for so large an increase.

The lack of earmarking in the governor's proposal was intentional. Alabama has the highest level of earmarking of any state (87 percent, compared with an average of 22 percent in other states). Citizens do not trust their officials enough to grant them discretion to spend public money as they see fit. With new, unearmarked revenue, the governor hoped to create enough flexibility in the budget to respond to downturns in the economy, but citizens refused to grant such discretion. In the face of such lack of trust, the governor's best chance for obtaining new revenues was to earmark them, which he did not do.[3]

Other missteps included calling opponents stupid or ignorant and describing the state as behind the times and behind other states. Misleading statements made the existing high levels of mistrust worse. For example, the governor claimed that the deficit was caused by an increase in Medicaid costs, when the federal government had more than covered the Medicaid increase. Another blunder was the governor's failure to demonstrate that all possible steps to reduce expenditures and increase efficiency had already been taken.[4]

Finance officers in Alabama conducted a survey to try to find out why the proposed taxes were rejected.[5] They found that some of the opposition related to specific tax increase proposals: 68 percent of tax plan opponents

(continued)

strongly objected to the provision to increase the tax rate on automobiles and light trucks; 63 percent were strongly influenced by the provision to assess real property at 100 percent of market value. Opponents also reported being put off by the fact that the governor was seeking twice as much revenue as was necessary to balance the budget; more than half expressed strong reservations about trusting the legislature to allocate the new revenues appropriately.

1. David M. Halbfinger, "G.O.P. Chief's Idea for Raising Alabama: Taxes," *New York Times*, June 4, 2003.
2. Ibid.
3. Eric Fleischauer, "Should the State Eliminate Earmarking Funds?" *Decatur Daily*, May 23, 2003, Decaturdaily.com (accessed August 24, 2003).
4. Karen Bailey, "Readin', Writin' and 'Rithmetic: A Back to School Guide for the Alabama Governor," Center for Individual Freedom, posted September 12, 2003, www.cfif.org/htdocs/legislative_issues/state_issues/bob_riley.htm (accessed August 25, 2004).
5. Jim Seroka, "Alabama's Tax Reform: What Went Wrong and Why?" Alabama Municipal Revenue Officers Association, December 5, 2003, http://web6.duc .auburn.edu/outreach/cgs/publications/Alabamataxvote2003.pdf.

blocking actions. Campaigns to earn public support and defuse opposition need to be carefully designed, and packages of tax increases need to be thoughtfully chosen and combined. The degree of earmarking and the programs to benefit from tax increases must be thought through as well.

Decision-Making Processes

The decision-making process to increase taxes has to be buffered from interest groups and the public to be effective. Individuals and interest groups tend to be both well informed and highly interested in tax proposals; they lobby intensively against proposals that will cost them money. When information about proposals is open to the public, the public in its various forms tends to turn considered technical proposals into mush. But tax-writing legislative committees can buffer themselves against public pressures and interest group pleadings in a variety of ways. Key elements in the process have to do with the degree of openness of the decision making to the public and interest groups, the kind of discipline legislative leaders can exert or the rewards they can provide for other legislative members, and the rules under which bills are considered by the legislative bodies. Open

---

Minicase: A Successful Municipal Tax Increase in Dayton, Ohio

In March 1984 the voters of Dayton, Ohio, overwhelmingly approved an increase in the city's income tax. The tax was presented as part of a package that included property tax relief of $50 per person, a benefit amounting to more than $1.5 million. Other elements of the approved package included pledges to reduce municipal employment by more than one hundred positions over the next five years and to maintain services at current levels, a limit on the city's cash reserves, and the establishment of a Chamber of Commerce review committee to study city expenditure patterns. The increase in the income tax had a sunset provision; that is, it was to terminate in 1990.

City officials engaged in a three-year campaign for acceptance of the tax increase. The campaign included quarterly reports to city council members, to build awareness of the problem, elimination of three hundred city positions by attrition, and meetings with a group of chief executive officers of businesses in the city to explain the need and ask for support. During the nine months immediately before the voting, the mayor and the city manager publicized financial problems, talked to neighborhood groups, and explained the plan to the city unions. The final package was put together by the city council, based on talks with those groups, and then publicized using "lots of personal contact, targeted selling techniques, and endorsements to explain and sell the package to the voters."[1]

1. This case study is taken from Timothy Riordan, "The Dayton Income Tax Increase: A Summary of Success," *Urban Fiscal Ledger* 1, no. 3 (August–September 1984): 1–3.

---

rules allow large numbers of often unrelated amendments, and closed rules prevent amendments after a bill has been passed by committee.

At the national level, the central role in tax decisions of the Ways and Means Committee in the House of Representatives has stimulated much thought on the effect of process on outcomes. For years, the Ways and Means Committee was dominated by its chairman, Rep. Wilbur Mills, D-Ark. He carefully worked out compromise legislation that had the full support of his committee; his recommendations were reported to the floor under a closed rule forbidding amendments and had full committee backing; they were seldom turned down by the House of Representatives.[1] The closed rule prevented House members from inserting tax breaks for special interests into the tax measure when it came to the floor for a vote, and it enhanced the power of the committee chairman. The closed rule, considerable secrecy in committee deliberations, and the selection of members for the Ways and Means Committee who were from safe districts made the committee less accessible to interest groups. Members of the committee were handpicked not only because they were from safe districts, but also because they were known to be disciplined party loyalists.[2] The committee operated as a whole, so its chair did not share authority with subcommittee heads. The chair offered support on special interest tax legislation to obtain backing on major issues. Once he had forged a coalition of support, it held through the legislative process.

The relative inaccessibility of Ways and Means Committee deliberations gave the impression of secrecy and of dominance of tax legislation by an "old-boy" power structure. The congressional reforms of the 1970s, however, opened up the committee's procedures. The chair no longer had the freedom to select members, the committee was expanded in size, and specialized subcommittees were formed. The decision-making process was more open to the public and the press. The ability of committee members to go directly to the press, and their greater independence in getting legislation through, made them less dependent on the chair's support for their special interest legislation, and hence they were less responsive to his rewards for their loyalty. Members were no longer selected to sit on the Ways and Means Committee because of party loyalty or because they had safe seats. Committee members became more vulnerable to interest groups.

Under this structure, the tendency to give away tax breaks (sometimes called "tax expenditures") increased. "Between 1975 and 1980 the revenue losses for tax expenditures rose faster—14 percent a year—than direct outlays, which increased 11 percent annually during that period. From fiscal 1974 to fiscal 1980, tax expenditures grew by 162 percent while outlays rose by 111 percent. In fiscal 1982 total tax expenditures exceeded $260 billion."[3]

After the changes of the 1970s, Ways and Means bills came to the floor under an open rule and were more likely to be amended. The Senate sometimes added amendments to House-passed bills, bypassing the Ways and Means Committee completely; these amendments went directly to conference, without any committee consideration. "The process has become so manipulable that in some ways it resembles an open caucus that can be taken over by virtually any group."[4] This environment strengthened interest groups.

After 1980, the structure changed back in the direction of more committee control over the tax writing process. Rep. Dan Rostenkowski, D-Ill., took firmer control over Ways and Means Committee members, negotiating support for committee positions and threatening punishment for those not supporting the final agreement. The open rule of the 1970s was replaced by a modified open rule, which allows a few specific and germane amendments but not an unlimited number for a range of purposes. In addition, more of the committee's bill writing was done in closed sessions, often without a formal vote. Appointments to the committee increasingly included more senior representatives from safer districts. These changes helped to insulate the committee from interest group pressure and have been credited with helping Ways and Means to design and pass the 1986 tax reform, which reduced the number of tax breaks.[5] After the 1986 tax reform, the rate of increase in tax losses slowed from 14 percent to approximately 6 percent a year.[6]

Process by itself cannot control politicians' desire to do favors. If the consensus to provide sound tax policy is there, the structure can be created to allow it to occur. The consensus tends to form when the environment leaves no doubt about the urgency of the need and when the environment suggests that tax increases are less risky for politicians, as when the opposition party is ineffective. Interest groups do not always determine the outcome if legislators choose to insulate themselves in the interest of avoiding a public policy disaster. But when legislators do not create such an insulating structure, they can be overrun by interest groups.

Tax-Raising Strategies

Public officials use a wide variety of strategies to try to get tax increases passed by the legislature and accepted by the voters. Some of these strategies have been suggested in the Dayton case, for example, convincing the public that there is a need for a tax increase and proving to citizens that their money will not be wasted. The Alabama case pointed out the importance of earmarking new revenues for popular or needed services and the consequences of failure to do so.

The chief executive who supports a tax increase can try to trade support on unrelated bills for support on the tax increase. If legislators feel the threat of being thrown out of office, such promises are often inadequate; the tax package has to be structured to maximize support. There are basically two ways to do that: (1) tie the tax increase to some highly desired service(s) or capital project(s), called "earmarking"; or (2) raise more revenue than is immediately needed to cover costs and distribute the extra income in such a way as to garner the needed votes.

Earmarking. Earmarking revenues means raising them for a specific purpose, so that the money must be spent on that purpose and not on anything else. If the purpose is popular, such as repaving miles of broken residential streets, citizens may be more willing to pay the extra tax for that desired purpose than they would be for general purposes over which they have little control. Those who support a particular program are often eager to have earmarked resources because it means that they do not have to compete with other expenditures in the budget; they can protect their program's funding into the future if they manage to earmark revenues for it. Sometimes powerful lobby groups actually manage to insert earmarking into the state constitution, to lock in a revenue source for the future. Earmarking is relatively common at the state level.

At the national level, one of the major examples of revenue earmarking is Social Security taxes, which are levied on individuals' paychecks and put into a trust fund that is not supposed to be spent on anything else. This arrangement is meant to protect Social Security funding from the demands of other government programs or demands to reduce taxation. There are also earmarked revenues at the federal level for airport construction, highways, and public transportation.

Although earmarking can help get a tax passed, it has a number of disadvantages. It sometimes prevents revenue from being spent on the highest priorities. It links specific revenue sources with specific spending programs, but often without any connection between the amount of revenues produced and the amount needed for the program. Often there is little programmatic connection as well. A portion of the income tax may be spent on local government, as in Illinois; a portion of income from parimutuel betting may be earmarked for mental retardation or indigent medical patients, as in Arkansas; or taxes on tobacco may be earmarked for education and welfare, as in Alabama.[7] Revenue from earmarked taxes may be erratic or even decline, a problem if the money is to be spent on programs that increase in cost as the population grows. These shortcomings may have helped limit earmarking.

Distributing Benefits from a Tax Increase. A second alternative for making revenue increases more palatable is to raise more money than is needed for the immediate problem and then design a package of expenditures that will gain support for the tax increase. This strategy does not always work, as happened in the Alabama case, where popular mistrust of the government was so great and the desire to keep taxes down so strong that raising more than was absolutely needed generated opposition to the tax increase proposal.

Some revenue-raising proposals have been bundled with tax reductions to gain supporters among those who would benefit from the tax revision package. Thus in the Dayton case property taxes were to be reduced for a large number of people, as income taxes were increased. The net amount of revenues is increased, but a large number of people felt that they were getting something positive out of the tax increase.

Some other strategies that public officials use when raising taxes include making the increase temporary, improving accountability, ensuring that the increases are gradual and predictable, and taxing those who lack the power or the means to protest.

Temporary Taxes. Temporary taxes are distinctly easier to pass than permanent ones, but if the need is not temporary (e.g., a short-term recession continues longer than expected), the problem recurs and the scene plays itself out again.

Accountability. Improved accountability can make the difference between whether a tax is accepted by the public or resoundingly rejected. It includes making it clear what the needs are and that there is no waste or corruption and detailing what will be done with the money collected. Not only must the financial records of the government be open to scrutiny, but they must be readable and easily interpreted, and they must answer key questions.

Predictability. Successful campaigns to increase taxes are also sensitive to the need for increasing taxes in a gradual, predictable, and unobtrusive manner. Taxes that increase in unpredictable jumps are apt to arouse the most vociferous opposition because people may be unable to pay them without making significant sacrifices. Sudden, sharp increases in property taxes often have preceded tax revolts. Rather than raise one tax by a large and visible amount, politicians may raise a number of smaller taxes by small amounts, so that no one group is seriously hurt and citizens feel that the burdens are being widely and equitably shared.

Taxing the Politically Weak. Although ethically questionable, another way of gaining acceptance for tax increases is to place the burden for paying for them on those who have relatively little political power. When business is relatively dominant, it shifts the burden of taxation away from business and onto consumers; when labor is dominant, it shifts more of the tax burden onto business and the wealthy. Another version of taxing those too weak to fight back is taxing outsiders, that is, those who do not vote and hence cannot throw politicians out of office. Severance taxes on natural resources are an example. States rich in natural resources tax those resources, and the tax is passed on as part of their price to residents in other states who consume the final product. At the local level, sales taxes in shopping centers are popular in part because they tax shoppers from other cities and towns. Hotel and motel taxes are also popular because they tax the out-of-town traveler rather than the resident.

To summarize, public officials plan very carefully for tax increases. They plan the timing, taking advantage of a lack of organized opposition and an environment that seems to require tax increases. They devise and use processes that insulate them somewhat from interest groups. And they strategize to minimize the pain to voters and build coalitions of support. When tax increases are necessary, public officials must be accountable for the way they have been spending money, in terms of the quality of management (lack of waste) and in terms of following the spending preferences of the public. Their strategies often include conveying to the public the appearance of good management and tying new revenues to particular, popular programs. They may back off from these efforts after the tax increase is passed. Hence the need for periodic tax increases is an important link between the taxpayers and the spenders—to keep the spenders in line with the desires of the payers.

The Politics of Protection

The politics of raising revenues has a mirror image, that of protecting the population in general or specific groups from taxation or lowering tax levels for individuals or groups. Just as raising taxes necessarily brings a certain amount of blame, the lowering of taxes brings, if not praise, at least a measure of gratitude. Interest groups may hire lobbyists to help deflect taxation onto others, or they may contribute to election campaigns to promote candidates who will protect them from tax increases. Groups seeking protection from taxation try to influence the choice of which taxes to use and the definition of taxable wealth; they also try to secure exceptions for themselves from broad-based taxes.

The acceptability of taxation is at least in part a function of where the burden falls. The choices revolve around three issues: (1) which taxes to consider; (2) what definition of taxable wealth is used; (3) what exceptions to broad-based taxes are granted.

The Choice of Revenues to Consider

Part of revenue politics involves pressure to adopt, or increase reliance on, tax sources that burden others more than oneself. The major sources of revenue currently in use are income and wage taxes, sales taxes of various sorts, tariffs, property taxes, and user fees. Each works differently and affects the population differently.

Income Taxes. Income taxes are taxes paid on different forms of income, including wages and income from investments. They are paid by almost everyone who lives in a jurisdiction regardless of where they work or how they derive their income. Income taxes may burden the rich more heavily than the poor, or they can tax everyone the same percentage regardless of income. Income taxes are tied to ability to pay. Wage taxes are also tied to ability to pay, but they are taxes only on earned income, not other sources of income, and they tax those who earn their income in the jurisdiction whether they live there or not. Wage taxes are one way of taxing outsiders, commuters to a city who work there but live and vote elsewhere.

Sales Taxes. Sales taxes are consumer taxes, paid when people or businesses buy something, usually (but not always) a finished product. Retailers, who are the ones who collect the tax, may be inconvenienced, and they have to deal with price increases and a possible reduction in demand. Consumers are the most directly affected, but they pay sales taxes in small, almost invisible amounts during the year, so they tend not to mind them too much. Sales taxes are not very closely linked to ability to pay; they often fall more heavily on the poor than the wealthy because the poor spend a larger proportion of their incomes on taxable items.

Tariffs. Tariffs are fees that foreign producers pay to be allowed to market their goods in this country. Tariffs protect domestic industries from foreign competition by raising the price of imported products, but they also raise prices for consumers. Tariffs are ultimately paid by the consumer, without much regard to ability to pay. Tariffs are levied only by the national government.

Property Taxes. Property taxes are levied on a proportion of the worth or sales value of property people own. This may be personal property (e.g., cars or horses) or real estate (land and houses and buildings). Property taxes on real estate are loosely related to ability to pay because wealthier persons are likely to own more expensive homes, but the relationship is not tight. Older people on fixed incomes may find property taxes rising because the value of their homes is increasing over time. Or a business may own expensive property and equipment but not be making much income on it proportional to the value of the property. Owners of commercial property may pass the tax on to their tenants, who may have less income than the owners.

User Fees. User fees produce revenue when citizens pay in proportion to how much they use a service. For example, you may pay a fee each time you use a public golf course or swimming pool, and you typically pay per gallon for water you use. User fees have the advantage of allowing those who pay to select only the services they want, and not to use them, and not pay, if the cost is too high. But they have several disadvantages as well. First, they often have little to do with ability to pay. And second, others who are not currently using the services directly, and hence not paying for them, may benefit indirectly. Because indirect users are not sharing the cost with the direct users, the direct users have to pay the entire price themselves. One the one hand this is unfair; on the other, the price may be too high to be affordable by many would-be service users.

Business groups often prefer sales taxes on consumers and oppose income taxes, especially those levied on corporate income. Labor groups usually favor income taxes, but as wages have risen, labor rank and file have become more reluctant to support high individual income taxes and more supportive of higher corporate income taxes. Many groups support user fees because they seem to be both fair and voluntaristic. Those who favor smaller government tend to favor user fees.

Because different forms of taxation affect different kinds of wealth, and the regions of the United States depend on different kinds of wealth, the politics of taxation has historically had a strong regional cast. Until the late 1930s, "the Northeast favored first tariffs (which protected their industrial goods) and excise, license and land taxes if needed; the South and West resisted all these taxes, whose impact fell disproportionately on them, and favored taxes on income and wealth, of which they had little." [8]

The regional character of lobbying for or against particular forms of taxation becomes particularly visible when a new tax is proposed. For example, when a new tax on imported oil was proposed, representatives from the New England states opposed it vigorously because it would raise the cost to them of gasoline and fuel oil, but the oil-producing states of the South and West supported the tax, because it would help raise the price of domestically produced oil.[9]

Those who have sufficient political power may seek to bar what they consider unacceptable forms of taxation in constitutions and charters. For example, for many years, the U.S. Constitution contained a prohibition against an income tax, as did a number of state constitutions. Writing such constraints into constitutions slows down the rate of change, but constitutions can be amended.[10] Introducing a new tax in the face of constitutional restrictions may require larger legislative majorities, public referendums, or even constitutional conventions. The courts are often involved to determine if a new tax is constitutional. Thus the number of actors is often greater, the size of groups with veto power often smaller, and the time required longer for new taxes than for increasing traditional taxes.

Defining Taxable Wealth

Once the type of tax has been determined, the actual burden of it may depend on how taxable wealth is defined. For example, governments might choose to measure the taxable worth of property based on the square footage, or the number of linear feet along the street, or the number of windows in the building. Two people with nearly identical houses might pay different amounts of tax depending on how many windows they have. Choosing how taxable wealth will be measured is not merely a technical decision; it is also a political decision, and it necessarily hurts some and helps others.

Historically, rural areas have wanted to make sure that the basis of taxation, the measure of wealth, was something they had little of and cities had much of. They worked to define property taxes in terms of both realty (houses, buildings, machinery) and personalty (other forms of wealth, including bonds, mortgages, and other money instruments). Farmers wanted to define the base of taxation to include the new wealth of the cities, of which the farmers had little; they also sought exemptions of various kinds for their own equipment and herds.[11]

Tax Breaks

As passed, a tax may place its burden on one group or another, but the weight of that burden may change over the years as politicians grant exemptions from the tax. Such exemptions can be viewed as political protections for certain groups or economic classes. Regardless of the level of government at which they occur, tax breaks share some common features:

1. They represent dollars that the government is theoretically owed that it has decided not to collect.
2. Analysts estimate the size of losses to the government, usually based on how much taxpayers save because of the tax break. But if the tax break were eliminated, the government might not get all the revenue that the analysts estimated it lost because taxpayers might take advantage of some other tax break instead. Because of this potential interaction among tax breaks, estimates of losses from different tax breaks—termed "tax expenditures"—cannot be added up reliably.
3. Absent dollars are much more difficult to count and account for than dollars one receives in one's hands. As a result, tax expenditures tend to be less visible than direct expenditures and often receive less scrutiny than direct budget outlays.
4. Over time, broad taxes may be eroded by exceptions for particular groups. Sometimes when a tax is passed or the structure of a tax is changed in a way that hurts a particular group, that group may pressure lawmakers for tax breaks to lessen the burden on themselves. How responsive lawmakers are to these pressures depends somewhat on the political strength of the group making the demands. At the state level, officials are often responsive to pressure from the dominant industries in their states. California taxes the movie industry lightly, and Wiscon-

sin favors the beer industry. North Carolina favors the tobacco industry, and Michigan protects its auto industry.[12]

5. During a period of economic stress, the tendency to give tax breaks to businesses gains momentum. When the economy began to falter in the middle 1970s, pressure increased for government to stimulate investment and capital formation. The national government responded with a number of tax breaks, aimed primarily at businesses and upper-income taxpayers. The number of tax expenditures greatly increased between 1975 and 1981, compared to the preceding twenty-nine years.[13] Many states have responded to economic problems in similar ways. In the middle 1970s, when unemployment hit 8 percent, governors were "under tremendous pressure to do something—anything. Most states responded with conventional medicine: they cut taxes and offered large firms in other states a host of tax and financial incentives to open new plants across state lines." [14] Cities have responded similarly to weakening economies, granting additional tax breaks to businesses.[15]

6. Tax breaks are often rationalized in terms of the public policy objectives they are supposed to achieve. However, it is uncommon for governments to supervise or evaluate these tax grants to see if they are really necessary or are achieving their claimed goals. Thus the federal government provides a tax break for investors who loan money to cities, so that cities can borrow at less expense than private sector companies. The public purpose is to encourage the building of infrastructure, such as streets, buildings, and drainage, that is needed for the economy to function. But there is no supervision to see if the borrowing has indeed gone for such purposes.

Within these overall similarities, there is considerable variation in the nature, use, and politics of tax expenditures at the federal, state, and local levels.

Some of the differences are in the amount of secrecy or reporting: The national government has reported the size of tax expenditures since 1974, and some thirty three states report on their tax expenditures, but only a handful of local governments do. At the state level it is difficult, and at the local level virtually impossible, to figure out the amount, the purposes, and the effectiveness of tax breaks because there is almost no information about them.

A second difference has to do with the way the tax breaks are worded and hence how rapidly they spread and increase in cost. At the national level, tax breaks are generally written as entitlements, so that the more individuals or companies are eligible for them and apply for them, the more they cost. Costs thus increase without additional legislation. There is also a logic by which tax breaks tend to expand to different groups—if oil companies can get for themselves a tax break based on the fact that they are depleting natural resources, then other companies that use natural resources should also be eligible for the tax break. The companies with more clout thus open paths for those with less clout. At the state level, there is a combination of entitlement programs and project-by-project funding. Project-by-project funding is somewhat more controllable, although the costs of particular projects may be very high as politicians seek high-profile successes. Larger cities often have some entitlement programs, but mostly project-based tax breaks, and smaller ones use only project subsidies.

A third difference has to do with the cost of the money being given away and who is paying it. At the national level, it is federal taxes that are being given away, and the consequence of a frenzy of tax expenditures is a budget deficit and/or forced cuts in spending. Although states cannot run deficits over a multiyear period, they can give away not only their own revenues but also those of the local governments, sometimes reimbursing the local governments for the losses and sometimes not. Cities can give tax breaks that reduce federal revenues, as when they give their tax-free borrowing status to businesses, and they can reduce the revenue growth of school districts and other special-purpose governments through tax increment financing, which uses increased property tax revenues that results from public infrastructure improvements to pay off the costs of those projects. Cities use not only tax revenue due to them, but also that due to other jurisdictions located in the tax increment district boundaries. Tax breaks financed from such sources may seem low cost or free to state and local governments, and that encourages their use.

A fourth difference has to do with the drivers of tax expenditures. At the national level, although some of the push for tax breaks is based on programmatic goals, much is also based on political goals and the aim of pleasing constituents. Tax breaks are seldom enacted for the purpose of making taxes more equitable, though they may be used to roll back new burdens created by increased taxation. This is done in lieu of tax reform and often creates greater inequities. At the state level, however, tax expenditures function not only to support major industries in the state that have political clout and to try to offset recessions, but also to make taxes more equitable. The federal income tax is progressive, but many state and local revenue sources are not; tax exemptions for the poor, elderly, or handicapped can help ameliorate the negative impacts of this more regressive tax base. Exemptions and tax breaks are also used to help temper public anger at taxation more broadly. Both state and local governments compete in bidding wars for businesses with other states and cities, a process that pushes up the cost of individual deals. This particular problem is not one that affects the national government.

**Table 2.1   Estimated Total Revenue Loss from Tax Expenditures,
FY 1988–2004 (in billions of dollars)**

Year	Individual	Corporate	Total
2004	689	80	769
2003	680	87	767
2002	665	92	757
2001	635	82	717
2000	569	75	643
1999	539	64	603
1998	487	69	556
1997	423	56	479
1996	407	57	464
1995	381	63	444
1994	352	57	408
1993	340	48	389
1992	328	46	374
1991	309	46	355
1990	284	58	343
1989	269	62	331
1988	253	49	302

Notes: Figures are rounded to the nearest billion. Figures for 2003–2004 include estimates for reduced rates on long-term capital gains from the Joint Committee on Taxation, *Estimates of Federal Tax Expenditures 2003–2008.* All other estimates are derived from the *U.S. Budget, Fiscal Years 1990–2006, Analytical Perspectives.*

Federal-Level Tax Expenditures. One of the functions of tax breaks at the national level is to reduce the burden of taxation on particular classes of people or businesses when the structure of a tax changes. As the burden on a group increases, the demand for exceptions for that group is likely to increase.

Some tax breaks have been policy responses to currently perceived problems, such as the gasoline shortages of the 1970s. In 1978, as part of its response to the energy crisis, the Carter administration requested, and Congress passed, a package of tax-incentives for individuals and businesses to insulate their homes and save energy. The estimated cost to the Treasury in 1979 was $935 million.[16] (See Tables 2.1 and 2.2, which display the increasing amounts of foregone revenue.)

The dollar amounts of tax breaks at the national level have been enormous, exceeding the size of even the largest deficits. After a major tax reform in 1986, dollars lost to tax expenditures began to grow again, edging up slowly at first, at 3 percent or 4 percent a year until 1997, and then much more quickly after that.

Table 2.2 Federal Tax Expenditures as Percentages of Income Tax Receipts, FY 1988–2003

Year	Individual	Corporate	Total
2004	85	42	77
2003	82	66	80
2002	78	67	75
2001	64	54	63
2000	57	36	53
1999	61	35	57
1998	59	37	55
1997	57	31	52
1996	62	33	56
1995	65	35	59
1994	65	41	60
1993	66	41	54
1992	69	46	65
1991	66	47	63
1990	61	62	61
1989	60	60	60
1988	63	52	61

Notes: Estimates for 2003–2004 include estimates for reduced rates and long-term capital gains from the Joint Committee on Taxation, *Estimates of Federal Tax Expenditures 2003–2008.* All other estimates are derived from the *U.S. Budget, Fiscal Years 1990–2006, Analytical Perspectives.*

By 2004 over $700 billion of revenue was forgone annually in the form of tax expenditures. The increase appears even more dramatic when viewed as a proportion of personal and corporate income taxes collected. (Keep in mind that any figure that sums tax expenditures is only a ballpark estimate.)[17]

The Bush administration expanded several tax expenditures in 2001 but at the same time reduced marginal income tax rates, particularly for upper-income payers. When marginal rates are lower, then tax breaks save people less money, and the estimated losses due to tax expenditures are lower. The reductions in the marginal rates were to be phased in over time. As a result, for recent years the rate of growth in losses to the Treasury has slowed somewhat. Nevertheless the absolute level of losses to the Treasury is an astounding amount of money, especially now that the government is once again running huge deficits.

If tax expenditures could be reduced, there would be more money available—translating into smaller program cuts or a more balanced budget. Hence curtailing revenue losses from tax expenditures has been tempting to supporters of federal spending programs and advocates of balanced budgets. Tax expenditures, however, have proved a difficult target. Over time, the list of tax expenditures has grown to include breaks supported by both Democrats and Republicans. Attacking the whole list tends to provoke the whole of Congress. But attacking only some of the list has not been successful. When a group of reformers on Capitol Hill proposed reducing so-called corporate welfare (a partisan approach), meaning a series of tax breaks for businesses, they did not attract enough support to pass the measure. Their next approach was to form a commission that would make tax expenditure reduction decisions impartially and take the political onus off individual members of Congress. That approach failed also.

Tax expenditures have proved enduring, despite pressures to balance the budget. There are several reasons for this impressive record of persistence. One is that tax expenditures for individuals are considered entitlements. People and corporations build these tax breaks into their lives and business operations and are unwilling to consider giving them up. Second, the tax breaks cover a wide range of interests and constituencies; nearly every elected official has some constituency to protect. Pork—grants and projects that members of Congress can direct to particular constituencies—had been sharply limited while the country was trying to balance the budget (before 1997). To the extent that tax breaks substituted for pork, members of Congress were extremely unwilling to give them up. The budget process at that time made it easier to create new or expanded programs through tax expenditures than through direct, discretionary expenditures, which were tightly capped. It was easier and more politically acceptable to find an offset to a tax break than it was to raise the caps. A tax expenditure looked simultaneously like a tax cut and a program expansion, and that combination—appearing to give more services for fewer dollars—fit the spirit of the times. More recently, the requirement that tax reductions be offset by enhanced revenue elsewhere was eliminated, making tax expenditures easier to pass. Finally, tax breaks do not receive the level of scrutiny in Congress that more direct expenditures face.

Tax breaks at the federal level have often been justified in terms of achieving programmatic goals. They are, in this sense, the equivalent of direct outlays. Thus tax reductions to homeowners for the interest on their mortgage payments are explained in terms of encouraging a stable home-owning class. The good to be achieved also includes stimulation of the economy, as home building requires not only lumber and other raw materials but also products such as washing machines, refrigerators, air conditioners, and heaters, all of which require raw materials and processing. Such tax breaks benefit the home-building industry and realtors, but they are rationalized in terms of a national good.

This attempt to use tax breaks as a policy tool or to rationalize them in terms of national goals opens tax breaks to several tests: Will this tax break help resolve some existing social or economic problem? Would some other form of subsidy achieve more of the goal less expensively than this tax break? When evaluated in these terms, tax breaks often do not look very good.

Lower taxes on capital gains have been justified in terms of encouraging investment and capital formation, but they have been used in periods when capital was generally available as well as when capital was in short supply. This anomaly makes one question whether this tax break was really intended to solve an economic problem or whether it was just a benefit to those earning substantial income from investments.

Even when tax breaks are clearly intended to solve a problem, they may be much more expensive than solving the problem another way. For example, the federal government allows local governments to borrow using tax-free municipal bonds. Cities can pay less interest because investors loaning money to the city will accept a lower rate, as they do not have to pay federal income tax on the earnings. (Instead of getting all their return on investment from interest payments from local governments, investors receive part of their return from reduced payments on their federal income taxes.) The federal government loses revenues that it would otherwise have earned; wealthy individuals and corporations that invest in municipal bonds get a substantial portion of the benefit; and only a limited portion of the money the federal government loses goes to cities to help lower borrowing costs. It would be cheaper for the federal government to give dollars to local governments to build infrastructure than to subsidize construction through tax breaks.

When tax breaks do not meet tests of efficiency and effectiveness, one wonders why they are used instead of more efficient and effective alternatives. One possibility is that the stated policy goals of creating the tax break were just a loose cover for granting favors to constituents or political supporters. Whether a tax break does or does not achieve a stated policy goal may be irrelevant if it is achieving desired political (distributional) goals.

Another reason for using inefficient tax breaks is that they sometimes increase the number of people and institutions that benefit from a program and hence enhance political support for that program. For example, the tax break on interest from municipal bonds creates a large pool of beneficiaries of a program ostensibly designed to reduce the borrowing costs of local governments. On their own, local governments in recent years have not had enough political power to retain many of their direct program benefits from the federal government, but the subsidy on bonds has proved difficult to remove because all those who invest in tax-free municipal bonds become a potential lobby to maintain this subsidy to local government. Local governments are aware of this political advantage and have tried to prevent a shift of their subsidy to the direct spending side of the budget, which they see as more vulnerable to cutbacks.

Another possible reason for preferring tax breaks over direct outlays is that they are somewhat less visible to the public. Since 1974 the Congressional Budget Reform Act has required that tax expenditures be listed and at least roughly summarized in the budget, and tax expenditures have to be passed by Congress and the president just like other legislation. The federal government is much more open about tax expenditures than are other levels of government. Nevertheless, it is in the nature of tax breaks to be less visible than program outlays. For example, it is reasonably easy to estimate the welfare benefit payments to a mother with five children in a particular state, but it is very difficult, if not impossible, for a journalist or citizen to figure out what the dollar benefit to a business is from combined tax breaks. The public is generally not aware that benefits to the middle class from tax breaks equal or exceed direct spending for the poor in some program areas. Partly because of the lower visibility of tax expenditures to the public, tax expenditure programs can be passed that would not be passed if they were open to the same kind of scrutiny and examination as direct outlays.

Paul McDaniel has spelled out the policy implications of the tax break for employer-provided health insurance, for example, and then asked if a direct spending program with these features would pass Congress: This tax expenditure covers only those who are employed; the unemployed are not covered. The decision whether employees will participate in the program is left to the discretion of the employer—neither the government nor the employee has any say. There is no limit on the size of the tax expenditure. The federal contribution is proportional to the marginal tax rate of the taxpayer; thus wealthier folks get a bigger subsidy on their health insurance. If a couple earns $80,000 a year, McDaniel argued, the federal government pays $31 per $100 of premium; if the couple's taxable income is below $10,000 a year, the federal government pays none of the couple's premium. It seemed to McDaniel that Congress was unlikely to design a health care spending program that would have these features.[18]

The Government Performance and Results Act of 1993 required evaluation of the efficiency and effectiveness of tax breaks in achieving programmatic goals. But the initial administrative response was that the data were inadequate to establish performance measures; data would be gathered for a handful of tax breaks, and measures set up for them. Progress has been slow, even for this limited number of test cases. Though the idea is clear—that tax expenditures should be chosen as a vehicle for program delivery only when they are more efficient and effective than other delivery methods—this long-desired integration of tax expenditures with other budgetary resources still seems a long way off.

Writing in 2003, ten years after the Government Performance and Results act was passed, Leonard Burman, a former Treasury Department employee, explained why so little progress had been made:

> Clinton's Treasury Department, of which I was a part from 1998 to 2000, was unenthusiastic about performing these evaluations, reasoning that a comprehensive evaluation of tax expenditures would necessarily raise serious objections to measures enthusiastically advanced by the Administration. The result would either be a waste of staff time, as a credible analysis would never be published, or a whitewash that would damage the credibility of the Treasury staff. Although the menu of favorite tax expenditures changed when President Bush took office, the Office of Management and Budget has not published any new tax expenditure analyses as part of GPRA, suggesting that the same concerns still hold sway.[19]

To summarize, because the federal government's budget is so large, tax breaks, even relatively small ones, can have impacts on the economy and on people's behavior, whether they are buying a house or drilling an oil well. Tax breaks can have legitimate policy goals. But these legitimate policy goals can easily become confused with more mundane political matters, such as responding to pressure from an interest group that wants to reduce its tax liability. These latter tax expenditures are often rationalized in terms of national goals to be achieved. When programs funded through tax breaks are compared with programs funded with direct outlays, they may be less efficient and less effective, but they may be more politically potent.

The rationalizations used to legitimize political giveaways to powerful lobbies can also be used by others who are less powerful to leverage further tax breaks. If the powerful oil lobby can get a tax break for depleting natural resources, then so can those whose business is to turn shells into paving materials in the south, and even those who use sand as a raw material. Nevertheless, federal-level tax breaks are not completely uncontrollable. Congressional committees can buffer themselves from interest groups. When it chooses to, Congress can require offsets for every reduction in revenues. When offset requirements are in place, legislators are more likely to watch the number and size of tax breaks awarded.

After balance was achieved (more or less) the spending caps and offset requirements of the Budget Enforcement Act (BEA) remained in place but were widely ignored. The discipline they imposed was considered too constraining in a period of budget surpluses. Deficits returned quickly and with gusto. Nevertheless, when

Minicase: Tax Expenditures and the Battle over Offsets

The temptation to give away tax breaks is strong because their visibility is low and they are always appreciated by constituents. However, unless tax breaks are offset, by closing other tax loopholes or otherwise increasing taxation or cutting expenditures, they contribute to the growth of deficits. To help control the granting of tax breaks, the Budget Enforcement Act of 1990 required that their costs be offset. On the one hand this requirement made the costs real at the time when the break was passed, and on the other, it forced trade-offs, making legislators say what it was that was less important than granting this particular exception to the tax code. Tax breaks were permissible only if they didn't make the deficit worse. This and other features of the Budget Enforcement Act, such as caps on direct spending, were credited with helping to achieve budgetary balance by 1998.

the caps and pay-as-you-go requirements of the BEA expired in 2002, they were not renewed. The Senate passed a temporary measure requiring a 60 percent majority to pass any tax reduction without an offset, but the House had no such provision, setting up tension between the House and the Senate over extensions and expansions of tax expenditures. Since one of the key policy goals of President George W. Bush and the Republican majority was to reduce taxes, there was enormous pressure to extend existing tax breaks, regardless of the effect on the deficit.

What made the issue more politically problematic for the Democratic opposition was that the specific proposals to extend tax expenditures that came before Congress in 2004 were billed as tax reductions for the middle class. Some senators held out for months, arguing that offsets were necessary for any tax expenditure, popular or otherwise, but in the end the so-called middle-class tax cuts (eliminating the marriage penalty, the extension of a 10 percent tax bracket for the first $7,000 of taxable income, and the expansion of the child tax credit) were passed without an offset. The package also included extension of exemptions to the Alternative Minimum Tax, a law that ensured that wealthy people paid some taxes. The appearance of benefiting the middle class (even though wealthy people benefited even more), combined with the timing of the proposals (just before a major election) made it nearly impossible for Democrats to resist voting in favor of the extensions, despite the loss of revenue and the resulting increase in the size of the deficit.[20]

The State Level. On the state level, tax expenditures have expanded since the 1970s and 1980s. They have traditionally been used to protect key industries and powerful lobbies. More recently they have been used to stimulate the economy and as a response to protests against taxes.

In Illinois, twenty-eight tax breaks were enacted between 1979 and 1989. Twenty of those were enacted between 1979 and 1984, just after Proposition 13 in California demonstrated the depth of antitax sentiment and just following the deep recession of the early 1980s. Roughly categorized by purpose, nine of the tax breaks were to encourage economic development; six were efforts to make taxes more equitable or otherwise reduce pressure for tax limits; nine were responses to powerful local industries; and five were responses to other requests or worthy causes.[21] Between 1979 and 1989, Washington State passed a whopping 110 new tax expenditures. The rate slowed in the early 1990s but picked up again in the mid-1990s. In 2003 Washington State passed a record number of new tax expenditures, thirty-eight in one year, at least in part in response to the recession of 2001 and its aftermath.[22]

Even granting that states are more likely to adopt tax expenditure reporting if they are extreme in the dollar amounts of tax breaks granted, the amounts of revenue that these states report losing due to tax breaks is dramatic. California reported tax expenditures of about $19.2 billion from the state income tax in fiscal year 2004, an additional $4.3 billion in annual losses from the corporate tax, and $340 million in losses from sales and use and other tax expenditures.[23] Massachusetts reported a combined $14.1 billion in tax expenditure losses for 2004.[24] In 2005, Texas reported exemptions from sales, franchise, gasoline, and motor vehicle sales taxes of $25.8 billion for the year.[25]

States are less able than the federal government to use tax breaks to stimulate the economy by giving people more money to spend and increasing aggregate economic demand. Instead, they have tried to use tax breaks and other incentives to lure businesses in from other states and retain businesses threatening to leave the state. States have used this competitive logic extensively and expensively.[26] States argue that they have to offer expensive tax breaks to lure and retain businesses because other states do. For example, the Illinois State Fiscal and Economic Commission has argued:

> As demonstrated, Illinois offers a wide variety of incentives to corporations as a way to lure them into our state. Illinois must do this in order to compete with other states that also want the economic opportunities that these businesses can create. Because of this competition, new incentive programs are continuing to be created in an attempt to stay one step ahead of other competing states. . . . The fact is, state and local governments, in the face of competition, are forced to put up incentives or risk losing desired investment. Because of this, right or wrong, business incentives are not going away in the

near future. Many scholars, economic development professionals, and state legislators have called for federal intervention to stop incentives. However, this cannot be accomplished on a state by state basis because any state that does not remove its incentive packages would immediately be the welcoming target of businesses looking to relocate, leaving other states behind. It is for this reason that a resolution can only come at a national level.[27]

This competition has increasingly led states to offer businesses the same set of tax breaks. For example, in 1974 six states offered tax exemptions to encourage research and development, but by 1992, thirty-one states offered this tax break. In 1974, eighteen states offered an exemption to industries on the corporate income tax, but by 1992, thirty-five states offered this break. One study reported that "by 1998, more than 40 states offered tax concessions or credits to businesses for equipment and machinery, goods in transition, manufacturers' inventories, raw materials in manufacturing and job creation. . . . Similarly, the number of states with financial-incentive programs also increased over the past two decades. By 1998, more than 40 states offered special low interest loans for building construction, equipment, machinery, plant expansion and establishment of industrial plants in areas of high unemployment."[28] The trend is uniform across a variety of tax breaks, with most of the competition and resulting imitation taking place before 1989.[29]

As the tax incentives became more similar, states had to outbid each other in the size of the tax breaks to compete successfully. The costs of tax breaks per job created in the automobile industry increased from $11,000 in 1980 (the Nissan plant in Tennessee) to $65,000 per job in 1992 (the BMW plant in South Carolina) to $200,000 in 1993 (Alabama, Mercedes).[30] More recent subsidies for automotive plants, while lower than the Alabama Mercedes plant, are still high. The state and local subsidy to Ford for the manufacturing campus in Chicago in 2000, at $119,000 per job anticipated, was well above the state's goal of $10,000 per job.[31] In Michigan, in March 2004, state and local tax breaks to General Motors for a plant conversion amounted to $30 million, with the hope of saving (not creating) 518 jobs—roughly $58,000 per job retained, under the assumption that all the jobs would be lost without the subsidy. Paying to keep jobs in the state is the flip side of offering incentives to companies from outside the state to relocate.[32]

The direct costs of particular deals with companies often underestimate the real costs, which may extend well beyond the individual company and the particular deal. Tax incentives for economic development are often phrased as entitlements. For example, some benefits, such as reduced taxes to companies that expand and hire twenty or more additional employees, are generally available to all who meet

Minicase: Boeing and Washington State

States sometimes get into a competitive mode and try to outbid other states in providing incentives to corporations, even when the number of jobs in question is not great or, as in the case of Boeing and Washington State, actually negative. In the case of Boeing, the company was threatening to take its jobs assembling a new plane to some other state. Washington State offered not only major tax breaks for Boeing but also reductions in worker compensation payments for all businesses in the state.

To justify the deal, state officials claimed they were helping to safeguard existing jobs. Boeing was only promising to perform the final assembly of the new plane in Washington, and that only if the state promised major subsidies. The plane parts were being manufactured elsewhere. Boeing had been the major employer in the state for many years, and the state legislature had always provided whatever Boeing asked for. With this particular request, Democratic lawmakers were reportedly afraid to criticize the deal, lest they be labeled as the people who lost Boeing.

The state provided nearly $4 billion in tax and other incentives without requiring a single net new job. After the deal was struck, Boeing continued to reduce employment in Washington State in other product lines, creating a net loss of jobs to the state.[1]

What is especially interesting about the subsidy to Boeing is not only its expense and lack of guarantee of public benefit, but also its secrecy. The Evergreen Freedom Foundation, a conservative watchdog organization, worked hard to learn the provisions of the deal with Boeing and complained that the state was refusing to release various details. After months of effort and freedom of information requests, the Evergreen Freedom Foundation listed what it had been able to find out about some of the "extras" in the contract:

- Seven full-time employees to be hired by the state (with Boeing's approval) to expedite the company's permitting requests, coordinate workforce training, work on the company's transportation needs, provide advice and consulting on state tax policy, pursue and apply for grants, coordinate relations between the company and state and local governments, etc.
- Special exemptions from sales, use, and property taxes
- Rate freezes for water, sewer, wastewater treatment, and solid waste services
- Favorable treatment in environmental impact analyses

(continued)

- State payment for and management of all recruitment, screening, and training of the workforce needed for Boeing's 7E7 project
- A state-bought (or built) facility to serve as Boeing's Employment Resource Center, with all costs associated with operation, maintenance and repair of the facility paid for by the state[2]

The Evergreen Freedom Foundation also reported that there was a provision in the agreement "instructing all parties with access to 'withhold or redact' all details of the agreement 'to the fullest extent permitted by law.'"

The *Seattle Weekly* added another layer to the story, and a possible explanation for some of the secrecy, when it revealed that the state paid Deloitte Consulting $715,000 to help it woo Boeing. Boeing is a client of Deloitte, which reportedly put the massive subsidy request before the governor. Deloitte, like many other consulting firms, makes its money by maximizing the benefits it can extract from the state government for its clients. For the state to hire this same company to do a study to figure out whether and how much to subsidize Boeing does not seem like a good way to safeguard the public interest. Apparently all parties knew that Deloitte was working for Boeing when the state hired the consultants—in its advertising, Deloitte lists Boeing as a famous customer. Both Deloitte and Boeing were reportedly delighted with the deal, having gotten all they asked for. The result was not surprising, inasmuch as no one represented the public in this process.[3]

1. Bob Williams, "Boeing 7E7 = Washington Jobs?" *Policy Highlighter* 14, no. 11, May 11, 2004, Evergreen Freedom Foundation Web site, www.effwa.org (accessed August 26, 2004).
2. "Details of Boeing Agreement Revealed," Evergreen Freedom Foundation, Media Center, press release, January 21, 2004, www.effwa.org.
3. Rick Anderson, "The State's Two-Timing Consultant," *Seattle Weekly,* March 17–23, 2004.

certain conditions. Even in case-by-case negotiations, the design of an individual deal may open the way for other companies to obtain the same tax break. For example, in the Alabama-Mercedes case, to benefit Mercedes the state passed a law that would allow any company that was investing over $5 million and creating at least fifty jobs to use the money it would have paid in state income taxes to pay off its debt. The law allowed such companies to use the income taxes deducted from employee wages to pay for land, equipment, and plant.[33] In Illinois, the deal made to keep Sears in the state required the state to pass new legislation broadening the use of tax increment financing districts, watering down the legislation that required the land to be blighted or in need of redevelopment. And sometimes deals include not only specific benefits but also law changes that apply to all businesses, such as changes in regulations on unemployment benefits and worker compensation.

In this competition among states, bigger plants promising more jobs are likely to get bigger subsidies on a per-job basis. Although these large companies look like great prizes, the number of jobs expected, especially auxiliary or secondary jobs, is often exaggerated. Not only do many businesses fail to reach the total number of jobs promised as a condition of getting aid and cost more than state or federal policy guidelines suggest is appropriate, but states sometimes do not try to get back their subsidies when businesses fail to deliver on their promises.[34]

Consultant studies may exaggerate the public benefit that a state can expect from a project to justify a larger set of incentives. For example, when Illinois was trying to lure Boeing's headquarters to Chicago, decision makers relied on a study by the now-discredited Arthur Andersen firm. Andersen wildly exaggerated the number of secondary jobs that the subsidy would produce. Illinois came up with major incentives for Boeing but has refused to make the Andersen study public, although it was paid for with public funds and therefore legally should be open to public scrutiny.[35]

The Boeing cases in both Washington and Illinois illustrate the kind of secrecy that often veils these deals. Unless the press or a particular watchdog group follows the cases carefully, it may be impossible for the public to know how much subsidy was given to which company, in return for what kind of promises. Hence it may be impossible to sort out the claims from the actual results. Recently in Hawaii, an internal staff estimate of the costs of tax breaks to businesses was withheld from a journalist.[36] Some states do not even make public the estimated cost of the tax breaks they have passed, making them appear free not only to the public but also to the decision makers. As of 2002, thirty-three states had tax expenditure reports of some sort, with the District of Columbia coming on board later that year.[37] Among the states that do report tax expenditures, most do not list the costs of tax breaks on a business-by-business basis.

To summarize, tax breaks to businesses may be justified as a way to stimulate the economy or create jobs, but the decisions about such subsidies may not be made on any rational calculus of cost and benefit. State officials sometimes get caught up in a competition with other states and feel they have to win, regardless of the cost, or feel that they will be blamed if a company leaves a state because they didn't offer a big enough subsidy. Especially when there is no publicly justifiable reason for the size of the subsidy, states may yield to pressure to keep parts or all of a deal secret. One consequence is that the overall cost and the effectiveness of these deals are hard to gauge. Although many analysts and state officials have become skeptical about

Minicase: Iowa—How a Tax Incentive Program Was Terminated

Elected officials often argue that they have no choice but to offer an incentive program, as long as other states do. They argue that they cannot terminate their programs unilaterally. Hence the demise of a business tax incentive plan in Iowa in 2004 is worth examining. What happened?

Two principles compete in the use of taxes to facilitate the growth of the economy at the state level. According to one, tax breaks are targeted to specific businesses to bring new jobs and income to the state. According to the other, taxes are reduced for all businesses and business regulation is reduced to increase business profitability and ease of operations. In Iowa, the two principles—tax reduction for all businesses versus tax breaks for new businesses bringing in new jobs—collided, with an unintended outcome.

When Iowa governor Tom Vilsack, a Democrat, proposed a fund for economic incentives to bring high-tech companies to the state, Republicans added to the governor's legislative proposal two other features bound to be popular: a tax reduction and eased regulations for businesses. These pro-business measures would win the Republicans political credit with mostly Republican business owners, while the Democratic governor was trying to take credit for bringing jobs and businesses to the state. Moreover, the Republicans could put the Democratic governor in a bad spot by reducing revenues. Unlike the national government, states are required to balance their budgets, but to do that the governor would have to cut programs, making him unpopular with his constituents.

Between a rock and a hard place, Vilsack exercised his line-item veto power, crossing out of the legislation the Republican income tax reduction for businesses and the reduced regulations. Outraged Republican leaders of the state legislature quickly sued the governor for exceeding his powers, claiming he had used the line-item veto on a policy as opposed to a budget item. The court sided with the Republicans and determined that the governor had indeed exceeded his powers. Contrary to the Republicans' aim in the lawsuit, however, the state supreme court declared the entire law, including the incentive package, the tax reduction, and the deregulatory package, null and void. The Republicans had hoped the court would restore their portion of the bill, not kill the whole bill.

A compromise was eventually worked out that terminated the incentives program, set aside a hundred million dollars from federal funds to pay for obligations already incurred under the program before the court threw out the law, and gave business a smaller, temporary tax reduction of $87 million

(continued)

for new equipment purchases, instead of the $310 million reduction in income taxes originally proposed. The compromise included some changes in workers' compensation for workers injured more than once.

Although the outcome suggests that an individual state can terminate an incentives program, the termination did not result from an evaluation of the cost or the effectiveness of the program. Rather it was the result of intense partisan conflict and different approaches to economic development policy.[1]

1. "Iowa Supreme Court Strikes Down Vilsack's Veto," TheIowaChannel.com, June 13, 2004; Jonathan Roos and Frank Santiago, "Millions Approved to Spur Business Growth," DesMoinesRegister.com, September 8, 2004.

them, they often feel powerless to change practices and want the federal government to pass a law applying to all the states. As long as secret deals continue, however, they erode the openness of the budget document and process.

Besides trying to rebuild the economy during or just after a recession by providing incentives to businesses to locate in the state, states have used tax expenditures to improve equity and reduce the burden of highly unpopular taxes, in an effort to reduce anti-tax sentiment and curtail public efforts to limit taxes and expenditures. The tax breaks are a kind of stopgap solution, often called tax relief, rather than genuine or far-reaching tax reform. In this context, tax breaks on the property tax have been widespread.

At the state level, efforts to head off tax revolts have resulted in both reductions in taxes for people who live in their own homes (homestead exemptions) and so-called circuit breakers to reduce the property taxes of the poor, elderly, or disabled. They are called "circuit breakers" because they kick in to provide relief when tax levels become unbearable, just as circuit breakers cut off the flow when the amount of electricity exceeds the capacity of house wiring. The analogy is not perfect, as circuit breakers reduce the burden but do not eliminate it. By 1992, thirty-six states had adopted circuit breakers. Most of these provisions were adopted between 1971 and 1977, a time of rapid inflation in housing prices and massive discontent with property taxation. An even greater proportion of states (forty-five out of fifty, plus the District of Columbia) have adopted homestead exemptions. Of these, nineteen provide the benefit to all homeowners who live in their own homes, and most provide additional benefits to the poor, the elderly or disabled, or veterans. The amount of revenue lost by these exemptions is significant, especially in states where eligibility for benefits is broad. Five states lost over

Table 2.3 Estimated Costs of State Circuit Breaker Programs

State (fiscal year)	Amount (in thousands of dollars)	State (fiscal year)	Amount (in thousands of dollars)
Arizona (1991)	12,743	Nevada (1991)	2,636
Arkansas (1992)	3,950	New Jersey (1990)	n.a.
California (1992)	16,699	New Mexico (1991)	3,903
Colorado (1992)	14,462	New York (1989)	50,800
Connecticut (1992)	27,916	North Dakota (1992)	2,381
District of Columbia (1992)	8,854	Ohio (1991)	56,094
Hawaii (1991)	5,819	Oklahoma (1991)	398
Idaho (1992)	6,031	Oregon (1990)	6,365
Illinois (1990)	104,354	Pennsylvania (1991)	108,681
Indiana (1991)	n.a.	Rhode Island (1991)	653
Iowa (1990)	10,737	South Dakota (1991)	1,000
Kansas (1992)	8,700	Tennessee (1992)	7,026
Maine (1992)	7,494	Utah (1991)	n.a.
Maryland (1991)	48,397	Vermont (1992)	22,010
Michigan (1990)	773,555	Washington	n.a.
Minnesota (1991)	133,500	West Virginia (1991)	n.a.
Missouri (1992)	17,973	Wisconsin (1992)	105,505
Montana (1990)	4,090	Wyoming (1992)	n.a.

Source: Advisory Commission on Intergovernmental Relations, *Significant Features of Fiscal Federalism, 1994,* vol. 1 (Washington, D.C.: U.S. Government Printing Office, 1994), table 39.

$100 million in 1990, including Michigan, which lost $773 million in revenue to circuit breakers that year. Homestead exemptions cost California $3.2 billion in revenues in 1992; Florida lost $1.7 billion in 1991; and Texas school districts lost $1.1 billion in 1990. These are the high-end figures; most states lost considerably less than these amounts (see Tables 2.3 and 2.4 for details).

The Advisory Commission on Intergovernmental Relations, which reported these statistics, was phased out in 1996, and there has been no survey of the states in recent years. Fragmentary data suggest that the cost of these tax breaks is still substantial. Nebraska estimated that its 1997 homestead exemption losses were $35,095,569, compared to its 1991 figure of $29.3 million.[38] Texas reported that the cost of its homestead exemption to school districts in 1999 was $1.365 billion, compared to $1.169 billion in 1990.[39] Washington State reported that its circuit breaker for the elderly cost $80,614,000 in 1998, compared to $50,184,000 in 1992.[40] Illinois reported that the costs of its circuit breaker property tax relief and

Table 2.4 States' Losses from Homestead Exemptions

State (fiscal year)	Amount (in thousands of dollars)	State (fiscal year)	Amount (in thousands of dollars)
Alaska (1991)	9,585	Montana (1990)	1,400
Arizona (1990)	162,744	Nebraska (1991)	29,300
California (1991–92)	3,290,000	New Jersey (1991)	59,583
Connecticut (1991)	18,522	New Mexico (1986)	8,400
District of Columbia		North Carolina (1990–91)	19,072
(1989)	21,758	Oklahoma (1991)	56,639
Florida (1991)	1,700,000	South Carolina (1991)	37,650
Illinois (1989)	451,498	Texas (school districts	
Indiana (1991)	274,501	1990)	1,169,665
Iowa (1991)	99,613	Utah (1990)	1,847
Kentucky (1989)	9,711	Vermont (1991)	1,000
Louisiana (1991)	438,494	Washington (1991)	39,200
Maine (1991)	3,024	West Virginia (1991)	25,829
Minnesota (1989)	660,000	Wisconsin (1992)	177,600
Mississippi (1990)	110,387	Wyoming (1992)	0

Source: Compiled from Advisory Commission on Intergovernmental Relations, *Significant Features of Fiscal Federalism, 1991,* vol. 1 (Washington, D.C.: U.S. Government Printing Office, 1991), table 42.

Note: Other states have homestead exemptions, but their estimates of revenue losses were unavailable.

senior citizen homestead exemption were fairly stable. The cost of the circuit breaker actually went down, despite liberalization of eligibility requirements, from $70.5 million in 1990 to an estimated $59.6 million in 2004. The cost of the senior citizen homestead exemption held steady throughout the period at about $113.9 million.[41] Colorado's senior homestead exemption cost the state $55.5 million.[42] New York State added a new program of school property tax relief in 1997, which has been estimated to save taxpayers $2.2 billion a year.[43]

Despite some new or expanded exemption programs, there are some recent signs that using tax expenditures to buy off opposition to taxation is yielding to more fundamental tax reforms. Where states have rolled back tax levels for everyone there is less pressure and less need to roll them back for particular classes of homeowners. Where states have made more explicit and general efforts to keep taxes within a given proportion of income to improve equity, there is less need for circuit breakers in the property tax to protect the elderly, handicapped, or extremely poor.

The Local Level. At the local level, tax breaks are primarily used to encourage economic development projects, a somewhat narrower function than that at the state
level. Tax expenditures at the local level are even less visible than those at the state
level. They seldom appear in budgets or financial reports.[44] They are generally
granted on a one-at-a-time basis, though some are phrased as entitlements, especially in larger cities. The enabling legislation passes at the state level, rather than
the local level, so cities are less likely than states to ease regulations or create new
tax breaks for all businesses in order to facilitate a single deal.

The most striking feature of local tax breaks is their relative secrecy. The data
simply do not exist to evaluate their effectiveness or their impact on government.
For example, in 2004 the Tennessee Advisory Commission on Intergovernmental Relations, mandated by the state to do a study of the impact of tax breaks on
local school districts, reported back that they were unable to do the study because
of lack of reporting of the data. They indicated in the report that Tennessee was
not alone in having such poor reporting and concluded,

> As a general rule throughout the U.S., no one knows the actual magnitude of
> tax abatements; whether abatements are cost effective in creating jobs and
> promoting economic development; the total cost of tax abatements; how
> much revenue schools are losing because of abatements; [and] there is very
> little in the way of audits or legislative oversight.[45]

Because of the lack of data and oversight, the trade-off between costs and benefits is often obscure. Builders, contractors, and businesses are encouraged to ask
for the moon and see how much they can get. The element of competition that
was apparent at the state level is exaggerated at the local level because the government has so little possibility of influencing the economy, and the bargaining
tends to take place when the local community is desperate for jobs. Companies
can promise jobs or threaten to take them away unless they get most of what they
ask for. The bargaining power tends to be one-sided.

There are no aggregate estimates of the amounts of tax expenditures at the
local level, but what evidence there is suggests that they can be very expensive.
In 2004, New York City reported (based on 2001 data) that it had more than fifty
tax expenditure programs and that the city-administered property tax and city-
administered business and excise taxes accounted for revenue losses of about $3.1
billion dollars a year. In addition, the city reported losses of $326 million for the
city sales tax and $50 million for the personal income tax.[46]

A recent report of the city of Baltimore estimated the total cost of a single tax
break, the newly constructed dwelling tax expenditure, at more than $2 million
over the period 1995 through 2002. Moreover, the study argued that the tax break

---

Minicase: State Tax Break Prohibitions and Evasion

Local governments are creatures of the states and must follow the state's laws and constitution. This rule applies to tax breaks as well as other areas of operations, so what the cities can do depends on what the state allows. Because individual cities do not feel that they can deny tax breaks and still compete successfully for businesses and jobs, they depend on the state to pass laws prohibiting expensive competition between cities. Tennessee forbids tax breaks for businesses in its constitution. But the pressure to give businesses tax breaks is so strong that the state aids the local governments in evading the prohibition.

The way the system works is that local industrial development boards take title to business properties and lease the facilities back to companies. Because these development boards are nonprofits, the prohibition on tax abatements does not apply to them. The subsidized businesses usually make some level of payment in lieu of taxes, under agreements negotiated with development boards and local officials.[1] This clear evasion, if not corruption, of the state constitution raises the question of how subsidies to business justify the erosion of constitutional law in the minds of the participants. It also brings into question the effectiveness of state laws prohibiting expensive competition between cities. Ultimately, cities may have to realize that this strategy has limits, regardless of state laws.

1. Dave Flessner, "Incentive Breaks," *Chattanooga Times Free Press,* April 11, 2004.

---

had been ineffective in attracting new middle-class homeowners to the city: The result was all cost, no benefit. The report estimated the costs of all property tax exemptions and credits for 2002 at \$9,055,000 and noted that the city was budgeting \$10,119,000 for 2003. The costs were going up by over a million dollars a year, meaning that revenue losses were growing by more than 10 percent annually.[47]

The following quotation suggests both the amounts involved and the spirit in which they are determined in Tennessee: "Hamilton County gave more than \$2 million in tax breaks to local businesses in 2003. Commission Chairman Curtis Adams said he hopes it will be even more this year. 'We give tax abatements to get new industry and to help businesses to grow,' Mr. Adams said. 'We have to provide incentives to be competitive. And, frankly, I wish we had more to give away.' "[48]

By the mid-1990s Ohio local governments had granted more than $2 billion in property tax abatements, mostly for economic development programs. The amounts were such that some counties, such as Montgomery County, began to slow down the granting of new abatements. Although the rate of growth was lower, the absolute amount was still stunning: "Montgomery County granted tax exemptions worth about $1.093 billion in 1995." Officials argued that no deal had fallen through because they had not given away enough in tax incentives. While still generous with these tax breaks, county officials attributed their relative caution to desire to protect the school districts, to which they granted a veto over tax breaks. If the school districts felt that they would be hurt by a deal, they could scotch it. Without such a veto, the county could grant tax breaks that reduced schools' revenue.[49]

Cities and counties are often in a position to spend money that is not theirs. For example, cities have extended their tax-free borrowing status to businesses to save them money. These breaks are called "industrial development revenue bonds," and they cost the federal government money.[50] In many states, cities can use tax increment financing, which allows them to spend property taxes belonging to school districts for economic development projects that are supposed to increase the school districts' taxable wealth over the long run.

There are no reliable data on the extent to which cities reduce the tax revenues of school districts or force school districts to raise taxes to compensate for short-term losses. To make matters more confusing, some states partially or fully reimburse school districts for revenue losses from tax increment financing and tax abatements for economic development, whereas others do not.

The data that do exist are necessarily only suggestive of the larger problem. Texas keeps such data, and there the state comptroller reported $144.9 billion in reductions of the tax base for the school districts in 2002 and $149 billion in 2003. Of the 2003 total, nearly $5 billion was from tax increment finances, an amount determined by cities, not the school districts. To get a sense of the dollar losses to school districts from these losses to their taxable base, multiply by about 1.5 percent, a typical tax rate for the Texas school districts.[51] The resulting estimate of dollar losses in revenue for the school districts is about $2.2 billion. Incomplete data on Tennessee indicate revenues losses to school districts of at least $33 million.[52] One recent estimate of the impact on Ohio schools of taxes abated for economic development is $101,985,690.[53]

A peculiarity of local-level tax abatements is that cities and counties can often take the lead in economic development and negotiate with other governments' or districts' revenues, sometimes exacerbating their fiscal stress. The cities are encouraged to offer larger incentives because the money they offer is not their own.

As a result, the school districts may look badly managed and may have to come to the public more often for tax increases. To this point, no one knows how often this occurs or what proportion of school funding problems stem from this source.

The Politics of Reform

The gradual erosion of the integrity of general taxes is part of a larger process that also includes reform and at least the temporary curtailing of interest group power. Tax expenditures reduce revenues, and that means cutting back spending, finding alternative revenue sources, or tolerating chronic deficits. Each of these alternatives has negative political consequences, and the more extreme any of them becomes, the greater is the pressure to stop awarding tax breaks or curtail existing ones. Tax expenditures also give the impression of unequal treatment of equals, and that upsets taxpayers and encourages them to try to reduce their own tax payments. In the extreme, it may lead to tax protests. When voluntary compliance with tax laws diminishes, the cost of tax collection increases. Thus, despite the political coalitions that support existing tax benefits, there are often counterpressures to reform the tax structure.

The main goal of reforms is to simplify taxes and reduce special exceptions. The resulting revenue increases may be used to reduce tax rates for everyone, to reduce the size of the deficit, or to sustain services and programs. For some the goal of tax reform has been to see to it that the poor do not shoulder a disproportionate burden of taxation and that taxes overall are apportioned according to ability to pay. Because tax breaks are often relatively inefficient ways of accomplishing program goals, curbing tax expenditures may also be seen as an effort to improve efficiency.[54]

Such reforms are difficult but not impossible to achieve. Politically they have the general weakness that those whose benefits are taken away are likely to be hopping mad, while those whose tax burden is lessened are likely to feel that they deserved it all along. Opponents of reform are likely to be outspoken, and supporters likely to be passive.[55] In addition, the amount of money gained from closing a large loophole that benefits a relatively small number of people is not great enough, when spread around the entire taxpaying public, to win much applause. One way to make tax reform politically attractive is to take away enough tax breaks to moderate substantially the tax burden of large numbers of people.

There was nothing inevitable about the timing of the 1986 federal tax reform, but the conditions were certainly favorable for a tax reform by the mid-1980s. Several decades of accelerated granting of tax expenditures had eroded the revenue base, and the president's 1981 tax reduction program had gotten completely out of hand, with Democrats and Republicans in Congress competing to add more tax breaks; an increase in the national deficit ensued. President Ronald Reagan made tax reform an early priority of his second term.

The White House and the Treasury wanted a measure that would give tax reductions to 80 percent of taxpayers, and they set that figure as a guideline. The Senate Finance Committee struggled to reduce the top bracket of the income tax significantly in order to gain enough support in Congress and among interest groups to pass the reform.

Rather than a mobilized opposition and quiet supporters, the 1986 tax reform brought out active interest groups on both sides. Business groups were split. Those in danger of losing benefits lobbied heavily against the reform. Chief executive officers of some major corporations, such as IBM, Pepsico, and Reynolds, were active in support. Taxpayer groups also created a politically powerful presence. Citizens for Tax Justice, a tiny, union-financed group, turned out reports on the amount of taxes paid by major U.S. corporations, many of which paid nothing at all. The reports received major publicity in the two years preceding the tax reform and helped persuade Congress to remove some of the beneficial tax treatment of the corporations. Citizens for Tax Justice "gave us the fuel for tax reform and for tax increases on the business community," said Rep. Robert T. Matsui, D-Calif., an influential member of the Ways and Means Committee. "I'll bet every member" who favored overhauling the tax code "used CTJ statistics in speeches back home." [56] As an aide to the Ways and Means Committee chairman remarked, sometimes legislation is based on a few good horror stories, and Citizens for Tax Justice provided those stories.[57]

Despite pressure from proreform interest groups, lobbying to retain tax breaks was fierce;[58] the first time the Senate Finance Committee tried to hammer out its version of reform, it was overwhelmed by resistance to the elimination of a variety of preferences. The committee chairman, Robert Packwood, R-Ore., may have set the wrong tone initially by supporting Oregon's lumber industry. By the time other senators had protected their constituents, the proposal was no longer revenue neutral—more money was given away in tax decreases than was gained by reducing tax breaks.

Senator Packwood went back to the drawing board and started again with a stricter revenue-neutrality rule: No benefit could be added without closing a loophole or eliminating a special benefit to pay for it. The committee's recommended package arrived on the Senate floor with an understanding that any amendments would not change total revenues and would not increase the size of the deficit. This informal rule blocked many interest groups that would have tried to reinstate their benefits on the floor.

One of the particularly interesting aspects of the passage of this reform act was the major role of the conference committee set up to resolve the differences between the House and Senate versions. The many differences between the House and Senate bills created a relatively open conference. The chairs of both the Ways and Means Committee and the Senate Finance Committee were on the conference committee and conducted most of the negotiations themselves behind closed doors. Other members of Congress reported that such a procedure insulated them from interest groups because they could legitimately say they did not know what was going on.[59]

The final conference committee product did not eliminate all special tax benefits, but it eliminated some and reduced many others. The top individual tax rate was dropped from 50 percent to 28 percent, and 80 percent of individuals and families would be taxed at no more than 15 percent. The top corporate rate was reduced from 46 percent to 34 percent.

In at least one case, the dynamics of income tax reform played out similarly at the state level. In Wisconsin in 1982, the cost of tax breaks was just about equal to total taxes collected.[60] A major reform of the income tax occurred by 1985. The reform had the governor's support and was tied to tax reduction. The reduction was made possible partly by eliminating deductions and exceptions and partly by a favorable revenue projection. The top income bracket tax rate was lowered, apparently as an essential part of gaining political support for reform. A high degree of centralization and closed decision rules helped block interest group demands.[61]

To summarize, broad-based taxes are likely to be gradually eroded by the demands of the interest groups and individuals who feel the burden of the tax. The integrity of the revenue base and the perception that taxation applies equally to all gradually deteriorate. Growing complexity of the tax laws, revenue losses, and inequitable treatment of businesses and individuals in similar financial circumstances generate pressure for reform.

Summary and Conclusions

Public officials need to raise taxes from time to time, but they confront a political minefield when they try to do it. The result is that they raise taxes with great care and try to place the burden of taxation in such a way as to minimize opposition and gain maximum support. The more open the government has been about its finances, and the greater the public's belief that the resources are really needed and will be spent on items they approved, the greater the acceptability of a tax increase. Tax increases may be precisely the occasions when the government is held to account.

The actors involved in revenue decisions include the chief executive, the revenue committees of Congress and finance committees of legislatures and councils, interest groups, and the courts. Departments and agency heads are almost completely absent, except when the Treasury Department recommends tax reforms. Citizen commissions, blue-ribbon committees, and task forces of the chamber of commerce are also frequent actors, examining the overall need, the current revenue situation, and possible revenue alternatives. An array of interest groups are directly involved at different times. Public employees and service recipients get involved when service cuts are threatened; chambers of commerce and other groups of business representatives get involved when new taxation is being considered. Taxpayers' organizations, unions, and business associations represent broad groups, but there are splits within each broad group. For example, business associations are deeply split about tax reform.

The power that interest groups are able to wield does not depend solely on their finances; small, poor interest groups are sometimes more effective than larger, better financed ones. Small groups with little financial backing are sometimes able to manage major impacts through research and symbolic stories that catch the media's and legislators' attention. The ability of interest groups to form and maintain coalitions affects their success, as does the budget process itself. When legislators organize themselves and the budget process in such a way as to insulate themselves from interest groups, interest group power may be curtailed. This does not happen all the time, but it indicates that interest groups do not always call the shots.

The politics of taxation is characterized by a struggle to shift the burden of taxation away from one's own group, however defined. Pressure may be exerted to shift taxes from the relatively poor to the relatively rich, or vice versa. There may be pressure to shift taxation from individuals to corporations, or from homeowners to renters, or to owners of commercial property. Those in one region of the country may try to shift the burden of taxation to other regions. When representatives of any group are in power, they may shift the burden to other groups.

Overall, revenue politics is characterized by a relatively long time span, over which both narrow and broad societal interests compete for position, and by efforts to lock in benefits such as tax breaks and to lock out taxes on particular forms of wealth while backers are powerful enough to do so. Earmarking of revenues is another way of trying to lock in particular favorable patterns.

Taxation often changes by small amounts in a variety of tax sources, but at intervals, there are major changes. New taxes are passed; the burden of taxation is shifted; the definition of taxable wealth is changed; or tax reforms restore the tax base.

3. The Politics of Process

If the budget process is to produce anything, it must produce honesty. Only then will the American people learn of and support the difficult choices the Congress and the President must make to restore fiscal discipline.

—Sen. John Exon

The budget process divides up the work of budgetary decision making, assigns particular decisions to particular actors or groups of actors, and coordinates the decision making among them. The budget process sets the rules, determines the parameters of time and money within which the deliberations will take place, and selects the options that will be compared. It also determines the level of competition among agencies and constituencies for governmental resources.

The budget process is important because it indirectly influences policy outcomes and directly influences the distribution of political power. In terms of policy, process can make it more or less difficult to spend public money to solve collective problems, to balance the budget, to make long-term investments, or to borrow money. The budget process may tilt toward lower taxes and a smaller scope of government or toward higher taxes and more publicly provided goods and services. The budget process may influence who benefits from lower taxes or decisions to spend more. In terms of the distribution of power, budget process can give one group of actors a veto over the decisions of other actors; it can be inclusive of new groups or reinforce the power of long-entrenched groups; it can facilitate democratic participation or strengthen authoritarian regimes. Budget process directly affects the distribution of power between and within the executive and legislative branches of government and between government and the public, both as individuals and as organized interests.

The budget process is often a key instrument of democratic participation and accountability. The openness of the decision making, the responsiveness of the process to democratically determined priorities, and the quality of reporting on how much money has been spent for what programs all reflect the degree of democratic control. Because the budget process is such an important part of governance, if there is public participation in and control over the budget, there is likely to be public control over government more broadly.

Budget Process and the Characteristics of Public Budgeting

The characteristics of public budgeting described in chapter 1 help to explain the functions and design of the budget process. Budget processes are not just a list of decision makers and a set of steps to coordinate timely decision making. They help the budget decision makers adapt to changes in the environment, facilitate the resolution of competing claims, create a smooth flow of information between payers and deciders, and constrain decisions about taxation and allocations.

Budget processes facilitate adaptation to the environment. If the economy is weak, there may be pressure to change the rules of the budget process to allow higher spending levels and permit deficits. On the other hand, if public opinion turns to favor budget balance, the budget process may shift to emphasize balance. If public support for government is low, elected officials may change the budget process to give the public more direct control over budget options or to provide more public accountability.

Public budgets involve claimants who want different things from the budget and a variety of political actors who want to exercise control over budgetary decision making. The budget process has to regulate the process of making claims and the competition among claimants. Sometimes the process gives advantage or precedence to some claims over others, or to claims made in particular ways, or to claims for particular resources.

The process may make it equally easy for all applicants for funding to make their pleas or may make it difficult for some and easier for others. For example, nonprofits applying for grants from cities may be required to fill out lengthy questionnaires, including indicators of their financial solvency and descriptions of their client base, while small businesses applying for assistance may have only to ask for the money.

The budget process regulates the level of competition among claimants by determining which programs compete most directly with which other programs for how much money. For example, process rules may designate a group of claimants and assign them a particular pool of funds. Those claimants must then compete among themselves, sometimes intensely, for that limited pool of resources. At the other end of the continuum, some programs may be given their own source of revenue, with no other programs allowed to compete for those funds.

The budget process may favor some requests over others. For example, it may determine the order in which requests will be considered, giving money first to items such as debt repayment, or entitlements, programs that are structured in such a way that all those eligible for benefits are paid before any other requests can be considered. The process may assign decisions on funding of particular programs to decision makers who favor those programs, to those who oppose them, or to decision makers who have other priorities.

The separation of payer and decision maker also has important implications for the budget process. To facilitate communication between government and the taxpaying public, the budget process often mandates open hearings before allocations are cast in law. Extensive reporting may be required to assure citizens that their money was spent in the fashion agreed to in the budget.

Of all the characteristics of public budgeting, the budget process most clearly represents constraints. Guidelines often set limits to expenditures or to revenues at the start of the budget process, so that decision making has to take place within those constraints. Or the process may begin with other kinds of constraints, such as goals for reallocation or productivity savings or targets for cutting back capital or staff. The budget process can require prior controls (especially detailed controls of inputs, such as ceilings on the number of personnel that may be hired). It can emphasize post controls, based on after-the-fact reporting of costs and accomplishments. Or it can require a combination of both. The budget process can include constraints on the total level of revenue to be collected; it can require that revenues exceed expenditures by particular margins; it can include limits on borrowing and on accumulated debt. It can even put constraints on subparts of the budget, setting ceilings on revenue by fund and purpose (no more than ten mills of property tax rate may be levied for roads and bridges) or on expenditure (no more than $10 billion can be spent on the State Department and the Department of Justice).

One example of the kind of constraints that can be built into a budget process occurred at the federal level beginning in 1985. The decision-making rules were embodied in legislation called (after its legislative sponsors) the Gramm-

Rudman-Hollings act. That law included new deadlines for decisions, targets for reductions in the deficit over a period of years, and an automatic series of cuts if deficit reduction targets were not met. The Gramm-Rudman-Hollings process introduced a number of extremely constraining conditions under which budgeting was to take place.

Constraints on decision making may exclude many options. The options that remain may be very narrow, despite the size of the budget. For example, once borrowing has reached its legal limit in a city, decision makers can no longer consider the option of borrowing. Spending caps for particular areas of the budget may also eliminate particular expenditure options from consideration.

Although many constraints are determined by the political actors in any given jurisdiction, in the United States the budget process also reflects constraints imposed by other levels of government. For example, the federal government may constrain state and local budgeting by requiring particular programs without providing sufficient funds to carry out those mandates. States can limit the amount of borrowing that local governments engage in, require that local budgets balance, determine the format of budget documents, or specify who may put a budget request together, such as a finance director, a budget officer, or a municipal clerk. States can also mandate that their local governments spend money on particular programs or increase spending for particular purposes.

Macro and Micro Politics

Because the budget process influences policy outcomes and political power, political actors continually try to shape it. Some seek macro changes, in an effort to bring about major policy shifts and lock them in over time. Others seek micro changes, short-term deviations or alterations in the rules addressed to specific beneficiaries, often for partisan gain.

Macro policy goals can include stimulating the economy during a recession, reducing the gap in wealth between the rich and the poor, balancing the budget, or shrinking the size and intrusiveness of government. One example of political actors' trying to achieve macro policy change through the budget process occurred when some conservative Republicans in Washington restructured the budget process to encourage tax reduction. Presumably they hoped not only to reduce the level of taxation, but also to reduce the scope of government services. By contrast, when political actors are seeking micro political goals, they jockey for power to influence particular decisions that may affect only one company or interest group. This second group may ignore, bend, or change the rules without regard for long-term or broader policy consequences. For example, one group of congresspersons raised the caps on discretionary spending to increase outlays for highways and pork-type projects. These members of Congress did not argue that the caps themselves were wrong. They wanted to influence the outcome of a specific decision, not the rules that structure the outcomes more broadly. The rules were just in the way.

The two minicases in the boxes that follow illustrate macro and micro strategies with respect to the budget process. The first describes an effort of Republicans in Congress to change the process to control the growth of government,

---

Minicase: Republican Macro-Level Reform Proposals

By June 1998 it was clear that the federal budget was close to balancing after decades of deficits. Many cheered the contribution of the budget process, revised in 1990, to finally eliminating the deficit. But some in Congress were still frustrated with the budget process. The Speaker of the House, a Republican, had created a task force to come up with budget reform proposals that would advance the Republican agenda and "enhance our common goals of controlling spending, reducing the debt, and cutting taxes." Task force members argued, "Sensible budget process changes can greatly improve our ability to advance our legislative agenda and to build on the success of the Balanced Budget Act of 1997."

Rep. Christopher Cox, R-Calif., reported the recommendations of the Speaker's Task Force on Budget Reform to the House Budget Committee's Subcommittee on Budget Process Reform.[1] One recommendation was to enforce the spending caps in the budget by requiring a two-thirds vote to exceed them; the requirement would also apply to supplemental appropriations.

A second recommendation was an automatic continuing resolution, at a hard-freeze level. Congress uses continuing resolutions when members cannot agree to pass the regular appropriations bills on time; while Congress is working out its disagreements, it usually passes a temporary budget law to keep the government open. Such legislation is usually classified as "must-pass" because without it, the government shuts down. There is great temptation, therefore, to put a variety of riders in the continuing resolution. Representative Cox argued that if the continuing resolutions were automatic, rather than discretionary, there would be no threat of closing down the government and hence no swollen must-pass legislation. What Cox did not say was that such a feature would also encourage conservatives

(continued)

who want lower spending to hold up the budget, with the idea that a hard freeze would then be put in place instead of a new, more expensive budget.

Cox also argued for an end to "baseline budgeting," by which he meant considering budget increases and decreases compared to a baseline that includes inflation. Since the early 1980s, the federal government has used a "current services" estimate, figuring what it would cost next year to provide this year's level of services. A cut from that level was considered a cut in the budget. Conservatives objected that what was considered a cut could in fact be an increase in dollars. They felt that consideration of inflation pushed up budgeting costs, building in increases by at least the rate of inflation. They also felt, with some justification, that the baselines were not well understood by the public and served to confuse more than to clarify. They argued for elimination of the baseline.

Cox also did not mention that there has to be some baseline; there is no way to budget without one. The issue is what baseline will be used. If politicians are going to talk about cuts or increases, they have to have reference to some kind of base. There are many choices of baseline, including last year's actual budget. What Cox and others wanted was to eliminate the "current services" baseline, substitute a different one that would assume that agencies were cut back each year by the level of inflation, and then advance or retreat from that position. In their model, an agency's budget could in fact be cut, but it would appear to be an increase if the budget increase was less than the inflation rate. The result could be just as confusing to the public, but it would build in a bias toward decreasing spending every year.

The Speaker's task force wanted the budget process changed so that it would be easier to reduce taxes. It was difficult to reduce taxes when the budget process emphasized balance, because every cut in revenue had to be offset by reductions in spending or other increases in revenue. One proposal was to eliminate the requirement that tax cuts be specifically offset, assuming that revenues were generally sufficient to prevent a deficit. In other words, task force members wanted to eliminate the need for explicit trade-offs when reducing revenues; they wanted to make it less clear what would have to be cut to pay for such tax reductions or who would have to pay for them. Undoubtedly such changes would make it easier to cut taxation.

Perhaps most dramatically, Cox recommended the elimination of all entitlements other than Social Security, making them instead subject to annual appropriations. Entitlements are payments that go to all those eligible, based on criteria such as age, income, or unemployment status. The cost to the federal government of such entitlements goes up and down with

(continued)

the economy and the number of people in need. It would be substantially easier to cut back the entitlement programs if they were annually appropriated rather than permanently authorized and automatically funded.

It is easy to see how these budget process proposals would make it easier to reduce taxes and cut federal government expenditures. They would change the present bias toward growth by building in a bias toward shrinking the federal government—all by changing the rules of budget process.

After figuring out what process reforms would help them achieve their agenda and uncovering the areas of consensus within the Republican ranks for such changes, the next step was to introduce legislation embodying these understandings. The result was a bill, the Comprehensive Budget Process Reform Act of 1999, called the Nussle-Cardin-Goss Budget Process Bill. In some ways, it went beyond the suggestions of the Speaker's task force, but all the proposals were in the same direction. The liberal Center for Budget and Policy Priorities called attention to a number of features of this bill and how they would work. In a sign-on letter, the center argued that Congress should reject the proposals:

> Key aspects of H.R. 853 would likely lead to cuts in discretionary spending and impair the appropriations process. In addition, the bill contains troubling changes in the pay-as-you-go rules; it would allow projected non–Social Security surpluses to be used to finance tax cuts or entitlement increases, but if such tax cuts or entitlement increases were enacted and the projected surpluses then failed to materialize, cuts in many important programs—including Medicare, student loans, farm price supports, veterans' adjustment benefits, and the Social Services Block Grant, among others—would be triggered through sequestration [automatic cuts]. In a break with past practice, the bill also would allow reductions in the discretionary caps to be used to finance tax cuts. These provisions are deeply disturbing and should not become law.
>
> Other provisions also are objectionable. For example, the bill's "lock box" provision would lower the discretionary caps when either the House or Senate approved a floor amendment reducing funding for an item in an appropriations bill, even if the other chamber had soundly rejected the cut and the cut was dropped in conference. Moreover, the caps would be reduced for all years for which caps had been set, even if the item that was cut through a House or Senate floor amendment was a one-year project whose reduction or elimination would produce no savings in subsequent years. At a time when many

(continued)

in Congress and elsewhere agree the existing discretionary spending caps are not sustainable and need to be raised, we find the bill's movement in the opposite direction exceedingly unwise.

We also are disturbed by provisions of the bill that mandate use of baseline assumptions under which discretionary appropriations would be assumed to be frozen for all years for which caps have not yet been set. Under the bill, the funding level reflected in the rather severe cap set for FY 2002 would be assumed to remain in place through FY 2009, with no adjustment for inflation. The shrunken baseline would be used to make the surplus appear to be $436 billion larger over the next 10 years than the current CBO baseline shows, paving the way for even-larger tax cuts at the expense of discretionary programs.

Finally, we are concerned that H.R. 853 would weaken the appropriations process. In combination, provisions that would have the budget resolution be signed by the President, prohibit the Appropriations committees from sending appropriations bills to the House floor until work on the budget resolution had been completed, and institute a year-long automatic continuing resolution at the prior year's level if an appropriations bill has not [been] completed by the start of the fiscal year would create a risk of putting the discretionary budget on auto-pilot, with long-term freezes in funding levels. The bias would be toward the status quo, rather than toward setting funding priorities for a given fiscal year and being able to address pressing needs as they arise.

H.R. 853 would both weaken fiscal discipline—by effectively jettisoning the pay-as-you-go rules—and largely abandon a budget process that has helped produce budget surpluses for the first time in many years. It paves the way for sweeping tax cuts at the expense of other important needs. We urge you not to support this bill.

1. Prepared testimony of Rep. Christopher Cox before the House Budget Committee, Subcommittee on Budget Process Reform, June 18, 1998; see also John F. Cogan, Timothy Muris, and Allen Schick, *The Budget Puzzle: Understanding Federal Spending* (Palo Alto, Calif.: Stanford University Press, 1994), esp. chap. 3, "The Uses and Abuses of Budget Baselines," by Tim Muris; and Center on Budget and Policy Priorities, "Concerns Regarding the Nussle-Cardin-Goss Budget Process Bill," May 14, 1999, www.cbpp.org, and the related sign-on letter urging opposition to the bill.

reducing taxes and cutting spending. The second illustrates the way rules can be used and abused for short-term political and policy gain, without regard to broader policy issues.

The chief Democratic counsel for the Senate Budget Committee in Washington, Bill Dauster, gave a partisan speech in 1996, pointing out a number of rule changes or evasions that the Republicans had devised for short-term advantage or to benefit a single constituent. It is not only Republicans who do such things when they are in the majority, but in this example, a Democrat was commenting on Republican behavior.

Minicase: Micro Politics—Bending the Rules to Win Individual Decisions

Bill Dauster, then chief Democratic counsel of the Senate Budget Committee, argued in a speech that the Republican majority in Congress showed a willful disregard for rules and laws when it served their legislative purposes.[1] In one case, to approve some unrelated legislation favoring the Federal Express Corporation, the Senate Republicans changed a century-old, standing rule that limited conference committees to the subject of the legislation that was sent to the conference.

Dauster charged that the Senate overturned another century-old rule, this one limiting legislation in appropriations bills. At the national level, there is a difference between appropriations bills, which provide money, and bills that design and modify programs. Appropriations bills are supposed to contain money approved for each program; they are not supposed to contain new legislation modifying programs or creating new ones. New or modifying legislation can take years to hammer out, as compromises between interests are negotiated. By contrast, appropriations bills are "must-pass"—the government will shut down unless there is money appropriated to pay for its programs and services. Allowing legislation in appropriations bills empowers a simple majority of the Senate to add unrelated provisions to a fast-track budget vehicle that is likely to pass.

The reason for such an important change in the rules, according to Dauster, was to adopt an unrelated amendment sponsored by Sen. Kay Bailey Hutchison, R-Texas. Hutchison's amendment to an emergency supplemental appropriation bill was a rescission or withdrawal of funding for the rest of the year, so that no new endangered species could be declared while an authorizing committee was working on revisions in the law to make it

(continued)

more difficult to declare a species endangered. Hutchinson thus accomplished quickly and for the short term, without a reauthorization bill, what she hoped to accomplish with reauthorization legislation later in a broader, more deliberative setting.

Dauster also charged the Republicans with abusing their scorekeeping powers. He argued that on October 27, 1995, during consideration of an amendment by Chairman William Roth, R-Del., of the Finance Committee, Budget Committee chairman Pete Domenici, R-N.M., misrepresented off-budget Social Security savings as if they were on-budget savings and thus paved the way for adoption of Roth's amendment by circumventing procedural obstacles that would have required sixty votes to waive. Under the Budget Enforcement Act, Social Security was supposed to be off-budget, so counting savings in Social Security was a violation of the Budget Act. One senator raised a point of order noting the violation, but rather than recognize the point of order, Domenici used his discretion as chair of the Budget Committee to make a binding determination of how the cut would be "scored" (counted). It was not that the senator made up a new rule or disapproved the existing rule; it was just that he chose to ignore the violation of the rule in this case.[2]

Dauster argued that the Republicans had expanded the reconciliation process to include nonbudgetary matters and a variety of budgetary issues beyond the basic task of reconciling, or cutting back, budgets to the level required by the budget resolution. The 1974 Congressional Budget Reform Act contained a procedure requiring the budget committees to assign total figures to the appropriations and revenue committees, which then had to reconcile their own numbers with those of the Budget Committee. The reconciliation process in the Senate was fast-tracked: it allowed only germane amendments and it limited debate. Most important, reconciliation bills could be passed by a simple majority.

Outside the reconciliation process, the rules of the Senate that make that body more deliberate than the House give each member, whether of the minority or the majority, power to obstruct legislation. An individual senator could filibuster a bill, delay it by speaking on and on, and it would take a supermajority to cut off the speech. That could not occur with reconciliation bills. Thus when ordinary legislation was put into the reconciliations, the Senate bypassed its own traditions of individualism and debate. Only germane amendments would be considered, germaneness to be determined by the majority party in committee. In the short run, the Republicans therefore strengthened their ability to pass their preferred legislation in the

(continued)

Senate over Democratic opposition, but in the long run they altered the deliberative traditions of the Senate and its role in the legislative branch. Dauster concluded,

> This past year, the Republican Senate majority has thus repeatedly arrogated greater power to the majority to use fast-moving legislative trains to move unrelated matters of its choosing. This majority has thus repeatedly torn down the protections that the Senate affords minorities. This majority has shown a disturbing willingness to cast aside long-held precedents and institutions to serve immediate policy ends. That, then, is the unifying theme that runs through the procedural actions that the Republicans took last year and that they seek to take this year. The Republican Senate stands ready to sell its birthright for a mess of pottage. It shows contempt for the institution. It focuses solely on the immediate political gain.

1. Bill Dauster, "Stupid Budget Laws: Remarks before the American Association of Law Schools," January 5, 1996, and *Congressional Record*, October 27, 1995.
2. Ibid.

Designing Process to Achieve Policy and Political Goals

Budget actors try to design and alter budget processes to produce the results they hope for, whether on a broad scale or in specific cases. Participants' efforts to change the process help make clear how particular parts of the budget process are intended or expected to work to achieve particular policy and power outcomes. What follows is a discussion of the parts of budget processes that political actors can change and the goals they hope to achieve through those changes.

Budget Process and Policy

A variety of features in budget processes may be used to achieve particular policy goals. For example, if elected officials feel the need to build public trust, then the budget process should emphasize openness, solicitation of public opinion, and a variety of means of demonstrating not only that public priorities have been followed, but also that the programs are well managed and effective. Budget documents are likely to be laid out in programs, each of which has performance measures that show what was planned and what was actually accomplished.

If the goal of the budget process is to reduce spending, then the process may emphasize constraints such as spending caps and build in incentives for end-of-year savings. Budget rules may create lockboxes, or prohibitions on transfers between funds or accounts, so that savings in one area are not used to increase spending somewhere else. Budget actors may change the assumptions on which future budgets are built, reducing or eliminating baselines that include inflation costs. They may build in automatic cuts if various actions are not taken. Target-based or zero-based budgets may facilitate prioritization for cutting or reducing some programs.

The format of the budget, that is, the way the budget document lays out information for decision making, is one of the key ways in which process influences policy. One reason is that collecting particular information in a particular way, and presenting only that information in the budget, influences the analysis and discussion of budgetary decisions. The second reason is that some so-called formats are really shorthand versions of the decision-making process that led to the information in the budget. Frequently used budget formats are the line-item budget, performance budgets, and program budgets. Zero-based and target-based budgets are also used, but although they may influence the layout of the budget and frame budgetary decision making, they are more descriptive of process than of layout. Each is intended to accomplish a different set of policy and political goals.

A line-item budget lists each department and assigns a sum of money to the department or other administrative unit. The money is not granted in a lump sum, to be spent as needed, but is divided into categories for specific purposes—travel, payroll, commodities, and the like. Each category of expenditure is listed on a separate line in the budget document. The department then has to spend its allocation in accordance with the requirements of each line. If the budget is broken into many detailed lines, such as paper supplies, pencils, desks and chairs, computers, and stamps, the department head has very little discretion about how the money can be spent. This kind of budget emphasizes financial control. A line-item budget plays down competition because it does not compare programs and makes it difficult to introduce new programs. Its orientation is to maintain the status quo in the distribution of funds and spending power.

A performance budget lists what each administrative unit is trying to accomplish, how much it is planning to do, and with what resources. The documents report on how well administrators did with the resources they had last year. The emphasis is on getting the most service for the dollar. This form of budget is high on accountability and may be used especially when public skepticism of government is high. The goal is to show the public what government agencies are doing, how much work they are doing, and how well they are doing it, with the goals of demonstrating effectiveness and encouraging program administrators to improve compared to a series of well-chosen benchmarks.

A program budget divides expenditures by activities so that, for example, the costs for juvenile counseling are broken out from traffic patrol, and both of those are separated from crime detection. Sometimes program budgets are formally linked to a planning process wherein community (or national) goals are stated and expenditures allocated to reaching those goals. The emphasis in this format is on the appropriateness of current spending priorities and the possible need for trade-offs between programs. Program budgets have the most potential for allowing legislators to review the policy implications of spending decisions.

Zero-based budgeting is a particular kind of program budget. It associates service levels in each program with costs, and then it prioritizes all the options, treating high and low service levels as different program options. All those at the top of the priority list are funded. If there are more items than money, the ones on the bottom of the list are not funded. Zero-based budgeting formally allows for, and creates a mechanism for, reallocation: one department may suggest a higher level of service or a new program that is ranked high on the priority list, while another department's programs are ranked low. The new proposal may be funded at the expense of the older. The potential for generating competition and conflict is so great in this budget format that it is seldom used; but a less-extreme version, called "target budgeting," typically puts only 5 percent to 10 percent of departments' budgets at risk for reallocation. Target budgeting is common.

The information presented in each budget format allows different kinds of analyses to be made. The line-item budget forces attention to changes in accounting categories—why are office supplies more expensive this year than last? These are technical questions of limited policy interest. When a budget is presented in line items, it can be very difficult to examine proposed expenditures for sound management practice or appropriateness.[1] The program budget, especially with its zero-based budget component, forces comparisons between programs on the basis of stated priorities. These priorities are usually statements of policy, for example, that a program that benefits the poor should have a higher priority than one that benefits the rich, or that programs that emphasize prevention should receive funding before programs that emphasize suppression. Performance budgets lay out not only what programs cost and roughly what they achieve, but also the (implied) criteria of productivity for the choices between programs.

Because the different budget formats have different strengths and weaknesses, many actual budgets combine formats.[2] Everyone has to be concerned about financial control, so there is often a line-item budget conforming to administrative units; but sometimes program budgets are added to line-item budgets and, more rarely, performance budgets are added to the program budget. In times of financial stress or in response to demands to reduce spending, governments may adopt zero-based or target-based budgets and put them on top of program budgets.

Budget Process and Power

Elected officials in the executive and legislative branches, budget office staff, and interest groups try to change the budget process to enhance their power over policy, and the politicians also try to use it to ensure their reelection and the dominance of their party. Budget processes summarize the outcomes of those contests at any given moment. Sometimes the actors manage to make changes that are relatively long-lived, building them into constitutions that are hard to change; at other times they make rule changes that do not have the force of law, let alone constitutional backing. The latter changes are much easier to overturn or modify. The longer-term changes are sometimes considered structural, though their effects are not determinative and may be modified by actual practice.

In normal budgetary decision making, someone makes a budget request, someone reviews that request, and someone has to approve or cut or disallow that spending. But within that overall framework there is enormous variation in who makes which decisions and who can overrule whose decisions.

One of the key contests of power has been between the legislative and executive branches of government. In some cases the executive branch dominates the decision making, and in others the legislative branch has an equal or even larger role. In the model of executive dominance, the chief executive is responsible for formulating the budget proposal, which reflects his or her priorities and policy agenda, if any. The chief executive may keep the executive branch agencies completely away from the legislature, other than to present the chief executive's approved version of the proposal. The legislature may rubber-stamp the executive budget, that is, approve it without detailed examination or emendation. Should the legislature make any changes that the chief executive opposes, the chief executive can veto the changes and sometimes even rewrite the legislation. In the legislatively dominated budget process, the bureau chiefs write up their requests for spending with the assistance of legislators who want some particular expenditures. The requests are not scrutinized by the chief executive but are handed directly to the legislature for review and approval. The role of the chief executive in the legislative dominance model is slight.

Budget processes normally fall between the extremes of total dominance by either the executive or the legislature. Formally and legally, legislatures often have the power to approve taxation and proposals for spending, but they may delegate much of that power to the executive. One reason for delegating that authority is the belief that expenditures are out of control and that the legislature cannot discipline itself, especially on capital projects and jobs for constituents. The chief executive is expected to be able to cut out proposals that legislators make to please constituents and impose discipline on the legislature. The belief that legislatures are more vulnerable to interest group and constituent demands than the chief executive leads to pressure to shift budget power from the legislature to the chief executive. One way that the executive is supposed to exercise control is to veto any increases the legislature adds to the executive's proposed budget.

Although the allocation of budget power between the executive and the legislative branches of government is a major and highly visible area of contested power, it is not the only one. A second politically significant characteristic of budget processes is their degree of centralization. Centralization refers to two related concepts: (1) the degree to which the budget process is bottom-up or top-down; and (2) the degree to which power is scattered among independent committees, commissions, and elected officials without an effective coordinating device.

Bottom-up procedures begin with the budget requests of bureau chiefs. These requests are scrutinized either by the chief executive and his budget staff or by the legislature, or by both, but the requests form the framework of decision making and set the agenda. There is little or no prioritizing of programs in this model in its extreme form. Each request is judged on its merits, independently of other requests. A loose coordination is achieved by setting revenue or spending limits at the beginning of the process; cost increases are kept within rough limits by giving no agency an increase much higher than the total percentage increase in revenues.

Top-down budgeting at its extreme virtually ignores bureau chiefs. The chief executive may not ask bureau chiefs for their budget requests or may give them detailed instructions on how to formulate their requests. The proposal can be made from whole cloth at the top of the executive branch by taking last year's actual budget and making changes in it in accordance with policy preference, giving more to one and less to another, regardless of what those running the bureaus would have asked for. A more moderate top-down procedure takes the bureaus' requests and gives more to one and less to another based on policy choices.

Minicase: How the Governor's Veto Is Used

One of the major arguments for strong veto powers for the executive is that they enable the executive to remove "pork" that legislatures irresponsibly slip into the budget. According to this view, the executives are financially responsible—they seek the public policy goal of balanced and efficient budgets, with the minimum of waste. Legislators presumably are interested in narrower, more partisan issues, such as bringing projects home to their districts so as to be reelected. Most of the governors have powerful vetoes over the state legislatures.

How is this veto power actually used? Is it used to maintain fiscal discipline, or to remove projects and appropriations added by members of the opposite political party, making their reelection more difficult?

The question of how governors use their veto power was addressed in a now-classic article by Glenn Abney and Thomas Lauth. They argued, on the basis of a survey of state officials, that governors were no more likely to use line-item vetoes in states where the legislature was heavily inclined toward pork projects than in states where the legislature was more fiscally responsible or less wasteful. What these authors found instead was that the line-item veto was more likely to be used by governors when they faced legislative majorities of the opposite party. Line-item vetoes, at the time of their study reported in 1985, were used as a tool of partisan contestation.[1] James Gosling refined this finding to include policy issues as well as partisan ones; he confirmed that for the state of Wisconsin saving money did not seem to be a major reason for the use of line-item vetoes.[2]

What about now, twenty years later? Is the line-item veto still used in a partisan fashion? During the 1980s, in Illinois as in other states, the line-item veto was used for partisan purposes in a divided government. The Republican governor used strong constitutional and institutional powers to dominate the Democratic legislature. However, in the 1990s a new way of making budget decisions evolved; budget decisions were negotiated by the governor and legislative leaders. Item vetoes nearly disappeared because the budget was negotiated in advance.

The conditions that facilitated this shift included fiscal stress and deficits on the one hand, and a highly competitive and more-or-less evenly divided legislature, with shifting majorities between political parties. The fiscal stress encouraged the governor to negotiate to avoid confrontations, delays, and veto threats late in the session. The divided legislature had the effect of encouraging negotiations to gain a clear majority for the negotiated budget

(continued)

agreements. If the governor had large and stable majorities of his own party in both houses, he could have passed whatever budget he proposed, without the need for vetoes but also without the need for negotiations. But when neither party held a firm majority—sometimes one party had a majority in one house of the legislature, and the other party had a majority in the other house—the governor welcomed the opportunity to come to an agreement before the budget was handed to the legislature for approval. With a Republican governor, even when the Democrats controlled one house of the legislature they did not have enough votes to override a veto. For them, negotiation meant the possibility of some influence, rather than being locked out of budget decisions completely.

For Illinois, then, when the governor faces opposition control of the legislature he is likely to use the line-item veto extensively to impose his policy preferences; when he controls both houses by comfortable margins, he can get his proposals through easily and does not need to use the veto. But when there is a relatively even split, with shifting majorities in each house from one election to the next, the governor negotiates with the legislative leadership, coming to agreement before the budget is formally submitted to the legislature. The leadership of the legislature has to control the rank and file sufficiently to ensure that the agreement with the governor is approved.

The major means of winning over the rank and file is what Illinoisans call "member initiative grants," providing funds for legislators to spend in their districts. The funds were allocated to the rank and file by the leadership in return for votes on the budget deal. The governor was also able to award funds from various state grant-in-aid programs and capital development funds. These tools, too, could be used to reward the faithful. Voting against the leadership's negotiated budget could mean losing access to funds beneficial to a legislator's district and thereby endanger his or her chances of reelection.

Rather than using the line-item veto to eliminate pork—in this case, member initiated grants—the governor actually increased the use of those grants. In Illinois, it turns out, the governor has not been interested in eliminating pork; it is too powerful a tool for gaining legislative support for the budget.[3]

1. Glenn Abney and Thomas Lauth, "The Line-Item Veto in the States: An Instrument for Fiscal Restraint or an Instrument for Partisanship?" *Public Administration Review* 45, no. 3 (1985): 372–377.

2. James Gosling, "Wisconsin Item-Veto Lessons," *Public Administration Review* 46, no. 4 (1986): 292–300.

3. Douglas Snow and Irene Rubin, "Budgeting by Negotiation in Illinois," in *Budgeting in the States, Ten Years Later,* ed. Ed Clynch and Tom Lauth (Westport, Conn.: Greenwood Press, forthcoming 2005).

In the legislature, too, budget processes can be more top-down or more bottom-up, depending on whether spending and revenue committees receive budget and revenue targets to work with or do their own work and give the totals to the body as a whole.

Budgeting processes normally combine some top-down elements and some bottom-up elements. Budgeting tends to become more top-down when there is a revenue problem or a defined budget crisis that requires reduction in expenditures. Top-down budgeting is associated with spending control and a policy orientation in the budget. That is, if the chief executive has a marked preference for achieving some goal, he or she is more likely to use a top-down process to select some programs and reject others as a means to achieve that goal.

The second dimension of centralization is the extent to which power is scattered among relatively independent actors. For example, the chief executive may have to share power with other elected executive branch officers or with independent commissions. When power is widely shared, the effect may be to immobilize decision making. No one has responsibility or can tell anyone else what to do; approval for any action has to go through a number of different actors. The purpose of a highly fragmented and decentralized budget process may be precisely to limit spending and activist government. More centralization of budget processes is usually more activist and more policy oriented but may be either economy oriented or spending oriented.

A key element in the design of budget processes is the degree to which the public has access to the process, through participation in planning, direct access and access through the media to useful information, and the chance to testify at hearings. The most open processes are those that make all decisions in plain public view, before the press, the public, and interest groups. Meetings are held at convenient times for visitors and are announced well in advance. Representatives of various interests are invited to share their views during budget hearings and on advisory boards. The process is closed if the public, the press, and interest groups are not permitted to watch the decision making or to express their views during the budget process. Or their views may be solicited but routinely disregarded. Budget processes are seldom completely open or completely closed.

Open budget processes are more accountable to the public, but they are also more open to interest group pressure. Closing the budget process is often considered one way to help control increases in expenditures; opening it is usually a way of increasing expenditures. Closing the process is also a way of helping to pass revenue bills, as noted in chapter 2, which means that a more closed process should favor budget balance as a goal.

Because there is so much contestation for control, and because the outcomes of that contestation depend on existing structures, party dominance, the economic and political environment, and public opinion, as well as skill in using existing resources, laws, and rules, there is considerable difference in budget process between federal, state, and local levels of government, as well as among state and among local governments.

Variation between and among Federal, State, and Local Governments

For years, scholars used the federal budget process as a model against which other processes could be compared and understood. But during the 1980s the federal budget was put together in a different way every year. The advent of ad hoc budgeting at the federal level shifted attention to the states and to local governments in the search for a pattern that would convey the idea of a budget process. However, a survey of state and local budget processes reveals enormous variation. To come up with an idea of budget process based on them requires a description of that variation and the mechanisms that generate it. This chapter illustrates some of the key ways that budget processes differ from one another. The next chapter describes how, and to some extent why, federal, state, and local budget processes have changed and discusses some common themes in their evolution.

Variation between Levels of Government

Federal, state, and local budget processes differ in the way power over the budget is negotiated between the legislative and executive branches of government; they differ in the degree of dispersion or coordination of power within the executive and legislative branches; and they differ in terms of the composition of the budget and the integration or separation of budget processes for different kinds of resources and programs.

Executive and Legislative Budget Powers. One way of describing budget processes is according to the balance between the executive and the legislature in drawing up and reviewing the budget. Over the past decade, there has been a more equal balance between the branches at the federal level than at the state or local level. At the state level, the executive tends to be stronger than the legislature, although they are becoming more equal in recent years.[3] At the local level, for all but the smallest cities, the model of executive dominance generally holds. Mayors often hold powerful vetoes, and city councils may be prohibited from increasing the mayor's estimates. Councils have little or no budget staff. However they must approve the budget in most cities, and in some they play a substantial role in budget review.

Governors generally have broader veto powers than the president. Constitutionally, the president of the United States has to veto all of a bill or none of it, which permits Congress to package bills to discourage vetoes. Forty-three state governors have line-item vetoes that allow them to strike out any expenditure that appears as a separate line in the budget. Thirty-five governors have the power to veto funding for an entire program or agency. A number of governors have amendatory vetoes, which let them rewrite parts of the law. Only six governors have a veto like the president's, that is, one limited to rejecting a bill in its entirety.[4]

At the national level, Congress sometimes puts a number of measures together, including some that the president wants badly, to make it difficult for the president to veto. These combined measures are called omnibus bills. One type of omnibus legislation is a continuing resolution. These are passed when one or more of the thirteen money bills (appropriations bills) required to fund the federal government's operations are not passed on time. Congress funds the departments whose money bills have not yet passed with one (usually temporary) continuing resolution, which combines appropriations that are normally passed separately. The large scope makes it difficult to veto without harming some absolutely essential spending.

A second occasion for omnibus legislation is the budget reconciliation bill. Reconciliation is a part of the congressional budget process, in which separate committees take action to comply with the budget resolution. The budget resolution is a kind of plan or road map for spending and taxing that is approved by both houses of Congress, ideally before the budget deliberations begin. Based on this overall plan, the budget committees give instructions to the committees on tax and spending legislation. After the committees have done their work, Congress gathers up the committees' changes and passes them as one omnibus piece of legislation. As pointed out by Bill Dauster in the minicase on page 83, much unrelated legislation has been put in the omnibus reconciliations. Again, the broad scope makes them more difficult to veto.

At the state level, budgets may be passed in a single measure or in a series of separate bills—practice varies from state to state. But the use of omnibus legislation to avoid vetoes is virtually nonexistent: Only nine states have a mechanism for continuing last year's budget in case this year's budget is late, and omnibus reconciliations are a peculiarity of the federal budget process. State legislatures lack the motivation to package legislation in large clumps; because the governor can generally veto parts of bills, omnibus legislation provides no protection against a veto. However, if the governor can only veto an appropriation if it appears in a line in the budget, the legislature can avoid putting that one item in a line by itself. Or the legislature can combine many budget lines into one, so the governor has to accept the whole section of the budget or reject it all. For example, in Texas, the legislature responded to the governor's political use of the line-item veto by creating a lump sum appropriation for higher education, rather than breaking down expenditures and appropriating them line by line.[5]

At the local level, most budgets are passed as a single ordinance, without any unrelated provisions. Agreement on the budget is often worked out in advance by the mayor and council,[6] so the council approves the mayor's or manager's proposed budget, and the need for a veto is slight. City staff typically monitor council statements throughout the previous year, weigh the spending and tax proposals embodied in such discussions, and incorporate the ones that make sense to them into the budget. By the time the council gets the budget, the things they wish to see are usually already incorporated. The mayor or budget office sometimes lays aside a small amount of money for a limited number of addbacks in case council members insist on adding some project the mayor, manager, or budget office intentionally deleted. To the extent that the budget is negotiated with the council, it is generally done in advance, with little open confrontation.

Sometimes, however, negotiations break down and the mayor threatens to use, or actually does use, his or her veto. Because municipal politics is normally not linked directly to Democratic or Republican Party politics, the use of the veto is less clearly linked with partisanship and may be more closely related to fiscal policy. For example, in a recent instance in Detroit the mayor vetoed council restorations of staffing cuts that had been made to help close a budget gap of $263 million. The mayor also argued in his veto that the council's plan for avoiding the layoffs resulted in some illegal cuts elsewhere in the budget of items the city was required to provide.[7]

Although party loyalty is seldom an issue at the local level, relations between the mayor and council over the budget can become confrontational if a council member is a potential rival for mayor; even then, the lack of a budget staff for the council makes it difficult for council members to pull the budget apart and make their own proposals. The council can become a noisy opposition and in some cases can prevent the passage of the budget or force compromises as the price for their support.

In short, there are major differences in the formal powers and patterns of negotiation between the executive and legislative branches at the federal, state, and local levels. At the federal level, where the balance is relatively even, executive and legislative members must engage in extensive formal or informal bargaining.

The results of these negotiations tend to frame the budget and set limits for departments. While bottom-up budget requests continue to be generated and examined, they may play a small role in determining outcomes because the agreements reached by the executive and legislative branches take priority over the expressed needs of the departments and agencies.[8] The federal government has put a great deal of time and energy into trying to devise budget agreements across branches. The result has been a considerable shift to top-down budgeting.

The situation is quite different at the state level, in part because the governors have more powerful vetoes and in part because the budget process itself is so different at the state level. There is no reconciliation process at the state (or local) level and so no occasion for an omnibus reconciliation. Only a handful of states have any form of continuing resolution if the budget appropriations are late,[9] so there is no occasion for omnibus legislation through continuing resolutions. Moreover, since most governors can reduce or amend legislation or veto parts of it, there is little to be gained from creating omnibus bills at the state level.

Dispersion of Power.   Despite the policy orientation of the federal budget and its relatively top-down process, budgetary power is the most dispersed and fragmented at the national level, partly because the decisions are so important that everyone wants a piece of the action. Before 1974 Congress divided budget responsibility among legislative committees that designed and authorized programs, revenue committees, and appropriation committees. In 1974 it added budget committees to set spending and revenue targets and coordinate the other committees. The summit agreements between the executive branch and Congress that occurred from time to time during the 1980s and 1990s added an additional level of fragmentation because they performed some of the key roles of the budget committees, they occurred at unpredictable intervals, and they were negotiated by a shifting set of actors.

By contrast, state and local governments have simpler and less-fragmented decision making, in part because the executive branch tends to dominate budgeting. Responsibility for budgeting in the legislature tends to be more concentrated in appropriations and revenue committees although, as at the federal level, sometimes the leadership of each house overrides committee decisions.

The level of coordination between committees is relatively high in state legislatures. In the cities, the structure is even simpler. In 1997, fourteen states referred revenue bills to the appropriations committees in the house, and fifteen did so in the senate, a powerful form of coordination. Fourteen states had joint appropriations committees between the house and senate, five always had joint hearings, and twenty-four sometimes had joint hearings.[10] At the local level, leg-

islative consideration of the budget may be confined to a single finance committee that is responsible for both revenue and spending approval.

Entitlements, Grants, Loans, and Operating and Capital Budgets. Federal budgeting is really two processes that are only loosely linked. Some expenditures are
approved annually by the appropriations committees, but a substantial portion
of the federal budget is composed of entitlements, which do not go through the
appropriations process and are approved for long periods of time, rather than
annually. Entitlements are special programs, the spending for which is determined
by how many people or organizations meet eligibility requirements.

In essence, there are at least two budget processes, one that applies to entitlements and one that applies to other spending. Among the other spending, however, is some that doesn't conform to normal operating budget characteristics.
The federal government deals in loans and loan guarantees. Ideally these loans are
all repaid, but at below-market interest rates. Figuring out how much these loans
(and guarantees) actually cost the government has been difficult, but in recent
years the budget has included a separate section estimating the costs over time.
These estimates are not equivalent to budget estimates for, say, employee salaries
in the Office of Personnel Management, and so they are not merged and added
to each other in a direct way.

Both state and local governments budget separately for capital and operating
expenses, which the federal government does not do. The process for formulating and approving the capital budget is often distinct and separate from the
process for formulating the operating budget, though they may be merged and
considered at the same time. Capital budgets have a different time frame from the
operating budget, as the projects they fund often drag out over several years.
When projects are complete, they are removed from the budget. While the operating budget may look the same (or nearly so) from year to year, the capital budget does not. States also have entitlements, some in cooperation with the federal
government and some of their own. State governments are also the recipients of
federal grants, both for themselves and as agents for the local governments. Such
grants are now generally appropriated by the legislature, but they used to form
a kind of second budget that was handled differently from normal appropriations.
State budgets are thus complicated mixes based on different kinds of resources
that can remain segregated or be merged in different ways into the budget. States
often have different processes of decision making for each of these different categories of programs.

Local governments generally do not have entitlements and appropriate all or
nearly all their budgets every year. Grant revenue from the federal government or

from the state may be incorporated into the budget, or it may be budgeted separately. Tax breaks, which operate as entitlements at the federal level and often
at the state level as well, are usually handled on a case-by-case basis at the local
level, so the costs are known in advance on a yearly basis. There are few open-
ended responsibilities. Balancing the budget is thus technically easier at the local
level. Expenditures typically do not go up at the same time that revenues go down,
as they do for the states and the national government.

Variation in Budget Processes among States and among Cities

Not only do federal, state, and local governments differ from one another in their
budget processes, but states differ from states, and cities differ from cities. Two
examples at the state level illustrate the range of possibilities. The budget process
in Texas is legislature dominated; the Georgia model is executive dominated.

In Texas, the governor and the Legislative Budget Board (LBB) prepare a broad
policy statement that informs the agencies' planning process. The LBB is composed of the lieutenant governor; the speaker of the house; the chairs of the Senate Committee on Finance, Senate Committee on State Affairs, House Committee on Appropriations, and House Committee on Ways and Means; two
additional members of the Senate appointed by the lieutenant governor; and two
additional members of the House of Representatives appointed by the speaker.

The governor also creates some goals and performance standards for the agencies. The agencies use this guidance to draw up plans, which have to be approved
by the governor's budget office and the LBB. Later, the LBB sends out instructions
to the agencies for the preparation of their budget requests, which must include
performance measures they described earlier in the process. Then the budget
office and the LLB together hold hearings on the agencies' strategic plans and
budget requests. Based on feedback the agencies receive during the hearings, they
revise their plans and requests. The revised submissions form the basis for the
LBB to put together the appropriations legislation. It can recommend different
amounts of money than the agencies request, even after the negotiations that
occurred during the hearings.

The legislative bills then go to committees in each house, and each house holds
hearings with the agencies requesting funding. The committees mark up the bills,
making whatever changes they decide on at that point. From there, the budget
must be approved by each house, and then there is a conference committee to iron
out differences. The conference committee report must then be approved by each
house. The approved budget goes to the governor for signature, though he has a
line-item veto should he decide to use it. Oversight of budget implementation

is done by the LLB and by legislators and is reportedly detailed and forceful, to ensure that the agencies are doing what they promised to do and are taking the performance monitoring system seriously.

The Texas governor actually has little formal budget power, except at the conclusion of the process through line-item veto power. His or her power is based more on indirect influence. Both the governor's policy guidance and detailed instructions to the departments from the budget office are blended with instructions from the Legislative Budget Board to the departments before they prepare their strategic plans and budget requests. The legislature is unusually active and powerful throughout the budgeting process.[11]

The picture is reversed in Georgia, where the legislature has had very little influence over the budget process. As one scholar described it, legislators have virtually no role in discussing budget reforms. The legislative session is extremely short, only ninety days, during which the legislators see only the parts of the budget that the governor has proposed to change. Legislators discuss a few politicized programs and pay attention to pork-barrel-type spending for their districts.

> The legislative institutions available to provide oversight have atrophied from over a hundred years of single party dominance. The legislative budget office consists of few staff many of whom are political appointees rather than professional budget analysts and the residuum of an early effort to create some audit and evaluation capacity, the Budget Research and Oversight Committee has been underfunded and understaffed. Institutionally, the legislature is hardly prepared to consider a regular budget much less make use of increased information that would result from a budgetary reform.[12]

The budget requests are prepared by the agencies, submitted to the executive budget office, and then the governor has hearings with the agencies to discuss their budgets and work out differences. The Legislative Budget Office also reviews proposals. The governor then makes his recommendations to the legislature, which are initially reviewed by the Legislative Budget Office and subject to hearings by the appropriations committee. Then subcommittees of the appropriations committee in the House meet and report to a budget subcommittee composed of the leadership of the House. That subcommittee makes recommendations to the appropriations committee; after approval by the appropriations committee the appropriations bill goes to the floor for a vote. From there the budget goes to the Senate, and thence to a committee appointed by both houses to work out differences.[13]

If the legislative bodies in charge of budgeting were fully staffed by professionals, and if there were time during the session to really examine the budget recommendation, or even make their own recommendations, power would be more nearly equal, even with the governor's powerful veto. In the past few years, one-party dominance has ended, with the result that there is some pressure from the legislature to play a more active role in reviewing the budget, but change has been slow.

Most states fall between the extremes of executive and legislative dominance, but they lean more toward executive budgeting. It is common for agencies to submit budget proposals to the legislature either before, or at the same time as, the governor submits his or her proposal to the legislature.[14] The legislature can choose between the governor's proposals and the agencies' where the proposals differ. This arrangement dilutes executive power over the agencies, when legislatures choose to use this power. If the legislature is of the opposite party to the governor, members may spend more time and energy examining the governor's requests or coming up with their own.[15]

The major systematic source of variation in municipal budget processes is the form of government. In the town meeting, citizens vote directly on the budget, providing the maximum imaginable level of accountability. This structural form is necessarily limited to small towns and relatively simple issues. In the commissioner form, which was widely adopted in the early 1900s, the department heads sit as the council and jointly make budget decisions. This form makes no distinction between the executive and legislative branches. It has become rare in recent years, in part because it created problems of accountability.

Most cities today have either a mayor-council form or a council-manager form of government. In mayor-council forms, the mayor may be chosen by the council and may have little more authority than other council members, or may be chosen by the citizens directly and have considerably more power than other council members. While small cities may still budget legislatively, with spending recommendations coming from the departments to the council finance committee for review, in medium- and large-sized cities, the mayor and members of his staff generally prepare the budget, and the council has limited ability to make changes or even to review it. In council-manager cities, the executive-legislative distinction is blurred because the city manager, who prepares the budget, is hired and fired by the council. If the manager insists on a budget that departs from council priorities, he or she is fired. Councils tend to play a more active role in budgeting in council-manager cities, at least to the point of making their policy preferences known and ensuring that their interests are represented in the budget. The council-manager form is more common in middle-sized cities, while strong (independently elected) mayors are typical of larger cities.

Summary and Conclusions

Budget processes are partly technical, coordinating decision making and keeping the flow of resources to the agencies timely, and partly political. Because budget power is perceived as such an important component of overall political power, there is considerable jockeying for decision-making power within the budget process. More broadly, many budget actors try to change the budget process to help achieve the goals they value, whether those be public policy goals, such as growth or decline in the scope and size of government, or short-term partisan and electoral goals, such as the distribution of pork or deregulation that benefits specific constituents or contributors.

A decentralized, legislative budgeting process is very open to interest groups and short-term issues and not as open to longer-term policy concerns. A more top-down, executive-dominated process can be more responsive to policy concerns. Budget formats that make comparisons among programs also encourage a policy orientation. The process can rein in interest groups to some extent; and it can exaggerate or tone down competition and encourage and frame budget trade-offs.

Not surprisingly, budget processes differ at the federal, state, and local levels, as well as across states and between cities. The differences depend in part on the structure. For example, in our federal system of government, state and local governments receive grants from the national government, but not the other way around. The separation between the executive and legislative branches is more marked and clear at the national and state levels than at the local level. Budget processes also vary among states and among local governments, partly as a result of structural differences, such as those between strong mayor and council-manager forms of municipal government, but also as a result of divided government—in states where the executive and legislature are of different parties budget processes differ from states where they are of the same party. But above all, budget processes differ depending on how particular actors have changed the process to suit their needs, values, and contemporary problems over time.

4. The Dynamics of Changing Budget Processes

Sometimes budget actors change the process because it does not seem to be working—it does not reduce the size of the deficit, as promised, or, contrary to expectations, it does not produce a budget in a timely manner. Perhaps as often, budget actors change the budget process to enhance their own power over policy outcomes. At the extreme, budget processes may collapse into ad hoc decision making either because they fail to adapt to changed circumstances or because the rules have become too constraining and actors cannot agree on new ones.

It is useful to observe the changes in budget process over time. These changes sometimes capture political actors in the middle of increasing or losing power, so the observer can examine that which is normally accomplished behind the scenes. Also, because budget process influences (though it does not determine) outcomes, changes in process help to explain changing budgetary outcomes. Examining budget process change also provides a way of seeing and analyzing some broader issues of governance: What stimulates an increase or decrease in openness or accountability? How far can the outcomes veer toward or away from democratic governance without provoking sufficient backlash to force a change?

To analyze changes in budget process one has to look not only at the formal processes, but also at the informal ones. Formal processes may be supplemented or supplanted by informal ones. For example, the formal process might include a fine division of responsibilities among legislative committees and between the executive and legislative branches, but actual budget negotiations may be restricted to representatives from the chief executive and the leadership in each house of the legislature, bypassing legislative committees completely. Though the committees seem to be doing their jobs, they may be taking their cues from summit agreements in which they had no part. This informal negotiation process occurs at times at all levels of government. When and why does this informal, less-visible process take over, and when does it subside or yield to the more formal and visible one?

One possible answer is that more and tighter rules encourage evasions and informal adaptations. Another possibility is that divided government contributes to the need for informal and secret negotiations because the executive and legislative branches, controlled by opposite parties, use the formal process to thwart each other's priorities. Third, actual power may be highly one-sided, leaving one or more parties to the process with a limited scope of decision making. The minority side might try to hold the budget hostage to increase its power and hold quiet negotiations rather than follow the formal process that disempowers them (see Minicase, page 104). Finally, if the formal process produces outcomes that are generally disliked or embarrassing, participants may switch to a less-visible process from which it is easier to distance themselves, generating the "Who, me?" defense.

When informal processes take hold, secrecy may increase (few people know how decisions are made; selected stakeholders may have disproportionate access) and the information content of the budget may deteriorate, as definitions erode, categories blur, and outcomes (such as the size of the deficit or the implications of borrowing) are obscured. Democratic participation, openness, and accountability may diminish.

Overview

Over the past hundred years there has been considerable change toward more centralized budget processes, to facilitate financial control, and toward a more explicitly policy-oriented executive budget review process. The practice of departments' submitting budget requests directly to legislative committees, with limited executive review, gradually has yielded to a process in which the chief executive is responsible not only for assembling agency requests before handing them to the legislature, but also for reviewing and trimming back those requests. As part of this change, executive budget offices were created, grew in professional staff, and became more politically sensitive and policy oriented. Over time legislatures have granted more power to chief executives to formulate and execute the budget, enhancing the policymaking power of the executive.

Minicase: New York State and Pressure to Change the Formal Rules

When the formal rules of budgeting do not seem fair to all the actors—when power is highly imbalanced—the formal rules may still frame the process, but informal negotiations may take over. The informal negotiations do not solve the underlying problems and in fact may generate new ones. Committees that go through the motions but make no decisions, and disagreements on what the budget numbers mean generate public cynicism and frequent critique. The behind-closed-doors aspect of the negotiations challenges democratic process. Under such circumstances there may be intense pressure to change the formal rules and redistribute budgetary power.

New York State is one of three states in which the executive budget reforms of the early 1900s radically disempowered the legislature. Left with nearly no power to shape the budget, the legislature routinely held up its passage to force the governor to negotiate. To underscore the one-sidedness of the executive powers, a recent court decision granted broad power to the governor to include policy in his budget. Governor George Pataki has gone further than his predecessors in using budget bills to pass new initiatives, an area where the legislature feels that it has legitimate authority.[1]

In addition, there is no independent estimate of the amount of revenue that would be available. No two actors accept the same projections for revenues or deficits. The governor and legislature discuss the proposed budget without numbers, a significant omission. The actual numbers are determined in negotiations between the governor and legislative leaders, not by professional technical staff or legislative committees. Besides being routinely late, budgets in general have been based on political trade-offs rather than technical estimates.[2]

After years of failed efforts, in 2004 both the New York Senate and Assembly passed a reform bill that would change the date of the governor's budget submission and build in incentives for the legislature and governor to get the budget done on time. The governor opposed the measure.[3]

Historical context makes it clearer what the legislature was trying to accomplish and why the governor opposed the proposal. New York State has one of the nation's strongest executive budgeting laws. The legislature in recent years has tried to gain back some discretion over the budget but has lost in several big court cases. Then it passed the 2004 reform bill, whose ostensible goal was to ensure that the budget would be passed on time, but

(continued)

which contained incentives and mechanisms to shift some budget power from the governor to the legislature.

The reform proposed to establish an independent budget office, appointed by the legislative leadership, that would referee disputes on spending and revenue forecasts. Such an office would give the legislature a capacity to question executive proposals with some authority when executive projections seemed too low.[4] If it worked, the proposal would help eliminate instances of the legislature's making higher estimates of revenue, and hence of spending, than the executive and then facing a series of exasperating gubernatorial vetoes.

A central feature of the reform provided that if the budget is not passed on time, an automatic provision kicks in to continue appropriations at the previous year's level, with the exception of welfare payments, state employee health benefits and pension costs, and debt service. This continuing appropriation is called the "contingency budget." The legislature granted itself the authority to amend the contingency budget.

Another feature of the reform proposal addresses the requirement that the legislature must take final action on the governor's budget proposal before taking up any of its own. In the reform plan, the contingency budget is treated as "final action" on the governor's bill, freeing the legislature to act on its own instead of only reacting to the governor's proposal. All the legislature has to do under this plan is stall action on the governor's budget until the first day of the new fiscal year, and it would have greatly enhanced decision-making power over the budget. Even with this expanded power, however, the legislature's budget additions would be subject to the governor's line-item veto, which can only be overridden by a supermajority of the legislature.

Governor Pataki vetoed the reform proposals in late 2004. Although he had earlier called for budget reform, he apparently did not want this particular set of proposals. The legislature did not try to override the veto, but the major legislative promoter of the vetoed reforms promised to put them forward again. Although not in place, the plan is significant because it shows how an extreme imbalance—in this case, extreme executive powers over the budget—generates efforts to go in the other direction, to modify those powers and share them more evenly. An extremely informal process that operates behind closed doors generates pressure to make the process more open. A symbolic discussion, without agreed-on revenue assumptions, creates pressure for a process based on credible and widely disseminated revenue projections. Regardless of these

(continued)

pressures, a change in the formal distribution of budget power is difficult to achieve.

1. The decision found that the main budget power the legislature has in New York is the power to hold up the budget. Michael Cooper, "Budget Is Job of Governor, Judges Rule," *New York Times,* December 17, 2004.
2. Editorial, "A Hocus-Pocus Budget," *New York Times,* January 21, 2004.
3. Opinion, "State Budget Reform: Hand It up Now, Albany," *Ithaca Journal,* October 6, 2004, www.theithacajournal.com/news/stories/20041006/opinion/1362658.html.
4. William F. Hammond, "Albany Leaders Retreat Behind Closed Doors," *New York Sun,* December 9, 2004.

Sometimes the shift to centralized executive budget making was the work of reformers through constitutional amendments, but sometimes the legislature delegated authority to the executive. Though one might expect legislatures to hold tightly to budget control as an important source of institutional as well as personal and political power, they have not uniformly done so. Two factors stand out as reasons for legislative delegation of budget authority to the executive branch: If the legislature and the executive are of the same party and have similar policy goals, the legislature has been more willing to delegate budget power to the chief executive. Alternatively, if there was some sense of crisis and simultaneously a demonstration that the legislature was not able to organize itself to deal with the problem, the legislature was more likely to shift budget-making power to the executive branch.

Legislative delegations have not always been successful or permanent. Sometimes delegated policymaking power has been used for purposes explicitly forbidden by the legislature or used to bypass legislative approval. Legislators have sometimes responded by trying to strengthen their own ability to perform the functions they had formerly delegated to the executive, increasing budget staff, improving their capacity to review budget proposals, and enhancing their capacity to evaluate executive branch performance.

When the legislature and the executive share somewhat equal powers, tumultuous budget battles can result when different parties control the two branches, leading to vetoes, late budgets, and sometimes failure to pass a budget at all—the so-called train wreck. Though often considered indicators of failed budget process and as evidence of a need for reform, in fact these battles may be the result of effective systems of checks and balances, which allow government to go only so far from public will or trust before self-destructing in a highly visible way. The cost of creating order in such volatile situations may be more extended negotiations between the executive and the legislative leadership and more (judicious, one hopes) use of distributive politics—pork. Ironically pork is generally considered bad and blamed on legislators, but it may be generated by executives trying to pass a negotiated budget in a two-party democracy where power is evenly divided. Executives may include the pork projects of particular legislators in their budget proposals (or in supplemental appropriations) in an effort to win legislative support for the whole package or for other, unrelated legislation. However, the cost and visibility of pork may undermine trust in government, generating new waves of budget process reform.

Major Changes in the Federal Budget Process

The federal budget process has undergone major formal change several times. In 1921 the executive budget process was adopted; in 1974 the Congressional Budget Reform Act was passed, limiting some of the president's budgetary discretion and enhancing Congress's ability to check executive branch revenue projections and economic assumptions; in 1985 the Gramm-Rudman-Hollings act was passed in an effort to curtail the deficit. After several iterations, that act was replaced by the Budget Enforcement Act in 1990 (BEA) in a further effort to help strengthen the norms of balance.

In addition to these formal, structural changes, there have been many informal adaptations. After the 1974 Congressional Budget Reform Act, the more equal budgetary power of Congress and the president during the 1980s and 1990s, compounded by government frequently divided between the parties, encouraged budget negotiations between Congress and the president. These summit agreements led to more centralization of control in the executive Office of Management and Budget and the congressional leadership to reach and carry out agreements.

The most recent phase of informal change occurred after the budget achieved balance in 1998. At first, the requirements of the BEA were widely ignored; then in 2002 its provisions were allowed to lapse. The result has been an upsurge in ad hoc budgeting and an increase in the size of the deficit. The war in Iraq has been funded primarily through supplemental appropriations. The 1974 act is still in effect, but it, too, has been ignored or waived in recent years. The result has been a highly unpredictable budget process, often playing out behind closed doors. Secrecy has increased, as has budgetary fragmentation, with more of what should be regular appropriations being treated as emergency supplementals and less serious scrutiny of the president's or Congress's budget proposals. The 2005 omnibus appropriation bill was reportedly voted on so quickly that few legislators had any idea what was in it.

The Creation of the Executive Budget at the National Level

At the national level, the 1921 Budget and Accounting Act created the executive budget and the Budget Bureau in the executive branch. This major change in budget processes illustrates both (1) the competition between branches of government for power over budgeting and (2) the role of environmental shocks and emergencies, which fostered increases in expenditures and debt, generating problems that were addressed through budget reform.

A major stimulus for the 1921 reform was the increase in spending that occurred from 1899 to 1912, in part because of a more activist government. Federal spending during the last third of the nineteenth century was $200 million to $400 million a year. From 1899 to 1912 the level jumped to $500 million to $700 million a year.[1] The full proposal for reform in budgeting at the national level included not just presidential review of agency requests but also a line-item veto for the president and restrictions on the powers of the Congress to change amounts the president proposed. Presumably the president would control expenditures and reduce waste using these tools. President William Howard Taft supported the executive budget proposal, but Congress did not initially approve of the idea.

The pressure on Congress to give up some of its traditional power in the interest of economy was reduced by budgetary surpluses in 1911 and 1912.[2] The Democrats in Congress preferred to strengthen Congress and let it do the job of controlling expenditures. World War I intervened, reducing the salience of the issue in the short run but raising expenditures and deficits to such a point that congressional opposition to the presidential budget proposal was reduced. Something needed to be done, and this reform promised lower taxes, lower spending, and elimination of deficits.

In the event, Congress reformed itself in 1920, before the shift to the presidential budget. The House of Representatives consolidated appropriations into a single committee in 1920. Complete integration of revenues and expenditures and comparisons of spending among programs were not fully accomplished, "but the reconsolidation of [the] appropriations power of several committees over the objection of the members of those committees and of the agencies and interest groups involved was still a considerable achievement."[3] As a result of the congressional reorganization and centralization, some of the pressure for the executive budget was reduced, and the eventual shift of power to the president was not as extreme as the reformers originally envisioned. The president got the Bureau of the Budget, which was transferred to the Executive Office of the President in 1939, and responsibility for preparing and presenting the budget, but Congress did not give the president a line-item veto and retained for itself its powers to accept, reject, or alter the president's proposed budget.

Entitlements and Congressional Fragmentation, from the 1930s to the 1970s

During the Great Depression of the 1930s, in response to massive unemployment and resulting poverty, a new kind of program was initiated, which gave money to individuals who satisfied criteria the programs established. Called "entitlements," these programs bypassed the appropriations committees and were scrutinized only by the authorizing committees of Congress. Considerable spending power was shifted to authorizing committees, which often favor additional spending, and control over spending was divided up among a greater number of committees, fragmenting the budget process and making coordination more problematic. In addition, World War II caused staggering spending increases during the 1940s. Congress responded with several unsuccessful efforts at reform.

From 1966 to 1973 several environmental changes took place that strained the budget process and gave additional impetus to congressional reform.[4] First were the costs of the Vietnam War. Rather than curtail domestic expenditures to help pay for the war and risk exacerbating domestic conflicts, the government ran bigger deficits. There was pressure to reduce both overall spending and the size of the deficits. At the same time, there were major policy splits between Congress and the president over the conduct of the war and over domestic spending. President Nixon withheld billions of dollars of domestic spending that Congress had approved. Mistrusting the president and fearing the loss of policy control over spending, Congress increased its budgetary role and strengthened its capacity to examine and determine budget policies.

Congress Takes Back Some Budget Control, 1974

These two pressures—to reduce spending and control deficits and to take back some of the budget discretion that Congress had granted the president—combined to produce the 1974 Congressional Budget and Impoundment Control Act. The act moderately increased centralization and coordination, but equally important, it provided a professional staff of budgeters to help Congress do the analysis that underlies a budget proposal. It also revised the procedures that allowed the president to withhold funds that Congress had approved.

Congress centralized budgeting only to a limited extent, however. To the existing authorizing, taxing, and appropriations committees, the 1974 act added budget committees, whose responsibility was to come up with overall estimates of revenues and targets for spending in broad areas. Their plan was called "the budget resolution" and needed to be approved by both houses of Congress. The other congressional committees were generally supposed to stay within the guidelines the budget resolution established. The new arrangement provided for some coordination between revenue and expenditure committees and some fiscal policy formation; at the same time it did not overly threaten the existing division of power.

Congress's reorganization of the budget process was also intended as a way of taking back some budget initiative from the president who, in the eyes of some, had abused the discretion he had been granted. The budget committees could accept presidential policies or, relying on the new Congressional Budget Office, could differ with the president on projections concerning the economy, the anticipated deficit, and the inflation rate. Congress could make its own fiscal policy. The new budget process also curtailed the president's ability simply to withhold spending that Congress had approved but which did not accord with presidential policy preferences. Congress was given the opportunity to object to proposed deferrals of spending, and it had to act positively to give assent to rescissions, or permanent withdrawal of legislative appropriations, or they would not take effect.

Though Congress tried to enhance its own power to devise and implement fiscal policy, most of the distribution of power within Congress was left as it was to ensure that threatened appropriations, tax, and authorizing committee members did not quash the whole proposal for change. The compromises resulted in budget committees that had little real power or influence. Their ability to act as a brake on spending was limited.

Deficit Controls 1986, 1990

Despite the new congressional budget process established in 1974, deficits continued to rise, taking an upturn at the end of the Jimmy Carter administration and then growing even more rapidly throughout the Ronald Reagan administration. Slow growth of the economy and the effects of rapidly growing entitlement programs contributed to the mounting deficits, but tax reductions, military buildups, and overestimates of economic growth also contributed their share.

Because many of the causes of deficits were seen as difficult to control or politically off-limits, there was renewed focus on changing the budget process instead of tackling the deficit sources directly. Supporters of a strong executive proposed stronger presidential vetoes; proponents of smaller government argued for a constitutional amendment that would take discretion away from public officials of both branches by requiring a balanced budget and revenue limitations. Advocates of congressional power suggested further reforms of the legislative budget process. What finally passed was a peculiar compromise that did not change the balance of power much between the Congress and the executive branch but markedly limited the discretion of both branches if they could not meet guidelines on the reduction of the deficit.

The compromise legislation, called Gramm-Rudman-Hollings after its sponsors, called for the setting of deficit reduction targets each year, with the goal of a zero deficit in five years. Failure to achieve the annual target for deficit reduction triggered an automatic, across-the-board cut (with some exemptions for entitlements). In theory, the across-the-board cuts would be so obnoxious to all parties that they would choose to achieve the deficit reduction targets on time, so the automatic feature of the cuts would not be invoked. What actually occurred, however, was that the rules were bent and most of the cuts never occurred. Gramm-Rudman-Hollings was modified several times before it was finally replaced by the Budget Enforcement Act in 1990.

Gramm-Rudman-Hollings was not particularly successful. It may have had some marginal effect in reducing the rate of growth, but the deficits continued to grow. Both Congress and the president began "gaming" Gramm-Rudman requirements, to reduce the apparent size of the deficit just before the calculation would be made on whether to invoke Gramm-Rudman cuts (called "sequesters") to get down to the mandated deficit levels. Gimmicks included overoptimistic estimates of growth in the economy, pushing back spending from one fiscal year to the previous one, and keeping new spending off-budget. Gramm-Rudman's one-year focus encouraged quick-hit, temporary revenue raisers that would do nothing to help balance the budget in future years.

Many legislators were reluctant to give up Gramm-Rudman because the symbolism was bad—it would look as if they were giving up on deficit reduction. Hence they decided to overhaul the legislation, trying to close the loopholes that had appeared and eliminate some of its worst features. In fall 1990, after five months of negotiations between the administration and Congress, a new plan for deficit reduction was passed,[5] with a number of features. First, the Social Security surplus was taken out of the deficit calculations, so that the true size of the deficit problem would be clear. Second, the legislation included a "pay-as-you-go" requirement, meaning that proposed increases in mandatory expenditures had to be balanced by compensating increases in revenues or decreases in spending for other entitlements, and proposed reductions in revenues had to be balanced by decreases in expenditures or an increase in some other revenue source. Third, the agreement set separate spending ceilings for defense, domestic, and foreign discretionary spending, in an effort to keep spending down.

The legislation addressed several problems that had arisen during Gramm-Rudman days. Congress had cut the defense budget but had used much of the savings on domestic spending increases; the new process prohibited such transfers. Each area of the budget had to come in at or under ceiling, and savings in one area could not be transferred to other areas. Those constraints made it easier to achieve savings to reduce the deficit.

Another problem of Gramm-Rudman was that the target had to be reached only briefly; there were no sanctions if the deficit estimates increased later in the year. The new law added a feature called "look back," a check on conformity with the new limits later in the year. If any of the three caps were breached (defense, domestic, or international), then automatic, across-the-board cuts would be invoked in the area that breached the limits. Sequestration, or automatic cuts, would also be invoked if pay-as-you-go provisions of the mandated portion of the budget were violated. If such breaches occurred late in the year, the legislation provided that the amount of the breach be subtracted from the next year's ceiling.

An additional problem with Gramm-Rudman was its one-year time span, which encouraged temporary revenue increases that did not solve the problem for future years. The Budget Enforcement Act included a five-year resolution that discouraged that kind of action.

The new budget process was less rigid than the previous one because it provided exemptions for emergencies and built in flexibility related to changes in the economy. The rigid deficit targets were gone, but the mechanisms to help achieve balance were strengthened. The new process was easier to live with and hence more likely to be observed. The process was still laden with constraints, as Gramm-Rudman-Hollings was, and it explicitly regulated and redefined what programs must compete with what programs.[6]

Evaluations of the Budget Enforcement Act suggest that it worked better than Gramm-Rudman-Hollings. One scholar observed, "A complete reckoning of what has happened since the rules were devised in 1990 would show that Congress has achieved substantial deficit reduction by increasing revenue and cutting direct spending under existing law while also offsetting any deficit increases resulting from new legislation."[7]

The Budget and Accounting Act of 1921, the Congressional Budget and Impoundment Control Act of 1974, Gramm-Rudman-Hollings in 1985, and the Budget Enforcement Act of 1990 mark the major formal structural changes in the federal budget process. In addition, there have been some informal and less structural changes.

Budgeting after 1998: Ad Hoc Budgeting

By 1998, after years of effort, the national government achieved budgetary balance and was looking at surpluses over the next few years. But the budget process was geared for the elimination of deficits, not for allocation of surpluses. The level of discipline inherent in the Budget Enforcement Act was difficult, if not impossible, to maintain after balance was achieved. Legislators no longer adhered to the spending caps in the BEA and ignored rules requiring offsetting revenue decreases with increases elsewhere or with spending cuts. They ignored some provisions of the budget process and worked around others. Writing in 2002, budget scholar Allen Schick described the evasion of the spending caps:

> The arrival of a surplus a few years ago triggered a spending frenzy that vitiated the discretionary spending caps established by the 1990 Budget Enforcement Act and made a mockery of the BEA requirement that increased spending be offset by cuts in other spending or by revenue increases. In 2000 and 2001, discretionary spending soared more than $200 billion above the legal limits on annual appropriations. The caps expire at the end of 2002—which will at least enable politicians to be more honest about what they are doing. They no longer have to pretend that the census and other ongoing operations of government are national emergencies.[8]

When the BEA formally expired in 2002, it was not renewed. But the result was not more openness or integrity in the budget process. The process became less predictable, less open, and more ad hoc. Deficits swelled, but neither the president nor lawmakers seemed to care enough to do anything about them.

The Budget Enforcement Act of 1990 had been layered on top of the 1974 Congressional Budget and Impoundment Control Act. With the expiration of the BEA in 2002, the budget process was still guided by the 1974 act. That process depended on Congress's ability to pass a budget resolution, balancing revenues and expenditures, either adopting the president's assumptions and totals or substituting its own. Once agreed on the totals and roughly how they should be spent, Congress was to divide up the totals among various committees and subcommittees according to the plan. The two-step process helped coordinate the work of the committees, maintain control of budget totals, and put Congress's policy imprint on the budget. After 2002, however, the provisions of the 1974 act were again often ignored or bypassed.

As former Congressional Budget Office staffer Phil Joyce observed, there was insufficient consensus to come up with congressional targets and adhere to them. The lack of agreement meant that the budget process was operating without a notional budget constraint. As a result, Joyce claimed, "no one knows how much is enough—or too much—spending. And nobody knows—or everybody knows, but nobody agrees—when the deficit is too large or the surplus too small." [9] The congressional budget process could have retreated back to the 1921 executive budgeting process, but the executive budget proposal was not balanced, either, and so could not operate well as an informal budget constraint.

Perhaps not surprisingly in this environment, for 1999, 2003, and 2005 Congress failed to pass a budget resolution, the central feature of the 1974 act.[10] Even in the years when there was a resolution, the process was not always predictable or open to scrutiny. In 2003 Congress passed a budget resolution, but House and Senate appropriators decided not to give spending targets to the appropriations subcommittees, at least not in public. The targets would be fluid until the subcommittees had done their work and crafted their portions of the appropriations for 2004. The consequence of not making spending targets public was to obscure the impact of President George W. Bush's tax cuts, which ought logically to have translated into programmatic spending cuts. Had Congress implemented its budget resolution in the normal fashion, it might have roused considerable opposition to the president's policies by showing the cuts made necessary by the tax reductions. Such a result could have jeopardized the chances of passing budget legislation. By obscuring the appropriations subcommittee ceilings, legislative supporters of the Bush policies made the tax cuts look as if they had no consequences.

The result was damaging to the budget process. Appropriators indicated that they would allocate as they went along, rather than set targets in advance, but other participants, including staffers, were not sure how that would work or if that would be the final process. Some observers wondered how a subcommittee could operate without a limit of some sort. They argued that the budget numbers didn't add up, which was a good reason not to allocate totals to the subcommittees, but that at the end of the legislative process, the Senate, according to its rules, had to conform to the budget resolution; that meant that appropriators would likely get caught at the end if they didn't work with some sort of limits built into the budget resolution.[11] It seemed likely, then, that spending targets of some sort would have to be in operation, even if they were informal and kept from public view or operated after budget appropriations had been crafted rather than before.

For 2005, Congress was not able to pass a budget resolution to guide the committees' work. The issue was disagreement on budget process, namely the lack of offsetting spending reductions to compensate for the Bush tax reductions. Moderate Republicans in the Senate refused to go along with a process that legitimated this budgetary imbalance, insisting on reinstating the part of the Budget Enforcement Act that required decreases in spending or increases in taxes to compensate for lost revenue. Enormous pressure was brought on these holdouts to concede and vote for the budget resolution, but they did not yield. Appropriations in the Senate proceeded without a budget blueprint. The result was a kind of first-come-first-served approach to budgeting. Spending items with the highest visibility in an election year would be approved, while more routine but equally important priorities would be left on the cutting floor:

> Without the budget resolution and its cap on fiscal 2005 discretionary spending at $821.4 billion, Stevens' panel [Sen. Ted Stevens, R-Alaska]would be limited to $814 billion [the limit in the previous year's concurrent budget resolution] in total spending but with no budgetary points of order on the floor capping funds for each individual spending bill. That would lead to a situation where funds could be increased on the floor until reaching that $814 limit, meaning some spending bills could be left out of the process.
>
> Without a budget, Stevens said, they would "pray and connive to work something out," but election-year politics would necessitate amendments increasing spending on fiscal 2005 Defense and Homeland Security Appropriations bills on the floor and "there won't be any money left for anything else."
>
> "My problems are just enormous without a budget," Stevens said. "Just enormous." [12]

In the end, it was the House's cap of $821 billion, which mirrored the president's proposal, that framed the final agreement on appropriations. Appropriators had to come down to that total. The various subcommittees that prepare the thirteen appropriations bills agreed to an across-the-board cut to their recommendations to bring in the total near the president's proposal. "In the end, Congress kept the total defense and non-defense discretionary appropriations below the $822 billion spending limit set by President Bush by cuts to several programs originally scheduled for more funding and by a 0.8% across-the-board non-defense, non-homeland security programs reduction." [13]

The appropriations process did proceed without a detailed blueprint, but it did not proceed smoothly. Only four appropriations bills had passed by the beginning of fiscal year 2005, so Congress had to pass an omnibus appropriation bill to fund the remaining agencies. This legislation was put together hastily and was huge (3,000 pages), tempting legislators to stick in a variety of pet programs, projects, or policies, in the certainty that other legislators would be denied sufficient time to read the legislation and oppose provisions of which they disapproved. Some such provisions were caught, but an unknown number survived in the must-pass legislation. The result was described by legislators as chaotic. House minority leader Nancy Pelosi argued that the chaos was intentional:

> In the House, Democratic leader Nancy Pelosi (Calif.) accused Republicans of abusing House rules requiring a three-day delay so members can read bills before they go to the floor and held up final action on the measure until yesterday to bring pressure on GOP leaders to stop short-circuiting the rules.[14]

The *New York Times* editorialized,

> The pork-stuffed omnibus spending bill that Congress rushed to passage without reading largely remains a $388 billion national secret. But laugh lines are gradually leaking out. For instance, why not spend $100,000 for the Punxsutawney Weather Museum in Pennsylvania, considering the annual drollery of Groundhog Day? And once the lawmakers put the taxpayers in for $25,000 to finance mariachi music in Nevada, hey, why not go for $350,000 for the Rock and Roll Hall of Fame in Cleveland? As for that $50,000 for wild hog control in Missouri, it's in the same spirit as the $335,000 to protect sunflowers from blackbirds in North Dakota.
>
> If only the bill were a mere laugh riot. But the truth is that the measure, cobbled together from 13 bills that Congress failed to weigh separately and thoughtfully, legislates the costs of next year's government by blindfold and bludgeon.[15]

Unable to come up with its own budget proposal, Congress relied on the president's proposal, but that was not a useful source of fiscal discipline because it was unbalanced. The executive budget was highly dependent on emergency supplemental appropriations, which did not require a revenue offset. In particular, the Defense Department was systematically underfunded during the budget process, with the idea that it would be funded separately, after the budget was approved, by a supplemental appropriation that would simply add to the deficit. At the time the omnibus budget legislation was passed for the 2005 budget year, the amount left out of the budget in defense alone was rumored to be around $75 billion. The previous year's supplemental was $87 billion.

In fact, the wars in Iraq and in Afghanistan were largely funded through supplemental appropriations, even though substantial parts of the need were known in advance, to the frustration of some members of Congress. Not having any idea of how much money would be required for defense during the year made it nearly impossible to budget for the remaining items or to judge how large a tax reduction would be possible; no one knew how much money would be left over after defense was accounted for. Defense experts predicted that funding through supplementals would continue for at least several more years. House Budget Committee chair Jim Nussle, R-Iowa, argued for at least some planning. Complaining about the ad hoc budgeting, Nussle stated, "This committee and this Congress must have a solid plan, a blueprint, a financial blueprint to set our priorities for the year and for long-term." [16]

In sum, since 1998 the budget process has fallen into disarray and become increasingly improvisational, or ad hoc.[17] Allen Schick has argued that when the budget process produces outcomes that are disliked, such as big deficits, decision makers distance themselves from the process, procrastinate on accomplishing key tasks, and sometimes encounter policy stalemates. Despite intense conflicts, they still have to produce a budget, so they resort to inventing new ways of getting the budget passed each year. Large deficits contribute to this deterioration of process and evasion of the rules, but deficits are also the result of the lack of agreed-on process. Without such a process, to help manage deep conflicts, time and energy are consumed on policy disputes, leaving participants with no time or inclination left to fix the process itself. The breakdown of budget processes is often accompanied by instability in policy and ad hoc scoring rules that make it nearly impossible to compare spending from year to year. Schick was describing the 1980s, but with respect to budget improvisation he might as easily have been describing the period from 1998 on.

Schick has contended that the cause of the breakdown of budget processes in the 1980s was a mismatch between a budget process geared for a rapidly growing economy and growing revenues, and the reality of a slow-growing economy generating inadequate revenues. The budget process was unable to adjust in a timely manner. This structural imbalance led to deficits and from there to a deterioration of routines and generation of ad hoc budget processes. Since 1998, however, a somewhat different sequence has occurred, though some of the same elements have reappeared. The budget process was geared to reducing or eliminating deficits and was unable to adapt quickly to a period of budgetary balance, creating enormous pressure to ignore the difficult choices inherent in the established budget process. While the economy slowed a bit, the major revenue problem was due to policy choices to reduce taxes. Politicians had a specific agenda, in this case to reduce the tax burdens on the wealthy, and were determined to carry it out regardless of the deficits and disruption of budget processes that resulted. Controversy about those policies led to stalemates and generated adaptations to get around the roadblocks, including omnibus appropriations bills that could not

Minicase: Ad Hoc Scoring Rules

Ad hoc budgeting is often accompanied by instability of rules. Decision makers create new rules as they go along, not only rules for how to make budgetary decisions, but also the rules for counting how much is being spent, estimating the size of the deficit, and figuring the size of revenue increases or decreases. Without stability in these rules, it is impossible to compare from year to year, or from committee to committee, or between the houses of the legislative branch. Once rules are up for grabs, the temptation is overwhelming to change them for short-term political gains, changing back again if additional political gains can be obtained that way. The result is chaotic not only for the budgetary decision makers, but also for the press and the public, who find it increasingly difficult to know the impact of current policymaking.

The Bush administration has allowed deficits to grow as a result of its policy of reducing taxes. Reducing the tax burden was a political priority, but the consequent growth of deficits is something of an embarrassment. The administration distanced itself from the results of its policies in a number of ways, one of which was to change "scoring rules" that help measure the cost of legislation. On measuring the costs of tax cuts, the administration first argued that its cuts would be temporary, so that under the scoring rules, OMB would only have to count a few years of the consequences, even though the financial impact increased after the end of that period. Then, a couple of years later, the administration argued that the tax cuts should be treated as permanent, so that their extension would not be scored as having any increased costs. The administration sought to dodge the implications of the tax cuts first in one way, and then it serpentined back to dodge the implications the other way.[1]

It was not only the executive branch that engaged in creative scoring and rules changes to make deficits look smaller, or vanish, to justify the policy of tax cuts. House Republicans adopted what has been called "dynamic scoring" as a way of measuring the impact of revenue cuts. Dynamic scoring tries to take into consideration the increase in economic activity, and hence the increase in federal revenue, that would result from any tax cut. The problem is that no one knows how big that effect might be, and the temptation is to inflate the estimated effect sufficiently to cancel out the apparent negative effects of a tax cut on revenue receipts. The Congressional Budget Office has not adopted dynamic scoring, and neither did the Senate, meaning that budget estimates are likely to differ between committees and between the two houses.

(continued)

The administration's eagerness to change the rules to make the consequences of its policies disappear continued on into President Bush's second term, when the administration proposed not counting the borrowing that would be required to set up private accounts for Social Security. Since those who pay into Social Security are in fact paying for the benefits of those who are currently receiving Social Security, setting up private investment accounts for young payers—diverting their contributions into their own private accounts—means that the government would have to borrow to pay benefits to current retirees—vastly expanding the deficit. Determined to adopt this privatization plan, the administration is seeking to make the borrowing disappear through new scoring rules.[2]

Ad hoc budgeting and rule making favor short-term partisan and political gains over long-term collective and institutional interests and in the process erode the quality of information available to participants and the public. They also foster public cynicism that corrodes the trust necessary for democratic governance.

1. Robert Greenstein and Joel Friedman, "Budget Rule Change Would Make the Cost of Extending the Tax Cuts Disappear," Center for Budget and Policy Priorities, February 27, 2004, www.cbpp.org/2-27-04bud4.htm.
2. Jason Furman, William G. Gale, and Peter R. Orszag, "Should the Budget Rules Be Changed So That Large-Scale Borrowing to Fund Individual Accounts Is Left out of the Budget?" Center for Budget and Policy Priorities, December 13, 2004, www.cbpp.org/12-13-04socsec2.htm.

possibly have been read by those who voted for them. The desire to hide the negative consequences of those policies led to increased dependence on supplemental appropriations and favored the use of omnibus appropriations that would obscure cuts by burying them in 3,000 pages of legislation. It also led to misleading and gimmicky accounting rules.

Can the budget process recover and stabilize? The enormous deficits, consequences of prior and continuing tax reductions and war, are not likely to go away without major spending cuts, even assuming economic growth. Spending cuts of the magnitude required will not be able to be obscured indefinitely by omnibus appropriations and will undoubtedly generate controversy and possibly stalemate. Dissent within the Republican ranks over the sustainability of deficits and required budget cuts may continue to disrupt the budget process. Funding defense through emergency supplementals is also likely to continue for at least several more years. It is not clear how great a deficit, or what confluence of political events, will be necessary to motivate Congress to reinstitute a budget process and adhere to it.

In the face of absolutely enormous deficits, the idea of a constitutional amendment requiring a balanced budget has been resurrected. In the past, the rigidity that a constitutional amendment would impose and the loss of legislative policy control that it would imply have motivated budget process reforms; those threats may do so again if a balanced budget amendment gains sufficient support. For now, however, the deficit seems out of control. The capacity of the federal government to budget, in the sense of prioritizing limited resources, has diminished. The huge buildup of debt is constraining future budgetary choices.

Changes in Budget Process at the State Level

Budget process doesn't always work well at the state level, either. The arrangements for sharing budget power between the executive and legislative branches are sometimes contested, as in the New York State example in the first box. Especially when there is divided government, or when legislative and executive powers are severely unbalanced and the governor flaunts his or her powers with many vetoes of legislative decisions, legislators may use their limited powers to hold up the budget, forcing the governor to negotiate. Behind-closed-doors negotiations may take the place of the formal process, sometimes leaving the legislative committees with little to do other than appear to be busy.

While many of the same themes emerge at both the state and the national levels, the distribution of power between the legislative and executive branches is a little different in the states. The same reform movement that brought executive budgeting to the federal government in the 1920s influenced the states first and went further there. In three states, New York, Maryland, and Illinois, the legislatures were disempowered (Maryland is the most extreme), leaving them still struggling for a meaningful formal role over eighty years later. The remaining states balked at implementing the reforms in such a strict way. In three states, the legislature maintained primacy in budgeting. In most states, the governor may propose a budget, but the legislature may form its own or ignore the governor's proposal if it wishes. Overall governors have more authority over state budgets than the legislatures.

History of State Budget Process

After an initial period of strong legislatures in the 1700s, state legislatures declined in public trust and responsibility. They tended not to be representative

Minicase: Maryland's Legislative Budget Power

Maryland has gone the farthest in disempowering its legislature and empowering the governor with respect to the budget. Because of fear that the legislature would spend money irresponsibly, the legislature was permitted only to reduce, not increase, the governor's budget proposal. This restriction has been in place since 1916 and is embodied in the constitution, which makes it very difficult to change. There have been several recent legislative efforts to put before the voters a constitutional amendment to let the legislature add to the governor's budget, but they have been defeated in the Senate, most recently in March 2004, in a reasonably close vote of 25–20.

One interesting feature of the Maryland case is that even when the reason for limiting legislative budget powers was gone, the strong gubernatorial powers remained in place. In recent years the legislature has been fiscally responsible; moreover, the proposed constitutional amendment prohibits the legislature from going above the governor's total, even when it adds items. It also gives the governor a veto over any added items. If the proposal to allow the legislature to add items to the governor's budget were to pass, the legislature would still not be able to spend recklessly.

A second feature of the Maryland situation is that because the legislature is formally without this key budgetary power, the budget process has adapted over time to reduce the gap in power between the governor and the legislature. Some of the adaptations reduce efficiency and flexibility, as well as accountability and the quality of decision making.

One adaptation is the redefinition of the purpose of supplemental appropriations. Under the state constitution, supplementals are intended for unanticipated needs. "In practice they are often used to reallocate funds deleted by the General Assembly or to reward or punish legislators based on their levels of support of the Governor's agenda." [1] In other words, the legislature has used its limited powers to cut out some items the governor wanted, and the governor retaliated by adding those items back in a supplemental appropriation. But in order to get legislative approval of that supplemental appropriation and to build support for other, unrelated policy initiatives, the governor added the pet projects that key legislators wished to include. As long as their projects for constituents can be obtained in this way, legislators may be content to leave the process as it is; that may be part of the reason why it has been so difficult to pass reform legislation.

Supplemental requests often do not get the same level of scrutiny as the rest of the budget, and projects in a supplemental are not compared in any priority ranking with normal budget items. Moreover, the negotiation of

(continued)

which items will be included in the supplemental tends to be a backroom affair, not open to the public.

Second, because the legislature cannot add to the governor's proposal, legislators often pass expensive programs with budget implications for future years instead. In the 1970s, the legislature passed a law requiring the payments of one program to match the costs of a second program, a law signed by the governor, but without funding. A court ruled that the governor could not be forced under the constitution to fund such a law. The legislature responded with a constitutional amendment to require the governor to fund programs that were legally passed. This provision was approved by the public and amended the constitution, providing a limited channel for the legislature to address needs not perceived or given high priority by the governor. When the direct budgetary path was blocked, in essence, the legislature chose the path of substantive legislation with budgetary implications. Program expenditures that are mandated in this way can push out other legitimate and routine needs because there is a constitutional requirement for a balanced budget. This mandated expenditure process interferes with the ability to prioritize expenditures. Also, with the mandated expenditure approach, program decisions are divorced from budgetary implications, so legislators can pass more expensive programs than the state can afford.

Third, the legislature can add or expand programs if it can pass legislation establishing dedicated revenue specifically to pay for them. This ability leads to an excessive number of accounts and reduced flexibility. Revenue dedication means that revenue sources are tied to particular expenditures and can be spent for nothing else. When revenue is divided into many small pieces, each of which is necessarily connected to a particular program, there is insufficient flexibility in the budget to adapt to new situations.

The fourth adaptation is that the legislature has compensated for its relative powerlessness by micromanaging the agencies, a role that is inappropriate and inefficient.[2]

1. Roy T. Meyers and Thomas S. Pilkerton, "How Can Maryland's Budget Process Be Improved?" Maryland Institute for Policy Analysis and Research (MIPAR), University of Maryland, Baltimore County (UMBC), September 2003, http://userpages.umbc.edu/meyers/improveMD.pdf; also available at www.umbc.edu/mipar.
2. The material in this minicase is taken from Roy Meyers's testimony to the House Appropriations Committee, Maryland General Assembly, March 9, 2004.

of voters, and they were often too big and overly responsive to interest group and constituency demands. These flaws sometimes led to structural characteristics intended to limit their influence, including short sessions, constitutional constraints on what they could do, and early awards of line-item veto power to governors.

To compensate for legislative weakness, the governor was strengthened in budget dealings with the legislature, but the executive branch, reflecting that same early distrust of state government, remained highly fragmented. Many key state officials were elected rather than appointed by the governor, so they had their own power bases and were not under the governor's control. A governor and his lieutenant governor might be rivals rather than teammates, and the elected controller might be out to blame the governor for budget problems. Legislatures also tended to create many independent commissions. Departments were often headed by commissions that appointed their own heads. Thus the governor's control, even when he gained the power to present an executive budget, was often very limited. In many states, the competing elected officials were gradually eliminated in favor of appointees loyal to the governor, and the governor instituted accounting controls over the departments. The governor and his budget staff would examine the requests coming from the departments, formulate a budget proposal, and pass that proposal along to the legislature for response. Often the governor was granted a veto over legislative changes to his or her budget proposal. Forty-four states and Puerto Rico have given the governor line-item veto authority—the ability to eliminate any item in the budget that appears as a separate line.[18] Forty-one states and Puerto Rico have provisions that allow the governor to reject particular items in a piece of legislation, such as a sentence, a paragraph, or part of a sentence (known as an "item veto"). Of those forty-one, thirteen allow a veto of selected words, and three allow the veto to change the meaning of the words.[19] These veto powers obviously are much more powerful than those of the president of the United States.

Although the governors generally dominate the state budget process, the capacity of state legislatures to review the governor's budget and question the assumptions underlying it has improved since the 1960s. In the 1960s, as a result of the Supreme Court's one-man, one-vote decision, the redrawing of electoral districts, and the election of more representative legislatures, state legislatures began to reform and prepare themselves for a more active policy role. The budget was a key focus of that increased capacity. Many legislatures increased the length of their sessions, changed from meeting every two years to every year, and added staff with expertise on fiscal and budgetary matters to advise them.

From 1975 to 1988 the professional staff of legislative fiscal offices nearly doubled, to an average of about fifteen people.[20] From 1991 to the present, fiscal staffing has been reasonably stable, at about twenty per state legislature.[21] A National Council of State Legislatures staff member who works closely with the section on legislative budget staff confirmed in 2004 that there had been little change in the number of staff in these budget offices over the past decade but argued that their responsibilities had increased.[22] These staff do many of the same things for legislatures that the Congressional Budget Office does for Congress at the national level. They empower the legislature to question the assumptions in the executive budget and to formulate its own alternatives without jeopardizing budget balance.

In the standard model of executive budgeting, the governor's office gives budget advice to the agencies, then collects proposals from the agencies, cuts them back, and forwards the whole budget proposal to the legislature for its consideration. In that model, the governor's policies form the framework for consideration of the budget. Most of the states have some form of executive budget, but most of them do not actually carry out the budget process in the way prescribed by the model. In reality many state agencies submit their proposals to the legislature at the same time as, or before, they submit them to the governor's budget office. This submission process enhances the legislature's budget power. On the other hand, it may leave the legislature mired in details of agency operations because the executive budget office has not sifted through the requests before the legislative branch receives them.

In 1983 the legislatures in forty-one states received budget proposals from the agencies before the governor's office had put the budget proposal together. By 1988 that number had risen to forty-three, but by 1997 only thirty-two states reported that the legislature received the proposals from executive agencies before the governor prepared his proposal. In 1983 three state legislatures received agency budgets only through the governor; by 1997 eight did.[23] Thus there was more willingness on the part of the state legislatures to work with the governor's proposal. Most legislatures have the right, and now the ability, to second-guess the governor's proposal if they want to. They may not feel the same need to do the budget themselves if they can exert influence over the executive's budget proposal or reject or amend parts of it. Slowly the legislature has become more of a watchdog and less of a hands-on, detail-oriented examiner of line items.

In states where there was a strong executive budget and a weak legislature, the legislature has gained power in budgeting in recent years; in those states where the legislature was strong and the governor weak, the governor's position has been strengthened. The state of Florida offers an example in which power over budgeting has gone back and forth between the legislature and executive, favoring the executive in recent years (see Minicase, page 126).

Minicase: Nevada—Legislative Access to Agency Budget Requests

In Nevada the legislature has a culture of paying attention to the details of the budget, which is presented in line items. The legislature expects Legislative Council Bureau (LBC) staff to review the Executive Budget for technical merit and to make recommendations on policy issues. Due to formal (state statute) and informal (agreements between the budget director and LCB leadership) arrangements, LCB fiscal analysts have access to information while the Executive Budget is being prepared, including copies of the agency requests, and can attend agency budget hearings during the executive preparation phase of the budget. Budget office analysts and LCB staff often work together on technical aspects of the budget so that consideration of the budget later is smoother.

Nevada is thus a state where the legislature and the executive have access to the budget proposals at the same time, rather than in sequence. If the governor got them first, he or she could probably make policy and technical changes before handing the budget proposal over to the legislature for its consideration. Under that scenario, the legislature might never know what it was that the agencies were requesting.[1]

1. Paula E. Yeary, "Nevada at the Crossroads," in *Budgeting in the States, Ten Years Later,* ed. Ed Clynch and Tom Lauth (Westport, Conn.: Greenwood Press, forthcoming 2005).

Throughout the 1970s and 1980s, the general direction of changes in budget processes in the country was clear: legislatures were becoming better organized, with more professional staff, and were taking a larger role in budgeting. That change led some to question whether governors overall were losing budgetary power. For the present, however, it seems that gubernatorial dominance of budgeting is safe. It is difficult to change constitutional provisions; it is even difficult to pass reform legislation if it threatens the governor's powers because the governor has to sign the bill. The governors retain many important formal powers, such as very strong vetoes, and use them when they feel it is necessary.

Governors on average have not lost power with respect to the legislatures, but when government is divided, that is, when the legislature is controlled by one party and the executive branch by the other, legislators scrutinize the governor's budget proposal with an eye to policies with which they disagree. When the legislature and the governor are of the same party, they are likely to have a similar philosophy and similar policy goals, so legislators are more inclined to go along

Minicase: The Executive and the Legislature in Florida's Budgeting

The evolution of Florida's budget process comprises not only shifts of power between the executive and the legislative branches, but also changes in the degree of centralized control the governor has over the budgets of the departments and programs.

Since Reconstruction, Florida has been governed by a multiple executive. Written into the constitution of 1885 was a requirement that six other officials besides the governor be independently elected from a statewide constituency. Each had his or her own power base equal to the governor's. Each of the six statewide officials had a set of administrative responsibilities, so the governor had minimal control over many of the state's most important programs. This structure reflected the distrust of government prevalent at that time and the consequent desire not to give much power to any elected official.

In 1968 an amendment eliminated the words "the governor shall be assisted by the cabinet" from the state constitution. The result of this language change was to make the statewide elected officials equal to the governor; they would not be required to help carry out the governor's policies. In the aftermath of this constitutional change, and confronted with the problem of dealing with the governor and six other independent executives, the legislature in 1969 granted the governor the sole authority to propose a budget. Agencies were required to submit their requests through him or her.[1] Shortly after delegating this authority, however, the legislative appropriations committees began to build their own professional budgeting staff so that they could analyze the agencies' requests without relying on the governor's staff.

Governor Bob Graham, elected in 1978, expanded his role in budget preparation by implementing a "program budget" and creating an office of planning and budgeting in the executive office of the governor. Program budgets grant the agencies broader discretion over spending and give the governor more policy control. The legislature reacted negatively to the program budget format and the enhancement of executive budget-making power. In 1983 it began mandating the format and content of the budget in considerable detail and requiring the governor's staff and the legislative staff jointly to develop the budget instructions sent to the agencies. Most important, the new law directed the agencies to "submit their independent judgment of their needs to the legislature," so the governor could not change the agencies' requests before the legislature saw them. The legislature also strengthened its budgetary oversight role, extensively reviewing budget changes initiated by the executive during the year.[2]

(continued)

At this point, Florida's executive was considered relatively weak in budgeting. Although the governor developed budget recommendations that were released with great fanfare six weeks before the opening of the legislative session, the agencies (the governor's and those outside his purview, such as those controlled by the other six officials elected statewide) and the judicial branch released their budget proposals to the governor and to the legislature at the same time. The legislature was free to consult with agency personnel, and the legislative staff developed its own set of budget recommendations for the appropriations committees. Agency heads could make end runs around the governor to the legislature, and the governor's budget recommendations were essentially dead on arrival in the legislature. One observer summarized, "The balance of power in state budgeting in Florida is only slightly less legislatively controlled than in Texas, where a joint legislative council creates the budget." [3]

The governor gained some control over the agencies when Florida's constitution was successfully amended in 1998 (effective in 2002) to reduce the number of independently elected statewide officials (besides the governor) from six to three. The three positions elected statewide are a chief financial officer, an attorney general, and a commissioner of agriculture. Two of the former elected executive positions, the treasurer and the controller, were combined into the chief financial officer's position, and two were eliminated, commissioner of education and secretary of state.

The governor was further strengthened vis à vis the legislature in recent years because the governor and majorities of both houses of the legislature have been of the same party (Republican). As a result, the legislature generally has been willing to go along with the governor's priorities, including his demands for more budgetary power. It retained some budgetary power for itself, redefining its role.

When Governor Jeb Bush was elected in 1998, he made it clear that he would not tolerate a system in which the governor's budget proposals were ignored by the legislature. [4] He insisted that all projects, including legislators' projects for their districts, go through appropriate review process in the agencies. In 1999 Bush declared that in the budget for year 2000, "all items, including member projects, must fall within the statewide budget policy priorities as set by the agencies. And they must be within the established spending limits for the agencies and programs affected. Furthermore, member projects may only be funded with non-recurring dollars and those projects will be evaluated for their effectiveness in the next budget cycle." [5] In other words, if legislators try to put their special projects into the requests

(continued)

of the agencies, the projects would increase the spending request total, forcing the agencies to cut other needed items. Bush had found a way of limiting member-requested projects without the governor's taking them out of the budget request, which he was not empowered to do. If legislators added projects to the agencies' requests later in the legislative process, the governor vetoed them. Governor Bush vetoed many more projects in legislators' districts than had his predecessors, using the item veto against Republicans as well as Democrats.[6] He threatened to veto any appropriations that did not contain the projects or programs he supported.

Legislators protested the 550 vetoes of Bush's first year and then responded with various strategies to make the items they put in the budget less visible as a way to avoid the governor's veto pen.[7] In 1999 and 2000, Bush vetoed about $313 million in legislative projects; in 2001, the figure was $290 million. Then in 2002 the amount dropped to $107 million, and in 2003 to a mere $33 million. It is not clear if legislators were hiding their projects better, were more selective in what they proposed so they passed gubernatorial muster, or the governor was backing away from using the veto against his allies in the legislature. Interestingly, however, in 2004, the governor returned to using the veto heavily, vetoing $349 million in legislative projects.[8]

In 2000 the Jeb Bush administration proposed a number of modifications to the budgeting system, which the legislature approved. Some of the changes were similar to those Graham sought earlier without success, such as a performance orientation embedded in a program budget. Along with the program budget, the legislature granted the executive branch more budget flexibility to move funds around. Most important, the legislature "removed the requirement that agencies submit preliminary Legislative Budget Requests, and thus limited opportunities for legislative intervention in framing departmental submissions."[9] With this provision, the governor could (finally) shape the agencies' budget requests.

At the same time that these reforms gave reality to executive budgeting in Florida, the legislature retained enough power to maintain its influence and some policy control. The new budget law increased the ability of agency heads to move money around from similar accounts, but only if in doing so they did not create any future obligations for spending or violate the intent and policy of the legislature. The new law required agencies to draw up plans and submit budgets that meshed with those plans, but it also required that the plans be submitted to the legislature for approval well in advance of the legislative session. The new law required agencies to come up with, and report on, performance measures but also to present those measures to

(continued)

the legislature for approval. By changing a few words in the older budget process law, the writers of the new law made sure that if key legislators felt that the governor was overstepping bounds, they could intervene to stop the offending spending. Furthermore, the reforms created the Legislative Budget Commission, consisting of fourteen members of both houses, including the chairs of the appropriations committees. One function of this high-powered legislative commission is to do zero-based reviews of all the executive branch agencies on an eight-year cycle. Thus although the executive's powers are greater than they were, and the legislature normally defers to the governor, the legislature retained for itself the authority and capacity to make decisions, enforce its policy preferences, and question the governor's policy proposals should the need arise.[10]

By 2003, new problems had begun to occur in the process. The two houses of the legislature quarreled with each other over policy matters, delaying the budget. At the same time, the legislature was no longer going along with all the governor's proposals. When the governor called for a reconsideration of two recent amendments approved by the public, one for high-speed rail and one to reduce class sizes in schools, leaders of both houses initially said no. The governor was sure that the public would not have approved the measures if their costs had been associated with the votes. Some legislators disagreed with the governor, particularly on the class size limits.[11] Others worried that asking for a reversal looked like a rejection of the public's expressed preferences. In 2003 the legislature passed funding for the high-speed rail line, but the governor vetoed it. After extensive pressure from the governor, the legislature agreed to put the high-speed rail before the public a second time, in 2004, and this time it was rejected. However, the class size limit remained in place despite gubernatorial opposition.

Observers noted that the tensions between the governor and the legislature were not along party lines:

> Lobbyist James Krog—former Gov. Lawton Chiles' former chief of staff—said it's not unusual for a governor to face legislative challenges when his party dominates both the Florida House and Senate. He said Chiles was confronted by the same situation. "You can be in the same party and still have your own priorities," said Krog, who has worked for two governors. "Tallahassee is not just Democrats versus Republicans—it's also the Legislative branch versus the Executive branch. There are differences that cross party lines all the time because there's

(continued)

a built-in friction in a representative democracy that encourages dissent," he said.[12]

Thus, despite the much-enhanced budgeting powers of the governor and same-party domination of the executive and legislative branches, the legislature in Florida remains strong and somewhat independent of the governor. It maintains its own staff to make revenue projections based on monitoring the economy; it monitors budget implementation; it reviews programs; and it can and does reject some of the governor's policy proposals.

1. R. B. Bradley, "Budgeting in Florida" (paper presented at the Association for Budgeting and Financial Management meetings, Chicago, October 7–9, 2004).

2. Gloria Grizzle, "Florida: Miles to Go and Promises to Keep," in *Governors, Legislators, and Budgets,* ed. Edward Clynch and Thomas Lauth (Westport, Conn.: Greenwood Press, 1991), 98ff.

3. Karen Stanford, personal communication, March 18, 1999.

4. Richard S. Conley and Richard K. Scher " 'I Did It My Way': Governor Jeb Bush and the Line Item Veto in Florida (with apologies to Frank Sinatra)" (paper prepared for The Citadel Symposium on Southern Politics, Charleston, S.C., March 7–8, 2002).

5. Fishkind and Associates, "Florida's New Budget Process," August 31, 1999 (Hank Fishkind, 90.7 FM, WMFE News), www.fishkind.com/radio/fnbspot.html (accessed March 25, 2005).

6. Conley and Scher, " 'I Did It My Way.' "

7. Ibid.

8. Jackie Hallifax, "Bush Trims $349 Million out of State Budget," *Naples Daily News,* May 29, 2004.

9. Bradley, "Budgeting in Florida."

10. Ibid.

11. Alisa LaPolt, "Governor's Reversal Requests Fall Flat," *Florida Today,* March 6, 2003, www.floridatoday.com.

12. V. J. Epstein, "Where Was Bush? Governor's Job Gets Tougher," *Florida Today,* April 29, 2003, www.floridacapitalnews.com/legislature2003/stories /0430bush.htm.

with the governor's proposals. One recent study argues that the governor gains more in power from times of unity in government than he or she loses in times of divided government.[24] It is not so much that governors have lost power over recent years, as that the legislatures have gained power. One way that legislatures can gain power without the governor's losing it is that each may care about a different area of the budget. Also, as the Florida case suggests, as the legislature cedes control to the executive over budget formulation, it changes its role to increase its power over budget implementation and program evaluation; as it gives up micro-management of the executive through line-item budgetary controls, it increases its scrutiny over agency plans and performance measures.

One fundamental difference between the state and the national level is that at the state level, the budget process, or parts of it, is often embodied in the constitution, rather than in laws, making it especially rigid and difficult to change. This fundamentally antidemocratic feature of some state budget processes has resulted in the growth of many informal rules that allow change and adaptation to occur. These informal rules may last a long time and they may differ considerably from the formal rules. By themselves, then, the formal rules may not be good indicators of process, and they may obscure the ongoing process of adaptation. The formal rules have to be viewed together with the set of informal rules they breed.

Changes in Budget Process at the Local Level

Budget processes at the local level are different from those at the state or national level. These differences affect not only budget processes in general, but also the direction and manner of budget process evolution. It is not only that local governments are much smaller, more numerous, and less partisan; they have a completely different structure. Most important, local governments are not independent but subordinate to the states. In many key ways they do not determine their own budget processes. As a result there is continuing tension between the states and their local governments on the degree of local autonomy over the budget process. There is some tension as well between the legislative and executive branches, but this manifests itself mostly in adoption and abandonment of council-manager and strong mayor forms of city government. While the former tension is constant and nearly universal, the latter occurs at intervals in some cities.

The states grant limited and often ambiguous autonomy to local governments through home rule laws or regulate the local governments directly through statutes, often called "municipal budget laws." Although cities do not, strictly speaking, have constitutions, the state may grant them a charter that outlines what they may do and how they may do it. These charters typically include the form of government, including the powers of the mayor and council, and may embody detailed rules about the budget process. They can be changed in much the same way that constitutions can be changed, by a massive campaign and vote of the citizenry, and hence charter changes, while they do occur, are infrequent. Changes in the form of government also change the budget process, giving more budgetary power to the legislative body, to the mayor, or in some instances, to a commission.

State Control over Local Budget Process

In the 1800s, states controlled the finances of cities through legislation. Sometimes legislatures passed laws specific to individual cities, and sometimes the laws applied to a whole class of cities. Mayors would negotiate with the legislature for exemptions from tax limits, or permission to borrow above a mandated limit, or permission to provide a particular service. Although there are still some remnants of the process of special legislation for each city, states gradually adopted a pattern of legislating for classes of cities or for all the cities and villages in the state. The local budgeting laws in many states are of this latter type.

States may control local budget process in greater or lesser detail. In some states, the laws specify nearly all aspects of the local budget process, including the forms on which budget requests are to be made, the accounts that may be used, the kind and amount of contingency funds, and the ability to transfer revenue between funds. In other states, the laws are less restrictive and may only require submission of a balanced budget, a public hearing, and an independent audit at the end of the fiscal year. State governments specify which taxes or fees local governments may use, and they may limit the amount of revenue that local governments may collect or mandate the provision of particular services. The states may pass tax exemptions that apply to local governments, and they may or may not replace revenue that is lost in this way. When they limit taxation and mandate service levels, states may preempt local priorities, which is to say, local budgeting.

To the extent that states have mandated budget processes in the localities, several major questions arise. The first deals with persistence: Are the rules so rigid and long term that they prevent local governments from adapting to new situations? The second question deals with the neutrality of the rules, their orientation toward improved financial management or toward specific policy outcomes. The third deals with the extent to which states have encouraged or hindered democratic participation in the budget process or have overridden local priorities.

Persistence. States have generally responded to problems of the cities, but the statutes they have passed have tended to be rigid, often across-the-board, and enduring well past the time when the problems were resolved. Some states have provided a set of minimum standards for city budget processes, which cities can adjust and modernize; in other states, budget rules have locked cities into clumsy processes designed for another time and another set of problems. In the latter cases the result has been a need to continually finesse the state regulations or ask for exemptions or changes to a system that has become too complex, as one system of rules overlaid another.

Many states have included in their municipal budget laws a kind of incrementalist, line-item approach to budget formats. At the time when it was coming into use in the early 1900s, line-item budgeting was a major reform and a considerable improvement over the way budgeting had been done. Before line-item budgeting, it was common to budget by naming particular expenses and how much they cost. A municipal budget might include an item for the police stables that read, "horses and stables, $50,000." The reader would have no idea of the number of horses, the size of the barn, the number of employees, the quality or quantity of the feed, or the health of the horses. There was no way to tell if this was a successful operation at reasonable cost. When line-items were introduced, the purpose was to put each component of expense on a single budget line, so it would be visible and comparable to the price of such items available elsewhere. The costs for a stable might be broken out into 30 pounds of feed at $30, 5 stablemen paid $5 a week each, and $10 for repairs to the roof. The idea was to make it known if the city was overpaying for supplies, personnel, or capital infrastructure.

The state budget laws typically required cities to include in the budget the expenditures in the last year or two, the current year's expected expenses, and the projection for the next year. The goal here was to make sure that the line items did not grow too quickly or without reasons. In the early 1900s, just after the major expansion of municipal programs in the Progressive Era (roughly 1895–1910) and the inflation caused by the expense of World War I, keeping costs down was a major consideration, and state requirements for local budget processes were designed to deal with those cost increases.

The emphasis on cost controls became exaggerated during the Great Depression. State rules for local budget making often broke revenues into small, earmarked portions, with tax caps for each function. The idea was that savings from one function should not be used to increase spending somewhere else, and revenue that came in over expectations could not be spent without formal rebudgeting and approval. The rigidity of this model led many cities to put expenditures where there was money, transferring costs into funds that had unspent totals, because it was illegal to transfer revenues out of those same funds. In other words, the system was so inflexible that it was often gamed. Where these rules still apply, cities still game them in the same fashion.

Out-of-date rules concerning municipal budgeting have persisted nearly unchanged in many states. For example, Oregon, an otherwise-progressive state, includes in its mandated budget procedures a focus on year-by-year changes in projected and actual spending. The following example is from a training manual for local governments prepared by the state of Oregon to implement its uniform local government budget law:

> Expenditure and resource estimate detail sheets are part of the budget document under ORS 294.376. These detailed estimate sheets show the actual expenditures and resources for the two preceding fiscal years for each fund (ORS 294.376). This requirement provides a two year record of what actually happened. It compares the earlier actual resources and expenditures with those estimated and budgeted for both the current year and the upcoming fiscal year.
>
> The historical data are figures confirmed by audit. Display the audit-confirmed revenues and expenditures in the budget at the same level of detail used for the estimates of the current year and coming fiscal year.[25]

A second example of the persistence of state requirements describes some of the old and detailed constraints still operating and the effort it takes to budget efficiently despite the regulations:

> Maricopa county in Arizona, the county in which Phoenix is located, ran into fiscal difficulties, and in getting out of them, became aware of how outdated the state laws were that controlled local budgeting and finance. These outmoded regulations held back improvements. The state law was passed in 1912 when Arizona became a state. The county found it could not legally pay bills by wire, even though that would help the cash flow, because warrants had to be approved individually by the board. Once the expenditures were determined for the year, that total could not be exceeded, even if more revenues were available during the year. And totals for departments could not legally be shifted around at the end of the year without declaring an emergency. The accounting system was required to be cash based. However, exceptions were granted on an individual basis. The result was that staff had to fight the system continuously to do a good job of budgeting and financial management. The county planned to propose some changes in the state law.[26]

In 1997, the law in Arizona was changed to allow local councils to make transfers between funds if the money was available and the purpose appropriate, without declaring an emergency. State laws regulating local budgeting do change, but slowly and with much effort.

Lack of Neutrality. States tend to be vulnerable to interest groups and lobbyists. They have been periodically pressed by businesses and homeowners to lighten the

burden of taxation. Some states responded to this pressure, especially during the
Great Depression, by creating budget processes in cities that were biased toward
reduction of property taxes and away from service delivery. Some states created
constitutional constraints on local revenues or spending, and others modified
their budget laws to reflect the demands of these organized interests. Some states
remained focused on the quality of financial management and avoidance of fiscal distress in their cities, but others, responding to antitax groups, structured
local budget processes to keep taxes down and to keep the scope of government
narrow. They created boards and commissions that could override local priorities and budget requests so as to keep expenditures down. Over the years, most of
these state-mandated budget processes have been changed to become more neutral. Indiana's budget law, however, has not changed much over the last eighty-
five years.

Indiana's old budget process, established in the early 1920s, emphasized holding taxes down. To do that it empowered the State Board of Tax Commissioners
to respond to citizen petitions. Any ten taxpayers could petition the tax commissioners on budgetary matters. The system was slanted to favor taxpayers who
wanted lower taxes, even when the majority of residents in a community was willing to have higher taxes and more projects and services.[27]

Disproportionate influence over budgetary matters was precisely what the
organized taxpayers sought. The fact that they could bring a case before the tax
commission gave them more power in local decision making. The secretary of the
Indiana Tax Association described the influence of the county chapters in these
terms:

> County associations have become so efficient that they consider and settle all
> of the perplexing questions arising from taxation matters, and the weight of
> their opinion has become so great in their respective communities that the
> elected officials abide by their decisions rather than attempt to fight the
> appeals, which they know will be taken if there is any hint of waste in the pre-
> pared budgets, or if the proposed levies are higher than necessity demands.[28]

During the Great Depression, when communities were in desperate need of
more funds to help the impoverished citizenry, the state relented and allowed
some increases in taxation.

One of the earliest major changes in the Indiana system occurred in 1927,
when the state allowed the state tax board to increase the levy allowed by the
county tax adjustment board up to the limit of the request of the local officials. Further flexibility was introduced in 1932 and 1937 when the county

tax adjustment boards were allowed to declare an emergency that required taxation above the state tax limits; the state board was required to review these requests.[29]

The flexibility and responsiveness of the Indiana system may have helped keep the basic structure intact. After all these years, Indiana's system still has some built-in biases toward low taxes, although it has become a bit more neutral. There is still a county board of tax adjustment; it still reviews local budgets, levies, and tax rates and can revise or reduce but not increase them. Ten or more taxpayers can still raise formal objection to the tax rates, and the local government is bound to hear their petition and respond in writing. The request and the reply become part of a review by the state, which makes the final decision. No citizens may petition on the grounds that the tax rate is too low, unless it is below minimums mandated by statute. Now, however, local officials can appeal the decision of the local boards to the state, which can increase the levy or tax rate if it wishes.[30] Indiana's mandated budget process is exceptional in its bias toward lower taxes, but even the Indiana system gradually accommodated to the needs of local governments and the preferences of local voters, in addition to responding to the desires of organized antitax groups.

Indiana changed over time from a system in which the state readily overturned local priorities to one in which the state focus was on assuring that the local governments adhered to the state's mandated processes and forms. A similar shift has characterized most states.

Democratic Controls. Nearly all the states require some level of direct citizen input into the local government budget process. Requirements include public hearings, which are often specified in great detail in terms of when they must occur, their scope, who must be present, and how long before budget adoption they must occur. Such rules have been in place for many years and demonstrate a desire to foster and preserve democratic responsiveness at the local level. However, at least in part because of the states' vulnerability to interest groups, the states have often mandated that local governments do certain things, such as increase police pensions or spending for public schools.[31] They also sometimes tell the local governments that particular classes of taxpayers should get a particular tax break. When the states do not reimburse the local governments for costs they impose, the local governments are stuck: They have to either cut back spending on some other service or project, or they have to increase revenue, often a difficult or even impossible task when the local governments are operating under state or local tax caps. Such unfunded mandates override local priorities. Unfunded mandates alter the budget process by telling the local governments in effect, Do this first; subtract the cost from your available revenues and then you can use the rest according to your own priorities. If used extensively, such mandates can erode local democracy by narrowing the decisions local governments and their citizens are allowed to make.

Local government officials, and the local citizens more broadly, have been frustrated by unfunded state mandates. Citizens fear that their property taxes will go up to cover the new costs. When they have had the opportunity, opponents have put measures on the ballot to curtail unfunded mandates, sometimes resulting in constitutional amendments. In response to intense pressure, legislatures have sometimes passed measures to limit unfunded mandates and allow local governments to opt out of programs or avoid complying with rules if the state does not provide the funding. The effectiveness of such measures is questionable, however; it seems too easy for legislators to evade laws prohibiting unfunded mandates.

The experience of states with unfunded mandates legislation has varied. In Massachusetts, an unfunded mandates provision was included in legislation sharply limiting property taxes. Under new, tight revenue constraints, local governments would be unable to absorb increases in spending mandated by the state, so a provision was included in Proposition 21/2 that if the state passed a mandate without fully funding it, then compliance with the mandate would be optional. To make the law workable, the state set up a Local Mandates Office in the Office of the State Auditor, which would, on petition from a local jurisdiction affected by a mandate, investigate how much that mandate would cost. The local government could use the Local Mandates Office's assessment as evidence in its petition to be exempted from the law. The office would try to figure out the aggregate costs and advise the legislature how to proceed and whether to fund the mandate for all jurisdictions. The law was passed in 1980, and since then the Local Mandates Office has several times declared that the legislature had indeed passed an unfunded mandate and recommended funding from the state. The state now funds local governments for keeping polls open three extra hours on election day, at a cost of $13.5 million between 1993 and 2004. A 1998 gun control act was also judged to be an unfunded mandate, and on the recommendation of the Local Mandates Office the state assigned more of the fees it collected to the local governments to cover their costs. Other funding recommendations were less successful.[32]

Despite the law and occasionally successful challenges to the legislature, local governments in Massachusetts are still burdened by unfunded mandates. First,

Minicase: Florida and Unfunded Mandates

In 1990 Florida citizens approved a highly popular constitutional amendment to prevent the state government from mandating expenditures by, or reducing revenues of, the local governments. There were three exceptions: if the legislature states that the public interest requires the legislation, if the mandate is necessary to fulfill a law or a requirement of the federal government, or if the cost is negligible. To enact a mandate that didn't fit into one of these exemptions would require a two-thirds vote of both houses of the legislature. Otherwise the local governments were free to ignore the mandate.

The legislature nevertheless continued to pass mandates, many of them unfunded. The legislature could grant a tax break to some particular group, and as long as the tax break was passed by two-thirds of each house the resulting reduction in revenue at the local level was legal under the constitution. Also there were a number of mandates whose financial impacts were individually less than the minimum, but which became expensive when added up. Nonrecurring losses, such as those due to tax holidays, were also legal under the constitutional ban on unfunded mandates. Anything to do with criminal justice was automatically exempted, so that legislation directing local police to arrest people for graffiti, for example, did not come under the limits of the law. Equally important, because the legislature did not stop trying to pass unfunded mandates, the cities and counties had to fight back after a law was passed that imposed large burdens on them.

The constitutional provision has been useful in that when the counties took the state to court over recent legislation shifting responsibility for juvenile justice to them, the court agreed that the shift was an unfunded mandate and illegal under the constitution. Using the constitutional provision effectively has been an uphill battle for local officials. One official in a Florida county explained,

> Cost shifting and unfunded mandates mean that the state of Florida says that you will pay for a program. Whether it's something we like or don't like, they tell us we have to pay for it. Now we have a constitutional amendment that says that they can't do that without a two-thirds vote in the [Florida] Legislature. Sometimes, we've been successful because they didn't get the two-thirds vote, but they also have this loophole about health, safety and welfare. So, they put something in the legislation about health, safety or welfare—then they can do it without the two-thirds vote. . . . It really goes to the efficiency. If it's

(continued)

a state program, they hire, they fire, they make the rules, they set up the program and they have control over it. Here we have no control. We simply write checks. If we're going to write a check for a program we at least ought to be in charge, so that if we can save money by having a clerk over in another division doing something, we haven't had that opportunity. That was one of the big things about Article V. We tried for years to show them efficiencies, and they wouldn't do them.[1]

1. Douglas C. Lyons (interviewer), "Face to Face: A Conversation with Karen Marcus," *South Florida Sun-Sentinel,* October 29, 2004, www.sun-sentinel .com/news/opinion/ sfl-facekarenmarcus,0,1790581.story?coll=sfla -opinion-utility (accessed January 5, 2005). The *Sun Sentinel* keeps older articles in its archives, http://pqasb.pqarchiver.com/sun_sentinel/search.html.

the expensive mandates that preceded the 1980 law are not affected and remain in place. Second, the legislature has found a way of getting around the prohibition.

For example, Lexington and Newton prevailed in an unfunded-mandate lawsuit against the state, successfully defeating a statutory amendment that expanded the local obligation to provide private school transportation. The state responded, however, by passing a second statute conditioning all state reimbursements for pre-1981 mandates on local acceptance of the challenged amendment. When the new statute was challenged by the same municipalities, the Supreme Judicial Court found that there was no violation of the prohibition. The court explained that there is . . . nothing to prevent the Legislature from forcing the acceptance of [the private school transportation amendment] upon reluctant cities and towns by providing benefits it has no obligation to provide.[33]

Even when the state has promised to come up with money to pay for mandates, it has not always done so, especially when it is fiscally stressed:

[T]he state legislature recently established a special education reimbursement program that offers additional state aid for eligible instructional costs associated with implementing individual education plans, so-called, of students receiving special education services. This program has been placed on indefinite hold, however, due to the state's current economic constraints.[34]

Equally important, when the state does pay for its mandates the results may still distort local decision making. In Massachusetts, the professional development mandate passed by the state requires all schools to establish a training program for education-related employees within the public school system. The funding for the program comes from the local school budget; it can be supplemented by grants from the state, but those grants are conditioned on the locality's maintaining the level of public school spending of the prior year. Any municipality that reduces funding for public education from the previous fiscal year becomes ineligible for state funds for professional development.[35]

In short, the states have had considerable influence on the budget process at the local level, but that influence has sometimes resulted in rigid, biased, and undemocratic outcomes. Overall these negative consequences have abated in recent years, but unfunded mandates from the state are still a burdensome problem for local governments and are a bone of contention between the states and local governments, even when laws and constitutional amendments forbid them.

Forms of Government

Within the limits of state laws, cities have chosen different legal forms, which entail particular budget roles and processes. In the early days of municipal budgeting, after the Civil War, many cities adopted boards of estimate; later, in the early 1900s, there was a major move toward executive budgeting, concentrating power in the hands of the chief executive. Throughout the 1900s, at intervals, a number of cities, perhaps especially middle-sized ones, adopted the council-manager form of budgeting. Although many cities have adopted one of these forms and stuck with it for decades, there has been some shifting between forms, and hence between budget processes, in individual cities. There has also been some informal adaptation within forms.

Municipal budgets originated as a spending control mechanisms during the period of major spending growth after the Civil War. Early budgets were estimates of how much tax revenue would be required, based on detailed accounts of receipts and expenditures for preceding years. Officials submitted detailed requests. Typically, the head of the finance department, the controller, the auditor, or the mayor would receive and cut back these requests, or in smaller cities the departments would forward their requests directly to the council or its budget committee. To control nonapproved spending during the year, some cities adopted annual appropriations, fixing expenditures for the year.

The 1870s and 1880s were years of sharp economic and governmental contraction for most cities. The focus of budgeting became one of keeping government small and inactive. Beginning in 1873 in New York City, a form of budgeting appeared in which budget estimates from the departments went to a board of estimate, variously composed, but generally consisting of the mayor, controller, president of the board of aldermen, and others. It is difficult to get a board of independently elected officials to agree to the same projects, and that slows down spending.

The extent to which the boards of estimates were viewed as a way of curtailing tax levies is underscored by a description of how the Board of Estimates actually worked in New York City. In the early days of the board, aldermen would add to the recommended amounts. From 1873 to 1888 they added on average about $500,000 annually. But they were constantly overruled by the Board of Estimates. Over time, the aldermen added less and less. "Responding to consistent pressure for economy in government, particularly from middle-class groups experiencing the brunt of taxation, the Board of Estimates ignored the proposed increases of the council and continued to reduce the level of public expenditures." [36] By 1898, the charter granted the council some formal budget authority, but only to decrease the estimates. If the mayor vetoed any reductions made by the council, a five-sixths majority was required to overturn. There was to be no reconsideration by the Board of Estimates after council action.[37]

During the Progressive Era expansion of government functions (from about 1895 to about 1920), the focus of budgeting shifted from keeping government small and ineffective to combining activism with efficiency and accountability. The result was a major push for a single executive responsible for the budget— the so called strong mayor form of government. Executive budget reform reflected the Progressive Era sense of government as a necessary counterbalance to business and a major provider of services, but at the same time it reflected the perceived need to control government and provide accountability. The single-executive reforms also reflected the notion of government moving on a plan, of change in an agreed-on direction, rather than the random expenditures of a council and a pork-driven budget. At that time, under this form of government, councils were sometimes radically disempowered.

The council-manager form began to gain popularity after World War I. In the council-manager form of government, the council was reduced in size and elected at large to reduce the influence of neighborhoods, ethnic groups, and political machines. This new council was given more budgeting authority, but it operated by hiring a professional manager who was responsible, either directly or through an appointee, for collecting and sifting the budget requests from the departments before forwarding them to the council for approval. This council-manager form was intended to be less political and more management oriented than the mayor-council form. Accountability was to be formally provided by the frequently exercised right of city councils to fire the manager if he (early managers were males, frequently engineers) did not do as they wished. But accountability was also provided by improved budget documents that demonstrated how well public money was being spent.

Major spurts in adoptions of the council-manager form occurred after the two world wars. From 1945 to 1959 the number of council-manager adoptions increased from 637 to almost 1,500.[38] One reason was that the infrastructures of the cities were in a state of neglect, and technical problems seemed to require competent staff and an activist approach. In the past few years, the number of council-manager cities has actually exceeded the number of strong mayor cities, but what has caught the eye of the news media has been some major cities' abandoning the council-manager form and adopting the strong mayor form instead.

Often in these abandonments of the council-manager form a highly popular and well-known mayoral candidate pressed for charter changes or enhanced his or her own mayoral power. The shift often followed corruption scandals, long-term community decline, or severe financial problems with implications of incompetence or cover-up. In Richmond, Virginia, former governor Douglas Wilder campaigned in 2003 for a charter change to abandon the council-manager form and directly elect the mayor. Then he ran for the office, winning handily, after which, in early 2005, the council gave him the line-item veto and enhanced appointment powers. In Oakland, California, Jerry Brown, another popular ex-governor, got an amendment to the charter onto the ballot before his landslide victory in the mayoralty race in 1998; the measure passed by a wide margin. For a trial period, the city manager would report to the mayor rather than the council. In 2004 the measure expired, and after a campaign was made permanent by the public in March. Some claimed that there was little distinction in people's minds between the mayor and the form of government. San Diego had a successful abandonment election in 2004. There the mayor will get the manager's budget responsibilities, but the council will get its own budget analyst and the ability to override the mayor's veto with five votes. "The October firestorms exposed the severe underfunding of city fire services, the pension fund deficit has ballooned to $1.1 billion, and federal authorities are investigating errors and omissions in disclosure documents used to sell municipal bonds."[39] These issues weakened the city manager, and the mayor seemed to be distancing himself from the decisions by blaming the manager for them, though the mayor and council had accepted the manager's recommendations.

In each of these council-manager abandonments, successful elections to enhance the powers of the mayor followed years of unsuccessful efforts by mayors and their supporters. The time, circumstances, and candidates have to be right to secure a shift of budget responsibilities to the mayor.

Summary and Conclusions

At the federal and state levels, with clear distinctions between the executive and legislative branches, much of the change over time has to do with the shifting balance of budgetary power between branches of government. But at the state level more of the budget process is embedded in constitutions, rather than laws, with the result that it is harder to change. Reformers can lock their policy preferences into processes that are binding for generations, a result that makes it difficult to adapt to changing circumstances and has major implications for democracy, since later generations are bound by the decisions and preferences of earlier ones. To get around rigid rules there may be more informal budgeting at the state level, processes that occur behind closed doors, involving negotiations. At the local level, much of the ongoing tension is between the state government, which is legally responsible, and the local governments, which are legally dependent on the states, over the degree of autonomy the local governments have in budgeting. The tension is ongoing in part because the rigidity and durability of state laws make it difficult for local governments to adapt and to make decisions that match local preferences.

At all levels of government tensions occur between extremes. When a budget process becomes extreme in any way, there are pressures to move it back toward the middle, even when this takes many years. Thus in Indiana, state-mandated budget processes affecting the localities have changed only slowly, but gradually they have become more neutral and respectful of local democratic priorities. In New York, extreme powers of the governor have generated multiple efforts by the legislature to win back some budgetary say. Sometimes the pendulum seems to swing back and forth, and back again, as when strong mayor systems are replaced by council-manager forms of government, only to be replaced again later by a strong mayor form. At the national level, if the president takes too much policy control away from Congress, Congress responds by taking some power back for itself. Change is more likely when a budget process fails to accomplish that which is supposed to be its strength—Gramm-Rudman-Hollings failed to balance the budget; the council-manager form in Oakland failed to provide sound financial management.

Though change in the process will almost always be justified on the basis of its ability to solve some public problem, in reality it is difficult to distinguish between changes aimed at enhancing the power of individuals and factions and changes that are aimed to solve particular public policy problems. Citizens seem unable to distinguish between giving more power to popular elected officials and changing the structure for the long term. The politicians pushing for enhanced powers often seem to short-circuit the discussion of the process changes, making them referendums on their own popularity.

The shifts in process through time can be visualized as pendulum swings between extremes, but the reality is that the pendulum sticks in places. Several factors cause that stickiness and slow the rebalancing of budgetary powers or revamping of budgeting processes. Among them are structural rigidities, constitutions, charters, and laws, on the one hand, and highly unbalanced powers on the other. Those who are truly powerless in the budget process have trouble changing it because those who would have to give up power choose not to; powerful governors reject the reform proposals of legislatures that would reduce their power, as in the New York example. These sticky places hold up formal change and breed a variety of informal processes instead, some of which are dysfunctional. The informal processes may include holding up the budget to force negotiations or excessive use of vetoes to impose the executive's will. Informal processes are often changeable from year to year and carried out behind closed doors.

Though the ideal might be some kind of equilibrium—a budget process that avoids the extremes and balances the voices of a variety of legitimate stakeholders—sometimes equilibrium is not achieved. Budgets may not only be late, they may not arrive at all before the beginning of the fiscal year, with chaotic results for managers of programs and agencies. Fiscal discipline may dissolve, with spending routinely outrunning revenues, piling up debt for future generations and limiting their ability to address their own problems collectively. Much time can be wasted fighting over process each year instead of working out priorities. In short, budget processes can deteriorate into ad hoc negotiations behind closed doors, with key figures and consequences blocked from public view. These episodic failures of process highlight the importance of building consensus around relatively neutral rules that share budgetary power wisely, so there will be minimal pressure to work around the process or derail it.

5. Expenditures: The Politics of Choice

The politics of expenditures is the politics of choice. Revenue is never sufficient to satisfy all possible claims on the budget, so governments have a formal (and sometimes an informal) process for making budget requests, sorting through them, prioritizing them, trimming them back, and approving the resulting plan. If there is a tight ceiling on spending, those proposals low on the priority list may not be funded. The stakes are high, the competition may be intense, and the associated politics is often lively.

Most of the year-to-year changes occur around the margins of the budget. Zeroing out whole programs is relatively rare, as is adding completely new ones. Because allocations do not usually change dramatically from year to year, some scholars have argued that there are not many choices, and hence there is not much politics, on the expenditure side of the budget. One agency or program may get a little more of the new revenue than another, or one program may be cut while others are allowed to keep up with inflation. Over a several-year period, however, if one agency continues to get a somewhat larger percentage increase than others, the distribution of funds among public priorities changes substantially. Such changes may be hotly contested.

The choices in the budget are sometimes based on policy preferences. One such policy preference might be that crime suppression is more important than crime prevention, so police requests must be funded before education or job training. More narrowly, a policy might state that no population control program will be funded if it engages in abortion counseling or lists abortion as an option. Some expenditure policies favor spending for the poor; others lean toward the preservation of open space or natural resources, or support particular industries, such as energy or automobile manufacturing. Or policies can cut across sectors and programs, perhaps looking for spending proposals that encourage competition or that shift discretion over spending to lower levels of government, or to street-level bureaucrats, those meeting with clients or customers.

These policy preferences tend to come from the top down, that is, from the elected officials, in both the legislative and executive branches. These officials may compete with one another to shape the budget according to their own policy preferences. At the same time, these officials are responsible for assuring that expenditures do not exceed revenues over the long haul. These two sets of goals sometimes clash: At times, funding politicians' policy preferences trumps budgetary balance or results in pushing expenditures off on other levels of government. Budget requests that originate in the agencies are more likely to be technical and less policy laden, but they still cost money, so there may be a contest between programmatic requirements coming up from below and policy demands coming down from above.

Although policy sometimes governs budget choices, many, perhaps most, expenditure choices are made without the benefit of a clear policy to guide them. Decisions might depend on which claimant has enough political clout or can negotiate enough support to win approval for a budget request. Or decisions may be made on technical grounds, such as whether a request is financially sound, or whose turn it is to be funded, or which proposal is most likely to solve policy problems or avoid future difficulties. The way program administrators frame their requests—the arguments and appeals they make to the budget office and to elected officials—may influence whether or not a request is funded. In addition, the environment may favor some claims over others. Jobs programs have more appeal during a long and deep recession; scientific programs to study earthquakes are more likely to be funded just after a major tsunami that drowns a hundred thousand people.

The politics of expenditures depends on the interaction between those in the agencies requesting budgets to accomplish their programmatic goals and elected officials trying to implement their favored policies and advance their chances of reelection. How well agencies do in the competition for resources depends on how well they address the policy preferences of the elected officials, how much interest group and popular support they can demonstrate, the match between their request and the recognized and imminent policy problems the government faces, and the technical accuracy and appeal of their proposals. It also depends on how well their strategies match the current environment. Similarly, whether the elected officials can achieve all or part of their policy objectives depends on the environment, their budget strategies, their ability to line up political support, and to some extent, whether the policies they advocate address and potentially resolve widely recognized problems.

Strategies of Agency Heads or Program Directors

Because the budget process always includes—though it does not always take seriously—requests coming up from departments and programs, the budget request and its justification present an opportunity for an agency or program to compete for limited resources. To be successful, budget proposals have to appeal both to financial and policy analysts in the budget office and to political officials in the executive and legislative branches. Budget strategies of agency heads and their supporters can be loosely grouped into (1) those designed to promote successful competition and (2) those designed to reduce the need for competition.

Agency Heads' Competitive Strategies

Agency heads compete for limited funds by preparing budget justifications that are appealing both in a technical sense (they will improve efficiency or effectiveness) and a political sense (they implement policies preferred by, and provide political capital for, elected officials). The strategies I describe are not mutually exclusive; an agency head can use more than one of them. One approach is for administrators to make their requests seem more urgent or more necessary than other possible spending choices. Another is to make requests seem cheap, or free, or highly cost effective. A third is to appeal to the policy preferences of the chief executive or key legislators, or more narrowly, to provide in the request for the special projects or programs that legislators want. In all cases, the proposal must be sensitive to the immediate fiscal and political environment.

Climbing the Priority List. One way of increasing the priority of projects or programs is to represent them as life saving. Thus a fire department can argue that a new fire station will reduce response times and save lives, and the Defense Department can argue for new weapons systems because terrorists are out to destroy the nation and could attack at any time. The emergency, whatever it is, needs to be easily imaginable. At one local government budget presentation, for example, a fire department official presented a film of a fire in a residence, with the blaze going from room to room. The film showed the temperatures in each room, the smoke and toxic fumes, and the damage done, second by second. One had to conclude that the house could be one's own, and that the quicker the fire department's response, the safer one's own house and family. The department requested an extra ambulance that year, complete with emergency equipment, and got it. It could probably have gotten anything it requested after showing that film.

The probability of catastrophic events may have to be exaggerated to make a powerful case. During the cold war with the Soviet Union, supporters of the defense budget often gave different and sometimes questionable estimates of Soviet troop and armament strength to justify military buildups. The information was not blatantly false so much as misleading—saying that the United States had fewer divisions of men under arms than the Soviets, for example, without mentioning that the size of U.S. divisions was much larger.[1] The threat of disastrous consequences if expenditures are not made is particularly common in the area of defense. For example, in 1986 President Reagan argued for a real (above inflation) increase in Defense Department spending because failure to provide increases would risk a return to the problems of the 1970s, "a hollow army, ships that can't sail, and aircraft that can't fly"; it would encourage adventurism on the part of the Soviets, and it would weaken the administration's ability to negotiate a satisfactory arms reduction agreement.[2]

The "just imagine what would happen if this purchase were not made" argument has widespread applicability. To evoke negative possibilities in the mind of listeners, agency heads requesting budget increases sometimes use word pictures, films or photographs, or even props. A budget presentation at a state university included a seat back, to illustrate that the library furniture was falling apart. The staff member went on to paint a verbal portrait of a crowded library where there were tables but no seats, and the students had to sit on the floor. In another example, a city director of water and sewer argued that he had to have certain new equipment because if he did not, the city sewers would back up into homes, and council members would get angry complaints from citizens. His brief argument was suggestive as to both events and the probable political consequences.

In an effort to push their programs up on priority lists, advocates sometimes try to define their program outputs as so valuable and so politically untouchable that no tampering with allocations is possible. For example, the goal of paramedic service is saving lives. Politicians are politically unwilling to estimate the dollar value of a life saved. Hence they may be unwilling to calculate the cost of paramedic service or may not hold the program to the same standards of cost effectiveness as other programs. It is politically difficult to deny such requests when the implied consequence of doing so is loss of life.

At the national level, the Export-Import Bank and the closely related Overseas Private Investment Corporation (OPIC) have successfully used the strategy of linking their program to goals with unlimited value. Both agencies provide loan assistance and insurance to make it easier for U.S. companies to sell their products abroad. Program supporters argue that a war is going on, a trade war, and without such tools as OPIC and the Ex-Im Bank, other countries that do have such tools will win out. Moreover, they argue, such agencies create U.S. jobs as well as improve trade. They also argue that OPIC covers its own expenses and makes a profit, which opponents deny. The success of these agencies in obtaining reauthorization in the face of opposition depends at least in part on their ability to link their activities to successful trade, whether that trade would have happened without them or not. This goal is so valuable that it has been difficult to question the budget requests of the agencies designed to achieve it.[3]

A variant of this strategy is to create programs with symbolic outputs. To the extent that the outputs are symbolic, their worth cannot be priced; hence they seem to justify spending any amount of money. Putting a man on the moon was such a program. Its costs were not estimated or even estimatable at the time the program was announced. The outcome was symbolic. We were going to do it, no matter how much it cost. A positive climate for business is another of those symbolic goals that seem to justify a wide range of expenditures. How much is it worth? How much will it deliver in terms of economic expansion? No one knows, but a good climate is perceived as of value in itself. Bringing democracy to the Middle East is another example of a symbolic goal justifying a seemingly unlimited budget request.

For agencies that cannot claim that what they achieve is of unlimited value, a frequent strategy is to try to link their activities to more highly valued goals. Thus a local airport serving private airplanes is running at a loss; it is providing a service used by some but paid for by all. The ratio of costs to benefits will be a political and technical red flag, unless the airport can be tied to a more valued goal (preferably one with unlimited value), in this case economic development. Even if the case linking private airplanes and economic development is weak, if the agency in charge of the airport and its backers can gain general acceptance for the argument, the airport's funding can be treated as not requiring cost-benefit analysis. Similarly, at the state level university funding had been a fairly low priority among state programs, but it received a boost when higher education officials managed to redefine higher education as the nucleus of economic development.

One of the key strategies that supporters of farm subsidies used over the years was to link their programs to the symbolic worth of protecting the family farm. But as the number of family farmers decreased, it gradually became clear that a substantial proportion of the funding was going to wealthy corporate owners with huge holdings, not to struggling family farmers. The linkage to a valued goal has to be credible to work. Accordingly in the past few years the rationale justifying such subsidies has changed. In 2002 the secretary of agriculture acknowledged to congressional committees that the agriculture sector had shifted, that most agricultural output was produced by a small number of very large farms, and that small farmers were often farming only part-time. The secretary justified department spending by focusing on a goal of unlimited worth: protecting food supplies, especially in the light of recent terrorist attacks:

> The Department is addressing the Nation's new priorities in light of the September 11 events in a fiscally responsible manner. This requires recognizing our priorities and making difficult funding decisions. I can assure you that USDA has done just that in preparing its 2003 budget proposals.
>
> We have also taken actions to assure that the $328 million of emergency supplemental funds made available to USDA for security needs in 2002 will be invested in ways to meet high priorities, particularly to improve USDA's biosecurity operations for the long term. We are working closely with the Office of Homeland Security and we have established a USDA Homeland Security Council to coordinate our security efforts and track progress in using those funds to ensure that priority needs are met. The Council will play a significant role in establishing the final plans for use of those funds.[4]

Making Programs Look Cheap, Cost-Effective. One way of appealing to both the budget office and elected officials is to demonstrate cost-effectiveness or to make programs look cheap or free.

There are many ways of using the cost-effectiveness argument; one is to argue that unless the requested money is spent now, the project or program will cost more later. For this argument to be successful, the project or program has to appear inevitable, only a matter of timing. Public works directors routinely argue that if roof repairs on public buildings are delayed, rain will cause structural damage, and the eventual costs will be many times greater than if the work is done soon. If street maintenance is delayed, the streets will fall apart and have to be rebuilt at much greater cost. Note the underlying assumption that the project will have to be done sooner or later.

Another way of making a program or project look cost-effective is to argue that it will either pay for itself, or more than pay for itself, returning a kind of profit. For example, the Children's Defense Fund argued that research proved that prenatal care and immunization save more money than they cost.[5] An expensive new water tower was justified in Dekalb, Illinois, one year because it would enable the city to pump water and use electricity at night, when electricity rates are lower. When it was experiencing deep budget cuts, the Government Accountability Office, in Washington, D.C., began to report how many dollars its recommendations to the agencies were saving, citing a ratio for how many extra dollars were returned to the government for every dollar it spent. The clear implication was that it would be foolish not to fund such a productive agency.

Generally agencies that are able to demonstrate their cost-effectiveness do better in budget allocations. Cost-effectiveness can be demonstrated through studies the agency contracts with neutral third parties that isolate the impact of its program and show how much those outcomes cost. For example, the federal Economic Development Agency contracted with Rutgers University to study its job creation programs and figure out how much money the agency spent for each job created. The study demonstrated very modest costs per job created, suggesting the program was highly cost-effective, and it was frequently cited when agency officials or program advocates testified before congressional committees.

A related argument is that money spent on a particular program is an investment. Money spent on medical research, on preventive health care, on capacity building, and on education is often justified in these terms. Spending for children's programs is often described as an investment. Grants for research and development are justified as investments for the society as a whole.

Agency administrators may not have to deal with cost-effectiveness questions if their programs do not cost much in the first place, so one strategy is to argue that a program is cheap. Sometimes programs really are not very expensive, but sometimes they are, and then the budget strategy is to make them look less expensive than they are.

Many techniques have been employed at all levels of government to make programs look inexpensive for example, substituting leases for purchases, which shifts expenditures from highly visible capital budgets to much-less-visible operating budgets. Sometimes governments make the costs of programs less visible by using tax breaks instead of outlays. In this manner, revenues are never collected or due, and hence they may never appear in the budget as an outlay, though the money is spent as surely as if the revenue were collected and then disbursed. Recent trends in tax expenditure reporting at the state level have made this strategy less effective, but there is very little tax expenditure reporting at the local level. Tax breaks may thus appear free, though in fact they may be very expensive.

Another way of making programs look inexpensive or free is to use grant money to fund them. Grants are transfers of money from one level of government to another, or from a governmental unit to an outside agency, to accomplish some particular program goal. The national government often awards grants to the states, and sometimes directly to local governments, as incentives for compliance with national policies. States may pass on federal grants to their local governments and add some further aid. Grants may seem free to the state and local governments that receive them. To the extent that the money comes from another level of government, the provision of a particular good or service by local government may be noncontroversial. If the local government has to put up some of its own money to get the grant, however, applying for or accepting the grant may be much more contentious. Still, a project with a state or federal match is cheaper to undertake than one without any grant support.

A whole set of techniques revolve around making project or program costs look less expensive by ignoring or underestimating later years' costs, or pushing current costs off into the future. One way of doing that is to budget a project's first-year costs starting in the middle of the year, so that the costs of a whole year do not show up until a year later. A second approach is to push costs off until after the end of the budget reporting period; if there is a five-year budget, the costs for the program might begin to balloon in year six. For example, the 1997 balanced budget agreement in Washington granted huge tax reductions whose costs swelled after 2002, but the agreement only went as far as 2002 in recording the costs. The result was to make the tax reduction look more affordable than it was.

Another way of making programs look inexpensive is to allow them to charge fees or otherwise recover their costs. Because the program seems to pay for itself, there may be no expenditure recorded in the budget. This sometimes occurs at the local level in economic development activities, when a city invests in extending water and services to an undeveloped parcel with the idea that it will recapture the outlays in the future when the land is developed and sold. The time lag between the initial outlays and the recapture may be many years, during which time the city has collected taxes and spent public money with no budgetary record. To a reader of the budget it may be unclear how much was spent and how much is owed; moreover, the land may never be developed. The federal government also has used fee income to offset spending, sometimes making spending appear lower than it is.[6]

Mobilizing Support. One of the best and most frequently used strategies for agencies to gain support for a proposal is to tailor it to the policy goals of the elected officials, where they are known and offer relatively clear guidance. Relatedly, describing how the agency is responding to criticisms leveled at it in the past may remove some obstacles to continued or increased funding. Agency heads may appeal to the chief executive, to the legislators, or to both at the same time, or they may appeal to program supporters to intervene with executive or legislative branch officials on their behalf.

Appeals based on compliance with policy guidance may be explicit in the budget justification and/or in legislative testimony. For example, agriculture secretary Ann Veneman stated in testimony to the agriculture appropriations subcommittee,

> For 2003, this budget supports the Administration's principles for the 21st Century as stated in our report: Food and Agricultural Policy: Taking Stock for the New Century, issued last fall. Specifically, the budget does the following:
>
> - Ensures that the new Farm Bill will be generously funded by providing an additional $73.5 billion in mandatory funding over the 2002–2011 period to develop sound policies for farm commodity and income support, conservation, trade, food assistance, research, and other programs.
> - Supports the Administration's goal of opening new markets overseas and expanding U.S. agricultural exports by providing over $6 billion in export program support.
> - Provides the largest increase ever for the Special Supplemental Nutrition Program for Women, Infants and Children (WIC) thereby supporting 7.8 million program participants.
> - Provides support for over 20 million food stamp participants including legislation to allow more legal immigrants to participate and other changes to simplify complex rules, support working families and improve program delivery.
> - Protects agriculture and our food supply from potential threats—intentional or unintentional—and requests more than $146 million in new spending for food safety, pest and animal disease prevention, and research.
> - Improves the Department's management of its delivery of programs.
> - Improves the stewardship of our soil, water and forests by making more resources available for conservation uses with less money spent for overhead expenses.
> - Maintains funding to support loans, grants, and technical assistance to address a diversity of rural development needs including financing electric and telecommunications systems, water and waste disposal systems, rural housing, and business and industry.[7]

By linking the Agriculture Department's budget to presidential priorities and policies, the secretary was arguing that disapproval of this budget request would thwart the president and pique his anger. Republican legislators would have to defy their party and president to oppose this request and presumably be prepared to pay the consequences. The secretary's testimony also plays to Congress in terms of offering to fix frequently criticized administrative problems with the Food Stamp program. The secretary also tried to please legislators and build support by emphasizing increases in WIC and Food Stamps, programs aimed at reducing urban poverty. This pairing of traditional farm support programs and urban poverty programs has long been a strategy to broaden legislative support for agriculture department programs beyond the farm states.

Broadening support for a program by adding elements that address different constituencies is widely practiced. It is difficult to fund programs that are narrowly targeted to a problem that occurs only in some parts of the country, state, or city or that apply to only a narrow portion of the population. As a result, programs may be designed to spread benefits widely, even when there are few dollars to go around or the result is inefficient, to gain enough legislative support to be passed.

Sometimes department and program administrators build pork-type projects into their budgets or include facilities or contractors within a legislator's district so that he or she can take credit for producing or maintaining jobs. This strategy is intended to win support from the legislator so targeted. It is practiced to some extent at all levels of government. In one city, for example, council members sometimes asked department heads to include particular projects in their budget requests, with the implicit quid pro quo that the council members would then approve particular expenditures that the department head wanted. If these legislator-requested items were deleted by the city manager as either wasteful or lower priority than other expenditures, the council members would add them back. The manager formally had the authority to remove the projects inserted by the council members, but doing so risked his job, since the council hired and fired the manager. At the national level, the Defense Department is reputed to include projects and contractors in congressional districts to win the broadest possible support for new projects, construction, and weapons systems.

Sometimes it is not clear where an idea originates—in the legislature, in a lobby group, or in the agency itself. Thus it may not be clear if an agency has designed a program to attract interest group and legislative support, or if legislators, working on behalf of interest groups, have asked the agency to insert particular expenditures in their budget proposals. Agency heads may be required to keep their distance from legislators to prevent this kind of collusion, but sometimes these relationships do occur. Relationships among agency heads, legislators, and interest groups or contractors in support of particular budget requests have been called "iron triangles" because they have three participants (corners), and

---

**Minicase: The Department of Housing and Urban Development
and Boutique Programs**

The federal Department of Housing and Urban Development has had a
troubled history, its programs complex and not always well managed. From
time to time HUD has been the repository of political patronage positions
rather than talented and interested political appointees. With its top-level
administrators sometimes accused of benign neglect, HUD has endured
financial scandals and low levels of political support. Funding of its programs and even the survival of the department have sometimes been in
doubt. In this context, HUD has tried to find friends in Congress wherever
it could, while working hard to document its efficiency and effectiveness.

Some legislators have sought to create within HUD small, "boutique"
grant programs that earmark parts of broad grants for particular, favored
projects or small programs. Getting such programs up and running with
limited staffing has been difficult for HUD, and distracting, but the department was in no position to jeopardize congressional support by turning
down a proposal from a congressperson. For the representative or senator,
having a program designed by and named after himself or herself was
a measure of success. For HUD it was a way of earning support for its
budget[1]

1. Irene Rubin," *Balancing the Federal Budget: Eating the Seed Corn or Trimming
the Herds* (New York: Chatham House Publishers of Seven Bridges Press, 2003;
Washington, D.C.: CQ press).

---

when they occur they are hard to control or break into (triangles are very stable).
What may occur more often is that agency heads, when their key programs are
threatened, invoke or warn the interest groups that support the programs that the
budget is in jeopardy, and the interest groups then lobby Congress for continued funding. Sometimes agencies structure programs in such a way that powerful interest groups will benefit from them, so that if needed these beneficiaries can
be mobilized to intervene with the executive or legislators to demand support for
the program.

Strategies to Reduce Competition

Agencies that have narrow constituencies, or that cannot claim emergency status or highly valued ends, do not always compete successfully or fear that at some

time in the future they will not compete successfully; they prefer to get out of the part of the budget where competition is keen or tap into areas of the budget where resources are more plentiful.

There are a number of ways that agencies can reduce their dependence on competing for a limited pool of funds. They can try to get approval to charge fees for their services, creating their own earmarked revenues, or they can argue that the fees they collect should not return to general revenue but should be earmarked for their own projects and programs. They can round up supporters to argue that they should become independent of a particular department, or at the local level, have their own tax collection powers as a single-purpose governmental entity. They can negotiate for mandates to force them to spend money on particular programs.

At the local level there are various possible structures for delivering services. There may be a city government that provides a whole range of services, or a city that provides fewer services plus a number of special-purpose governments created to provide a single service or perform a single major function. In a city with many functions, budget requests are weighed according to importance or urgency, within revenue constraints. In this competition, some departments have historically succeeded better than others. Police and fire departments do well—they can claim they are saving lives—but streets and public works, which are less glamorous and cannot claim to save lives, are sometimes shortchanged. Parks and recreation are often at the bottom of the list—nice to have if there is plenty of money but the first to be cut if there is a dip in revenues. Advocates of parks and recreation sometimes have felt that if they didn't have to be a department of city hall and be compared with the police and fire departments, they would do better. Hence many of them sought to become special-purpose governments with their own taxing powers, and in fact, they have tended to fare better as independent, single-purpose governments. Some states have many special-purpose local governments, from airport authorities to mosquito abatement districts. There are disadvantages to fragmenting government in this way, but for the beneficiaries of these now-independent programs there is stability of funding and an end to sometimes unsuccessful competition with other governmental functions.

In Illinois there are special-purpose governments to provide library services, sanitary sewers, mosquito abatement, drainage, education, parks, special recreation, and airports. Special-purpose governments may charge fees, but they can usually also collect taxes and issue debt, much like any other local government. The difference is that other local governments provide a variety of services, while special-purpose governments provide only one.

The variation among metropolitan areas in the number of special-purpose governments led one researcher to investigate whether provision of a service by special-purpose government led to a higher level of spending than would have occurred in a multipurpose government. She found that pulling out a single function and providing it with its own taxing powers made that function more successful in getting and spending resources.[8] Thus, though creating a special-purpose government can be time consuming and difficult, it is often a successful funding strategy for supporters of services that are not doing as well in the highly competitive environment of general purpose local governments. From the point of view of public policy, however, special-purpose governments prevent the kind of prioritization and trade-offs that are part of democratic governance.

There are also degrees of budgetary independence. It may be sufficient to get revenues earmarked for a given program, while keeping it inside a general purpose department or government body. At the national level, the Patent and Trademark Office (PTO) charged fees to inventors, and the revenues were to be devoted to running the office. However, when the federal government was trying to eliminate deficits, Congress decided to increase the fees but use the extra money to reduce the deficit instead of dedicating the revenues solely to the PTO. The PTO gradually lost control of its own fees. Supporters of the agency argued that the PTO should leave the Department of Commerce and set out on its own, taking its fee revenue with it. A compromise was reached in which PTO would remain in the Commerce Department but become a performance-based organization, that is, it would be run like a business with its own revenue stream.

A different approach to minimizing competition is to get some authoritative body to mandate a particular level of expenditures. A mandated project or program is not in competition with any other project or program; it must be provided and paid for, regardless of other priorities. Mandates can come from accrediting associations, from banks or other lenders, or from federal or state legislatures. They are requirements that a particular good or service be provided at a given, required level or cost.

One form of mandating is the professional accreditation model. The model occurs in universities, where accounting associations, journalism societies, bar associations, planning associations, and public administration associations set standards for academic programs. In many cases accreditors restrict transfers of money out of a program (as in law schools) and set staffing as well as academic standards. These standards imply mandatory minimum levels of funding because if the program (or the whole school) loses its accreditation its ability to attract students seriously diminishes. The accreditation model also applies to some other public sector agencies. For example, cities are rated on their capacity to handle

**Minicase: The Economic Development Administration Uses
              Defense Funds**

If an agency sells something, or provides a service for which it can charge
fees, or if it can levy taxes to pay for its services, and if it has a large supportive constituency or an appealing function that is hard to say no to, such
as recreation for people who are wheelchair-bound, it can try to get out of
the competitive part of the budget and set up its own shop. But sometimes
agencies neither fare well in the budget competition nor have either special appeal or a service they can sell. The Economic Development Administration at the national level was such a body.

EDA had a difficult time demonstrating that it was cost-effective; it was
hard to prove what impact its programs really had. After years of severe
budget and staffing cuts and failure to reauthorize the program year after
year, the agency finally stabilized and was reauthorized in 1998. In addition
to paying much more attention to demonstrating its cost-effectiveness, the
EDA had increased its focus on economic redevelopment programs for
abandoned military bases. The program made sense given the EDA's mission, but equally important, it gave the agency a way of tapping into the
defense budget for a couple of years. Unlike the EDA, the Defense Department could claim that it was in the business of saving lives. Its budgets were
generally secure, and no one was threatening its existence. Once the EDA
had established its track record in this area, it received additional funding
whenever there was a new round of military base closings.

**Defense Department Economic Adjustment Funds
(in constant [2000] dollars, in millions)**

Fiscal year	Amount appropriated
1992	58
1993	90
1994	89
1995	113
1996	96
1997	94
1998	92
1999	87
2000	77
2001	33
Total	829

Source: David Witschi, director, EDA Economic Adjustment Division, in *EDA and
U.S. Economic Distress, 1965–2000,* by Robert W. Lake, et al., Edward J. Bloustein
School of Planning and Public Policy, Center for Urban Policy Research, Rutgers,
The State University of New Jersey, 2004, 120.

major fires, and fire departments use these ratings as arguments for what they must have in the way of staffing and equipment.

Although the accreditation process may be presented as an outside force, subject to no internal control, agency heads and interest groups can help form professional societies and urge them to set up standards in order to reduce the competition they face in the budget. Professional societies can play the role of accreditor or help to set standards that are set into law.

Mandates may also come from the federal government to the state and local governments, and from the state governments to their local governments. The federal government can pass a law requiring states to implement laws on clean air or water or require state and local governments to provide equal transit services for the handicapped. Carrying out such laws can cost state and local governments hundreds of millions of dollars. Even though these costs may be burdensome, and state and local governments may complain bitterly about the loss of their freedom to prioritize according to their citizens' demands, the fact remains that many state and local governments not only approve of such requirements but may have been actively involved in setting them in place. When the expenditures are mandated, there is no competition with other requests for spending.

Top-Down Strategies

Elected officials use many of the same strategies the agencies do, or similar ones, but they have a wider range of options open to them, some of which have negative outcomes for budgeting and democratic accountability.

Choosing Program Structures to Reduce Competition

Because competition can be fierce in parts of the budget, the participants sometimes strategize how to reduce competition rather than how to compete effectively. They seek to put constraints on budgeting that give their programs automatic funding or somehow make their programs untouchable, to take them out of the rough-and-tumble of policy-related trade-offs.

Entitlements. At the state and national levels—much less so at the local level—programs may be designed as entitlements. An entitlement is a particular kind of program that offers public money to individuals, companies, or governmental units that fit particular requirements. All those who are eligible and apply for the benefit receive it. The costs of entitlements are uncertain from year to year because they depend on the number of eligibles who apply. Entitlements make a prior claim on the budget; they must be funded first. Other expenditures may have to be cut to pay for entitlements; otherwise they would cause deficits. At the state level, for example, the cost of health care entitlements keeps growing. Because many states treat tax increases as politically unacceptable, the increase in entitlements often forces cuts in other, more discretionary programs, such as highway maintenance or higher education. Similar trade-offs have been required at the national level.

Under the Budget Enforcement Act of 1990, there were walls between mandatory and discretionary spending. Mandatory spending includes entitlements and other expenses, such as interest on the federal debt, that are more-or-less automatic. According to the budget rules then in effect, the costs of existing, mandatory programs could go up because of increased numbers of eligible applicants or inflation, without requiring reductions in discretionary spending. But if the increases were not offset in some way, they increased the deficit. Efforts to reduce and eliminate the deficit put pressure on Congress to cut the discretionary side of the budget to offset increases in the costs of entitlements. Appropriations committee members, who deal with the discretionary portion of the budget, freely expressed this relationship.

Some entitlements are so firmly rooted in beliefs about what government should do for citizens that they are treated as rights.[9] For example, people may have a right to basic protection, or a roof over their head, or a right not to starve or freeze to death in a society that can afford to feed and warm them. Basic health care may also be considered a right. Once an entitlement is treated as a right, it is virtually nonnegotiable in a budget. Entitlements, when they are treated as rights, represent an extreme form of the strategy of locking in program funding.

For program advocates, trying to design programs as entitlements is a strategy to reduce competition. They may also try to change the social definition of the right underlying an entitlement, by bringing dramatic instances of socially caused suffering to the attention of the public and of politicians. Documenting need is an important part of this strategy, and the ability to rouse public sympathy may be crucial.

Public Enterprises. Public enterprises are governmental services that are run like businesses, in the sense that they sell goods or services that they produce. Public enterprises may be owned or operated by government agencies. They are intended to pay for themselves through the sale of what they do or make. To the extent that they succeed, they involve no direct expenditures and hence appear free. They are segregated from the rest of the budget, and the revenues they generate are supposed to go exclusively for the expenses they incur. They typically do not compete with other programs or projects.

There are public enterprises at all levels of government. At the national level, the Tennessee Valley Authority (TVA), which provided electric power, is one example of a public enterprise; the postal service is operated as a public enterprise, as is Amtrak, the passenger rail company. States have historically run a number of enterprises, but currently the state university systems are probably the most widespread enterprises at the state level. At the local level, common public enterprises include water and sewer services and parking.

Revenue belonging to a public enterprise normally stays with that enterprise, but it may be coveted by other agencies, which sometimes manage to shift some of their expenses over to the enterprise. Enterprises are not airtight when it comes to hanging onto their revenues. A trust fund offers a stronger legal framework, though it turns out not to be airtight either.

Trust Funds. Trust funds are budget entities that separate out specific revenues and expenditures for a particular purpose. Money deposited in a trust fund is supposed to be spent only for those purposes specified in the fund's creation. Among the best-known trust funds are Social Security and the Highway Trust Fund. Social Security provides income to elderly people after retirement to ensure that there are not a lot of elderly poor people who cannot pay for food or shelter; it is supported by a payroll tax collected explicitly for Social Security. The Highway Trust Fund, which builds and repairs the Interstate Highway System, is supported by an earmarked gas tax.

Trust funds are different from enterprises in that they are not businesses, making a product and selling it for a fee. Trust funds normally rely on taxation rather than fees for services. Trust funds do not have the same meaning in government as they do in the private sector. Calling them trust funds evokes in people's mind the private sector definition, a legally enforceable agreement requiring a fiduciary, that is, a responsible person or company, to maintain the fund on someone else's behalf and spend the money only for legally designated purposes. That image is misleading when applied to government and causes people to feel unnecessarily disappointed that the government trust funds are not treated with the same hands-off approach. Government trust funds can be changed by the government that created them. For example retirement funds, which are the major category of trust funds, can be changed in terms of eligibility, the age of retirement at which benefits begin, and the level of benefits. Current policy proposals for privatizing Social Security would substantially change its structure and nature.

The most common form of trust fund in government is a pension, wherein money is held in trust for employees for their retirement. As elsewhere in government, however, these are not really trust funds, as the conditions of retirement

Minicase: Federal Trust Funds

In a true trust fund, money is held by one party for someone else who is the actual owner of the account. The responsible party is required to manage the funds wisely and spend them according to the legal terms of the fund, and in no other way. He or she cannot unilaterally change the terms of the agreement but is merely a guardian of someone else's money.

There are very few trust funds in this sense in the federal government. Most of the funds called "trust funds" are in fact alterable by Congress unilaterally. They operate more like revolving funds with earmarked revenue. It would be better if they had some other name, so that the beneficiaries of trust funds would not think they owned the money in the fund and ought to be controlling its use, and feel angry and disappointed if they are not allowed to do so.

There are some real trust funds in government, however. One is the Indian Trust Fund. These monies are in fact owned by individuals or tribes but held for them by the government, in this case the Department of the Interior. The Federal Accounting Standards Board decided that these funds should not be reported along with the Department of the Interior's general purpose financial reporting, as they have nothing to do with the department's funds.[1]

1. "FASAB Interpretation Number 1—Reporting on Indian Trust Funds, Interpretation of Federal Financial Accounting Standards," March 12, 1997, available at www.fasab.gov. FASAB, the Federal Accounting Standards Board, sets standards for what entities should be covered in an agency's accounting reports and what numbers should be reported at the national level.

can be changed legislatively, nearly at will. Mostly such changes are phrased so that they apply only to newly employed personnel, so each person retires under the system in place when they were first employed by the agency, but sometimes changes also apply to those who have already been admitted to the system or even already retired. In Illinois, many changes were considered that would affect present employees and retirees, including changing the inflation adjustment formula.[10] Changes in pension systems are popular not only because they can save a lot of money but also because they tend to be less visible to the public. The only ones who protest reductions in benefits are the government employees themselves or the labor unions that represent them.

In short, trust funds are not inviolable in the public sector. They are sometimes competitive with other budgetary priorities. Pensions may be underfunded, so that the money that should have gone into them is spent on something else; revenue that is earmarked for trust funds may be shared among several purposes—used to balance the budget in one way or another; and benefits may be changed. Even so, however, trust funds are generally less competitive with other programs and projects than spending programs that are not in trust funds.

Locking in Priorities

When elected officials choose the legal framework for a program, they are often establishing the level of competition that that program will face. They may try to lock in their policy priorities and make them difficult for successors to change. For example, entitlements are typically authorized for multiple years or indefinitely. By giving money directly to recipients, who build the funds into their future decisions, they create a pool of recipients who will demand the program's continuation. Such programs are very difficult to cut back or eliminate. Public enterprises, too, establish a long-lasting structure. Other ways of locking in priorities include earmarking, formula allocations, and specific rules for priorities when cuts in spending occur. More rigid locking mechanisms include borrowing for present priorities and putting spending requirements in constitutions or charters.

Earmarking. A spending earmark means that a legislative or constitutional mandate requires a particular level or amount of spending for a specified purpose. Earmarking is the opposite of lump-sum budgeting, in which a total amount of money is granted, with agency administrators maintaining discretion on how the money will be spent.

One of the main reasons for spending earmarks is the failure of a program to compete successfully in a free-for-all, despite its importance to some constituents or interest groups. The group or the program may not have a large constituency; it may not have the resources to compete successfully; but it may have powerful symbolic appeal or strong support among key legislators. Earmarking is highly controversial. Public managers often resent earmarking because it limits their discretion. Legislators use spending earmarks as a way of forcing the executive branch to implement their preferences. Without such earmarks, small programs or projects that a few legislators care intensely about might be starved of resources by agency heads trying to protect broader programs.

Sometimes earmarks are authoritative restatements of priorities that are legitimately determined by legislative committees. At other times, earmarks are just pork—distributive benefits to particular companies, organizations, or geographic areas in the home district of a legislator. Distributions of pork often result in lower-priority spending being pushed up to the top of the list; they may result in the funding of projects that would not survive on their merits. But even pure pork may have positive functions. As a reward for support on particular bills, pork provides a way of building coalitions for important legislation. Small amounts of pork can be the lubrication that makes the political system work, but pork looks, and sometimes is, wasteful, and it can generate substantial controversy.

Formula Allocations. Like spending earmarks, formula allocations may lock in priorities. Formulas may be very simple; for example, requiring the same percentage increase for each department or program. More elaborate formulas may govern the distribution of grants or shared revenue to other levels of government. Such formulas may allocate funds based on measures of need, such as the average age or condition of housing, or measures of demand, such as the size of caseloads or school enrollment. The policy driving the original allocation is locked into the formula, which is used year after year. Thus if the formula says that communities with a high unemployment rate should get more money than communities with a low unemployment rate, and that this factor is more important than the age or condition of housing, water mains, or streets, that policy is built into the formula for grant allocations. Similarly, if a school funding formula weights heavily the relative wealth of a community compared to others in the state, a policy of equalization of educational opportunity is built into the formula and may last unquestioned for years.

Prior Rankings. Another way of locking in priorities is to provide a list in rank order of the programs that will be cut, in case revenues are less than projected or deficits make cuts necessary. In this situation, some programs are more vulnerable than others. Some state governments use this kind of process to deal with declines in their revenues. In an extreme model, some programs are exempted from cuts. For example, Gramm-Rudman-Hollings, which revised the federal budget process in 1985, specified that if deficit reduction targets were not met, there would be across-the-board cuts in defense and domestic spending, but specified programs would be exempt.

Referendums and Constitutional Amendments. Along the same lines, public referendums, often spearheaded by elected officials who vote to put such a measure on the ballot, sometimes establish a floor below which a program cannot be cut. Successful referendums may result in constitutional provisions that require funding at some given level. For example, the successful Florida referendum to limit class sizes in public education required more spending for teachers and classrooms to accommodate the number of students. An outcome of this sort is more likely to occur when a program has been competing unsuccessfully. Thus if education is losing out to entitlement programs such as Medicaid, supporters of education may push for a referendum to set a minimum level of funding for education, to strengthen its claim on the budget. In general, putting a requirement for spending on a specific program in the constitution of a state or the charter of a city makes it more rigid and difficult to reverse, locking in present policy decisions for the indefinite future.

Borrowing for Present Expenditures. A very important locking mechanism is to borrow money to spend on a particular project or program, and spend the money now, obligating taxpayers of the future to continue paying the debt. Since the money will have been spent, those who come later cannot undo this spending even if they would have preferred to spend the money on something else. By borrowing for current spending priorities, a coalition that is currently politically dominant can make policy decisions that lock in its preferences for many years to come. An example occurred in the city of St. Louis when a mayor and his supporters borrowed heavily to redevelop the downtown. The underlying policy position was to spend money on the downtown renewal, rather than on services for everybody or on the neighborhoods. The successor to this mayor was unable to change these priorities because the city was saddled with debt, which had to be paid off, and there was no money left to change priorities. At the national level the proposal to borrow money to fund the privatization of Social Security would have a similar effect, locking in the policy priority for privatization and forcing future generations to pay for it.

It is important to recognize, though, that with the possible exception of the borrowing strategy, even seemingly ironclad and irreversible funding decisions may be subject to intense pressure and ultimately be changed. Trust funds may be forced to share revenue with other programs; constitutional and charter provisions can be revisited and eroded or reversed by later referendums; formulas for the distribution of grants can be changed. Even rights-based entitlements can sometimes be reduced or denied. The political system generates counterpressure to restore flexibility, choice, and adaptability, as well as responsiveness to future elected officials.

Broadening the Base of Support

Not every program or service benefits every taxpayer in even measure. Leaf pickup may disproportionately benefit the wealthy, who have large wooded lots on tree-lined streets; municipal airports may benefit the owners of private aircraft; various federal programs benefit middle-class students, or underprivileged youngsters, or owners of private boats. Elected officials need budget strategies to get sufficient support to gain funding for programs when the group of potential beneficiaries is too small to assure legislative approval.

Geographic Dispersion. One way is to make a narrow program serve a number of different beneficiaries. For example, a program for repairing naval ships may be divided into ten locations, so that legislators from ten different states will support it. Such a tactic will gain more geographically diversified backing for the program.

Positive Spillovers. Another approach to winning support for a narrow program is to convince the public that there are positive spillovers, that is, that people in general benefit from the program even if they do not use it directly and never intend to. Public subsidies to mass transit are often justified in terms of positive spillovers: It is not just riders who benefit from mass transit. The users of automobiles also benefit because if all the riders on mass transit took to their cars, there would be immense traffic jams, and the costs of road repairs would be much higher. Downtown businesses and mall owners also benefit from mass transit because buses and trains bring in not just customers but also employees, increasing the quality and reducing the cost of labor. Mass transit is more fuel efficient, slowing down the need for imported oil and the depletion of nonrenewable resources and helping to keep gas prices down for everyone. In addition, some elderly or handicapped people can become economically self-sufficient through the use of mass transit, reducing the public cost of supporting them.

Programs can be sold by advertising their actual positive spillover effects or by exaggerating potential ones. An example of an exaggerated positive spillover effect is the claim that local airports should be subsidized by general taxpayers because they aid economic development. The argument is that small airports, which directly serve only wealthy owners of private planes, contribute to economic development because businesses will not locate in the city unless it has an airport. Every taxpayer presumably benefits from economic development because there will be more taxpayers sharing the burden of paying for public services, and so taxes for each resident will presumably drop. The actual impact of the airport on economic development may never be measured or questioned, but it becomes a rationale for public support of a program with a narrow group of beneficiaries.

Balancing Benefits to a Variety of Groups. If a program benefits a particular group, and there are not clear positive spillovers to help rationalize public spending on it, then several other strategies may be employed. One is to see that everyone gets a little something from different programs. Thus there may be rent subsidies for the poor, and low-cost loans for education to the middle class, and a Coast Guard fleet to maintain the safety of pleasure boaters among the wealthy. There may be water subsidies to farmers in the Southwest and dairy subsidies to farmers in Wisconsin and New England. The Interstate Highway System that serves primarily rural areas may be balanced by the public transit program that serves primarily urban areas.

To make this model work, not only must each of the key interests get something, but the benefits should be roughly even to each, or those receiving less are likely to protest. For example, a program to provide long-term home health care for the elderly was defeated in the House of Representatives at least in part because the elderly had just been given an expensive new program to protect them from the costs of catastrophic illness. Critics of the proposed home health care measure argued that the elderly were being greedy, that they had just had a turn, and that now other needy groups should get their turns.[11] Opposition to the home health care bill was framed in terms of an intergenerational split: the elderly were getting more benefits, while the young were actually losing theirs. Lobbyists for the elderly tried to redefine the situation to create the perception that care for the elderly helped the entire family (positive spillovers to everyone), not just the elderly. They argued that if family funds went to take care of the elderly, families would have less money to send young people to college.[12]

In the case of the elderly, less money for them does not automatically translate into more money for the young and the middle class; there is not an explicit agreement among supporters of these programs to balance the spending. Since the elderly have been so politically powerful, they have been able to get much of what they want without forming any coalitions. But among some competing interests, informal agreements to balance expenditures may emerge.

One example involves urban and rural interests and subsidies for agriculture. The politics of farm support has a geographic bias, since rural states are more likely to benefit directly, and more urban states are likely to pay the bill in higher food costs as well as higher tax bills. To offset this potential urban opposition to agricultural subsidies, advocates of agricultural subsidies have supported programs like food stamps, school lunch programs, and mass transit, which aid the poor and big cities.

When farm subsidies were being reconsidered by the budget committees in Congress in 1990, advocates of continued subsidies testified at the hearings. Charles Rose, of North Carolina, chairman of the Agriculture Subcommittee on Tobacco and Peanuts, argued not very subtly that he expected loyalty from representatives of large northern cities who had received his votes before:

Mr. Downey had a good time poking fun at wool and mohair and laughing about that and about the honey bee program. I would like for you and him to know that a lot of people I represent do not think subsidies for New York City and the Long Island Railroad and mass transportation up north are very funny, either, but we continue to vote for them and we continue to support them. . . .

I remember when Eddie Koch [later mayor of New York City] was here and he led the whole Congress against the farm bill. I believe he even beat major farm legislation . . . and then he turned right around and said everybody has to sign on in the bailout of New York City. I wrote Eddie Koch a letter, and I said I believe that must be what you call "chutzpah," Mr. Koch. I think that you need to know that the problems of this country extend beyond the Hudson River and the Long Island Railway. Do not ask us who represent the farms of America to come to your aid when you take cheap shots at us in the farm bill.[13]

Dan Glickman, representative from Kansas and chair of the Subcommittee on Wheat, Soybeans, and Feed Grains, of the Agriculture Committee, made a similar argument that sounded just short of a threat. "I have supported food stamps, urban programs . . . as have most of us. . . . I would hate to see a lot of programs jeopardized because of an attempt to drive a train through agriculture programs. That could happen. I am serious about that." [14]

Obfuscation, Invisible Decision Making, and Secrecy

Elected officials are sometimes so determined to get some particular item of expenditure into the budget that they are willing to defy what they perceive as likely public rejection of the choice, the beneficiaries, or the consequences of the spending; they do this through strategies of obfuscation or various levels of secrecy. Sometimes expenditures are taken off-budget, which not only makes them less visible but also reduces competition. Secrecy may hide the budgetary consequences of the actions elected officials want to take. Some modicum of secrecy may occasionally be necessary in budgeting, but it is a dangerous strategy in a democracy and easily abused. Budgets, which ought to be tools of public accountability, can become ways to hide public policies and their consequences from the public.

Complexity and Obfuscation. Sometimes legislators and other elected officials make programs so complex or processes so arcane that it is difficult if not impossible to figure out what is going on. Some of this complexity is not intentional, but some unknown portion probably is by design. When the complexity is so extreme that it defeats the best efforts to figure out what decisions have been made, the result is a strategy of obfuscation.

One example of intentional obfuscation is the way baselines are used. Budgets are analyzed and presented in terms of baselines. A baseline is a standard against which increases or decreases can be measured, a way of comparing last year's budget or this year's budget with the proposal for next year. Baselines can be relatively simple and easy to understand or complex, and they can be implemented uniformly or inconsistently. Decision makers have a choice of baselines to use—for example, they can compare the next year's proposal with the proposed budget for the present year, or with last year's actual spending; or they can create a baseline called "continuing services," that is, how much it would cost next year to provide this year's level of services. Such a baseline includes inflation, subtracts out one-time expenses of the current year, and adds one-time expenses for the coming year. The proposed budget may be higher or lower than this baseline, telling citizens and elected officials not whether dollars will be increased or decreased, but whether service levels will be increased or cut.

The idea of a present services budget is clear and simple, but it is often used in a highly confusing manner. It is not only that an increase in dollars might be represented as a decrease in base and hence a cut, which some people find confusing, but that the base itself is not consistently calculated or used. How inflation is calculated may vary from one agency to another, so one may be granted an automatic increase of 4 percent, to keep up with inflation, and another a much smaller amount. One program may be described in terms of last year's budget or actuals, while another agency is described in terms of a constant service budget.

In some governments, at some times, the base is calculated with an automatic reduction included. For example, salary increases may be estimated on a base that consists of last year's salary figure minus 5 percent to 10 percent. The amount of the reduction varies from year to year. The idea is that when there is employee turnover, some savings can be squeezed from the personnel budget when there are vacancies or by hiring junior people to replace senior ones who have retired. The problem is that the base figure is not necessarily linked to the actual amount of turnover or the dollars saved by not filling some positions. In some years the base calculation forces an agency to leave positions unfilled to create savings to fund salary increases. How much money has to be saved from unfilled positions varies from agency to agency. Typically, these cuts are not discussed, and their impact is not measured. They are just endured.

A second way of obscuring policies behind budget choices is to make program designs so complex it is difficult to figure out not only how they work, but who

Minicase: Calculating the Base in St. Paul, 2005

The budget for the city of St. Paul, Minnesota, describes how that city calculated its base budget for the 2005 fiscal year.[1] Actual allocations would be compared to this base. Note that the base includes cuts and would be different for 2005 than it would be for other years. The size of the base cut is not specified in this description, nor is it clear whether the base cut was across the board or was different for different departments. Finally, a change in which expenditures were attributed to the departments was put into effect, which would make the base look bigger for 2005 than for 2004, when in fact it might be the same or less.

Some budget scholars have maintained that elected officials only pay attention to additions or deletions from the base, however calculated, but sometimes there are additions or deletions in the base itself, which are nearly invisible. How much was the base cut in each department or program? Given the following presentation, it is difficult, if not impossible, to know:

> The 2004 adopted budget was adjusted to set the budget base for the year 2005. The actual 2004 salary rates were implemented and the cost of one pay day was removed because 2004 was a leap year, with one extra work day. The base includes the planned salaries and growth in fringes for 2005 for employees related to the bargaining process, and a small 2% growth for normal inflation on goods and services. The budget base also reflects the city-wide policy decision to alter the way the costs of workers' compensation are accounted for: moving away from an indirect allocation method and to a direct charge approach recording each department's costs in their own department budget. So, a separate line item budget for workers' compensation was included in specific department activity base budgets. Finally, one-time 2004 spending amounts were removed from the budget base and a spending reduction was imposed on the department's adjusted general fund budget to help control city general fund spending, and meet the third round of announced cutbacks in the State's 2005 local government aid funding.

1. Available at www.ci.stpaul.mn.us/mayor/05budget /AdoptedSummaryBook.pdf.

benefits from them. When the beneficiaries are ones the public might not approve of if they knew about them, observers might suspect that the complexity is intentional. Consider for example the following excerpt from the *Congressional Record*, in which Rep. Nick Smith, R-Mich., was objecting to the amount of farm program money going to large agribusinesses rather than family farmers. Smith suggests that the American public was duped by the complexity of the program into believing that its benefits were not disproportionately going to large agribusinesses:

> One concern that I have that has been in a lot of the media and newspapers is the generosity of the farm bill that was passed in terms of giving million-dollar payments to many of the very, very large farmers in the United States. I met with Senator Grassley last week, and we are trying to strategize how we can change that farm bill so that we have some kind of a cap, some kind of a limit on those exceptionally large million-dollar-plus payments that are going to the super-large landowners in this country. We are looking now at the appropriation bills and language we might put in the appropriation bills.
>
> Very briefly, Mr. Speaker, this is somewhat complicated, so we have sort of hoodwinked a lot of the American people saying, there are limits on the price support that farmers can receive. But there is a loophole. That loophole is called "generic certificates," and that means that when you reach the limit on monetary price supports, you can still forfeit the grain back to the government, and the government will give you a certificate that a farmer can exchange for money, because the limits are on cash payments to farmers and certificates are not considered a cash payment. That ends up being a loophole, allowing the very large farmers to get millions of dollars in price support benefits.
>
> ... I am in hopes there can be a better understanding by the American people, by this Congress, of what the loophole is; and that it is reasonable to set limits on price support payments. Our public policy should be to help and hopefully strengthen the traditional family farm in this country. That family farm might be 500 or 5,000 acres, but it is not the 80,000-acre farms.[15]

It is not only program structure that can be so arcane that no one but an expert can figure it out, but also financial deals. Although most state and local programs are reasonably clear and easy to understand, elected officials sometimes create such complex financial deals that it is difficult to know where the money is coming from or how much is being spent. Consider, for example, the arrangement worked out by New York City and New York State to pay off the bonds that New York City issued to survive its fiscal meltdown in the 1970s. Its complexity may not have been intended to deceive the public, but it certainly got around the rules, and its content would have been widely criticized if it had been more transparent.

By 2004, New York City still owed about $2 billion that traced back to its mid-1970s fiscal crisis; the money was payable over four remaining years of the debt. Now, however, the $2 billion will become about $5 billion, payable by the state instead of the city, over a thirty-year period.

To sell the bonds in the 1970s, an entity was created called the Municipal Assistance Corporation (MAC), and the city owed it the money it had borrowed. In 1991, a new entity was created, the Local Government Assistance Corporation (LGAC), which was intended to help the city borrow long term, to avoid annual, short-term spring borrowing at high interest rates. This debt was to be repaid by dedicated funds, consisting of the first percentage point of the state's sales tax. Those dedicated funds are much more than the amount needed to pay off the interest and principal on the LGAC bonds, so the rest of the money ends up in the regular state budget. The mayor of New York found a way to tap into that fund to help pay off the MAC loans from the 1970s, with support from New York State legislators. The city will get $170 million a year from the LGAC sales tax fund. "The mayor in turn will assign this money to an all-new entity (the Sales Tax Asset Receivable Corp., STARC), which will use whatever it needs to issue bonds to pay off the MAC debt. Anything STARC doesn't need will be returned to the city budget, creating the very real possibility that the city will actually make money on the deal." [16] While the use of the funds in this fashion is not illegal, it is expensive, and so complex that few people are likely to understand how much is being spent by whom for what. A simpler deal, in which the state merely assumed the city's debt, might not have passed the legislature or withstood the governor's veto.

When financial deals involve multiple units of government and oral agreements carried out over years, they can be nearly impossible to track and describe, let alone understood by the public. At the local level, the cost of subsidies to bring in businesses can be obscured in a variety of ways, one of which is to use complex financing schemes that look free, enabling elected officials to make whatever deals they wish at whatever cost they come up with, with little scrutiny or opposition.

Reconstructing the events in one city concerning paying for a highway exit illustrates the complexity that can occur: A mayor agreed with a highway authority to pay for an exit to the city near a parcel of land that was to be developed. The cost was nearly $3 million, but the revenue was to be produced by the developed parcel, so it looked free. The development never materialized, and the city was stuck with the bill, which if publicized would have made the costs of development suddenly very public. The city did not have the money and would have to borrow it. Instead, it made a deal with the county, which had the cash to pay off the bill the city owed to the toll authority. The city and county agreed that the city would not contest a tax-sharing deal between the city and the county on a piece of property the county owned. By entering into this agreement, the city was pledging revenue over an indefinite period of time to pay back a one-time debt. The amount the city would actually pay was unknown and unknowable, but it would certainly eventually exceed the size of the debt it owed initially to the tollway authority and later to the county. What makes the deal more ambiguous is that it is not clear whether the city, had it contested the tax-sharing deal, would have won and been able to keep all the future revenue from certain parcels for itself. Was this a good deal for the city? Nobody knows. It may well be that some of the costs, if not all of them, were transferred from the city to the county, but they still had to be paid, and by many of the same taxpayers, as the city constituted a substantial portion of the population of the county. What is clear is that the costs of the original, failed economic development project were buried so deeply that no one could track them with accuracy.[17]

Invisible Decision Making, Secret Budgets. Most budgetary decision making takes place in public view, but not all of it, and not all the time. Sometimes controversial decisions are made out of public view, behind closed doors, where they are not open to scrutiny, objection, or modification and compromise.

Perhaps the epitome of invisible decision making in budgeting is the Defense Department's "black budget," the portion of defense spending that is classified. It includes the budgets of most of the Central Intelligence Agency and all of the National Security Agency and the National Reconnaissance Office. It pays for secret wars and secret police, at the discretion of the president. Although there are undoubtedly some legitimate national secrets in the black budget, during the 1980s it expanded to include controversial weapons systems and by extension the policies that drive their invention and intended deployment.

From 1981, the beginning of the Reagan administration, to 1985, the Pentagon budget doubled, but the secret portion for weapons increased eightfold.[18] During that period there was no outside scrutiny of secret spending, not by the General Accounting Office and not by the Pentagon's own auditors.

After the GAO was allowed in, it discovered that the air force and navy refused to tell "their civilian overseers about new black programs they . . . created." [19] The military had created hundreds of unauthorized programs during the 1980s. The lack of oversight suggested not only that civilians had lost control of the military but also that the quality of management might be worse in the secret portion of the defense budget than it was in the overt part. Secrecy made it possible to hide mistakes and made economizing unnecessary.

Congress began to try to take control of the black budget in 1986. Procurement horror stories in the regular Defense Department budget made many wonder about the waste that might be occurring out of sight. Congressman John Dingell, who chaired the Subcommittee on Oversight and Investigations, of the House Committee on Energy and Commerce, spearheaded the effort; also important was Les Aspin, who took over the House Armed Services Committee and was the first chair in many years who was willing to question what the generals asked for. Dingell asked the secretary of defense for a list of Air Force black programs over $10 million; the secretary ignored the request. Then Representative Aspin and the ranking minority member of the House Armed Services Committee, writing for the committee, argued with the secretary that too many defense programs were being put into the black budget and that the budget numbers for the Stealth Bomber and the Advanced Cruise Missile should be released. The secretary did not release the figures. In the face of this intransigence, Congress passed a law the following year requiring the Defense Department to reveal the information. The information was not revealed until 1989, by which time much of the weapons research had been completed.[20]

By 1989, the black budget reached a peaked of about $36 billion a year. The declassification of the Stealth Bomber and MILSTAR, a complex computerized communication and coordination project to run a nuclear war, brought the black budget down to $34 billion by 1991.[21] In 1992 the secret satellite program was made visible; its budget was about $6 billion.[22] Though technically still part of the secret budget, the satellite program was open to financial oversight. By 1995, newspapers were estimating the size of the black budget at about $28 billion.[23] In 1997 the CIA reported, as the result of a freedom of information lawsuit, that the black budget totaled $26.6 billion.

Looking at only one portion of the black budget from 1987 to 2005, analyst Steven Kosiak found that the trend toward lower black budget expenditures for procurement and for research and development had reversed since they reached a low in 1995. By 2005 this component of black budget expenditures reached over $26 billion. Kosiak noted "In real (inflation-adjusted) terms the $26.1 billion FY 2005 request includes more classified acquisition funding than any other defense budget since FY 1988, near the end of the Cold War, when DoD received $19.7 billion ($27.3 billion in FY 2005 dollars) for these programs." He also noted that classified acquisitions funding had nearly doubled since 1995.[24]

Estimates of the costs of intelligence gathering or the total black budget remain approximate because the government has not released the figures since 1998.[25] A recent estimate is about $40 billion, up from $26.7 billion in 1997.

Kosiak argued that while some classified acquisitions programs have been successful, others have had a troubled history, with performance problems and cost increases that he attributes in part to lack of sufficient congressional oversight. If officials can get a favored project or policy into the black budget, it will then be subject to little or no competition or scrutiny. The public and the press cannot be told about it, and those who might oppose the project if they knew about it are typically never told. If a project is included in the black budget, it may never come to a direct vote in Congress. As a result it is tempting to put controversial projects that Congress might reject, and that would anger allies and provoke enemies, into the black budget. This strategy may be engaged in by either elected officials or by political appointees.

The national government and the Defense Department rationalize making some expenditures unavailable for public scrutiny on the sometimes questionable basis of national defense, but state and local governments have to come up with other, even more questionable arguments for doing so. A recent episode at the state level suggests that sometimes the motivation may simply be to give legislators freedom to spend without accountability. If expenditures can be kept secret, legislators can spend what they want and not have to persuade others that the expenses are legitimate.

In 2001, the *Pittsburgh Tribune-Review* reported that legislators' spending on themselves and on running their offices was not being shared with the public. "[T]he information that is available is difficult to access and interpret, and there is little oversight to ensure the money is spent properly." Furthermore, the newspaper reported, "Internal guidelines are lax, secrecy guards the details of most House expenses and an annual audit doesn't examine the propriety of expenses. The Legislature also is off-limits to the auditor general, the state's fiscal watchdog." [26]

The justification given for not making the expense reports public was that "the reports are personal." Another was that the documents were just internal spreadsheets, working data, and hence should not be made public. One legislator argued that lawmakers should not have to show receipts for how they spend the money.

When the newspaper spent six months investigating who received how much expense money and how they spent it, they found some embarrassing results. For example, one legislator charged per diems for days the legislature was not in session, and others took trips to Germany, San Diego, San Francisco, and St. Petersburg, Florida. While the legislators might have been able to justify these trips, they were never required to do so. What is equally interesting is that although

Minicase: Black Project Failure—The A-12 Navy Fighter Plane

Many projects in the black budget work out well, but darkness encourages all kinds of misbehavior. The A-12 navy fighter plane, located in the black portion of the budget, was an acquisitions disaster, costing billions of dollars without producing a single plane. The program was scuttled completely in the early 1990s, but lawsuits continued on throughout the decade.

Many things went wrong with this project or were done incorrectly or illegally. For example, the so-called stealth technology needed for the plane was not ready; the air force, which had more experience with the new technology and materials, didn't share its knowledge with the navy, which had to reinvent it; the original mandate from Congress that the airplane be bought by the navy, air force, and marines was ignored, as the air force and marines backed out of the deal, increasing the price per plane.

The navy didn't have the funds necessary for the contract, so it offered a fixed-price contract with a ceiling on the bids. Two out of the three bidders refused to bid under these conditions because of the high risk of unknown technology. With only one potential bidder, the navy would have to go to a sole-source contract, which meant that it would have to pay on a cost reimbursement basis, which is more expensive than a competitive bid for a fixed-price contract. "In the face of this dilemma, Navy procurement leadership realized that with the entire program then 'black,' no one (not even superiors in DoD) would need to be told that there was, in fact, no competition for the program and that, among the three potential teams, only the team that believed erroneously that the program could be accomplished under the required terms was willing to bid. To carry this off, Northrop would be told that it was a viable competitor and would be kept in the 'bidding.' "[1] In a second highly questionable action, the navy let the contract without having sufficient funds to pay for it.

One of the attorneys working for the contractors later described another problem: the plane would be overweight. "Regulations required that the Navy report to DoD that the aircraft would not meet its weight threshold. DoD, in turn, was then required to disclose these facts to Congress. Because it would have put congressional support for the program at risk, no such disclosure was made. Instead, the Deputy Chief of Naval Operations for Air Warfare told the Naval Air Systems Command to proceed with the program and report the overweight condition only when it became a reality."[2]

Presumably most if not all of these problems would have been caught— the lack of viable technology, the lack of competition for the price the navy

(continued)

> could afford, and the letting of the bid with inadequate funding—if the program had been in the open rather than the secret portion of the budget. Ultimately the program was terminated by DoD, not because of these problems but because its budget was being cut back, and a plane designed for a situation that no longer existed apparently had lower priority than some other projects at the time. In times of budget cutback, it turns out, there is competition even within the black budget.
>
> 1. Herbert L. Fenster, "The A-12 Legacy, It Wasn't an Airplane—It Was a Train Wreck," *Proceedings,* February 1999, U.S. Naval Institute, Annapolis, Md., www.usni.org/Proceedings/Articles99/PROfenster.htm.
> 2. Ibid.

spending reports are compiled by each house of the legislature for the use of its members, the numbers that are released are not aggregated. In other words, in response to queries administrators release a mass of details that are difficult to put together to form any kind of picture, forcing anyone who wants to know to spend months of painstaking effort, even though a summary report exists and could, in theory, be released. Burying information in a mass of details is one way of keeping information from public view.

Another way is to contract for services. There can be many good reasons for contracting out rather than providing services with public sector employees, but one consequence of contracting is that information that would be provided if public sector workers produced the services vanishes. Sometimes only the total for the contract is reported, and often not even that much appears in the budget. A number of contracts may be lumped together and reported as a total for contractual services. It may no longer be possible for the public to see what services were purchased, at what costs, and with what quality requirements. If an elected official wants to spend money on favored constituents by awarding them profitable contracts, there is often little oversight to ensure that the public gets its money's worth or to guarantee that the contract is the best way to spend public money. For some elected officials, contracting out is a strategy to reduce oversight and conflict when a project would not otherwise pass muster. It can also be a way of locking in policy preferences over a fairly long period of time. These issues arise at all levels of government.

The costs of contracts may be obscured, but equally important, the decision making may also be done off-stage. The result can be noncompetitive contracts, so called no-bid contracts, awarded to one favored company. Even the number of such contracts can be difficult to track. The federal government, which used to keep a record of contracts that was open to the public, contracted out the record keeping. The contractor is charging a substantial fee for using the database, making it less accessible to citizens, reporters, or academics who might want to track no-bid contracts. Information about contracts may not be available at all in some state and local governments. Overly expensive contracts may become exposed only if they are flagrantly illegal or the services they provide are so far below expectations that the recipients who are able to complain do so in a public fashion.

Contract failures sometimes stimulate reforms to make the contracting process and costs more visible. For example, in Wisconsin, two widely publicized contract controversies have precipitated proposals for opening up the contracting process by requiring bidders to register in the same way that lobbyists do. In one, the State Elections Board is facing a lawsuit challenging the way it entered into a $9.7 million contract to build a statewide voter registration list. The chief executive of the Elections Board signed a contract himself, without consulting the rest of the board as the law requires. The process was challenged by state employee labor unions, which claimed that they could have done the work for less money and that doing the work with public employees was not considered. The decision was also challenged by one of the losing bidders, who was rejected on the basis of qualifications, namely lack of experience with a database the size of the one Wisconsin was putting together. The plaintiffs claimed that the deal was secret and therefore violated state open records laws.[27]

Contracting out often involves the same three interested and contesting parties: the elected or appointed official who wants to award the contract to a particular contractor; public unions, which react to the loss of possible jobs; and disappointed bidders who wonder at the whole process. Sometimes contention among these three groups makes a particular contract more visible or raises the issue of transparency more broadly.

In the voting database case, the issue was that the decision was made behind closed doors. In the second case, which involved the Wisconsin Department of Transportation, the issue was no-bid contracts with high price tags. A contract to build a basic Web site was reported to cost $685,000. Not only did the agency make questionable decisions to award the contract to a particular company, but when called on to examine that decision making, it stonewalled, delaying the release of a report on the subject, a step that was not legal under the state's open records law.

While Wisconsin is considering reforms to curtail the possible damage from contracting by making the bidders more public, the city of Chicago has responded to contracting scandals by increasing the amount of sunshine on the contracts as well as the contractors. The fact that the reforms included opening the contracts to public scrutiny suggests that the mayor believes that sunshine will help prevent corruption and, conversely, that secrecy fosters it, allows it to grow and fester. In a highly unusual move, Chicago has put up on its Web site a complete list of recent contracts by year, not only describing the amounts involved but also linking the contracts to a file with the contract in it. Thus all the details of the contracts are public and easily and freely accessible. The mayor has called on the press to help him clean up the contracting scandals, a further indication that he believes that openness is the best defense and preventive measure. Both the Chicago and Wisconsin cases indicate that the amount of secrecy can vary within the same jurisdiction over time and that there is a pattern in which excessive secrecy fosters corruption, which eventually becomes so flagrant and embarrassing that it generates pressure for more openness.

Like contracting, loans, loan guarantees, and subsidies are sometimes completely invisible to the public, although the federal government, through credit reform, has improved public reporting on their real costs. Because loans look free, as they are usually paid back in full, they may not appear in the budget at all. It is at least theoretically possible to put loans in the budget, but loan guarantees, which are only contingent obligations, to be paid only in case of default, are conceptually difficult. A loan guarantee is not the same thing as either a loan or an expenditure and probably should not be mixed in with other expenditures, but ignoring loan guarantees misleads legislators and the public about possible future costs. Loan subsidies—that is, the degree to which the government's lending rate of interest is below the market cost—can be estimated, but as these are not direct costs to the government, they are typically excluded from budgets.

Various other kinds of subsidies may also escape budgetary treatment, such as waiving fees for a new development, sharing future sales tax revenues with a new commercial business, or land writedowns. In the latter a government unit acquires land, often using eminent domain to get a property at a lower cost than the private sector could do, then pieces parcels together to greatly enhance their value, and resells the now-enhanced property to a business for much less than it would have cost the business to get that property on its own. Because these expenditures often do not appear in the budget, they seem free, and hence one strategy of elected officials who wish to subsidize various businesses is to use these loans, guarantees, and subsidies.

Loans, loan guarantees, and subsidies are difficult to represent accurately in a budget, so not reporting on them isn't necessarily intentional concealment, but there can be little question about intent when a whole program is removed from the budget. At the federal level, the strategy of taking programs out of the budget led to an odd outcome in the 1970s and 1980s. Congress took the Export-Import Bank off-budget in 1971, making it more or less disappear, and restored it to on-budget status in 1976. Section 202 Housing for the Elderly and Handicapped was taken off-budget in 1974 and restored to budget status in 1978; the Strategic Petroleum Reserve program was declared off-budget in 1981 but restored to on-budget status, along with every other off-budget program other than Social Security, in 1985, by the Deficit Reduction Act (Gramm-Rudman-Hollings).[28] The result was a sort of peekaboo effect: Now you see it, now you don't, now you see it again.

Program supporters try to take a program off-budget when they think they will be more successful in spending money that way. Most legislative efforts to take programs off-budget fail (see Minicase, page 181), but some programs are defined administratively (as opposed to legislatively) as independent and are not considered part of the budget, such as the Postal Service and Federal Reserve System.

The pressure to take programs off-budget receded when the Budget Enforcement Act, with its caps on total spending, was allowed to lapse. However President's Bush's 2005 budget proposal promises to reduce the enormous deficit built up during his administration and asks for restoration of spending caps and constraints on entitlement growth. If his requested process changes take effect, they will intensify competition over federal spending and may reinvigorate efforts to take programs off-budget to protect them from cuts.

State and local governments do not use the off-budget mechanism in the same way as the federal government, but the issue of scope—what is and what is not reported in a consolidated budget—is as important at the state and local levels as at the national level. For example, for many years, grants from other levels of government were often budgeted and reported separately from the main budget, as they were often not technically in competition with other spending. The result was a kind of shadow budget, often controlled more by the executive, rather than jointly controlled by the executive and legislative branches.

Among the negative consequences of taking programs off-budget and shadow budgets is that the reported spending totals and the totals for different functional areas of the budget become misleading.

The Environment Can Affect Spending Priorities

A change in the environment can overwhelm all strategies, temporarily reducing the scope of activity of individual budget actors. Or it can create a situation in which policy mandates are clear and urgent.

Minicase: The Aviation Trust Fund

Not every effort to take a program off-budget is successful, but even the unsuccessful efforts demonstrate how the strategy is supposed to work. In 1999, when the Budget Enforcement Act was still in effect, supporters of the Aviation Trust Fund put forth legislation (H.R. 1000) to take the fund off-budget. This legislation passed the House of Representatives. Had it been successful, the strategy would have meant that the trust fund was exempt from spending ceilings, as well as other budgeting rules, and it would have a lower level of presidential and legislative scrutiny:

> Advocates of the proposal to move aviation spending off budget argue that this special privilege would protect the tax revenues generated by the airline industry and airline passengers from being diverted to non-aviation spending, tax relief, or debt reduction. And because none of the existing congressional spending limitation efforts and mechanisms apply to off-budget spending, this privilege also would allow Congress to raise future aviation spending substantially above levels that would be permitted for such other, unprotected programs as national security, health care, and law enforcement.[1]

Because the legislation built in escalating funding levels for five years, not only would legislative scrutiny be less each year, but the incentive to improve management to get more funding would be nil.

1. Ronald D. Utt and Gregg Van Helmond, "Moving Aviation Trust Fund Off Budget Undermines the Budget Process," Heritage Foundation, Backgrounder #1305, July 9, 1999.

The environment can change in a variety of ways. There can be natural disasters; there can be wars, cold or hot, and arms races; there can be elections and changes of policy resulting from the change of officeholders; and there can be a change in popular opinion, elevating some benefit programs to rights and demoting others from rights to formula-funded grants. In addition, the environment continually affects the politics of spending because it influences the level of resources and rate of growth of revenues, and because it influences the certainty that revenues will appear.

One major change in the environment that affects budget strategies is the difference between relative abundance and continuing growth, on the one hand, and ragged stability or revenue decline, on the other. Agencies can add new people with specialized skills or fancy equipment during growth; during decline, the existing staff have to do more different kinds of jobs, and new equipment may be nearly impossible to obtain. The model of incremental growth—making changes only at the margins and generally allocating revenue increases equally across the board—is premised on moderate, gradual, but continuous growth. If growth is more rapid or if there is no growth, this pattern is likely to be disrupted. Rapid growth in revenues may lead to a burst of planning and searches for new missions and programs; there may be an outreach to new potential interest groups or service beneficiaries; new needs may be documented and new programs designed. A change in the environment from rich to lean may mean the elimination of the increase in revenues from last year to this that is the focus of the internal actors' bargaining in the incremental model of politics. Budget processes are likely to become more centralized, subordinating the competition between individual actors to the achievement of collective goals. If there is a need to cut back departments and programs, then each department's budget may be at some risk, vastly increasing the scope of competition. Agency heads are more likely to use defensive strategies, such as linking current programs to politically valued ends, distorting program goals to make them look like they are within an approved policy set, and trying to reduce competition and lock in current spending levels.

Even governments that are reasonably well off financially may not be able to count on their revenues—the environment may be unstable, or revenue sources unpredictable. At all levels of government there may be reductions in budgets during the year if revenues were overestimated or if the economy declines unpredictably. Uncertainty can be introduced for state and local governments by changes in tax laws at other levels of government. Taxpayer revolts may change the amount of revenue that can be collected or redefine taxable wealth. As national economies are increasingly open to the world economy, changes in the price of oil or droughts in other parts of the world can have an impact on spending programs. If the price of fuel suddenly increases, then operating costs go up; if other countries purchase unforeseeably large amounts of grain, the cost of agricultural subsidies may suddenly go down.

When revenues become uncertain, spending behavior may change. Planning assumes long-term stability; with continual disruption and reallocation from project to project, planning makes little sense. The idea of being patient and giving up current programs or capital projects to someone else, with the assurance that you will succeed in the future, vanishes. Being at the top of the current list is all that counts. This pattern makes it difficult to save money for a large project, or to allocate one large project in one area one year and another large project somewhere else another year. Instead, the emphasis is likely to be on a number of smaller projects each year, even if none of them can solve real problems because they are too small. Also, one is not likely to break a larger project or program into parts, assuming that one part can be achieved this year and another next year; the later parts may never arrive, and the project may remain incomplete and useless.

Uncertain revenues also affect spending by encouraging higher-level executives to hold back on the budget, allocating a little at a time, so that there is uncommitted money to eliminate from the budget if cuts come suddenly. Requests for spending may pile up, generating a continuing competition between agencies to get portions of their budgets released.

In short, changes in the environment can override other considerations. They may directly impose policy mandates that cancel out other kinds of politics; thus a war, or a warlike peace, may impose defense spending. Or environmental changes may make policy directions clearer, as in a change in the political party in power or a major transformation of public opinion. Such a shift may be the result of urban uprisings, which have spurred increases in police spending, or of changes in the balance of trade, which may generate a variety of policies. Changes in the environment may alter the budget process and thereby budget strategies. Changes in revenue levels are likely to affect the politics of spending as well.

Analysis: Accountability and Acceptability

The separation between those who pay taxes and those who make the decisions about how those taxes should be spent introduces the concepts of accountability and acceptability. "Accountability" means transparency to the taxpayers about what budget decisions have been made; "acceptability" means that whatever decisions are made should not stir up too much public opposition. In some circumstances, accountability and acceptability go together; in others they are clashing opposites.

For example, if elected officials' spending decisions agree with the opinions of the majority of citizens, as when a service clearly benefits everyone, then accountability and acceptability go together. The decision is acceptable and can be openly arrived at and be highly visible. But if spending decisions favor only one small group, and the majority of citizens would not approve the expenditures if given the choice, then accountability and acceptability may be opposites—to gain acceptability may mean obscuring what the decisions were or how much they cost.

Spending decisions at some level have to gain public support, or at least acquiescence. That may mean providing services that nearly everyone wants, and no others; or it may mean trying to deliver programs to smaller or more targeted groups and either convincing the whole public to go along, or offering other programs to the people who do not directly benefit. When neither of these options seems to work, then supporters may represent the costs as low or free, and hence not important, or obscure the costs in a variety of ways so that they do not rouse too much opposition. If program supporters feel that their programs will lose out in a tight competition—because of the need to reduce deficits, or lower taxes, or because of a decline in revenues due to a recession—they may choose strategies that reduce competition or make costs less visible.

The amount of transparency or complexity, visibility or secrecy, in the budget process and outcomes is not fixed; it changes over time. If politicians are elected on a platform that benefits narrow constituencies, that not everyone would approve of if they knew, there may be an upswing in secrecy and obscurantism. The public may be charged for information, or information may be released in highly disaggregated fashion, requiring weeks or months to sift through for meaning and context. But black budgets and opaque spots invite the press to make the effort to find out what is going on; hidden budgets invite abuses which eventually become embarrassingly public. Scandals create pressure to restore openness and let the sun shine in.

Summary and Conclusions

In the public sector, because of the wide variety of budget actors and the variety of their preferences, the amount of competition underlying the budget is necessarily high. The chief executive and his or her staff, the department heads, and legislators and their staffs all play a role in formulating or approving proposals for expenditures. A variety of interest groups may lobby for particular expenditures, and the public at large may have marked preferences about what government should and should not spend money on. The level of competition may be exaggerated or reduced by changes in the environment and in the budget process. The budget process frames choices and hence determines what expenditure proposals compete with one another.

When programs or departments are forced to compete with one another for resources, they develop a variety of strategies to improve the priority of their spending goals. In the capital budget, project supporters may argue that the technical requirements for some project absolutely require this expense immediately; or they may argue that delay will only increase the cost. In the operating budget, program supporters may argue the political consequences of failure to provide a popular service, or they may try to link their programs to widely accepted policy goals.

Competition in some parts of the budget and under some budget processes may be so keen that the actors, rather than try to compete successfully, switch to strategies to reduce the level of conflict. They do this in a variety of ways. In the capital budget, competition can be defused through the use of a long-term plan; projects not funded this year can be kept alive and possibly funded later. There are winners but no absolute losers. In the service portion of the budget, competition may be defused by norms forbidding sudden termination or deep cutbacks in one program to build another. Change occurs in small amounts at the margins, limiting the scope of competition. In trust funds and enterprises, competition is defused by taking revenues and expenditures out of the general fund, isolating them from potential trade-offs. For some programs, competition is defused by setting them up as entitlements, distributing funds by formula, or imposing particular expenditures by mandates. One cannot understand these adaptations and the direction of change without appreciating the intensity of competition that underlies them.

The direction of change over the past fifty years has been to lock up more and more of budgets, to take programs and projects out of the competition for funds. There has been an increase in the use of trust funds and, especially dramatically at the national level, in the use of entitlements. At the local level, services that charge fees have been increasingly segregated from the municipal budget, and in some states have been set up as special, single-purpose governmental units. Contractors may push for long-term, sole-source contracts, to lock in spending for capital projects; coalitions of interest groups, legislators, and bureaucrats may, when the environment favors them, push to lock their programs into the budget for as long a period as they can manage.

The result of the changing composition of the budget is that budgets may now look more interest group dominated, and it may be difficult to perceive competition over the short term. But trying to lock in expenditures at the peak of one's power is part of budgetary politics; if anything, it underscores the waxing and waning of interest group influence and the responsiveness of expenditures to outside contingencies. Coalitions of support for a particular program may peak at some point, and at that point supporters try to lock in the program through a trust fund structure or an entitlement. The coalition may not be able to stay together after that, or the environmental conditions that made the program seem desirable may disappear. But if the coalition was successful in locking in the program or project, it will survive future changes in environmental conditions.

The process of locking up expenditure decisions and reducing budgetary competition is not permanent and one-directional. There are major pressures in the opposite direction—to reduce or weaken entitlements, to borrow from public enterprises or use their revenues for other purposes, to use trust funds for other purposes, or use general funds to pay for programs that have trust funds. But the time required to unlock expenditures may be relatively long. Politicians find it extremely difficult to terminate entitlements that are popular with a broad segment of the public. If over a long period that support erodes, politicians may be able to change programs from entitlements to block grants, making them easier to cut. It took many years and a massive reduction in the number of family farms before cuts in the agriculture support programs became acceptable. Efforts to break into trust funds may take years but have sometimes been successful.

Handling competition is one key theme in the politics of expenditures; the second one is managing accountability and acceptability to the taxpaying public. Budget choices do not depend only on what the budget actors want and can get from one another; they are constrained by the preferences of the public that pays the taxes. Accountability and acceptability are handled differently depending on how popular particular expenditures are and what techniques are used to gain support for less-popular programs.

The delivery of services that benefit citizens broadly is generally publicly acceptable, and the costs are open and clear. In situations in which benefits are targeted at a narrower group, and when costs can be pinpointed, program supporters may offer their support to other groups to help them get their programs, so as to widen their support base. Thus supporters of agricultural subsidies to rural areas supported school lunch programs for the urban poor. Coalitions of support may be engineered among various interests. Spending under these conditions may occasionally be controversial, but the strategy generally works. In areas of spending where individual groups or geographic areas benefit, without any apparent trades of support, the costs may be deeply submerged or invisible. Controversial issues may be kept off the policy agenda.

The politics of expenditures is not dominated by the motives and strategies of a limited set of actors. Instead, varying groups of actors, with strategies framed by the budget process and the environment, strive to achieve their goals. Elected officials who make budgetary decisions are ultimately accountable to the public; the need to gain public acceptance of spending decisions influences the openness of spending, the geographic distribution of beneficiaries of spending, and the formation of coalitions among rivals for spending. The result is simultaneously highly competitive and highly constrained, open to the environment and accountable, more or less, to the public.

6. The Politics of Balancing the Budget

We still need to constrain the deficit. We still need ways to impose budgetary discipline. . . . Gramm-Rudman has accomplished neither reduction nor restraint. . . . the time has come for something more effective.
—Sen. Jim Sasser

The most important constraint on budgeting is the requirement for balance: revenues must equal or exceed expenditures. Balancing is a key part of budgetary decision making, but it is not always successful. Both raising revenue and cutting expenditures are politically difficult, and granting tax breaks is politically tempting. As a result, the definition of balance may be loose, applying only to some portions of the budget or only to the proposed and not the approved budget. Or budgets may look balanced but not really be balanced, for example, if borrowing is allowed.

Even if budgets are truly balanced at the beginning of the budget year, they may become unbalanced during the year. This may occur by accident, if revenue projections were not good enough or if some expenditures were unintentionally underestimated. But governments sometimes run deficits intentionally. There may be an emergency—a war or a natural disaster—that requires spending whether budgeted or not. Especially at the national level, and to a lesser extent at the state level, governments can run deficits to moderate negative trends in the economy or to maintain spending for unemployment benefits and welfare during a recession. Governments at all levels can also run deficits because the budget actors are unwilling to make difficult choices.

When deficits are caused by emergencies or by declines in the economy, the borrowing required to cover them is temporary and is not usually particularly harmful. Budgets have to be flexible and responsive to the environment, and some borrowing may be necessary to that end. But sometimes deficits occur because revenues are growing more slowly than expenditures and decision makers are unwilling to make politically difficult choices. Or, as in recent years, elected officials may be so bent on reducing taxes that they ignore the resulting deficits, at least for a while. This kind of deficit spending is attributable to a lack of discipline or a lack of will. The proposed solution for growing deficits is often new budget processes and more rigid budgetary constraints.

Although the decisions that have to be made to reduce or eliminate deficits may be politically unpopular, the solution of ignoring hard decisions and running deficits is not popular either. Both the public and the financial community oppose deficits. After the federal budget was balanced in the late 1990s, public concern with deficits naturally fell off, but it reawakened with the resurgence of massive deficits in the George W. Bush administration. "[A]lthough deficits have not been a paramount political issue during recent years, a recent survey by the Pew Research Center found that 56 percent of voters now identify the budget deficit as a 'top priority,' up from 51 percent a year ago and from 35 percent three years ago." [1] These figures are a bit lower than they were in the mid 1990s, when nearly two-thirds opposed the deficits and thought them a top priority, but the numbers are climbing.

Because deficits are publicly disapproved, they are politically embarrassing, especially for conservative governments that promised to keep spending and deficits in line. Consequently when governments run chronic deficits, those responsible for them tend to deny them or minimize their size and importance. For example, the Bush administration has routinely omitted the costs of the war in Iraq and Afghanistan from annual budget estimates and hence has underestimated the deficit by approximately $80 billion in each of the past few years. Also, the deficit is usually presented including the Social Security surplus, which is misleading because Social Security is off-budget and its surplus cannot be used to defray the deficit. The quality of the budget numbers suffers under these circumstances, and it can be extremely difficult to figure out the real size of the deficits.

By the time those in charge of the budget decide to act, the deficit may be very large and proportionately difficult to cut back. Whose programs should be cut back, and by how much? Where can cuts legally be made? How can resistance from interest groups be minimized? Whose taxes should be raised, and by how much? Can expenditures be shifted to other levels of government to reduce the size of the deficit? How can the appropriate actions be taken while maintaining accountability and acceptability to the public? How can politicians make such unpopular choices and still maintain their support base?

The politics of budget balance revolves around how and why budgets become unbalanced, as well as how to rebalance them. In exploring this decision stream it may help to return first to the characteristics of public budgeting outlined in chapter 1: This decision stream is marked by constraints, and the requirement of balance is itself a constraint; the politics of balance involves multiple actors with different budgetary goals; budgets are open to the environment, which requires a certain amount of flexibility; and deficit politics has to resolve the separation of taxpayer and budget decision maker through techniques of accountability and acceptability.

Balance as a Constraint

Governments define what "balance" means, at times making the constraints looser or tighter. Balance may include or exclude savings from prior years. The requirement for balance may cover all funds or only some of them. The balance constraint is eased if surpluses from one fund can be used to defray shortages in another fund. Some governments allow the budget to be balanced with borrowed money, drastically loosening the balance constraint. Another way that the constraint of balance can be loosened or tightened is to change the point at which the budget must be balanced: when the executive proposes it, when the legislature passes it, or at the end of the year. For example, in some states, such as Pennsylvania and New York, the governor is required to present a balanced budget to the legislature; after that, anything can happen. In forty states the legislature is required to pass a balanced budget, but twelve do not have a requirement that forbids carrying over deficits into the next fiscal year, so deficits can occur during the year, after the legislature has passed the budget. California used to have one of the looser requirements for balance. Until recently, the governor had to propose a balanced budget, but the legislature was not required to pass a balanced budget, and the state could pass a deficit forward into the next year. However, a referendum in 2004 changed the requirements, so that the legislature has to pass a balanced budget, midyear shortfalls have to be resolved midyear, and the state is forbidden to borrow to cover end-of-year shortfalls.[2]

Most of the time, balance is determined year by year, but sometimes balance occurs over several years. If all outstanding obligations were to be deducted from this year's revenue, the budget might not be balanced, but if those same obligations were matched against several years' anticipated revenues, that same budget might be balanced. The Federal Highway Trust Fund illustrates this somewhat looser definition of balance (see following box).

Regardless of how balance is initially defined, when officials do acknowledge deficits they often respond by increasing the number and severity of constraints as a way to restore balance. The additional constraints can vary from a moderate change in the budget process that makes the linkage between revenue and expenditure decisions tighter and more authoritative, to a change in statute making the requirements for balance more inclusive and more difficult to get around, to a change in the constitution narrowly specifying the conditions under which deficits may be run or forbidding deficits or borrowing to pay them off.

Multiple Actors, Ideologies, and Deficits

Who gets involved in the politics of balance, and how do these actors come down on the variety of policy issues involved in budget balancing?

The public plays an indirect role by putting pressure on elected officials to balance the budget. Citizens argue that their personal budgets have to balance, and hence governmental budgets should also balance. At the same time, citizens often want something for nothing, demanding lower taxes without cuts in their services or benefits. When elected officials comply with the demand for lower taxes and more services and programs, they create deficits; when the elected officials try to reduce or eliminate deficits, the need to give the impression of not raising taxes or cutting services leads to a variety of complex evasions, distortions, and distancing mechanisms. Acceptability often trumps accountability.

Interest groups may contribute to deficits by making it difficult to raise specific taxes or cut particular programs. When cuts are being proposed, interest groups may be vociferous in protecting programs that benefit them. But interest groups that represent narrow constituencies do not generally have distinct policies toward deficits (as opposed to policies toward maintaining the programs that benefit them) or play much of a policy role in the politics of deficits. Politicians sometimes use the requirement for balance as a vehicle for arguing about the appropriate size of government and level of taxation. These are issues that affect the rich and the poor differently, and thus class-based coalitions often take sides in debates on budgetary balance. A coalition of labor unions may oppose a coalition of business groups.

Minicase: Balance in the Federal Highway Trust Fund

The Highway Trust Fund is an account based primarily on user fees that is set aside for building and repairing the nation's highways. It operates through contract authority rather than more normal budget authority: when projects are finished, the states bill the federal government for reimbursement out of the Highway Trust Fund. As a result, a simple definition of balance (and surplus) is not possible for the Highway Trust Fund. That is, if the fund defined itself as balanced because its revenues this year were greater than its outlays this year, it would be misleading. Revenues have to be greater than obligations, not just greater than outlays, because the states are running up bills that they have not yet submitted for reimbursement. By next year there will be more money in the fund to pay off the bills that are being incurred now but that will not be presented until next year or the year after. So how can anyone tell if the trust fund is really balanced at any time? How can Congress or the president ensure that the states do not exceed revenues in their spending? And if there is a surplus, how does anyone know how much it is?

When money is committed by the states, it shows up in the trust fund as obligated but not yet spent. So the total in the fund remains high, although much of the money is already committed and cannot be spent on anything else. The result of not subtracting this committed money from the trust fund total is to make the balance in the fund look greater than it really is. This can help to make the federal budget as a whole look balanced, if the "surplus" in the Highway Trust Fund is counted as part of the consolidated balance of the federal government. But the result is misleading:

> In FY 1994, for example, the highway account showed future commitments of $42.6 billion. If these commitments had been charged against the balance in the highway account at that time, it actually would have shown a deficit. To guarantee the ability to make good on these commitments, Congress, through the Byrd amendment to the Federal-Aid Highway Act of 1956, as amended, restricted the growth of these commitments to a level not to exceed the current year's unexpended balance plus projected income for the following two fiscal years.[1]

The result does provide some protection against overspending, but it does not yield an exact figure for budgetary balance or an exact estimate of the surplus. To calculate a surplus in this situation, one has to subtract the actual obligations from the present and future revenues. The number is spongy, in part because until bills are actually presented for projects approved or under way, the exact amount is not known. Also, the calculation depends on estimates of revenues for the present and the next two years.

1. John W. Fischer, Congressional Research Service report for Congress, *Transportation Trust Funds: Budgetary Treatment,* Economics Division, updated April 6, 1998, 98–63 E.

Officials at different levels of government also become actors in the politics of deficits because of the possibility of one level of government's balancing its budget at the expense of other levels.

These actors take sides on at least four major policy issues in the politics of balance: the appropriate size of government, the role of the budget in the economy, the appropriate role of each level of government, and the outcomes, that is, whose taxes will be increased and whose programs will be cut, by how much and with what effect.

The Appropriate Size of Government

Budgets can be balanced by allowing revenues to increase; by freezing revenues at current levels and cutting expenditures to match; or by reducing revenues and cutting expenditures deeply to create balance at a new, lower level of spending. Allowing revenues to increase to reduce deficits is a fiscally conservative but socially more liberal position, without major implications for current program spending. Liberals hope to increase taxes on the rich to pay for programs for the poor. Achieving budget balance by deeply cutting programs is a more politically conservative position. Some conservatives press for cuts in taxes as a way to force cuts in expenditures, using the requirement of balance as a vehicle to reduce the scope of government. They hope to reduce the tax burden on the rich and simultaneously reduce services to the poor and dismantle regulations that hamper businesses and reduce profitability.

The Role of the Budget in the Economy

Should the budget be a tool of control over the economy to dampen economic swings, to control inflation and unemployment levels? Political liberals have accepted the need for deficits during recessions because the need to increase unemployment benefits and welfare spending occurs at the same time that government receipts decline as a result of falling incomes. Some conservatives oppose deficit spending as a technique to help stimulate the economy when it is weak. They prefer that the budget not be responsive to economic cycles at all and argue that expenditures should be cut back when revenues fall during recessions. Other political conservatives will tolerate deficits during recessions if the deficit is caused by tax reductions to businesses and the wealthy. This policy is supposed to increase the supply of capital and thus stimulate the economy. Not only conservatives and liberals line up on this issue, but also aggregates of interest groups that represent business and labor.

The Role of Each Level of Government

Where should the burden of providing services and benefits be placed? If balancing the budget becomes a valued goal at the federal level, there may be a strong temptation to balance it at the expense of other levels of government, cutting back grants and passing on program responsibilities. The states may do the same with local governments. Local governments may try to give service responsibility back to the state government or to townships, counties, special districts, or the private sector. In theory, each level of government has an interest in passing on expenditures to other levels and preventing expenditures from being passed to themselves.

The Choice of Outcomes

Which functions should continue to be performed? Whose benefits and programs should be maintained or cut? The politics of balance may lightly veil a bitter politics of outcomes, with protection or termination of particular programs or benefits as the goal. Interest groups, service recipients, and agency heads may take sides on this issue to protect their programs.

These four issues summarize what many of the actors in this portion of the budgetary decision-making process are trying to achieve. Liberals are trying to maintain the scope of government, while conservatives are trying to shrink it. Working people and their representatives want the budget to be used to keep the level of employment high, while businesspeople and their representatives prefer that the budget be used to keep taxes low. Each level of government wants to balance its budget, possibly by shifting the costs of programs and the burden of taxation elsewhere. Interest groups, legislators, beneficiaries of programs, and agency heads try to protect their programs from cuts that are proposed to balance the budget.

The Environment, Unpredictability, and Deficits

The four policy issues—scope of government, role of government in the economy, shifting of responsibilities between levels of government, and shifting the winners and losers in terms of tax increases and program decreases—are part of the politics of budgeting even when public officials work hard and openly to achieve balance each year. Deficits occur in part because budgets are open to the environment.

The courts may declare that mental patients cannot be committed to a mental hospital without treatment or that overcrowding of prisons is cruel and unusual punishment, so governments have to increase treatment in mental hospitals and build more prisons and hire more guards. Or natural events can provoke increases in expenditures, for example, hurricanes, floods, blizzards, or exceptionally cold or hot weather. Violence, such as riots, crime waves, or political demonstrations, can require extra staff hours, more communication equipment, improved training, or better public relations. War, with its overriding urgency, can increase expenditures without reference to current revenues.

Unexpected losses of revenues can result from courts' declaring some tax unconstitutional, which may require the restoration of the revenues to the taxpayers. Or sudden declines in tax revenues can result from changes in state laws that affect local governments. There may be a change in the type of bonds that cities may legally issue, or borrowing may become more expensive just when a government is planning to borrow for a large project. The costs of medical insurance or gasoline can surge unexpectedly or relentlessly. A sudden downturn in the economy can shrink revenues below expectations. At the local level, a business may close unexpectedly or move to another state, causing a decline in property tax revenue and leaving people without jobs and income, reducing sales tax revenues.

The intergovernmental revenue system introduces considerable uncertainty for state and local governments. Some grants are competitive, and so the potential recipients do not know in advance whether they will receive the money. Sometimes intergovernmental aid is set up as an entitlement, so that all cities, for example, that have over 6 percent of their population unemployed for longer than a certain number of months are eligible for particular kinds of aid. Those paying for the program cannot estimate its cost; those who might receive the aid do not have any way of knowing in advance whether they will be eligible. They may find out in the middle of a fiscal year that they will get the aid.

When state governments give aid to local governments in the form of entitlements, the problem is exaggerated because the state governments have to balance their own budgets. To meet unexpected increases in costs, they have to set aside contingency funds, which may be inadequate to the purpose. At times states incur obligations to their local governments that they do not have the money to fund. Local governments that planned on revenues from the state and included them in their budgets have to guess how much they will receive of what they were entitled to.

Another, related problem with intergovernmental revenues is that when the donor-level government is in financial trouble, it may hang on to the money it is supposed to give to the recipient for weeks or even months, so that it can earn interest on the money to help with its own financial problems. Or it can simply delay payments into the next fiscal year, forcing those who needed the money and planned to use it at the normal time to borrow in anticipation of receiving the money later. Donor governments may cancel or reduce shared revenue programs when they run into fiscal stress.

Some expenditures are demand driven rather than revenue driven. That means that the cost depends on the demand; the supply of the service is not determined by how much money is budgeted. For example, fire departments are to some extent demand driven; they respond to calls, and the calls are not limited to, or even related to, the supply of resources. One response to such a situation from the budgetary perspective is to create an overcapacity and budget for it, so that no matter what the demand, it is budgeted for. But that is a very expensive solution. Ambulance calls are demand driven; social service agencies that deal with battered spouses or abused children are demand driven. You should not turn someone away in the middle of a crisis in which they are in physical danger, yet costs are proportional to the number of clients. Environmental changes may push such costs up beyond plans or expectations. For example, increasing use of crack, an especially addictive form of cocaine, seems to increase the number of abandoned children and the incidence of spouse abuse, but it is hard to predict when it will hit a particular community or with what force. A poor economy in other parts of the world may set the jobless migrating, and an influx of non–English speaking immigrants may tax the capacity of the Immigration and Naturalization Service and all the social agencies that deal with poor immigrants.

The problem of demand-driven costs is particularly acute at the federal level because so much of federal spending is now composed of entitlements, many of which are open ended. That means that if there is an increase in the number of people eligible for a given benefit, the money must be found to pay them, regardless of what is happening on the revenue side. Entitlements decouple revenue and expenditure decisions and hence make budgets more vulnerable to deficits.

Long and severe recessions contribute most directly to budgetary imbalance because they simultaneously increase expenditures for unemployment relief and welfare and reduce revenues because so many people are out of work or earning less. It is politically very difficult to raise taxes when many people are unemployed and perhaps equally difficult to reduce the benefits of people who are desperate for them because they have been thrown out of work. Moreover, reducing public spending to balance the budget may worsen the recession because people have even less money to spend to keep the economy going.

The environment may also contribute to deficits when the economy of a whole region is gradually declining and with it the amount of taxable wealth. The costs of delivering programs and projects may continue to increase, since costs are often proportionate not to the size of the population but to the number of lane miles or the number of square miles of area. There may be a long-term disequilibrium between the cost of government and the availability of revenues. Either governments must continue to raise tax rates, taking a greater and greater share of people's income, against which the public will eventually rebel, or they must continue to cut back programs and projects, potentially exaggerating the decline. In the face of such continuing negative choices, officials may from time to time run deficits.

In short, many deficits, perhaps most of them, stem from changes in the environment. These changes may require more flexibility than the budget can deliver. Despite the best of intentions, deficits happen. Forbidding deficits—which is one response to them—seems futile in the face of the openness of the budget to the environment. The budget can be made less open to the environment, and it can be made more flexible, so that it can adapt without deficits. But the most common response seems to be to run the deficits and then worry about how to eliminate them in a timely and fair manner.

Increasing Stress between Payer and Decider

The potential difficulties created by the separation of payer and decider may become acute when governments run deficits. The public wants balance, but it simultaneously wants to maintain services and programs that it likes, and it does not want to increase its tax burden. Decision makers are faced with what appears to be a series of impossible choices from the perspective of political acceptability. Citizens may argue for taxing someone else and cutting someone else's programs, but for the decision maker there may not be many legal options that satisfy those conditions. The result in these cases may be a reduction in accountability.

The unpopularity of deficits, when combined with the unpleasant options available to reduce them, may lead to a tendency to hide or minimize deficits or to pretend that they are not there. The budget in this case loses much of its capacity to act as an instrument of accountability that transparently tells the citizens how their money is being spent. Balance may be redefined, the system of accounting may be changed to a cash basis to hide deficits, long-term capital borrowing may be used to cover operating deficits, expenditures may be pushed off into the next year, or funds may be borrowed between accounts inappropriately and possibly without record (presumably with intent to repay). Revenues may be overestimated or expenditures underestimated to make the budget, as passed, look more balanced than it is. The longer this hiding goes on, the more convoluted and uninformative the budget becomes. The worse the situation looks, the more unwilling those responsible for it may be to have the situation revealed.

How, then, can a deficit situation ever be fixed? Actually there are a number of pressures to reveal the problem and restore balance. For example, if there has been a lot of internal borrowing, those agency heads whose funds are being borrowed may become desperate enough to complain, especially if they are not being left with enough money to run their programs and they are being publicly criticized for poor management. Second, the problems of internal borrowing may become so tangled that auditors can no longer certify the honesty and integrity of the financial records, a sure warning sign of trouble that may bring the situation to public attention. Third, if the problem goes on long enough, there is likely to be an election, and if there is competition, the rival for chief executive is likely to be more than willing to discover his or her opponent's financial misdoings. If and when new politicians are elected, they have the incentive to reveal as much as they can attribute to their predecessor and make a highly publicized effort to clean it up, casting the blame on the previous incumbent. Fourth, the amounts involved may become so large that they are impossible to keep quiet. If the amounts grow large enough, they necessitate public borrowing, which means turning to a public market for funds. Banks and other investors normally require evidence of sound financial practice. The more desperate a government is to borrow, the more it needs to restore its fiscal integrity to be able to do so. If the government doing the borrowing is perceived as a poor risk, its costs of borrowing may become so high that they interfere with its ability to carry on its routine activities, adding to the pressure to restore balance.

Once the need is recognized, the difficult task of restoring balance remains. When many programs are entitlements and therefore difficult to cut back, and other programs have intense interest group support, it may be difficult to know where and how to cut expenses while maintaining acceptability to the public. These problems are particularly intense at the federal level, where the deficit sometimes becomes astronomical before serious efforts are taken to reduce it.

For some state governments, the problem is so acute, and they have so little time to deal with it, that borrowing, or spreading the deficit out over a period of years, seems to be the only sensible solution. That can mean borrowing internally, by not funding pensions fully, in essence borrowing against the future, with the idea that the situation will improve later and funds can be restored. In that case, the problems being created are not likely to come home to roost while current elected officials are in office. States may borrow against future revenue sources, such as tobacco settlement money they are due in the future but need now. These are one-time revenues and will not address a long-term structural imbalance between revenues and expenditures, but they tend to dampen the sense of emergency, lower the estimates of deficits in the short term, and hence reduce the embarrassment of deficits and the need to make politically unpopular cuts in services or programs. In extreme cases states have borrowed long term to cover an accumulation of short-term operating deficits. That makes the cuts more manageable and the levels of service disruption less noticeable.

When cuts are necessary, one response is to make them where they are least noticeable to prevent citizen complaints. Such cuts break the visible link between taxes paid and services produced; it appears as if cuts can be made without reducing services. The costs of such a strategy, besides the long-term decline in the trust of the taxpayers, include the increased costs of delayed maintenance and capital projects deferred and inability to downsize in a logical way. Agencies may face the peculiar task of arguing initially that cuts will hurt operations, but after the cuts are made, arguing that the agency can continue to be as effective as before, with fewer resources. The model of invisible cuts encourages elected officials to keep on cutting, as there never seems to be any damage or public outcry.

Another approach is to cut across the board, to give the impression of fairness. Elected officials and program administrators are more likely to accept cuts if they know the pain is widely shared, that they have not been singled out. To the extent that this strategy is employed, it prevents cutting more deeply the programs that have more waste or those whose services can be more easily dispensed with or provided by the market. It may work if the cuts are temporary but be inefficient if the problem is long term and structural. It can also be a difficult strategy to implement, as interest groups that perceive their programs being cut will fight to protect them, regardless of what is happening to other programs.

A third approach is to cut the programs that have the weakest interest group support, including internal service programs that have no external constituencies, such as personnel and training, foreign aid at the national level, and parks and recreation at the local level. A related strategy is to cut the programs of political opponents—either the ones that serve opponents' constituents or the ones into which opponents have in the past hired most of their political supporters.

The locking in of benefits makes it especially difficult to cut in a rational manner. Some programs are difficult to cut legally; they may be mandated by a higher level of government, for example, or they may be required to be performed at a given level by the constitution or a charter provision or an accreditation board. In such cases, spending is cut back not where the priorities are lowest, but wherever it is legal to cut and where there are funds to be gained from delays in spending or reductions in outlays. At the state and local levels, public works programs may be most severely cut because they have projects that are not yet committed, and delaying them will save some money in the short run.

The four characteristics of public budgeting—constraints, variety of actors and goals, openness to the environment, and the separation of payer and decider—provide some common themes for the politics of deficits at different levels of government. Nevertheless, there are some important differences between federal, state, and local levels that influence how they deal with deficits when they occur.

One difference between levels of government is that state and local governments are required to balance their budgets; the federal government is not. When changes in the environment push up the costs of entitlement programs at the federal level, the increased costs show up as increased deficits; at the state level, the costs have to come out of a contingency fund or reduced spending for other budgeted expenses. Because state and local governments generally have to balance their budgets every year, or at least in a short period of time, there may be more pressure to delay payments, push up revenue collection, or shift more program costs to local governments. States and localities sometimes built up budgetary surpluses to guard against deficits. Another product of the state and local requirement for balance is that efforts to hide deficits may be more intense.

A second difference between the levels of government is that the role of deficit spending in regulating the economy is most salient at the federal level. State governments are only marginally involved in efforts to control the economy, and local governments are generally too minor a part of the economy to control it no matter how they spend their money. Absolute and rigid controls that prevent deficit spending would make it difficult or impossible for the federal government to spend countercyclically, that is, to stimulate the economy in times of recession. But rigid prohibitions against deficits can be, and are, used at the state and local levels.

A third difference has to do with overall size. At the federal level, the tremendous size of budget deficits and their chronic nature create a noisy and stubborn problem with potentially major impact on the national economy. Deficits are rarer and more tractable at state and local levels. The requirements for balance make rebalancing the budget during the year a frequent activity, so that it is more difficult (though not impossible) for large deficits to accumulate from year to year.

The Politics of Deficits: The Federal Level

Deficits were a fact of life at the federal level for many years, but they became particularly large in the late 1980s and early 1990s (see Table 6.1 for the size of deficits by year from 1940 to 2005). They were brought under control by 1998, only to grow again, to record levels, after 2001.

From the beginning of the republic to the 1930s, deficits were associated primarily with wars, and debts were paid off after the wars were over. During the Great Depression of the 1930s, politicians responded to falling revenues and the urgent need for aid for the poor by allowing deficit spending. The depression forged a new role for the federal government to help minimize swings in the economy and the attendant social and economic distress. After the depression, an economic theory, Keynesianism, emerged, that argued that deficits for this purpose were not necessarily harmful and that spending during recession actually helped stimulate the economy. Deficits incurred to offset recessions and stimulate the economy are supposed to be temporary, but since the middle of the 1970s deficits have occurred nearly continuously.

Since the 1970s politicians who promised to eliminate deficits have often failed to do so, creating the impression that deficits were out of control. Whatever acceptance there was of moderate-sized and occasional deficits began to evaporate when the deficits became huge. In 1974 the federal government had a deficit of $6.1 billion, which was four-tenths of one percent of the gross national product (GNP). By 1992 the deficit had reached $290 billion, or $340 billion if the Social Security surplus was subtracted.[3]

David Stockman, director of the Office of Management and Budget during the Ronald Reagan administration, in a candid speech in spring 1985, just before his resignation, summarized the reasons for the deficits. Stockman argued that the first cause of the deficits had to do with demobilization after the Vietnam War. Instead of the government's reducing expenditures, the newly freed-up money was absorbed in increased income-support programs. Outlays for defense were reduced, allowing the massive inventories created by the war to be drawn down. But lower defense spending could not continue; the hostage situation in Iran highlighted U.S. military weakness, contributing to a consensus for increases in military spending, beginning with President Jimmy Carter in the late 1970s and continuing well into the Reagan administration. The rate of inflation increased,

Table 6.1 Federal Surpluses and Deficits, 1940–2005, in Current Dollars and as Percentages of GDP

Fiscal year	Surplus or deficit in current dollars (billions)	% GDP	Fiscal year	Surplus or deficit in current dollars (billions)	% GDP
1940	−2.9	−3.0	1974	−6.1	−0.4
1941	−4.9	−4.3	1975	−53.2	−3.4
1942	−20.5	−14.2	1976	−73.7	−4.2
1943	−54.6	−30.3	TQ	−14.7	−3.2
1944	−47.6	−22.7	1977	−53.7	−2.7
1945	−47.6	−21.5	1978	−59.2	−2.7
1946	−15.9	−7.2	1979	−40.7	−1.6
1947	4.0	1.7	1980	−73.8	−2.7
1948	11.8	4.6	1981	−79.0	−2.6
1949	0.6	0.2	1982	−128.0	−4.0
1950	−3.1	−1.1	1983	−207.8	−6.0
1951	6.1	1.9	1984	−185.4	−4.8
1952	−1.5	−0.4	1985	−212.3	−5.1
1953	−6.5	−1.7	1986	−221.2	−5.0
1954	−1.2	−0.3	1987	−149.7	−3.2
1955	−3.0	−0.8	1988	−155.2	−3.1
1956	3.9	0.9	1989	−152.6	−2.8
1957	3.4	0.8	1990	−221.1	−3.9
1958	−2.8	−0.6	1991	−269.3	−4.5
1959	−12.8	−2.6	1992	−290.3	−4.7
1960	0.3	0.1	1993	−255.1	−3.9
1961	−3.3	−0.6	1994	−203.2	−2.9
1962	−7.1	−1.3	1995	−164.0	−2.2
1963	−4.8	−0.8	1996	−107.5	−1.4
1964	−5.9	−0.9	1997	−21.9	−0.3
1965	−1.4	−0.2	1998	69.2	0.8
1966	−3.7	−0.5	1999	125.5	1.4
1967	−8.6	−1.1	2000	236.2	2.4
1968	−25.2	−2.9	2001	128.2	1.3
1969	3.2	0.3	2002	−157.8	−1.5
1970	−2.8	−0.3	2003	−377.6	−3.5
1971	−23.0	−2.1	2004	−412.1	−3.6
1972	−23.4	−2.0	2005 (est.)	−426.6	−3.5
1973	−14.9	−1.1			

Source: Adapted from *Historical Tables, Budget of the United States Government, Fiscal Year 2006,* 25–26, wais.access.gpo.gov.

contributing to higher interest rates and a major increase in interest payments on the federal debt. The Reagan administration's policy of tax reductions added another element. When these tax reductions were combined with the recession of 1981–1982, the deficits soared.[4]

Stockman pointed out that the Reagan administration strategy of cutting back discretionary programs, while maintaining support for defense and Social Security and cutting taxes, could not possibly reduce the deficits because there was not enough money in the discretionary programs. "We argue with Congress over $80 or $90 billion of nondefense appropriation, but those that are truly discretionary amount to only a few billion dollars a year—not enough to fix a $200 billion problem." [5] Taxes had to be raised, or entitlement programs reduced and defense curtailed. Thus deficit reduction was framed in terms of major policy priorities. There was no easy way, or even relatively easy way, to cut the deficits.

Citizens favored balanced budgets and increasingly supported efforts to control or limit the level of taxation. Moreover, taxpayer groups were organized and began to press the state legislatures to vote for federal balanced budget amendments. Under pressure from national taxpayer associations, many state legislatures did pass calls for a constitutional convention to add a balanced budget amendment to the U.S. Constitution.

President Reagan was interested in reducing the scope of government activities and wanted to reduce taxes. He advocated a balanced budget in his election speeches, but there is considerable evidence that his administration was not terribly interested in reducing deficits, in comparison to achieving other policy goals.

> The Reagan administration, while it does not like deficit spending, has opted for this course of action because deficits facilitate the achievement of some of its other policy objectives. Deficits have enabled it (1) to preserve the 1981 tax cuts; (2) to blame Congress for fiscal irresponsibility; (3) to pressure for cutbacks in domestic programs; and—at least in its first years—to finance additional defense spending.[6]

At least one of President Reagan's entourage admitted that the tax cuts of 1981 would increase deficits. He confided, "Reagan's main goal is not to balance the budget—it is to reduce the role of government. . . . if we don't cut taxes and generate big deficits, spending will never come down. . . . with huge deficits, their choices are tougher. . . . they'll have to cut spending." [7]

Pressed by its own policy goals to accept a growing deficit, the Reagan administration purposely underestimated the deficit's size. Discussing Reagan administration OMB director Stockman's book, the *New York Times* noted, "The economics of Mr. Reagan's successful drive to cut taxes and restrain government spending in his first year in office . . . was predicated upon an economic forecast for 1981 that its authors, Mr. Stockman and the president's chief economist then, Murray Weidenbaum, knew to be false but a politically expedient device." [8] According to Stockman, the administration used accounting gimmicks to make the deficit look smaller. In 1981, he reported, a series of spending reductions and revenue measures were inadequate to close the gap opened by tax cuts. "Book-keeping began its wondrous works. We invented the magic asterisk: If we couldn't find the savings in time—and we couldn't—we would issue an I.O.U. We would call it 'future savings to be identified.' " [9]

The administration also minimized the importance of deficits. In hearings before the Ways and Means Committee in 1983, after Chairman Dan Rostenkowski described the size of the deficits as in the $200 billion range, he asked Secretary of the Treasury Donald Regan if he still opposed new taxes. Regan responded that he did: "We think that to have tax increases over the next two years would be folly, because it is not needed at this point. The deficits can be handled." [10]

President Reagan pressed Congress for spending cuts, with considerable success in the first year of his administration. But as his ability to dictate cuts to Congress waned, he threw more of his support to the movement for a constitutional amendment that would combine a balanced budget requirement with spending limitations. Such an amendment would accomplish more of the president's goal of cutting back the size of government than the balanced budget amendment alone.

Constitutional approaches to eliminating the deficit vied for years with more flexible, legislative approaches. Every time a legislative approach failed, it gave impetus to the movement for a constitutional amendment; every time the constitutional amendment came up for a vote and appeared likely to win, it increased the incentive for finding a legislative formula that would work.

Proposed Constitutional Amendments

The U.S. Constitution can be amended in two ways: Congress can adopt an amendment by a two-thirds vote in each house and then put it before the states, three-fourths of which must ratify it, or two-thirds of the states can vote to hold a constitutional convention, at which an amendment would presumably be discussed. In that case also, three-fourths of the states need to ratify the proposed amendment. Partly because of the legal ambiguities in the second route (it is not clear that a constitutional convention could be limited to consideration of the balanced budget amendment), many in Congress preferred to head off the states and present a carefully considered congressional proposal.

As early as 1939 states began petitioning Congress to propose an amendment limiting federal taxing power. The movement continued on and off until 1963, when thirty-four states had passed such resolutions. By then, however, some of the resolutions were fifteen to twenty years old, and twelve states had withdrawn their applications, so the convention was never called.[11] More recent calls for a balanced budget constitutional amendment began in 1975. The National Taxpayers Union and the American Farm Bureau Federation were active in starting this movement.[12] By 1985, thirty-two of the required thirty-four states had passed resolutions calling for a constitutional convention.

As the movement grew in the states for a constitutional amendment, Congress began considering its own proposals. The Senate passed a proposed constitutional amendment in August 1982; the House of Representatives voted it down in October 1982. A budget-balancing amendment was voted on in the Senate in March 1986, where it narrowly failed because a competing form of limitation had been passed several months earlier, draining away some of the support for the constitutional amendment.

Proposals for a balanced budget amendment to the Constitution gained much support in 1992, 1994, and 1995 but did not pass both houses by the required two-thirds majority. In 1990 Congress had passed the Budget Enforcement Act, changing the budget process and strengthening the requirements for balance, but the deficit got worse in 1991 and 1992. Legislators kept telling each other that a balanced budget amendment was the only remaining possibility, that nothing else could possibly work.

Robert Reischauer, who was then director of the Congressional Budget Office, explained in fall 1993 why deficits kept going up despite tax increases and an improved budget process with more constraints. There was a slower than expected recovery from recession, and a number of technical factors went in the wrong direction, including better-than-average farm weather, large crops, and below-average prices, requiring high federal payments to farmers.[13] By the end of 1993, the deficit was finally headed downward, reflecting the 1990 spending caps and more technical factors going the right, rather than the wrong, way.

The version of the balanced budget amendment that came up before the House in 1992 included a requirement for a two-thirds majority to increase the debt limit or to suspend the requirement that outlays not exceed estimated receipts. A more moderate proposal that would have limited revenue increases to the rate of increase in national income died in committee. The proposal that was voted on (H.J. Res. 290, the Stenholm proposal) was inclusive in terms of covering all revenues and expenditures, including Social Security, and did not deal with the possibility of shifting the burden of spending to the states. This particular version of the proposal reportedly earned the opposition of the Chamber of Commerce because it suggested to them that state and local taxes might increase to balance the federal budget; organized labor and the American Association of Retired Persons also lobbied against the measure, fearing that cutbacks in Social Security and Medicare would result.[14] The measure was defeated in the House.

Although the deficit situation did improve, as the economy recovered from recession and the effects of the 1990 spending caps were felt, the prospect of large deficits resuming later in the decade as a result of entitlement spending remained in the foreground. When the elections of fall 1994 created Republican majorities in both the House and the Senate, an ideological passion for change swept over the House in particular, and new energy was expended to get a balanced budget amendment passed.

The question of where the burden would fall if a constitutional amendment was passed was partly resolved with the passage of a limitation on unfunded mandates in 1995. Although this legislation does not protect states from cutbacks in grants, it helps prevent the federal government from setting standards and requirements that states have to implement at great cost. With new and enthusiastic Republican majorities and with the problem of state opposition out of the way, it seemed more likely than ever that the constitutional amendment would pass Congress and go on to the states for ratification. The measure did pass the House of Representatives but failed in the Senate by one vote. The closeness of the vote suggested that legislators were trying to maximize their popularity by taking a public stance in favor of a balanced budget amendment, as long as the measure did not actually pass. In fact, legislators charged each other with taking symbolic stances.

The last time that the balanced budget amendment came before Congress was in 1995; the idea's popularity waned as the budget became balanced in 1998. By 2003, however, large deficits had returned, and conservatives demanded and were promised a vote on such a measure by 2004. Republicans were between a rock and a hard place because the deficits they were campaigning against were clearly run up by a Republican administration. In the end, a balanced budget amendment did not come up for vote in 2004. Perhaps chastened by conservative pressure, however, the president made a major push for spending cuts in his 2006 budget proposal.

Each time that the balanced budget amendment came up, fairly standard arguments were made for and against it. The arguments on the positive side included the following:

1. Deficit spending is detrimental to the economy, it increases inflation, and it crowds out other uses of capital.

2. The need for flexible economic policy is overstated. Keynesian politics doesn't work, and monetary policies (controlling the economy by regulating the amount of money in circulation and influencing interest rates) are sufficient to influence economic cycles.
3. Growth of government should be checked.
4. Congress, if left alone, will not act or cannot take effective action.

The arguments against a constitutional amendment requiring a balanced budget included the following:

1. There is little relationship between either deficits or the size of government and inflation, and a balanced budget/revenue limitation is likely to have major negative economic impacts.
2. Constitutional budget constraints will impede the government's ability to respond to economic and other crises.
3. A constitutional requirement for a supermajority to allow an unbalanced budget will have the effect of magnifying the power of a small minority of congressmen who could demand a high (and unrelated) price for their votes.
4. A constitutional amendment is unenforceable.
5. Spending cuts are likely to fall on social services and aid to state and local governments.
6. A constitutional amendment will shift budget-making power to the courts (because of enforcement issues).
7. This is not a proper subject for a constitutional amendment.
8. The same result can be achieved through legislation.

Ultimately, the rigidity of a constitutional amendment, the support for different versions of its wording that allowed or did not allow much revenue growth, and the loss of budget power in Congress that would result from such an amendment shifted support to a legislative solution. Unfortunately, it was not clear what an effective legislative solution would look like; it took several iterations and a number of years to work one out.

Statutory Approaches to Budget Balancing

In December 1985 the Balanced Budget and Emergency Deficit Control Act of 1985, popularly called Gramm-Rudman-Hollings, was passed. Gramm-Rudman-Hollings was oriented toward deficit reduction and budget balance rather than expenditure or revenue limitations. The legislation allowed some rise in revenues to balance the budget, rather than putting rigid limits on revenues. It protected entitlement programs such as Social Security. It reduced the shock of cutting back the deficit by phasing in balanced budgets over a five-year period. The law stipulated that Congress could vote to allow deficits in excess of targets in case of economic recession. The requirements for balance were to lapse during a war.

The goal of Gramm-Rudman-Hollings was to achieve budgetary balance by 1991 by reducing the size of the deficit by specified amounts each year from 1986 to 1991. If the deficit in any year was larger than the target for that year, an automatic provision would take over, cutting programs across the board after certain special rules had been considered. The cuts were to be divided evenly between defense and nondefense expenditures. The threat of cutting all programs was supposed to be not only more fair but so distasteful that it would force Congress to eliminate the excess deficit before the automatic cuts could take effect. In the event, in response to widespread pressure to protect particular programs from reductions, Congress exempted many programs from the across-the-board cuts, so that if such cuts, called sequesters, were necessary, they would fall disproportionately on a relatively small number of programs.

In an effort to reduce the deficit so that sequesters would not be necessary and the programs covered by Gramm-Rudman-Hollings would not be decimated, both the president and Congress began to "game the system," by such means as selling off assets, building trust fund balances by freezing spending from the Highway and Airport Trust Funds, and increasing revenue estimates. Spending was pushed over into the succeeding year to make the current year look more balanced than it was.

Gramm-Rudman-Hollings was not successful. It encouraged stopgap measures and overestimates of economic growth; created incentives to take existing programs off-budget and create new off-budget enterprises. Sen. Herbert Kohl, D-Wis., observed, "Since we enacted Gramm-Rudman, we have created five off-budget government sponsored enterprises. Only one was created in the previous thirteen years." [15]

Sen. Nancy Kassebaum, R-Kan., summed up the accumulated congressional frustration with the budget process in 1989 when she decried the use of such emergency devices as continuing resolutions as substitutes for a budget. She claimed that Congress had routinely failed to make timely fiscal decisions. "In doing so," she argued, "we lose the power to allot money among programs of greater or less merit. We lose the chance to weigh revenue options thoughtfully. In fact, we lose the ability to do anything other than affirm the aggregate spending, taxing—and borrowing—decisions of earlier years. That is not policy making." [16]

Pressure increased to reform the budget process as deficits grew beyond the ability of Gramm-Rudman sequesters to cure without doing unacceptable damage. The Budget Enforcement Act was passed in fall 1990. Like Gramm-Rudman, the BEA picked from and blended a large number of different proposals; it was a complex measure. But its essential feature was that it strengthened the constraints for balance rather than trying to reduce the size of the deficit.

One portion of the BEA focused on limiting spending on domestic "controllables," those programs that regularly go through the congressional appropriations process. Another part focused on entitlements and other mandatory spending. The goal for entitlements was less on keeping spending down than on maintaining balance; pay-as-you-go (often called "pay-go") provisions required compensating increases in revenues or decreases in other noncontrollables to pay for any increases in entitlements. Similarly, revenue reductions were to be controlled by strict requirements that they be offset with either increases in revenue or spending reductions. The linkage between revenues and expenditures was intentionally tightened in two key areas, entitlements and tax expenditures.

Part of the thrust of the reforms was to make the real costs of spending apparent when decisions were being made, so as to reorient incentives toward balance. For example, another part of the act made the costs of loans and loan guarantees more visible at the time when the programs are being approved. Before the reform, approval was separated by many years from the actual costs, which were routinely underestimated.

The removal of the Social Security surplus from the calculation of the deficit also had the effect of making the costs of current spending and revenue decisions more apparent. When Social Security balances were included in the deficit calculation, the deficit looked as if it were decreasing, even when it was growing, and that encouraged a lack of fiscal discipline. With Social Security surpluses out, each action that increased the deficit would have an immediate, visible, and negative consequence.

The Budget Enforcement Act of 1990 was especially significant because it shows the budget process starting to adapt to a slower-growing economy. The reform discouraged increases in expenditures and reductions in revenues and strengthened the expectations for balance. It helped make costs clearer. Its scope was broad in including regular appropriations, entitlements, loans, and loan guarantees, and it was more inclusive of time, requiring enforcement at several points during a year and over several years. Instead of a rigid series of goals intended to last only until the problem goes away, the new process was much more flexible, leaving room for choices among programs, for adaptation to the economy, and for emergencies. The Budget Enforcement Act did not set a specific date for the elimination of deficits; it linked revenues and expenditures more tightly and restructured the incentives to make it easier to achieve balance over the long haul.

The new law was much more successful than Gramm-Rudman-Hollings. Its more flexible approach to deficit reduction and its explicit closing of the loopholes in prior legislation markedly reduced the manipulations that marked the Gramm-Rudman-Hollings period. For a combination of reasons, including the budget caps in the BEA, strong revenue growth from a booming economy, and major tax increases, the budget was balanced, more or less, by 1998.

After budget balance was reached, however, the discipline that the BEA envisioned fell apart. Its rules were widely evaded, and in 2002 it was allowed to lapse. With huge tax reductions, the spending increases in response to the attacks of 9/11, and the wars in Afghanistan and Iraq, deficits soon replaced surpluses. By 2005, the president was proposing major spending cuts and new legislative budget processes.

Deficits in the States

Despite the unfunded mandates law, unfunded mandates to the states began to pick up again and became especially burdensome in the economic slowdown that followed 9/11. The National Council of State Legislatures (NCSL) reintroduced its Mandates Monitor, a device it had used successfully before the passage of the Unfunded Mandates Act in 1995, but which had not been necessary between 1995 and 2004. The NCSL estimated that unfunded mandates cost the states $29 billion in 2004 and would probably cost around $34 billion in 2005.[17] Those amounts were 6 percent of general fund totals for the year 2004 and 7 percent for 2005. In commenting on the president's 2006 budget proposal, the NCSL complained, "The budget as proposed would merely export the federal deficit to the states." It listed in particular programs that were mandated and unfunded or severely underfunded, such as the Individuals with Disabilities Education Act (IDEA), No Child Left Behind Act, the Help America Vote Act, the State Criminal Alien Assistance Program, and the mandated improvements to drivers' licenses in response to 9/11.[18] While the NCSL position is overstated—clearly not all the federal deficit will be shifted to the states—the temptation to achieve federal policy goals without paying for them at the national level has exacerbated state fiscal problems in the last few years.

From 2001 to 2004 states struggled to close deficits that have totaled approximately $190 billion.[19] The federal government, although it can spend money to counteract a recession, spent only $20 billion in the states in 2003 to help them manage this financial stress. State actions to increase taxes and reduce program

Minicase: Wisconsin Confronts Deficits

Wisconsin's fiscal stress and the state's responses to it illustrate many of the themes of this chapter. The state's financial problems were structural, rather than cyclical, but were exacerbated by the post-2001 recession.[1] Wisconsin lacked a functioning rainy day fund, which made its revenue problems after the 9/11 terrorist attacks larger than they otherwise might have been.

The state announced a $1.1 billion deficit in the 2001–2003 biennium. In light of this huge shortfall, Gov. Scott McCallum recommended in 2002 that the state shared revenue program, amounting to nearly a billion dollars, be terminated by 2004. This proposal would have put nearly the whole burden of eliminating the deficit on the shoulders of the local governments, saving state agencies and programs from major budget reductions. The local governments fought back, arguing that the program did not represent money that the state was just being nice about sending to local governments but was to compensate for tax breaks the state granted, and hence it was money that belonged to the local governments.

Legislators agreed that the state's budget should not be balanced on the backs of the local governments. Instead, the state relied primarily on one-time revenues from the tobacco settlement. It sold expectations of future revenue from the settlement at a discount, to create a current pool of funds, which were then used to securitize a revenue bond, bringing in more money in the short run but costing more in the long run. The state lost considerable money by selling the future revenue at a discount, and by borrowing it incurred interest costs that would have to be paid off over the years, in essence borrowing long term to close a single biennium's budget gap. This was a very expensive solution that met the requirements for balance but did not resolve the state's financial problems. The use of one-time funds merely put the problems off into the next biennium. Moreover, the biennium was still going to end with a deficit, despite the borrowing. The deficit at midyear was pegged at $452 million.

For the following biennium the deficit was estimated to grow to $3.2 billion by 2005. Since 45 percent of state revenues goes to schools and another 9 percent to shared revenues for local governments, to achieve something like the 15 percent cuts necessary to balance the budget without tax increases, shared revenue was put on the block again. However the proposal this time was less drastic than in the previous administration.[2] When the new governor took office, he argued that the previous governor and legislature had signed a budget they knew to be out of balance. He used his emergency budget powers to trim $170 million immediately from the bud-

(continued)

get approved by his predecessor. Then in preparing his budget for the next fiscal year, he made major cuts:

> I cut spending by $1.5 billion—the largest cuts in the history of Wisconsin. In signing this budget, I will trim our state payroll by almost 2,300 positions. Instead of freezing the bureaucracy, I am actually cutting state agencies by 10 percent, or $400 million. And because I believe in leading by example, the first office I cut was my own. The result is that spending in the Fiscal Year that began on July 1 will decrease by 2.4 percent over last year. Over the course of the biennium, spending will increase by less than one percent—a record in fiscal restraint. I am signing this budget with a total of 131 vetoes—lowering spending by eliminating $315 million in appropriations. I am reducing the amount the Legislature added to our "structural deficit" by $258 million. When my vetoes become law, we will wipe out our $3.2 billion deficit and leave a $205 million balance. Most importantly, I am doing this the fiscally responsible way—without raising taxes.[3]

The governor cut shared revenue but not by as much as local officials had feared. Local governments were struggling to avoid property tax increases to make up the difference, but Republican legislators feared that reductions in shared revenues would trigger property tax increases and so proposed tax caps and freezes to prevent that from happening. These restrictions were rejected by the Democratic governor as falling too heavily on education. At the same time, the legislature passed a law requiring a zero-based look at state programs, with a third of the state's programs to be reviewed in the first year.

The economy had improved somewhat by the time preparations for the 2005–2007 budget had to be made, but the deficit did not disappear; for the biennium the state was anticipating a $1.6 billion deficit. The shared revenue program was again threatened, with a nonpartisan policy analysis suggesting the time was ripe to eliminate this funding. With the continuing threat of a legislatively imposed tax freeze, the local governments were particularly concerned about the possibility of losing the shared revenue and being unable to replace it. Republicans were pushing hard for a spending limit on the state government, as well as a tax limit for the local governments, using the deficit as a wedge to gain support for tax reduction and spending control.

With a Democratic governor and a Republican legislature, there was no consensus on how to regain structural balance in the state. The governor

(continued)

and the legislature continued what the press dubbed a duel of two tax freeze proposals. The governor's version held down property taxes by taking money earmarked for roads to spend on schools; the legislature was pushing a TABOR ("taxpayer bill of rights") proposal, a constitutional amendment limiting state and local taxing and spending authority. To pass a constitutional amendment the legislature has to approve it by simple majorities in two succeeding sessions and then put it to a public vote. The governor may not veto it.

The local governments responded that the increase in property taxes was not caused by them, but by the state's passing along unfunded mandates to local governments, whose major revenue source is property taxes. They put an advisory question on the state ballot for state assumption of courts and health and human services, so that those functions would be paid for by state revenues rather than local property taxes.[4] It is not clear, however, that even public approval of the assumption of these functions would move the state to pay for them while it is trying to eliminate a structural deficit of over a billion dollars.

While the outcome of the duel over the 2005–2007 budget is not yet known in early 2005, the outlines of the contest suggest that determination to control taxes and reduce spending has taken the place of thoughtful analysis of how to eliminate the structural deficit. The battle over where to shift costs and what level of government should take responsibility for which functions continued without clear resolution. What is clear is that, as elsewhere in the United States, the local governments in Wisconsin are at the mercy of the state government, which sometimes reduces their revenue sources, mandates functions without paying for them, or freezes taxes while program costs continue to grow faster than inflation or the population. An unbalanced budget exaggerates the possibility of the state creating structural deficits at the local level.

The fight about tax limits and a taxpayers' bill of rights amendment, or TABOR, combined with divided government to illustrate clearly the positions of the Democratic governor and the Republican legislature. The governor boasted of his accomplishments in preserving Medicaid and funding the public schools; he had vetoed the tax freezes that would have hurt the schools. The Republicans aimed to reduce taxes and force a reduction in the size of government, without much regard for which programs would have to be cut. When the proposal for reducing shared revenues threatened local governments, the Republican response was to block any increase in property taxes at the local level to make up for revenue loss.

(continued)

The chronic deficits and disagreements about how to address them resulted in long and contentious sessions as the legislature wrestled with the budget, bringing calls for a change in the budget process itself. In 2002 a legislative commission was established to recommend budget process changes, reporting its results about a year later. Most of its recommendations were introduced as legislation, but the major ones, which would have affected the way the budget was to be balanced and the size of, and rules for, a revenue stabilization (rainy day) fund, did not pass.

1. Andrew Reschovsky, *Wisconsin's Structural Deficit, Our Fiscal Future at the Crossroads,* LaFollette School of Public Affairs, University of Wisconsin, Madison, 2002, www.lafollette.wisc.edu/publications/otherpublications/wisconsin-primer/2002/StructuralDeficit2002.pdf.
2. Rick Olin, *Shared Revenue Program (County and Municipal Aid and Utility Aid),* Informational Paper 18, Wisconsin Legislative Fiscal Bureau, Madison, Wisconsin, January 2005, www.legis.state.wi.us/lfb/Informationalpapers/18.pdf (accessed March 28, 2005).
3. Text of Governor Doyle's budget address, *Milwaukee Journal-Sentinel,* July 24, 2003.
4. "Game Is on over Whose Tax Freeze Is Better," editorial, *Sheboygan-Press,* February 17, 2005, www.sheboygan-press.com.

expenditures may well prolong a recession by further reducing people's ability to spend and drive the economy. The huge deficits run up by the national government over this period contributed to the meagerness of its effort to help the states. Moreover, the national government's deficits probably also contributed to the underfunding of federal mandates to the states—program underfunding is not controlled by the federal Unfunded Mandates Act.

When they are facing deficits, the states, like the federal government, have to decide whether and how much to raise revenues or cut expenditures, with similar implications for the scope of government. Just as at the federal level, there are problems of defining what constitutes a deficit and of measuring the size and importance of deficits. Just as the federal government has to decide how much of a financial burden it can shift to the states or the private sector, states have to decide how much expense to absorb from, or pass on to, local governments and how much service burden they can unload on them. But the requirement of annual (or biennial) balance in the states creates some differences from the national-level government.

Because the states are not supposed to run deficits, they need to save up to cover declines in revenues in rainy day funds or other kinds of buffer funds, but some do this more successfully than others. Because balance is supposed to occur every year or biennium, states are especially stressed by recessions that increase the cost of entitlements while decreasing revenues. If only they could put off cuts until the recession was over and the economy had recovered, the states might avoid deep cuts, but because the law doesn't usually allow deficits to run for several years, the states have often adapted, finding ways that are more-or-less legal, if not fiscally conservative, to tide themselves over. Creative accounting and financing are common at the state level as a response to deficits. Moreover, as we have seen, most of the governors have more power over the budget than the president of the United States, including their stronger vetoes, which they use when confronting a deficit.

Although there is considerable variation among states in who has power to reduce spending to restore balance after the beginning of the fiscal year, the responsibility is generally given to the governor. In 1998 twelve states reported that the governor had unlimited authority to cut the budget during the fiscal year, if necessary. Ten states reported that the governor could make cuts during the year but that they could be only across-the-board cuts. Twelve states reported that the governor must consult with the legislature before making midyear cuts. In 1988 only seven state legislatures had required the governor to consult over midyear changes, indicating that the legislatures were taking a somewhat more active role in budget implementation issues.[20] By 2002, the Association of State Budget Officers reported that governors in thirty-six states had the authority to cut back the budget without legislative approval, leaving fourteen in which the governor must consult with the legislature before making cuts.[21] There has thus been a slow but steady increase in the number of states where the governor is expected to consult with the legislature before making midyear cuts. At the same time, however, in states where the governor can cut back the budget without consultation, there are fewer states that put strings on that power.[22]

The issue of which interests will be protected and which will be cut back has been less salient at the state level than at the national level because deficits, when they have occurred, have usually been caused by recessions and hence been relatively short. Because the deficits are considered temporary, states can adopt temporary measures to handle them, including temporary taxes or surtaxes. They can tighten belts and make across-the-board cuts. They can often avoid making difficult choices among programs or types of programs. Moreover, the states do not have enormous flexibility in what will be cut back, inasmuch as their biggest expenditures, and the ones that are growing most quickly, are entitlement programs such as Medicaid, which is shared with the national government, and public elementary and secondary education.

When budget cuts are necessary, the discretionary portion of state budgets—the nonentitlement, non–debt repayment portion—must be disproportionately reduced because other expenditures are either mandated or out of direct state control. The discretionary portion of state budgets includes highways and higher education and shared revenue or grants to the local governments in states that have such programs. When Colorado's TABOR amendment caused serious budget cuts year after year, it forced cuts in education, so citizens passed a referendum forcing funding for kindergarten through grade twelve schools. The result was that higher education was nearly the only expenditure left that could be cut, and the state universities' budgets were sharply reduced. It is partly this lack of options that makes it so tempting for states to pass along costs to the local governments or take local revenues to pay state bills.

Balancing with Gimmicks

When confronted with historically high deficits after 2001, many states did some cutting but also some temporizing. They frequently used budget gimmicks of various sorts to prevent deeper cuts in programs and staffing, hoping that if they put the tough decisions off into the future, the problems would go away—the economy would recover, and balance would be easier to achieve later. Many states borrowed against the money they expected to get in later years from their successful lawsuit against the tobacco companies; they drew down whatever reserves they may have had in rainy day funds; they delayed payments to local governments. "As states move paydays, delay tax refunds, speed up fee collections, accelerate seizures of unclaimed property, borrow billions of dollars, sell off buildings and lease them back in a chaotic rush to paper over record deficits, analysts say that many state budgets are as flimsy as the paper they are printed on." [23] Several states even engaged in a kind of arbitrage, borrowing money and investing it in the pension funds, with the hope that the market would increase the value of the borrowed funds, paying for the interest on the loans and helping to shore up the severely underfunded pensions. A number of states borrowed to close budget gaps.

Reluctance to raise taxes, combined with the size of the problem, has made this recent round of deficits more difficult, contributing to the level of budget gimmickry.

> Arturo Pérez, fiscal analyst for the National Conference of State Legislatures, said one-shot financing is increasing as the appetite for boosting taxes fades. In the previous recession, in 1991, he said, states raised taxes about 5.4 percent to close deficits. Last year, he said, they raised them only 1.4 percent.

Lawmakers in New York, Ohio, Arkansas and Idaho, among other states, have increased taxes this year, but most legislatures and governors remain opposed.

At the same time, they appear unwilling to cut spending enough to control deficits. Facing a $9 billion deficit, for example, the Texas state Senate recently passed a no-new-taxes budget that the state comptroller decried as being built on "smoke and mirrors," including a shift of almost $2 billion in state payments from one fiscal year to the next.[24]

Obscuring the Deficit

States wrestling with balanced budget requirements sometimes use budget gimmicks not only to react to deficits but to obscure or minimize them. If the deficit is small or defined away, they will not have to act to raise taxes or cut services, both of which are politically unpopular. For example, Rep. David Obey of Wisconsin reported a number of years ago, "I come from a state with a balanced budget requirement. In the six years that I served in the legislature, Wisconsin's indebtedness doubled, because they engaged in all kinds of phoney-baloney devices, off-budget accounting, dummy building corporations, all the rest, that simply defined out of the budget all kinds of spending that was really governmental." [25]

Another gimmick to make a budget look balanced is to accelerate tax collections, which produces a one-time windfall for the state. For example, if a state changes from a quarterly to a monthly collection schedule, it can collect fifteen months' revenues in twelve months. On a quarterly basis, it could collect taxes the first of the year for the preceding three months; the second payment would be at month three for the preceding three months; the third payment would be at month six for the preceding three months; and the final payment for the year would be at month nine for the preceding three months. But if the state goes to monthly collections at that point, it can collect the taxes for months ten, eleven, and twelve, which it would normally have to wait until the next fiscal year to collect.[26]

A similar gimmick is to delay some expenditures so that they occur in the next fiscal year. That increases the next year's expenditures, but by then the recession will have ended, it is hoped, and increased revenues will cover the extra expenditures. A way to push expenditures into the following year is to change the basis of accounting from modified accrual to cash. Under cash accounting, expenditures that are incurred this year, but not paid until next year, are officially counted as next year's expenditures. Under accrual accounting, they would be counted as part of this year's expenditures.

In Illinois the governor changed the accounting system from modified accrual to cash in 1978. He made the budget look more balanced in that year because the cash accounting system pushed off some expenditures into the next year's budget.[27] In addition, the cash budget changed the definition of a deficit. A cash budget measures deficits by looking at the available cash balance at the end of the year, rather than matching revenues and expenditures during the year. The result is an easily manipulable deficit.

The available cash balance is eminently suited for manipulation: Any cash on hand goes into the available balance, even if it is a loan. The available balance is also affected by speedups in revenue collections, or delays in paying vendors, or by manipulating the timing of drawdowns of federal funds. "When an administration commits itself to a specific end of year available balance, it can manipulate the revenue processing system to bring about an available balance consistent with its prediction." [28] Perhaps most important, the cash balance is always positive and hence makes it look as if the state is always running a surplus, even if it is in deficit.

Other common techniques include borrowing between funds and using one-time revenues to make the budget look more balanced than it is. For example, to address an incipient deficit in FY 1981–1982, California began its deficit reduction plan mainly with one-time revenues. These included financing capital outlays previously paid out of the general fund with one-time use of tidelands oil revenues; anticipation of increased federal funding for Supplemental Security Income/State Supplemental Income; and temporary elimination of the state payments to local governments to replace revenues lost because of Proposition 13. One-time revenue increases totaled nearly $514 million; one-time expenditure reductions totaled $208 million.[29]

Taking expenditures off-budget, manipulating the cash balance by borrowing or moving expenditures forward or revenues back, closing the gap with one-time revenues, and internal borrowing are all techniques to reduce the amount of spending cuts or tax increases that might otherwise be necessary. They are part of a politics of avoidance and delay to avert hard political choices, the kind that make enemies. These techniques are not necessarily bad; it makes sense to avoid deep cuts and expensive restructuring to eliminate a deficit that will disappear on its own within a year or two as the economy recovers. If state laws allowed more time to recover from a deficit resulting from a downturn in the economy, less effort would be exerted to hide such deficits.

Creating Buffers

Although some states minimize deficits with budget gimmicks, to get past the worst of a recession without deep cuts in service levels, these techniques can take them only so far. When the deficits are discovered and made public, the routines of handling deficits require action during the year. Since such cuts are typically painful, the states have sought to create funds that will help tide them over recessions without cuts to programs or staffing.

It is normally the governor's responsibility to make midyear cuts, which are perceived as a political liability. The governor may try to avoid them by creating buffer funds through underestimating revenue or holding back expenditures that have been appropriated. The politics of balance is intimately related to the politics of revenue estimation. In Illinois, for example, the governor and the state Office of Management and Budget have had a tendency to underestimate revenues, to build in a buffer in case some revenues do not show up. Such a buffer prevents deficits and hence the politically awkward cuts the governor would otherwise have to make in the middle of the year. The legislature has pressed for higher estimations of revenues, knowing that if a deficit occurs during the year, the governor, not the legislature, will have to cut back expenditures.[30] The higher estimates of revenues allow legislators to make a more generous budget and satisfy more claims.

Rather than raise taxes during a recession, which may exaggerate the economic downturn and will almost certainly raise a public outcry because taxes will take a bigger bite out of people's shrinking income, or cut expenditures, which are needed more acutely during recessions, most states have created so-called rainy day funds. They also may build their general fund balances during the good days and draw them down during recessions. The Advisory Commission on Intergovernmental Relations (ACIR) estimated that thirty-five states had some kind of stabilization fund in 1988.[31] By 1992 ACIR reported that forty-four states had such a fund.[32] The Center for Budget and Policy Priorities reported that forty-five of the forty-eight states they looked at had some kind of rainy day fund in 1999.[33] Some of these funds were tiny or even had a zero balance, however, so their impact during a recession would be minimal, especially if the recession lasted for more than a year. In what appears to be something of a turnaround, in 2002 the Center for Budget and Policy Priorities reported that nine states either had no rainy day fund or had no money in the fund. The states that did maintain the funds had more money in them than during the previous recession, but the amounts were still inadequate.[34] The recession following 9/11 depleted many rainy day funds, and in 2005 the Center for Budget and Policy Priorities listed seventeen states that either had no rainy day fund or had a fund with a zero balance.[35]

The farther away politicians get from the last recession and its painful cuts, the greater the temptation to spend down the year-end balances. Separate rainy day accounts, with automatic provisions for buildup and spenddown, may lessen this temptation somewhat. Rainy day funds are somewhat easier to defend than unearmarked year-end balances, which look as if the state has collected more revenues than it needed. The formula for funding the rainy day account is decided first; then the money is set aside each year and is drawn down when economic conditions cause a decline in revenues.[36]

Passing the Buck to Local Governments

Especially for states without effective rainy day funds, such as Wisconsin, there may be great temptation to balance the budget on the backs of the local governments. Because local governments are the subordinates of the states and have to take orders from state governments, the states can decide to pass the burden of paying for programs and projects on to them. The states can also claim local revenues if they choose. Richard Lamm, when he was governor of Colorado, described the politics of passing the buck:

> The Gramm-Rudman bill is the result of Washington's inability to deal rationally with its mounting deficit. My hope is that this bill will be a catalyst for more careful analysis of Federal programs. My fear is that it will be an excuse for fiscal federalism at the point of a budgetary bayonet. I would be more critical of the Federal Government but for the fact that Colorado state government plays the same tricks on its cities and counties. Every election year, legislators brag that Colorado ranks forty-eighth nationally in the level of state taxes based on personal income. What they don't tell the public is, local governments are having to shoulder the tax burdens that the state passes along.[37]

Cutting back revenue that the state would normally share with the local governments is a very tempting strategy, and one that the local governments fear because they are dependent on these fund flows. The fear is heightened when the states reduce revenues, or set taxing or spending limits, or experience recession-related declines in revenue. Reflecting such fears, when Michigan passed a constitutional amendment in 1977 to limit expenditures, it wrote into its constitution that the state had to maintain the current proportion of expenditures on local governments. The state was forbidden to economize by disproportionately cutting intergovernmental transfers to local governments. In 1979, the voters of Washington State passed a similar measure, illustrating the link between state spending limits, on the one hand, and curtailment of state unfunded mandates on the other. In Oregon, in 1996, the citizens passed a constitutional amendment prohibiting the state from imposing unfunded mandates on the local governments. What made this measure urgent was that the local governments were confronting rigid statewide limits on their ability to raise taxes. The provision required public reaffirmation of the amendment in four years, and it was enthusiastically renewed by the public.

States have generally found it difficult to abide by limitations on their ability to pass costs along to their local jurisdictions, but such laws or constitutional provisions do seem to help local governments fight back, despite the disproportionate power of the state compared to the local governments.

In 1979 the voters approved Initiative 62 (codified as RCW 43.135.060), which limited state spending and imposed restrictions on the state to prevent the state from shifting responsibilities to the local level without adequate funding. A number of lawsuits were brought against the state pursuant to Initiative 62, including an action by King County to recover costs related to the mandatory arrest requirements imposed by the state for domestic violence. This resulted in a settlement for $1.95 million.

In response to King County's lawsuit and a similar suit brought by Tacoma, the legislature amended RCW 43.135.060 in 1990, to make it impractical for any other jurisdiction to sue the state. However, this amendment was repealed by the voters with the passage of Initiative 601 in 1993, which reinstated the state's obligation to fund any mandate to local government occurring after July 1, 1995, by specific appropriation. When the voters approved Referendum 49 in 1998, the obligation of the state to provide a specific appropriation to fund mandates to local government was amended to allow the state to reimburse the cost of new programs or increases in service levels by making "increases in state distributions of revenue to political subdivisions after January 1, 1998."

In November 1998, twenty counties, including King County, filed an action against the state pursuant to RCW 43.135.060, alleging that the state had failed to fully fund the counties for processing alternative residential placements, children in need of services, at-risk youth and truancy petitions as mandated by chapter 13.32A RCW and chapter 28A.225 RCW (popularly known as the "Becca Bill"). This action was settled between the state and the counties for $4.7 million, including $1.35 million for King County.[38]

In California the situation was a little different. Rather than pass along costs, the state took control of local government revenues. In 1978 California voters passed a constitutional amendment known as Proposition 13, severely reducing property taxes for local governments. The state stepped in and helped replace the lost revenue, but in the process, state control of local government finance became much more centralized. When the state ran into fiscal difficulties, it eased them at the expense of the local governments. The state took over $40 billion from local government revenues over twelve years. Initially the state took property taxes that were going to the local governments and gave them instead to the schools and community colleges, reducing its own expenditures. Then after 9/11, when the state's financial position worsened, the state reneged on replacing revenues lost through a reduction in the car tax when the economy was flush. The state then delayed payments on mandated expenditures, leaving the local governments to find whatever money they could to fulfill the state requirements. Collectively, these losses aggravated financial problems at the local level, in some cases causing, or at least contributing to, staffing reductions in police and fire departments.

As the problem grew worse, the local governments initially reacted with dismay and then began to fight back with a proposed constitutional amendment to restrict the state's revenue grabs. Eventually a compromise was worked out in which the state promised to stop taking the local governments' revenues but retained some leeway in case of severe fiscal exigency. The amendment "prohibits the Legislature from taking car taxes, local property tax money and sales-tax money from local governments unless the governor first declares a fiscal emergency and two-thirds of legislators agree. Even then, the money must be paid back in full within three years." [39] In addition, the measure requires the state to pay back the costs of mandates for which it had not paid the local governments for several years, and it allows the local governments to decide not to comply with future unfunded mandates if they cannot afford to pay for them or disagree on their importance. The amendment protecting local government revenues had wide bipartisan support and passed easily in November 2004.

When a state is in severe financial trouble, the existence of a prohibition on unfunded mandates may not be sufficient to curtail them. The temptation to take local revenues either to carry out state policy or to fill state budget gaps can be overwhelming.

The city of Champaign, Illinois, described in 2004 the impact of the state's mandates on the city's budget:

> The state recently adopted legislation related to property taxes that will increase the City's costs and reduce its revenues, for an overall negative impact of close to $1 million. The first change is an increase in property tax exemptions that will result in a loss of about $300,000 to the General Fund for the 2004 levy year. . . . The second unfunded state mandate, an increase in firefighter pension benefits, will reduce property tax revenues to the General Fund as well. The fire pension benefit increase expense is estimated at $600,000 annually.[40]

To get some idea of whether the states generally refrain from passing along unfunded mandates, or yield to temptation to balance their own budgets at the expense of the local governments, possibly creating the need for revenue increases or service cuts in the localities, one can look at the laws states have passed requiring the state to absorb the costs of mandates they impose on local governments, and at the proportion of state and local spending that the states have picked up over time.

By 1988 fifteen states had passed laws and constitutional amendments requiring the state to reimburse localities for imposed costs. Those laws and amendments overestimate local ability to resist state imposition of costs, since half of them are statutory, and they may be overlooked in practice.[41] In 1995 New Jersey citizens approved an unfunded mandates amendment that required a supermajority, three-quarters vote of the legislature to pass an unfunded mandate and established a mandates board to examine complaints and petitions and decide what was and was not an unfunded mandate under the law. By 1996 the Wisconsin Legislative Reference Bureau reported that twenty-eight states had some type of mandate restraint program, established by constitutional provision, statute, or both. Of the twenty-eight states, seventeen provided for the reimbursement of all mandates; nine provide for reimbursement of selected mandates. The extent of reimbursement could be full, partial, or a combination.[42]

More evidence on trends can be deduced from looking at changes over time in the cost to the states of assistance to the local governments and changes in the proportions of the costs of direct service delivery that state and local governments pay. Are the states assuming more responsibility for direct services or handing more of those responsibilities over to the local governments, on average?

As the states have granted tax breaks, preempted local revenue sources, or applied tax limits at the local level, they have increased their payments to the local governments to compensate them for the revenue losses. State payments to local governments increased from 30.4 percent to 32.8 percent of local government revenues between 1997 and 2002; even more striking, those payments jumped from 31.3 percent to 45.5 percent of state revenues over the same period. While local governments are still responsible for the majority of direct expenditures, states are picking up a bit more than they had, increasing their share of direct state and local expenditures from about 43 percent to close to 45 percent between 1997 and 2002. These data, provided by the U.S. Census of Governments, only tap the beginning of the recession, but they do indicate why some states, after using temporary resources to balance their budgets, have been eyeing their shared revenues and payments to the local governments for possible cuts.

More direct evidence is seen when one looks at the state proportion of state and local expenditures (excluding federal aid) over a longer period. (If the state proportion is going up or is constant, then the state is not passing on any burden to the local governments.) The proportion of state and local expenditures the state governments picked up increased continuously from 44 percent in 1942 to 58 percent in 1982. But in 1983 and 1984 it began to decline, to 57 percent in 1983 and 56 percent in 1984. By 1991–1992 the state share had dropped to 43 percent. The figure has remained nearly constant since then, rising only to 45 percent by 2002.[43]

For the decade 1992–2002, on average, state aid to local governments was not cut disproportionately, but to manage their share, the local governments had to maintain or increase taxes, while the states were more cautious about increases. In 1997, the ratio of own-source local to own-source state revenues was roughly 40 percent to 60 percent, but only five years later, in 2002, the ratio was closer to 47 percent to 53 percent. With more states imposing tax limits on local governments' ability to tax, this trend may stop, but if it does, local governments will find it even more difficult to pay for state mandates, especially if the states curtail their shared revenues to balance their own budgets during recessions.

The Politics of Balance in Cities

Like states, cities are required to balance their budgets. But unlike the federal government, local governments have virtually no role in influencing cycles of the economy with their budgets. Generally, their budgets are too small and their economies too open for local governments to have an impact on the economy. The result is that cities do not have to worry about whether they should run deficits. They try to maintain year-end balances to tide them over when recession hits, but they are often unable to predict downturns in the economy and have to reduce expenditures during the year to balance the budget.

At the local level, as at the state level, considerable effort may be spent to hide or minimize deficits, especially ones that are not the result of immediate environmental exigencies. Cities use many of the same tactics that states do, including borrowing between funds (sometimes invisibly and without intent to repay), changing the basis of accounting so that some expenditures are counted in the next year's budget, delaying paying bills, and borrowing from pension funds by not making the required employer contribution. Cities may also hide deficits by borrowing outside the city for operating expenditures, pretending they are borrowing for capital. They sometimes shift expenditures from a fund that is poorer into another that is richer.

Depending on the definition of "deficit" used, cities can sometimes make the budget look balanced by drawing down reserves, which is usually technically legal but obscures the fact that the city is running an operating deficit. Or the budget can be balanced with revenues from the sale of property, grants or other one-time income. Overestimating revenues also makes the budget look more balanced than it is.

When deficits occur unintentionally during the year, the normal response is to gather unspent money and defer spending it until the crisis is over or until the council has had a chance to act on priorities. The result may be heavier cuts in some areas than in others; the intent is not to choose program areas but to find money that is as yet unspent. Capital projects are often delayed if the money is not yet spent or irrevocably committed.

When a deficit is imminent in the following year's budget, or when a deficit is carried over from one year to the next, then the manager or mayor makes recommendations for how the deficit gap is to be closed, and the council must approve or disapprove the recommendations. In this situation, program priorities must be decided, revenue increase and expenditure decrease weighed, and scope of services reevaluated. Formally, the council often has the legal power to make these decisions, but in reality the distribution of power between the mayor, manager, or administrator, on the one hand, and the council on the other, is highly variable.

The council may give the chief executive officer general policy for the upcoming budget, such as, "Balance the budget without tax increases this year" or "Figure in a 1 percent increase in local sales taxes." The manager or administrator may make recommendations for the figure to use for inflation and give estimates for revenue. Council members may accept or reject these estimates or give alternate estimates. The council may give general guidelines about which services may be cut and which must be sustained, or it may get involved in the details of line-by-line, program-by-program cuts. Whatever balance of power exists in one year may change the next, as council members lose interest, or the manager or mayor restructures the budget process and asks for a different kind of input, or asks for input at a different stage of the process.

The issue of scope of services is unlikely to arise in response to a midyear revenue decline, but it can arise as local governments wrestle with what appears to be an impending imbalance in the next year's operating budget. For example in the 1970s, when cities were dealing with fiscal stress, if they were responsible for a range of functions they often tried to shift some of them to other levels of government. Services such as courts, city universities, and museums were either shifted to other levels of government or to the private sector. Some cities gave their planning functions to the county. In some states, cities were able to shift some or all of their share of welfare to the state, as well as some of the cost of policing.[44]

One city wrestling with slow growth in property tax revenues and termination of federal revenue sharing tried to give a city sewer to the sanitary district, the city bus system to the local state university, the dog pound and animal control function to the county, and the airport and economic development office to regional authorities. A number of counties have given responsibility for the courts to the states.

The issue of scope arises not only in terms of shifting the level of government at which some services are performed but also in the question of what services will be cut back or eliminated. During the 1970s, when the public seemed determined to hold the line on revenues, cities perceived that they had little choice but to cut back services. They chose to do this, insofar as they could, in ways that would not affect the public too greatly. They cut back in invisible ways, such as delaying maintenance and deferring capital projects. When deep service cuts appeared necessary, their choice was to find some other unit of government to perform the task.

The example in the following box, of a city running deficits, illustrates several themes about how city budgets become unbalanced, the tendency to obscure deficits when they occur, and the kinds of pressure necessary to force a city to rebalance its budget. The case also illustrates how difficult it can be to cut

---

Minicase: The Politics of Deficits—An Urban Example

The city of Southside (a fictional name given to protect the anonymity of those involved) ran deficits that were hidden in the budget from 1972 to 1976.[1] During the later part of this period there was no recession to blame. The initial causes of the deficit included hiring at the same time a young and inexperienced city manager and an inexperienced budget officer. But the city's problems went well beyond hiring a few inexperienced people. It was suffering from long-term erosion of its economic base, as heavy industry in the region declined, leaving behind many unemployed and a reduced demand for housing. The result was frozen or slow-growing revenues from both sales and property taxes. Department heads and elected officials seemed unwilling or unable to cut back expenditures proportionately. Elected officials at one point actually reduced property tax rates despite increasing costs. The young city manager did not have enough power to

(continued)

force the elected officials and department heads to cut expenditures, so he tried to reduce labor costs instead, incensing the city's employee unions and actually increasing labor costs.

The young manager initially hid the deficits, then tried to publicize them as a way to force the council to make the requisite cuts. He used his budget message to warn council members about emerging deficits, but council members later argued that they did not understand that the budget had to balance fund by fund. They said they were looking at the bottom line, in effect, a cash balance. Cash balances are nearly always positive at the end of the year and are thus misleading indicators if there is a deficit. The council in effect chose a loose definition of balance.

The deficits were kept secret in part by inappropriate, secret internal borrowing, especially from the cash flow of the water fund. The director of the water department worried that he could no longer do his job properly. He pleaded his case at a budget hearing in an emotional tone. When auditors came to examine the financial records of the city, they refused to audit the water fund because the records were not complete—the first public acknowledgment of serious financial trouble.

The second key event in forcing the deficits into public view occurred as the council and manager struggled to deal with the long-term decline of the city's economic base. They helped promote a new regional shopping center on the edge of the city. To carry out their end of the bargain required annexations, property acquisitions, and capital outlays for water, roads, traffic signals, and a new police substation. The city had to borrow, issuing a bond. The bond issue meant that Moody's, one of the major bond evaluators, would have to examine and certify the city's creditworthiness, or potential bond buyers would not risk their money. The evaluation of the city's creditworthiness was a disaster; the staff had to struggle to retain any rating at all. The problem was now public, and the city had to take action to avoid complete humiliation, as well as to maintain the marketability of its bonds.

The manager tried to cut back spending by the departments but was hampered by the independence of the department heads. The police and fire chiefs were hired and fired by a police and fire board appointed by the mayor and so were not directly responsible to the city manager and felt free to ignore his budget advice. The fire department was spending more than its budgeted allocation; police department expenditures had grown rapidly in response to urban riots a number of years earlier, and the manager seemed unable to cut them back. He requested cuts from the department

(continued)

heads, which they refused to make. The manager also tried to cut out council members' pet capital projects but found that he did not have the power to do that either. In frustration, the manager tried to cut some of the union agreements and restructure the unions so that they would be easier to deal with, but he ended up with some very expensive, arbitrated settlements that further unbalanced his budget. The manager was fired and replaced with a more senior manager.

The new manager froze departmental budgets and increased revenue by increasing federal aid, an option still open in the late 1970s. Perhaps more important, he changed the budget process. He had control over the street department head, who was responsible to him, and fired him. The manager forbade department heads to communicate directly to the council without going through him, to prevent end runs in which department heads got protection for expenditures from the council before they appeared in the budget request. The new manager insisted on the right to hire the police and fire chiefs and was successful, so that they reported to him. The fire department was broken out of the general fund and set up with its own earmarked taxes, so the temptation for it to overspend by borrowing from other departments was reduced. These changes vastly increased the manager's ability to control the budget requests and spending of the departments. The departments and the council were burdened with more constraints, but the manager had more authority to enforce balance.

The case of Southside indicates that despite balanced budget requirements, cities sometimes do run deficits, but because of the balance constraint, the size of the deficits may be obscured. When that happens, the deficit can grow to a substantial portion of all spending and make remedies politically difficult. Because many of the actors shared a belief that the public would not tolerate an increase in the property tax, the option of reducing spending was explored. But the political coalitions that supported expenditures were stronger than the young manager, and he failed to make significant cuts. When the manager was finally fired and the city resolved to handle its deficit problems, it chose budget process reform as a key to the solution, giving the manager more power to make cuts and balance the budget and centralizing the executive budget process. The deficits seemed to result as much from failure of structure as from economic circumstances, and so a reform of structure seemed a logical response.

1. Irene Rubin, *Running in the Red: The Political Dynamics of Urban Fiscal Stress* (Albany: State University of New York Press, 1982).

spending when every expenditure seems to have a political protector or be exempt from cuts. A change in structure was required, with an increase in constraints, to force a linkage between revenues and expenditures and create enough central authority to cut back spending proposals. The case occurred in the 1970s, when the option of increasing federal aid was still open. The same story told today might have a different ending.

Summary and Conclusions

Budget balancing is more than a technical activity that readjusts spending and revenue decisions. It is fundamentally linked to issues about the scope of government, because balance depends on decisions to raise taxes and maintain scope or cut spending and reduce scope. Balance is also linked to spending priorities: when expenditures are cut back, some programs will be protected and others cut back disproportionately, or all programs will be cut across the board. Balance is linked to federalism because the scope of responsibilities and the relationship between revenue capacity and spending responsibilities can easily be changed, as one level of government seeks to balance its budget at the expense of others. Finally, the politics of balance is linked to the politics of process, as governments shift budget-making power in attempts to increase discipline, control expenditures, and systematically and authoritatively link revenues and expenditures.

Many of the issues involved in budget balance are not immediate distributional questions, but questions of the structure and size of government, the level of taxation, and sometimes even the form of government. These questions bring out ideological differences between people, between Democrats and Republicans, liberals and conservatives, business and labor. Even the public at large may be involved, in terms of preferences for taxation levels or insistence on the constraint of balance.

Those who want to limit the size of government have striven to link spending caps with balanced budget requirements and to reduce flexibility to a minimum via simply worded amendments in the constitution. Those who want government to continue to provide existing programs, or even expand them, have sought to maintain balance without constraints on revenues.

More specialized interest groups and department heads may become involved in the politics of balance if particular programs are threatened by cuts; they increase the constraints on cutting the budget, making the political choices more difficult, and hence encourage options that do not rely on deep budget cuts. The consequences of the political difficulty of making cuts are delay, minimizing the size and importance of the problem, hoping it will go away, and using gimmicks that make the budget appear balanced.

The politics of balance is closely linked to the politics of budget implementation. A budget can become unbalanced during the year because of environmental changes or because gimmicks used to make the budget look balanced cause problems during the budget year. Budgeters may overestimate revenues and underestimate expenditures, so that the budget as submitted looks balanced, but it will become unbalanced during the year. At the state and local levels the budget may have to be changed during the year to rebalance it. At any level of government, departments may request supplemental appropriations if their initial estimates of expenditures were too low. Requirements for balance also encourage interfund transfers during the year, to make the budget look more balanced than it is. The importance of changes that occur during the budget year is discussed in the next chapter.

7. Budget Execution: The Politics of Adaptation

Budget execution is the fun part of budgeting, and the most important part. You get to see how good your estimates were, and whether it all works. You can't just put a budget on the shelf and expect it to work.

—Neil Neilson, City Manager

A budget is passed at the end of a long period of analysis, debate, disagreement, and compromise. As a result, it often seems to be the outcome and end point of the budgetary process. But budgeting does not stop completely once the budget becomes law. Because of a changing economy, poor predictions of revenues and expenditures, continuing political battles, changed leadership, and the altered salience of public problems, the budget may change after it is passed. Making changes because of unavoidable circumstances, while ensuring that the policy agreements underlying the budget are observed, is the task of budget implementation.

The implementation stage often involves formulas for disbursements and rules about how much money can be shifted from one item or program to another after the budget has been passed. The emphasis in budget execution is on carrying out the budget exactly as it was enacted, which makes budget execution seem highly technical, the proper sphere of administrators and accountants, devoid of political content. In reality, budget execution is also political because it regulates the degree of public accountability in the budget, because it involves battles for policy control between the executive and the legislature, and because even the most technical of issues, such as the elimination of waste, fraud, and abuse, may become part of political campaigns.

Budgets are open to the environment; when the environment changes in the middle of the year, the budget must be flexible enough to adapt. The people who draw up a budget have to make predictions about revenues and expenditures based on guesses about the future performance of the economy, the rate of inflation, and even the weather. When the economy improves, revenues increase, and outlays for programs such as unemployment compensation and welfare go down. When the economy slows down, revenues drop off, and expenditures for unemployment compensation and welfare go up. Inflation affects the price of goods and services purchased during the year, as well as the payout for pensions that rise with the cost of living. Weather conditions affect the costs of heating bills, street repairs, and cleanups after hurricanes, tornadoes, or floods. In recent years, war has created a somewhat unpredictable set of expenditures, including everything from recovery costs from the attacks of 9/11 to military supplies. To accommodate unforeseeable events the budget may be adjusted in midyear.

A budget may change during the year because the budget process was not complete before the beginning of the fiscal year. The budget year may begin under one set of figures but continue under a different set after the decision making is finished. For example, at the national level, it is common for some of the thirteen appropriation bills to be completed on time but for others to miss the deadline. To keep the federal agencies functioning, Congress passes continuing resolutions, funding the agencies at the level of last year's budget or at the level of a House- or Senate-passed bill until their final budget is approved. Several continuing resolutions may be passed at different levels of spending before the final budget is passed.

Budget negotiations may seem to be complete sometimes when they really are not. Budget actors may tentatively resolve an issue, expressing the result in the formal budget that is passed in public view, but later back off from the agreement, bringing about new negotiations. Sometimes actors distort information to get an agreement that will pass, but end up with an unworkable budget, and have to modify it later.

When leadership changes, which often occurs during a budget year, the new insiders may be eager to implement their policies. Newly elected executives may make extensive revisions in existing budgets to reflect the promises they campaigned on.

For all these reasons—a changing economy or environment, continuing political battles, a changed leadership—the budget implemented may not be the same as the budget passed. A certain amount of flexibility and change during the budget year is both necessary and desirable, but once the door is open to changes, some of them may be inappropriate and may undo the agreements reached in public or challenge constitutional balance of powers.

Granting the executive branch wide discretion to implement the budget and make such changes as may be necessary may give chief executives a disproportionate amount of decision-making power not allowed during the regular budget process. If the chief executive uses that discretion to reverse the intent of the legislature, the result may be a battle between the two branches. Changes in the budget during the year, if they are extensive or clearly policy related, may create a shadowy, second budget process, outside public scrutiny, threatening the ability of the budget as originally passed to represent government decisions to the public. The need for flexibility in the budget, to adapt to changing conditions, conflicts with the need to implement the budget as it was passed. Public accountability requires that the budget passed in full public view, with public and interest group participation, be the budget implemented.

How is this dilemma resolved? First, budgets are generally implemented as passed. The requirement to do so is taken seriously, so that consideration of important policy issues that arise during the year is often delayed until the next full, open budget process. Second, the legislatures generally grant the executive branch discretion to make necessary, minor technical changes during the year. These technical adjustments may be carefully monitored to ensure that important policy decisions are not slipped in among the routine adaptations without due consideration and participation.

Policy-significant budget decisions may be allowed during the year under particular conditions. When a new president is elected, he may be given fairly broad discretion to reshape the existing budget to fit his policies. Or Congress may design and implement new programs for relief of farmers in the middle of a drought or to help the unemployed during a deep recession. These decisions are made in the normal way, by the usual committees; what is unusual about them is that they feed into the budget in the middle of the year and they may be made in haste. In these cases, the changes have high visibility and widespread public acceptance. They do not threaten public acceptability or accountability.

Despite the care with which budgets are normally implemented, deviations from the budget that are not routine and minor sometimes occur. These may be of two kinds: The first is a violation of fiscal control, resulting in overspending or waste, fraud, or abuse. The second is a violation of policy control, in which some budget actor makes policy changes in the budget without going through the whole formal, public business of lawmaking. If the consequences are serious enough, irritating enough, or embarrassing enough, the chief executive or the legislature may increase control over budget implementation to prevent a recurrence. The legislature may increase its control over the executive; the chief executive may increase his or her control over the agencies. The result may be an increase in the number and severity of constraints over budget implementation.

Tools for Changing the Budget

Budgets can only be changed in specific ways after the budget year has begun. These include supplemental appropriations and rescissions, building and depleting contingency funds, deferrals and other holdbacks, and interfund transfers and reprogrammings.[1]

A supplemental appropriation is a budget law that adds money to some existing function or new purpose during the year. The money can come from fund balances, unexpected revenue increases, or contingency funds, or it can come from rescissions, that is, withdrawals of previously granted legal authorization to spend money. In some cases, however, there may be a supplemental appropriation without extra funds to pay for it. In such cases, supplemental appropriations contribute to deficits.

A deferral is a delay in spending money that has been appropriated for a specific project or program. A chief executive may ask for a hold back, usually a fixed and small percentage of the approved budget of all or nearly all agencies. Holdbacks can be insurance against fluctuating revenues or unexpected expenditures, or they can be used to create a pool of funds to spend for special, politically favored projects.

Interfund transfers take money from one appropriation account or fund and purpose and spend it in a different fund or appropriation account, presumably for a related function. Such transfers normally go back to the legislative body for approval; they represent a sort of budget amendment and reprioritization. Reprogrammings are transfers that occur within funds or accounts, often within the same administrative unit. They may shift money from one line in the budget to another, from one project to another, or from one category of spending, such as capital improvements, to another, such as supplies or contractual services. Rules typically govern the allowable amounts of such within-fund transfers and sometimes govern where the money can come from. At the federal level, reprogrammings are typically also bound by reporting requirements. Some reprogrammings require advance notice and some require after-the-fact reporting. Without those reports, Congress could lose control of budget implementation and policy and have little idea how the money legislators had approved had actually been spent.

Supplemental Appropriations, Rescissions, and Deferrals.

Supplemental appropriations and rescissions are most common at the national level as tools for reshaping the budget midyear. Both are laws, passed in the normal manner. They may be initiated by the president or by Congress, and if initiated by the president may be raised, lowered, or denied by Congress.

Supplemental appropriations were used extensively in the 1970s and most of the 1980s. Table 7.1 shows the dollar amounts of supplementals, as well as the percentage of total budget authority and proportion of the deficit that they represented. Table 7.2 shows the relationship between growing supplementals and growing deficits for the recent period 2000–2005. It is clear that supplementals contributed substantially to the deficits.

The use of supplementals dwindled in the 1990s, to the point where rescissions actually exceeded supplementals in one year. The change shows the effect of efforts to rebalance the federal budget, particularly the Budget Enforcement Act. As we have already discussed, the Budget Enforcement Act mandated that supplemental appropriations be offset with additional revenues or spending cuts elsewhere, for all except urgent emergency spending. The necessity of making explicit trade-offs to fund new requests midyear helped reduce their frequency. Efforts were made to estimate in advance the costs of emergencies caused by storms, earthquakes, or floods and budget for them. Only amounts above the averages would have to be paid for with supplementals. Expenditures to help the economy adjust to recessions, which had been routinely picked up in supplementals in prior years, were drastically reduced in the 1990s—only $4 billion of a $16 billion antirecession initiative passed in the early 1990s.

After budgetary balance was achieved in 1998, the pressure to limit emergency supplementals was reduced and they began to grow again. Items that were not clearly emergencies or unpredictable crept into the emergency supplementals, where they did not have to be offset by new revenues or budget cuts elsewhere. Perhaps the most glaring example was the funding of the 2000 Census with emergency supplemental funding, which is to say by deficit spending. Obviously elected officials could not argue that the Census was not anticipated well in advance or represented an emergency.

After 2002, when the Budget Enforcement Act lapsed and the response to 9/11 began to cause increases in spending for antiterrorist activities and war, spending through supplementals soared, as did the deficit. The wars in Afghanistan and

Table 7.1 Supplemental Appropriations, Net of Rescissions, 1970s, 1980s, 1990s

Year	Supplemental budget authority (in millions of dollars)	Percentage of total budget authority	Deficit (in billions of dollars)	Percentage of deficit
1970	5,994	2.8	2.8	na
1971	9,871	4.2	−23.0	42.6
1972	11,599	4.7	−23.4	49.1
1973	11,371	4.1	−14.9	75.8
1974	14,796	4.7	−6.1	240.9
1975	27,588	6.7	−53.2	51.6
1976	24,636	5.9	−73.7	33.3
1977	36,724	7.8	−53.7	68.3
1978	16,054	3.1	−59.2	27.0
1979	13,858	2.5	−40.7	33.9
1980	19,461	2.9	−73.8	26.2
1981	6,923	.9	−79.0	8.7
1982	21,020	2.6	−128.0	16.4
1983	21,123	2.4	−207.8	10.1
1984	16,222	1.7	−185.4	8.7
1985	14,804	1.4	−212.3	6.9
1986	2,249	.2	−221.2	1.0
1987	9,370	.9	−149.8	6.2
1988	1,302	.1	−155.2	.83
1989	5,615	.5	−152.5	3.6
1990	4,329	.3	−221.1	1.9
1991	48,281[a]	3.4	−269.3	17.9
1992	11,229	.7	−290.3	3.8
1993	7,860	.5	−255.1	3.4
1994	10,358	.6	−203.2	5.1
1995	−12,524	—	−164.0	—
1996	668	.04	−107.5	.6
1997	917	.05	−21.9	4.1
1998	3,551	.2	69.2	na
1999	11,348	.6	125.5	na
2000	16,952	.9	236.2	na

Sources: Congressional Budget Office, *Supplemental Appropriations in the 1980s,* x. Total budget authority and size of the deficit were drawn from the *Historical Tables of the U.S. Budget;* calculations by the author. Supplementals net of rescissions for the 1990s, from CBO, *Supplemental Appropriations in the 1990s,* March 2001, Table A-1.

a. The year 1991 was an anomalous year; most of this supplemental was for Operation Desert Storm and was eventually paid back by our allies.

Table 7.2 Discretionary Supplemental Spending 2002–2005 (in billions of dollars)

Year	Supplementals	Total discretionary budget authority	Deficit
2001	20	664	128.2
2002	44	691	−157.8
2003	91	758	−377.6
2004	117	790	−412.1
2005	93 (anticipated)	823	−426.6 (estimated)

Source: Data on supplementals and total discretionary budget authority from Office of Management and Budget, *Budget 2006 Summary Tables,* Table S-2, Discretionary Totals. Edited by author; available at www.whitehouse.gov/omb/budget/fy2006/pdf/budget/tables.pdf. These data are not, strictly speaking, comparable to the data in Table 7.1, as they are based only on supplementals for discretionary spending, and it is not clear that the figures given are net of offsets.

in Iraq were funded through emergency supplementals, even though many of the expenses could have been anticipated in the regular budget. The effect was to swell the deficit.

Why fund wars with supplemental appropriations? By leaving a huge chunk of spending out of the regular budget and funding it later during the year, the president made the deficit look smaller when he submitted his annual budget proposal. If the real size of the deficit were widely advertised, there might have been more pressure to curtail it and hence to limit the tax reductions that have been the cornerstone of the George W. Bush administration. Second, emergency supplementals for war are nearly impossible to vote against; they receive very little congressional scrutiny and provide maximum flexibility to the Defense Department in spending the funds (although Congress has been reluctant to give the DoD as much of a blank check as it wishes and has asked for). The Defense Department has made it clear that it prefers supplemental appropriations because they give more discretion in spending than regular appropriations. Third, when the administration borrows to pay for a war, present voters do not have to pay for it, and hence they are less likely to oppose the policy that launched the war. The costs of the war are obscured.

While emergency supplementals do not have to be offset, sometimes they are, and nonemergency supplementals have routinely been offset. Rescinding or legally withdrawing permission to spend money for some other program is a common way of funding a supplemental appropriation. Sometimes, however, rescissions occur independently of supplemental appropriations; they must be passed by both houses of Congress and signed by the president just like other legislation.

Presidents have long coveted the line-item veto. Some kind of enhanced rescission powers could be granted to the president to strike out parts of legislation he did not approve of. Just as line-item vetoes strengthen the governors with respect to the legislatures, enhanced rescission authority for the president would tilt the balance of powers away from the legislature and toward the executive branch.

In the 1990s, some legislators thought that enhancing the president's rescission powers might provide a way to balance the budget because the president could cut from the budget all the pork that Congress added. Although its real potential to reduce expenditures was moderate at best, the misnamed Line-Item Veto Act, granting the president enhanced rescission powers, was passed by Congress in 1996. The president made limited use of the authority. Even so, members of Congress whose projects the president cut were predictably infuriated, requiring some of the cuts to be reversed. The president's relationship with Congress suffered, further ensuring that such presidential rescissions would be a limited tool at best. After only a short time in effect, enhanced rescission authority was declared unconstitutional.

Rescissions are common at the state level. Because states are forbidden to run deficits, when revenues drop unexpectedly during the year the state may have to rescind spending authority granted to its agencies in the annual budget. In anticipation of such rescissions, agencies sometimes hold back some of their budget, rather than spend at the normal rate, to have some money on hand to cut if a rescission occurs. New hires may be delayed until it is clear that a rescission will not take place or will not be large enough to prevent new hires. Capital projects may be delayed, with the idea that money set aside for them need not be spent this fiscal year and can be applied for again in later years. It is difficult, if not impossible, to cut in a rational manner to cope with rescissions that occur during the year; what is cut is what has not yet been committed. If rescissions become common, agencies are likely to organize their expenditures so there will be resources to cut midyear. They may change the ratio of permanent to temporary employees, for example, so that there will be enough temporary staff to cut, if necessary, on short notice.

Repeated rescissions are not unusual. For example, in Idaho in fiscal year 2002, the governor announced a 3 percent midyear rescission; he announced another one for fiscal 2003. State agencies were warned that the revenue situation was deteriorating and that they should expect cuts, but they were not told how much they would have to cut. The governor announced two separate holdbacks in fiscal year 2002, one earlier in the year and one later, as the revenue situation continued to deteriorate. Many other states also engaged in rescissions during the recession and fiscal downturn from late 2001 through 2004. Temporary cuts during the year sometimes become permanent and the base on which future budgets will be allocated.

The later in the year a rescission occurs, the harder it is to implement. An 11 percent rescission that occurs in the last half of the fiscal year effectively cuts 22 percent of the remaining revenues for the year. Efforts by Governor Blagojevich in Illinois to rescind spending in the last few weeks of the fiscal year caused havoc. Because money that been held back to accommodate a possible rescission had already been spent, agencies no longer had any money to give back to balance the budget. Occurring so late in the year, the rescission claimed a substantial percentage of the remaining funds.

> Cheryl Peck, Director of Public Relations for UIS [University of Illinois Springfield], said that the governor told public university officials last fall to set aside funding for a possible midyear rescission. [Governor Rod] Blagojevich asked for a 2 percent rescission in May [the fiscal year begins July 1], but by that point the U. of I. had already spent much of the funding it had put into reserve because the middle of the fiscal year had passed, Peck said.
>
> "I can't speak for the other public universities," she said, "but when we found out six weeks before the end of the fiscal year that we had to give back money, it was pretty shocking because we . . . certainly didn't expect to have to give it back at the end of the fiscal year." . . . The U of I has lost more than $75 million in midyear rescissions since fiscal year 2002. State appropriations to the university have fallen by more than $130 million within this time.[2]

Unlike supplementals and rescissions, deferrals are not based on formal legislation passed by the legislature and signed by the executive. Nor are they useful for balancing the budget, as they typically delay rather than eliminate or reduce spending. The executive decides to delay some expenditure, presumably for technical reasons, such as a project's not being ready to begin. In the past, however, presidents have found it tempting to use deferrals in somewhat the same way as governors use line-item vetoes—to take out of the budget congressional add-ons to their budget proposals. All a president had to do was delay indefinitely any expenditure of which he disapproved. Such policy-based delays, however, violated the balance of powers, essentially ignoring the decisions of Congress if the president disagreed with them. Such deferrals became highly controversial, and so Congress included in the 1974 Congressional Budget Reform Act a requirement that the president propose deferrals to Congress; if Congress did not disapprove, the spending could be deferred. Some or all of the money for a particular project or program could be delayed for some specified period, usually only months or until the end of the fiscal year.

Congress normally accedes to the president's requests on routine deferrals but gets very touchy when the president refuses to spend money that has been legally appropriated and that represents Congress's preferences. In 1981 and 1982, Congress allowed almost all of President Ronald Reagan's requested policy deferrals; Reagan was a popular new president with an apparent mandate to reshape the budget quickly, so Congress went along with his initiatives. From 1983 to 1988, Congress got more balky about approving the president's proposals to defer spending for policy purposes. Although Congress had approved $6.1 billion of policy deferrals in 1981 and 1982, it approved only $7.7 billion in such deferrals over the next six years.[3]

During 1981 and 1982 Congress acceded to many cuts it might have preferred to oppose; the political risks of opposing the popular new president were too formidable. During those years, the president not only invoked the reconciliation procedures of the 1974 budget reform act but also bypassed those procedures by substituting his own amendment for the work of the congressional committees. Reportedly the president applied pressure to get support on these measures and provoked considerable resentment for his seeming lack of respect for congressional ways. When in 1983 the Supreme Court nullified Congress's ability to veto presidential requests for deferrals (*Immigration and Naturalization Service v. Chadha*),[4] it must have seemed one more blow to congressional power. However, the congressional veto of deferrals was declared unconstitutional because it required only one house to take action and therefore did not have the force of law.

Congress responded to the elimination of its veto power over deferrals by putting its rejections of them into supplemental appropriations and passing them as they would other laws. In 1986 when Reagan deferred some $10 billion that he did not want spent, "Congress's response was to insert a provision in that year's supplemental appropriation bill nullifying most of the policy deferrals."[5] In 1987 the Senate report on the supplementals rejected the president's request for deferrals, arguing that the president was using them for policy purposes, not programmatic technicalities. The report questioned the president's legal ability to defer the funds.[6] Indeed, in 1987 the U.S. Court of Appeals for the District of Columbia barred any kind of policy-based deferral.[7] On April 1, 1987, the comptroller general advised Congress that twenty-five policy deferrals submitted by the president after the decision by the court of appeals were illegal. The administration decided not to appeal the decision to the Supreme Court. Consequently it became illegal to defer spending for policy purposes, although spending may still be deferred for technical reasons.

At state and local levels deferrals are not policy related. Projects are deferred when there is no cash to pay for them or because it took longer than anticipated to design and contract for them. Because governors usually have line-item vetoes, and sometimes have amendatory vetoes, it is not necessary for them to withhold spending on projects that the legislature might add to their budget requests.

Reprogramming

Reprogramming is taking some or all of the money that has been budgeted to one program or project and transferring it to another in the same account or fund during the fiscal year. Reprogramming may make good managerial sense if the money cannot be appropriately spent as budgeted and other urgent needs for the money occur during the year. A labor strike may result in budgeted salary remaining unused, or a change in accounting for pensions may free up some funds that were budgeted for that purpose. At the federal level, a change in program structure may reduce the amount of money it is necessary to keep in reserve in case of emergency. Or expenditures may have been inadvertently overestimated, such as money set aside for plowing snow. Such funds can and should be released for other purposes that arise during the year within the same fund or appropriation account.

Reprogramming can help an agency adapt to unexpected contingencies without requiring a supplemental appropriation. Some agencies, however, may intentionally underspend to create a pool of funds that can be spent elsewhere on items that have not been approved. Extensive reprogramming can alter the approved budget and change the legislative priorities reflected in the appropriations. To monitor changes taking place and prevent changes that threaten legislative policies, the legislative body may set guidelines for reprogramming, limiting the total amount that can be shifted, reducing the size of the units within which flexible choices can be exercised (say, from accounts to subaccounts), requiring advance notice and explanation of reprogramming, or requiring extensive quarterly reporting after the reprogramming has taken place.

Reprogramming does take place at the state and local levels and sometimes becomes controversial, but it has been a more visible issue at the national level. Congress has tried to maintain agencies' ability to adapt to changing situations, while preventing them from using reprogramming to thwart its will. It does this by issuing guidelines to control, rather than prevent, reprogramming. Guidelines often include wording such as, "Reprogramming may be used for unforeseen events but only if delay until the next budget cycle would result in excessive costs or damage." Proscriptions include any projects for which Congress has already denied funding, and reprogramming into areas where Congress has just cut the budget. These guidelines normally appear in committee report language, rather than in actual legislation, to convey the intent of committee members without binding the agency through law, although reprogramming and transfer authority may be included in appropriations bills. Committees often ask the agencies to report in advance reprogrammings above a given dollar amount, which gives the committee members a chance to object if the reprogramming has policy implications or is otherwise questionable.

Overall, Congress's experience in controlling reprogramming has been successful. The number of requests for reprogramming has been moderate over the years, and there have been few major controversies. Nevertheless, especially in those agencies where there has been a history of tension between the committees of jurisdiction and the departments or agencies over reprogrammings, Congress has remained vigilant. Moreover, efforts to balance the budget and reduce spending, especially in the discretionary portion of the budget, renewed interest in reprogramming. War and the antiterror campaign have also seemed to require more budgetary flexibility. Legislators needed to grant agencies more discretion to redeploy money that was not being fully used, but they worried that their legislative priorities might be cut if reprogramming authority was broadened.

In 1994, when congressional appropriations committees were wrestling with cuts to help balance the budget, several subcommittees reiterated or changed language in reprogramming guidelines. The Interior Subcommittee of the Senate Appropriations Committee included such revisions in Senate Report 103-294. The language simultaneously increased the minimums necessary to trigger a formal reprogramming action, thus increasing agency discretion, and tightened other areas of discretion. The minimum trigger for reporting a reprogramming to congressional committees was raised from $250,000 or 10 percent, to $500,000 or 10 percent, with exceptions for the Forest Service, the Bureau of Indian Affairs, and the Bureau of Land Management. In the Bureau of Land Management and some Forest Service programs, the reprogramming control level was made the line item, but the trigger level for changes to be approved was $3 million or 10 percent. Thus the unit being controlled was much smaller, but the trigger for invoking control was much larger. The change was the result of an intentional effort to give these agencies more budgetary discretion. While reprogramming requirements were loosened, the Interior Subcommittee added new strictures on other sources of flexible money. For example, the committee required that when secretaries took money from programs to pay for departmental overhead, the amounts and purposes of the assessments had to be spelled out clearly. Departments were forbidden to use such funds to pay for programs that Congress had cut, for new permanent staff positions, or for any spending that could have been foreseen. In other words, Congress was considering overhead assessments as a potential source of reprogramming funds that needed to be controlled.

As this example suggests, it is not always clear whether the level of agency discretion over reprogramming is going up or down. In agencies where the clear direction was to relax reprogramming controls, the results did not confirm expectations for improved management and therefore did not encourage more decontrol. For example, in 1995 there was a budget reform of the Forest Service, which had been cited by the National Performance Review as having a budget structure so complicated and controlling that it hampered management and efficient use of public money. The House and Senate Appropriations Committees agreed to increase the agency's budgetary flexibility, consolidating line items and increasing the agency's ability to move money between line items without approval. The appropriations committees expected improved performance and reporting in return for weaker line-item controls.

The GAO reported in December 1998, however, that the changes seemed to have made little difference to agency management. One reason seems to have been that the agency seldom requested changes between line items, either before the reforms or afterward. Part of the reform restructured the budget so that all the funding for a project was consolidated in the program that would benefit most from that project. Such an approximation to program budgeting should have improved accountability. The GAO reported, however, that for a variety of reasons, including underestimating of project costs, some programs did not have the funds needed to implement a project, so other programs that were providing support services were required to absorb some of the costs.[8] Under the newer, more program-oriented system, flexibility between line items within a program was not the major concern; paying for a project with inadequate budget was the main issue, and for this, a different kind of flexibility was needed.

Although there were many reasons for lack of results from the Forest Service experiment, one of them had to do with the politics of full costing, which sometimes makes programs or projects look too expensive. Simply removing or loosening some of the line-item controls did not address the agency's perception that it needed to underestimate costs. When costs are underestimated, they have to be made up somehow because of federal antideficiency regulations. In this case the costs were made up not by formal reprogramming but by informally putting more of the costs on supporting units.

Reprogramming can be an important problem or not, depending on whether the reprogramming guidelines are too strict to allow an agency to adapt to contingencies during the year, whether the agency is likely to try to evade reprogramming guidelines, and whether the legislative body has detailed priorities that it is trying to ensure are observed. In addition, if the accounts or funds are small, there is not much discretion to move items around inside them, but if the accounts or funds are very large, the possibilities for evading policy directives are more substantial. Budgetary cutbacks increase the pressure on executive agencies to reprogram as a way of adapting to reduced funding and, at the same time, intensify legislators' fears that some of their priorities may be cut as a way to pressure them to restore funding. Agencies that often deal with emergencies arising during the year are more likely to have to worry about reprogramming, especially when supplemental appropriations are hard or impossible to get. An agency history of prior evasions makes legislators who have followed the agency for years skeptical of current intentions, but agency insistence on the need for flexibility often dominates the outcome. To deal with this tension, Congress grants agencies considerable discretion but may require extensive reporting on how money is actually being used.

Contingency Funds

Contingency funds are sums of money budgeted for unknown or unstated purposes. There are some contingency funds, or discretionary funds, at the federal level, but they are less important than those at the state and local levels. At the national level contingencies are generally funded by supplementals, which often increase the size of the deficit; at state and local levels, it is illegal to run deficits, so a variety of special funds are set aside for different contingencies. At the local level departmental budget justifications are normally included in the budget, so a detailed plan of how money is to be spent is part of the budget legislation. Most city agencies thus do not have much flexibility regarding how budgeted money will be spent. To create discretion during the year, administrators have to build it into the budget by establishing pools of uncommitted revenue to be allocated during the year.

Cities and states can use their year-end fund balances, money left over from the prior fiscal year, as a kind of emergency kitty, and they can create separate accounts specifically to handle contingencies. The more money there is in contingency funds, the less is needed in the year-end balance, and vice versa. Or a city or state may intentionally not spend all the money that was budgeted so as to create a pool of money that can be rebudgeted if necessary. The latter category is called "holdbacks."

Minicase: Reprogramming in the Department of Defense

The Department of Defense has a history of conflict with Congress over how it spends appropriated funds and in particular whether the department shifts funds in ways that affect policy or evade congressional controls. While this history was in the background, in the foreground, after 2001, the nation was at war, and the military's need for flexibility caused Congress to increase the amount of discretion that the DoD could exercise over its budget and over reprogrammings in particular. Reprogrammings are divided into two broad groups: Below-the-threshold reprogrammings are typically small and not policy laden; they have minimal or no reporting requirements. Above-the-threshold reprogrammings are larger and more important and have extensive—sometimes advance—reporting requirements. With little or no reporting required on the smaller reprogrammings, many of them together could have substantial impact. Any reason for distrust can cause Congress to increase reporting requirements.

In fiscal years 2003 and 2004, the Appropriations Committee temporarily increased the threshold for a below-the-threshold reprogramming, to $20 million for procurement and $10 million for the category Research, Development, Test, and Evaluation, or 20 percent of the budget line, whichever is less. The result has been a considerable increase in DoD's discretion to make changes in its budget without reporting to Congress. Appropriations Committee members soon became concerned about how that discretion was being used, or abused, and asked the Government Accountability Office to investigate. Because DoD's data were so poor, GAO could not figure out whether the department was evading congressional guidelines, but it did find that the department was "taxing" its subunits and programs 2 percent or 3 percent, to create a pool of uncommitted revenue to reallocate as needed, using its newly expanded reprogramming powers to do so. The committee was worried about where those monies were going.

> [T]he Committee has observed increased use of BTRs [below-the-threshold reprogrammings] by both the Office of the Secretary of Defense (OSD) and the military services in a manner which is often inconsistent and in clear violation of congressional intent. Especially troubling is evidence suggesting below-threshold reprogrammings have been used to initiate new start development programs without congressional notification.[1]

Moreover, the projects started in this way did not have congressional approval.

(continued)

The House Committee on Appropriations was concerned that poor and vague information was being transmitted to it. The committee members worried that the holdbacks or unlegislated "taxes" on programs and services would provide a buffer for department administrators to cover up inefficiencies and failures, a kind of slush fund that would encourage poor management. They also worried that the guidelines for reprogramming might be violated. The committee report to accompany the Defense Department appropriation bill included some strongly worded recommendations for change.

The report argued that because the services and programs were being "taxed" 2 percent or 3 percent, those services and programs were increasing their budget requests to Congress by this percentage. Congress should not fund this slush fund margin, and the committee recommended cutting back the requested funds for the Research, Development, Test, and Evaluation appropriation (Title IV of the appropriation bill) by $685,000,000. Further, the committee forbade DoD to set aside funds in this manner other than by congressional direction. It required DoD to report on how it was complying with directives from Congress to create set asides, so that Congress could see that such burdens were appropriately levied against all units, not more heavily against some and less against others. The report further required the secretary of defense to report in detail on how flexibility mechanisms had been used in 2004 and to come up with a proposal for reporting for fiscal year 2005 that would include withholdings, "taxes," and reprogrammings, both above and below the threshold. The committee also asked DoD to create a committee to come up with recommendations for better ways to provide visibility, flexibility, and accountability, as well as oversight, internal and to Congress, for research and development appropriations.[2]

1. U. S. Congress, House, Appropriations Committee Report 108-553, Department of Defense Appropriations Bill, 2005, 108th Cong., 2d sess., June 18, 2004.
2. Sources include House Committee Report 108-553, and the GAO report *Defense Acquisitions: Better Information Could Improve Visibility over Adjustments to DoD's Research and Development Funds,* a report to the Appropriations Subcommittees on Defense, House and Senate, GAO 04-994, September 2004.

Pools of flexible funds can be created by overcutting in response to pessimistic revenue estimates. In a study of Cincinnati during a period of fiscal stress, the city cut back expenditures in line with a worst-case revenue scenario, creating moderate amounts of slack in the retrenchment budget. The council used the slack to add police and fire personnel after the 1976 cuts. In 1980, the manager elicited supplemental requests from departments to use revenues that had exceeded the pessimistic predictions in the budget. The manager then selected those that dealt with the problem that he saw as high priority, deferred maintenance.[9] How such "savings" are used and who will control them are policy-laden issues.

The use of funds built up through conscious overestimation of expenditures and/or underestimation of revenues also occurs in cities not experiencing cutbacks. The following excerpt from an interview with a city manager indicates that he believes that some cities use their balances to make minor but policy-related changes during the year:

Q. What about year-end balances, how are they used?

A. They are strictly an accounting device. We don't play any games at all with the statements. I could, because most people don't read accounting statements. Some managers do use it. They purposely underestimate revenues and overestimate expenditures, so that will happen. The council may ask the manager to find money to fund a project during the year. The manager then can do it. The council thinks it's magic.

The project for which the council is asking midyear support may be one for which the need developed during the year, or it may be a pet project with political payoff that could not be funded as part of the regular budget, but could be funded midyear without much scrutiny or comparison to other projects.

While the need for contingency funds at the local level is substantial, year-end balances combined with contingency funds seldom exceed 8 percent to 10 percent of the budget in midsized or larger cities. Such balances can be proportionately much larger for smaller cities, villages, or counties, which have limited discretion and small budgets. One of the major purposes of such contingency or emergency funds is to provide money for labor agreements, which represent no policy change. Contingency funds may be drawn down to fund a particular capital project or to tide the city over in a recession to prevent having to cut the budget during the year. In some cities, at some times, a portion of the contingency funds may be spent for special council projects, with explicit council approval. The budget may thus change somewhat during the year, with negative impact on public accountability, but the amounts involved are normally quite small, maybe 2 percent of the total budget.

Interfund Transfers

Interfund transfers are shifts of money between appropriation accounts or funds. At the federal level, because the amounts of the individual appropriation accounts can be very large, most of the need for transfers can be accommodated within accounts, with minor reprogramming and without fanfare. Why go between accounts, which requires legislative approval, when there is sufficient discretion to move small amounts of money within accounts, which requires no approval? In cities, however, individual funds (the local analog to federal appropriation accounts) are sometimes narrow, covering only one function and having only a limited number of dollars. Some of these funds may be spent for related functions, so interfund transfers may be planned and budgeted in advance. Formal transfers occurring during the year are treated as budget amendments and need to be approved by the council. Hence they are not secret and do not bypass the regular budget process, although they occur during the budget year.

There should be little reason for unanticipated transfers, and normally there are few of them. Sometimes, however, there is some informal borrowing, especially from cash-rich to cash-poor funds. If the borrowing is not approved by the council or becomes a long-term loan, or if a loan is not fully repaid, the implications are policy laden rather than technical. For example, if a general fund borrows from a water fund and does not repay the loan, the water fund may develop deficits.[10] The fund showing the deficit will have to cut services or increase user fees or taxes to eliminate the deficit. The result may be, for example, raising water fees to pay for police services, a result that is not only inequitable but secret. If the deficits are not eliminated, borrowing costs for the water fund may go up, forcing the city to pay unnecessarily high interest charges on future water projects. This practice is probably not common, but it does sometimes occur, and when it does, there are policy implications.

Summary and Conclusions

For the purposes of accountability to the public and managerial predictability, most of the budget is implemented as passed. Nevertheless, some flexibility has to be built into budget implementation because budgets are open to the environment. Rivers flood, countries invade each other, hurricanes knock down trees and houses. The economy waxes and wanes, reducing or increasing revenues beyond expectations and reducing or increasing the number of those eligible for entitlements. If more people commit crimes and are caught and sentenced to prison, there has to be some way to pay for their imprisonment, even if the numbers were not correctly predicted when the budget was put together. Budgets also adapt to the priorities of newly elected officials, who must initially work within the framework of budgets put together by their predecessors.

Budgets adapt through a variety of techniques, including supplemental appropriations, rescissions, deferrals, reprogramming, contingency funds, and interfund transfers. Some techniques are more common at one level of government than another. The federal government can run deficits, so it can respond to an emergency with a supplemental appropriation. State and local governments generally cannot run legal deficits and so have to build up reserve and contingency funds to draw down in emergencies, and they often hold back on spending during the year in case revenues do not materialize. Contingency funds and deferrals of this sort are common at state and local levels, but supplementals are relatively rare. Interfund transfers are fairly common at the local level; reprogramming within accounts is more important at the national level because accounts are so large that moving money around inside them usually provides sufficient flexibility.

Most of the changes in the budget during implementation are the results of technical changes and adaptation to the environment, but the flexibility that is absolutely necessary to budgeting also allows for some changes due to policy considerations. If Congress adds on to the president's budget, the president may try to rescind or defer that unwanted spending; to bypass the president's opposition, Congress may package the spending the president disapproves of with supplemental requests the president urgently needs. At the local level, revenues may be intentionally underestimated, so that when revenue not in the budget materializes, it can be put into a pool for allocation to council members' favorite programs or projects. Agencies may reprogram money approved by the legislature and the executive to spend on priorities they prefer. In general, the amount of money spent on policy-motivated changes during the year is quite limited and in some cases, as with policy-related deferrals at the national level, has been reduced to near zero. Supplemental appropriations at the national level were controlled for a time during the 1990s, but began to rise again after the deficit was eliminated in 1998, and became a major contributor to deficits in wake of 9/11 and the wars in Afghanistan and Iraq. Reprogramming is under reasonable legislative control. Once in a while, though, issues of budget implementation take center stage.

8. Budget Implementation and Control

The budget is generally implemented almost exactly as passed. Nevertheless, the discretion granted to the executive branch to change the budget during the budget year or biennium is sometimes used for political and policy purposes. Not all of this policy-related activity is unacceptable or threatening to democratic values. But sometimes changes in the budget during implementation have the effect of rendering the publicly circulated budget document obsolete. Sometimes the discretion to adapt the budget to changing circumstances is abused or is perceived as a perversion of legislative intent. If there is some indication of overspending or underspending, or of corruption, fraud, or purposeful thwarting of the policies and priorities in the budget, legislators are likely to increase their control over budget execution.

The Discretion-Abuse-Control Cycle

The dynamic of control tends to follow a pattern over time: (1) an initial grant of broad discretion to the agencies; (2) a perception of abuse; (3) increased budgetary control, in the form of increased supervision and oversight, increased reporting responsibilities, and additional constraints written into committee reports and statutes; and (4) agency reaction to reduced flexibility. If politicians become overburdened with politically irrelevant decisions about budget execution, or if the original problem seems to have been resolved, there may be (5) a gradual lessening of the intensity of oversight. Alternatively, the agency response may create a new set of problems, suggesting that the original controls may have been, or may have become inappropriate, forcing problematic evasive actions. Elected officials may then loosen controls or change them.

The central part of this process involves the perceived abuse of discretion and the reaction to that perception. Years ago, Sen. Edmund Muskie, D-Maine, described his impulse to increase control over implementation when an agency defies congressional or committee intent. When he learned that the Environmental Protection Agency (EPA) had misused its discretion to implement the budget, Muskie said, "The clear language and debate was what we were giving you, in what we understood to be legitimate administrative discretion to spend the money, not defeat the purposes. Then to have you twist it as you have, is a temptation to this Senator to really handcuff you the next time." [1] "Handcuffing" involves writing into legislation detailed constraints that reduce the agency's discretion over budget implementation.

The National Level

At the national level, for the most part Congress's control of agencies' budget execution is informal. Legislators converse with agency heads during budget hearings, or committee members put their suggestions for restrictions on spending into committee reports, which do not have the force of law. Congressional committees request and agencies prepare detailed budget justifications, but these justifications are not part of the appropriation legislation; they are just part of the informal understanding between agency officials and members of Congress. But if the agency does not adhere to informal advice, congressional committees may put restrictions into the appropriations act or authorizing legislation, giving them the force of law. "Usually when restrictive provisions are written into appropriations acts, it is because the agency has failed to comply with these less formal types of guidance or the Congress is not satisfied with how a particular agency is progressing toward some congressionally desired goal." [2]

One example of a broad grant of discretion followed by a perception of abuse and an increase in controls occurred in response to reprogrammings. Departments have sometimes taken money intended for one approved program and spent it on another program expressly disapproved by Congress. The problem of controlling reprogrammings accelerated after 1949, when Congress began to consolidate a number of appropriation accounts.[3] Reprogramming can occur only within a single appropriation account, so the move toward lump-sum appropriations, with many programs in a single appropriation, increased the amount of discretion and the amount of reprogramming that could be done.

During the Vietnam War the Pentagon used funds appropriated for other purposes to pay for projects that Congress had disapproved. Congress took control of this particular reprogramming in 1974, with legislation prohibiting the Defense Department from reprogramming funds to any items previously denied by Congress. As a further discouragement to reprogramming, Congress took a more active stance in recommending rescissions of unspent money, so there would be less money around that could be easily reprogrammed.[4]

Despite these congressional actions, some reprogramming problems remained in the Defense Department in the late 1970s and early 1980s, provoking congressional threats of more detailed control over spending. Rep. Joseph Addabbo of New York complained in 1981 hearings that the Department of Defense had avoided specific congressional instructions; he threatened to impose detailed, line-item control in the operations and maintenance section of the Defense Department budget. Addabbo asked whether Congress had come to the point "when we should get the Congressional Budget Office to prepare a computer printout and we line item. When we cut, say, 'this is it' and the money will be spent in all of the other items."[5]

Addabbo charged that the Defense Department was funding a number of items during the year that were not even in the budget request and for which funds had not been appropriated.[6] He also complained that Defense Department officials were reprogramming in such a way as to try to force Congress to pass supplementals to restore the lines from which the reprogramming funds were taken. Addabbo described this ploy in the following terms:

> Well, take the Indian Ocean operation, moving the task force in there, you proceed to do that and within that category, the same category, you have a ship overhaul. You take the money from ship overhaul, which is a high priority item, and use it for this. I am willing to venture a guess that within that same category there are many items which we discussed and which there should have been a more careful look at. . . . You don't grab where it's easiest to grab and say we are going to get that back anyway. That is what we have seen.[7]

Defense Department officials, according to this description, transferred money (reprogramming) out of top-priority rather than low-priority programs because they knew that Congress would have to pass a supplemental appropriation to replenish the funds for the high-priority programs. In addition to taking money out of ship overhaul, the DoD took money out of ammunition, which Congress would necessarily have to replace in a supplemental appropriation.[8]

The Defense Department did indeed come back later with requests for supplemental appropriations. During the hearings on the supplemental request, Rep. Addabbo pointedly argued that the department had tried to avoid cuts specifically recommended by Congress through reprogramming and had taken money for these revisions from programs specifically approved by Congress:

> Last year in R.D. and T.E. [the research and development programs] the Congress said you had too much budgeted for inflation. We cut, and all we got back was a lot of nonsense, a lot of wording that we cut so dramatically that many things are going to go wrong. You decided to teach Congress a lesson. You took the reductions out of add-ons by the Congress and we had to hold action on reprogrammings. Because action was required on the supplemental, you started taking it out of where you should be taking it out.[9]

The reprogramming Addabbo was describing represented an agency attempt not only to avoid specific congressional cuts, but also to implement the president's budget over congressional preferences. That is, the Defense Department chose to make the cuts in those areas where Congress had added to the president's request. The usurpation of congressional prerogatives by the executive branch was not lost on the appropriations subcommittees, which held up the emergency supplementals until the cuts were taken as specified.

The tension between the Defense Department and the congressional committees over reprogramming has continued over the years. Eventually the committees did resort to what Muskie had called "handcuffing" the agencies. Specific constraints were written into appropriations laws forbidding agencies from reprogramming money for specific purposes. For example, the 1994 Defense Department appropriation states that during the current fiscal year and thereafter, there was to be no reprogramming, transfer, or shift of money by other means between the CIA and the Defense Department for any intelligence or specific activity different from what was previously justified to the Congress, unless the director of the CIA or the secretary of defense had notified the House and Senate Appropriations Committees of their intent to do so and described the project. The legislation also included a series of rescissions, which would prevent the accumulation of funds that could be used for reprogramming. Moreover, the appropriation legislation specified where money could be transferred from and where it could go for particular purposes.

Reading the 1994 Department of Defense appropriation bill might make one sympathetic to the complaint of the Department of Defense that Congress is micromanaging it, especially because so many of the prohibitions in the legislation seem narrowly political—Don't move the 116th Fighter Wing of the National

Minicase: Abuse and Controls at the Department of Defense

At the end of September 1985, the House Armed Services Committee took the deputy secretary of defense to task for what many committee members perceived as a violation of the reprogramming procedures.[1] Apparently the Defense Department had proceeded with a contract bid even though the committee had denied the necessary reprogramming approval. The result of this bypassing of the committee's controls was considerable anger.

The committee wanted an explanation and also wanted the deputy secretary to reaffirm his understanding of the informal agreements between the committee and the department about the rules of reprogramming. The deputy secretary shifted the blame to a number of other locations and promised to try to do better in the future. He demonstrated a clear understanding of what the rules were.

Some committee members were not content with what they called "wrist slapping." They called in the General Accounting Office to review not only the department's procedures on reprogramming but all of its reprogramming requests to see if they complied with the committee's rules.[2] Then the Senate Armed Services Committee instructed the GAO to evaluate reprogramming in the Defense Department and suggest improvements.

The GAO found that the Defense Department was doing a reasonable job complying with the committee's rules but that the reporting procedure was such that the department did not sort out the reprogramming requests by fiscal year and did not highlight the items of interest to congressional committees. Nor did the department tell the committees of other pending requests that might give congressional committees a clue about what policies it was pursuing. The GAO also found that there was considerable reprogramming that went on below the limits required for reporting.

Part of Congress's concern was where the money for reprogramming was coming from, not just where it was going, and whether the object was one Congress had forbidden. As a GAO report described, the Defense Department had proposed a $60.8 million reprogramming from a single program, the Small Intercontinental Ballistic Missile program, without indicating that this request was part of a $330 million sum that it had reprogrammed out of that program or was in the process of reprogramming. When Congress understood the full impact of the proposed reprogramming, it denied use of the Small Intercontinental Ballistic Missile program as a source of most of the requested reprogramming funds. Then it rescinded $266 million of the program's funds, eliminating it as a source of reprogramming.[3] In 1989

(continued)

the defense appropriations conference report included language requiring
Congress to review decreases in spending resulting from reprogrammings,
not just increases.

1. U.S. Congress, House Committee on Armed Services, *Full Committee Consideration of Reconciliation Recommendations and Hearings on Reprogramming
Process and Procedures*, 99th Cong., 1st sess., September 30, 1995.
2. U.S. Congress, House Committee on Armed Services, *Full Committee Organizational Meeting and Consideration of Defense Department Reprogramming*,
100th Cong., 1st sess., February 5, 1987, 10–11.
3. General Accounting Office, *Budget Reprogramming: Opportunities to Improve
DoD's Reprogramming Process* (Washington, D.C.: U.S. Government Printing
Office, July 1989), 14–15.

Guard from Dobbins Air Reserve Base to Robins Air Force Base. However, in the
light of Congress's history of trying to obtain compliance on reprogramming in
gentler ways, and persistent Defense Department defiance, the degree of detailed
legislative control seems more understandable, if not ideal.

Part of the congressional effort to enforce department accountability was to
eliminate or reduce the discretionary funds that misbehaving agencies controlled.
For example, Congress went after carry-forward funds that were intended to tide
an agency over the beginning of the fiscal year in case appropriations did not
come through on time. The effort to control this type of fund only occurred after
an agency had flouted congressional directives. For example, the formerly secret
National Reconnaissance Office, after defying congressional oversight, was discovered to have accumulated a carryover fund of $1.5 billion (on a budget of
about $6 billion). Congress trimmed back the fund to one month of the agency's
budget (about $500 million), forbade the agency to allow the fund to grow any
larger, and invited the inspectors general of the CIA and Defense Department to
examine the agency's spending controls and recent financial history.[10]

Earmarking is another common congressional response to agencies that evade
congressional priorities through extensive reprogrammings; it is also a constraint
that, written into the law, may last for many years. Congress may specify in legislation that so much money, or a specific percentage of the appropriation, be
spent on a particular program. The earmarking may be less formal if it appears
in committee reports instead of in the law. For example, the Judiciary Committees of both houses of Congress initially granted wide discretion over spending
to the Department of Justice, but some committee members were concerned that

some programs in the department were not being funded because the department's priorities were different from those of Congress. One department activity the committee supported, but that members felt was being obliterated, was the program to catch and deport Nazi war criminals. The committee proceeded to earmark money for that specific purpose.

The discretion-abuse-control cycle applies not only to reprogramming, but to other midyear budget changes as well. A major example has been impoundments, the president's unilateral refusal to carry out expenditures that Congress has authorized. Historically Congress allowed the president to withhold some authorized spending for technical reasons. But under President Richard Nixon, such withholding was used to increase the president's power over the budget and defy congressional intent:

> Executive officials seized on discretionary language in statutes to suspend or cancel programs. Through strained legal analyses, administrative officials contended that permissive language in authorization and appropriation bills allowed the president to terminate programs. Also the Nixon administration treated the president's budget as a ceiling on Congress. Any funds that Congress added to the president's budget could be set aside and left unobligated.[11]

Congress was so annoyed by what it considered Nixon's abuse of his discretion over budget implementation that it increased congressional control of budget execution. In 1974 it passed the Congressional Budget and Impoundment Control Act, in part to control presidential impoundments. The act divided the withholding of funds into two categories: (1) rescissions, or formal retractions of a law appropriating funds, and (2) deferrals, or delays in spending approved amounts. The law required presidentially proposed rescissions to have the specific approval of Congress. Deferrals proposed by the president would take place if Congress took no action to deny them. Either house could block a deferral. The law made the GAO the watchdog, to make sure that the administration was not withholding funds from agencies without reporting the withholding to Congress.

President Reagan was still submitting policy-related deferrals in 1986 and 1987, but Congress was no longer able to overturn them with a veto by one chamber because the Supreme Court, in *Immigration and Naturalization Service v. Chadha,* had ruled such one-house vetoes unconstitutional. Congress then took the offensive to prevent the president from submitting policy deferrals at all and was successful in getting the courts to rule them illegal. Thus by 1988 Congress had good control over policy-related rescissions and had virtually eliminated policy-related deferrals.

Rescissions are highly visible; deferrals are somewhat less so, but with GAO oversight, they are more difficult to hide. One congressional strategy has been to make budget changes more visible so that any that have policy implications will stand out and receive consideration. The result may be to shift more executive attention to less-visible means of reshaping the budget according to the president's policy preferences. Consider, for example, salary increases for civil servants.

Salary increases have for years been determined governmentwide, without giving agencies enough money to cover the mandated salary increases. The logic is to force agencies to take money that had been unspent in other accounts to contribute to the salary increase, so as to reduce the need for, and the size of, supplemental appropriations. The process sounds like a technical and routine matter, but it has a definite political implication. First, Congress often sets targets for how much of the salary increase the agencies should aim to absorb. Agencies do not necessarily have that much unspent money in personnel lines. OMB has encouraged agencies to transfer surplus funds from other accounts to salary. This practice raises the questions of what is surplus, whether program funds are being used to pay for salary increases, and if so, which programs are being cut.

The agencies sometimes have to guess at how large a salary supplemental OMB will approve and create sufficient surplus to make up the balance. That may mean leaving positions unfilled, increasing the size of a reduction in force, or using a furlough (mandatory, unpaid leave of absence) to save money in the salary lines. In short, OMB can force an agency to cut its personnel budget to absorb some portion—not necessarily the congressional target—of salary increase costs. In this case, the issue becomes less one of efficiency and using unspent money and more a matter of forcing unpublicized cuts on an agency midyear without explicit congressional approval.

In the late 1970s OMB used salary absorption to discriminate against congressional add-ons.[12] OMB placed an inordinate burden on those agencies with salary and expense lines that Congress had increased above the president's request. "Administration officials were using their powers of implementation to frustrate congressional priorities."[13]

Congress responded to this arrogation of power with the threat of increased legislative controls and in some cases with a requirement that the agency seek supplementals for salary increases rather than try to absorb the costs from existing lines. Florida senator Lawton Chiles warned in 1979 that "continuation of this practice might prompt Congress to write into the appropriation bill the instruction that absorption cuts be made on a pro rata basis."[14] That restraint would eliminate discretion to cut some programs to fund the salary increase and leave others alone. The Senate Committee on the Judiciary added a section to the annual authorization bill stipulating that the Department of Justice would not be required to absorb any salary increases.[15]

The State Level

The cycle of broad discretion, abuse, and tighter control also applies at the state level. Traditional line-item controls (restrictions on spending according to the object of the expenditures, such as personal service, travel, or contractual services) became less effective as state expenditures grew from $27.6 billion in 1964 to over $100 billion in 1976. Not only is there a lot of money in each line, which creates a lot of discretion, but funds appropriated for a line item can be disbursed legally for a wide variety of purposes. "Moreover, expanded federal grants in aid—from $1.6 billion in 1948 to $16 billion in 1969 to over $40 billion in 1976—vitiate legislative oversight by creating opportunities for state administrators to initiate new programs or to transfer funds among activities during budget execution." [16]

The list of techniques widely used in the states to change the budget during the year is suggestive of the possibility of abuse of discretion, at least as the state legislatures see it. Techniques have included padded requests, artificial accounting balances, and improper interfund transfers. Transfer authority also has allowed funds to be shifted between line items and appropriation accounts.

In a survey in 1976, 62 percent of 324 state agency directors in eight states responded that they transferred money between line items; 66 percent reported that they engaged in reprogramming within appropriation accounts. These reprogrammings were used to compensate for cuts in priority items, to engineer expansions in programs, and to initiate programs that lacked legislative support. The more different federal programs the state agencies received money from, the more likely the agencies were to report that they were reprogramming funds.[17]

State legislatures gradually reacted to what they perceived as an abuse of discretion. One report noted in 1975 that "legislatures are paying increased attention to expressing their intent more clearly as a means of exercising policy control." The report continued, "[E]xecutive agencies' fun and games with the enacted budget are the cause of much of this concern." [18]

By 1984 major changes had been made in legislative control over state budget execution.[19] In the 1960s legislatures had begun to assume the postauditing function that had been independent of the legislatures. By 1980, four out of five state legislatures selected a postauditor responsible to the legislature. The activities of the auditors expanded to include program and performance auditing. In addition, "Legislatures began to appropriate federal grant-in-aid monies in an effort to assure legislative rather than executive priorities in the spending of state funds, to guard against commitment of future state dollars for matching programs without legislative approval, to avoid pursuit of programs the legislature had disallowed through use of substitute money, and to guarantee effective delivery of services." [20] As of 1988, thirty-six state legislatures made specific appropriations of federal funds, and seventeen controlled appropriations of federally funded staffing levels. Another six states controlled the federally funded staffing in some cases.[21] By 1998 forty-three states appropriated federal funds for specific agencies, and twenty-six appropriated federal grants.[22]

Generally legislative oversight of budget implementation at the state level works the same way as at the national level. The following excerpt from the State Department of Finance Web site, describing California's budget process, shows the breadth of discretion granted to the governor and the agencies, as well as the methods by which the state legislature oversees their use of that discretion:

> The Budget Act is the primary source for appropriations. Continuous statutory appropriations and special legislation also provide expenditure authority.
>
> Departments have the primary responsibility to operate within budgeted levels and to comply with any restrictions or limitations enacted by the Legislature. Further, the general expectation is that State agencies comply with the legislative intent. Although the general expectation is to conform to the enacted budget, the Legislature has recognized a need to establish some flexibility to adjust budgets. For example, the statutes provide a continuous appropriation for allocations by the Director of Finance to meet expenditures resulting from natural disasters for any emergency proclaimed by the Governor. The Legislature has also provided provisions in the Budget Act to allow for budget adjustments. Most of this authority requires Director of Finance approval; many require a formal notice to the Legislature and a waiting period to provide the opportunity for legislative review and response before final approval. Budget Act provisions to allow adjustments include authorizations for:
>
> - Changes to federal funding levels
> - Deficiencies
> - Changes to reimbursements
> - Intra-item transfers
>
> The Department of Finance approves budget changes using Budget Revisions, Executive Orders and letters. These changes are transmitted to the State

Controller's Office, which maintains the statewide appropriation control accounts.

The Governor has certain powers to adjust expenditures. Although these powers do not permit for adjustment of appropriations, the expenditure plan may be changed. For example, past Governors have issued Executive Orders to implement hiring and equipment purchase freezes and delayed capital expenditures. Under emergency conditions, the Governor is also authorized to direct State resources to meet emergency needs.[23]

On the one hand, the legislature grants the executive branch broad discretion to adjust the budget for technical and unavoidable reasons, but on the other, it monitors and regulates those changes to be sure that discretion is not being abused.

The Local Level

At the local level, the discretion-abuse-control cycle is even clearer than at state and federal levels, although it is primarily state control over local governments, rather than the legislature controlling the executive. Local governments are creatures of the states, and when their finances get out of hand, the state governments step in. The historical example in the following box illustrates, in addition to the abuse and control cycle, managerial problems resulting from too-tight control and gradual relaxation of control under changing conditions. It thus shows not only steps one, two, and three of the discretion-abuse-control cycle, but also steps four and five, agency response and the relaxation of controls.

The control cycle does not necessarily end with ever-tighter controls. At the federal level, for example, the consolidation of appropriation accounts represented a lessening of legislative controls on expenditures, and it increased agency discretion over reprogramming; the cycle of control began with a lessening of control from the previous cycle. At the state level, it was clear that line-item controls were weakened both by increases in total dollars and by the complexity resulting from federal grants. At the local level, overly harsh state controls have generally loosened over time.

When controls are tight, they make routine management problematic and adaptation difficult. Managers under these circumstances will often try to re-create flexibility within the existing constraints. For example, managers dealing with tight line-item controls have generated a system of invisible swaps between line items. Legislative controls on impoundment spawned ways of getting around them, such as executive reduction in staff. It can be difficult to devise a system of controls that will not be evaded but will not be so rigid as to make

Minicase: Massachusetts Overcontrols the Cities, 1875–1933

After the Civil War, local debt grew enormously in Massachusetts.[1] The growth was in response to rapid urbanization and the need for infrastructure, but it also reflected a desire to keep property taxes low. Some of the borrowing was for current expenses and for railroads. The growth in borrowing was accompanied by increased valuations of property for tax purposes until the fiscal crisis of 1873, but during the subsequent recession the burden of debt was keenly felt. Taxes had to go up to cover debt payments when people could least afford increased taxes.

By 1875 the state had stepped in to curtail and regulate local debt, and in 1876 the state limited cities' investments in railroads. The debt limit was lowered in 1885, from 3 percent of assessed valuation to 2.5 percent, and then to 2 percent. Also in 1885 municipal tax levies were curtailed in an effort to control municipal expenditures, which were increasing rapidly. Debt declined from 1875 to 1882, then climbed slowly until 1890. But from 1890 to 1905 net debt more than doubled, and the annual tax levy increased 80 percent. The increases continued after 1905.

A growing population and changing social and economic conditions created new administrative problems for local governments, and a rising standard of public consumption pressed on the tax and debt limits. Cities had begun to petition the legislature for exemptions from the limits almost immediately after the 1875 legislation. More than 1,500 special exemption acts were passed between 1875 and 1911. These exemptions allowed about $73 million in debt outside the limits.

In addition, cities got around the limits on long-term indebtedness by borrowing more short term, in excess of anticipated revenues, and through demand notes. They refunded these notes without appeal to the legislature, rolling over short-term debt for ten, twenty, or even fifty years. Cities also borrowed for operating purposes for periods of less than ten years, another loophole in the law. Taxes that remained uncollected for long periods contributed to the buildup of debt.

Part of the cause of the buildup of debt was the limitation on property taxes. Because cities could not tax to cover their expenses, they resorted more frequently to borrowing. State mandates for spending also added pressure on local governments to bypass restrictions. The tax limit, like the debt limit, was loosened in actual practice by legislative exemptions.

By 1913 the state had passed a new law attempting to fix some of the problems with the previous legislation. Tax limits were taken off all cities

(continued)

except Boston; debt limits were raised somewhat; and the state tried to improve record keeping and data presentation so that the legislature would have some independent basis on which to evaluate requests for borrowing outside the limits. Short-term debt was controlled.

Borrowing for current purposes was reduced by this legislation, until the Great Depression of the 1930s increased welfare expenditures and reduced revenues. From 1913 to 1920, debt increased only moderately, partly because of World War I and the suspension of improvement projects. From 1920 to 1926 aggregate debt grew by 41 percent; then the rate of growth tapered off until 1930. In the early depression years, debt grew rapidly. The state responded to the depression-caused financial problems of the cities by loosening debt limits and loaning cities money.

To summarize, the state stepped in when debt got out of hand and popular pressure against increased taxes provided a base of support for state intervention and control. For a time, the controls had their intended effect, but they also had unintended effects; the tax and borrowing limits increased short-term borrowing beyond expected revenues. When controls are too tight, there is enormous pressure to evade them, and some of the evasions cause additional abuses that invite a new round of controls. Over time, the circumstances that brought about the original controls disappeared, and changing circumstances, such as the depression of the 1930s, required that controls be loosened.

1. This case is taken from Royal S. Van De Woestyne, *State Control of Local Finance in Massachusetts* (Cambridge: Harvard University Press, 1935).

good management impossible. When legislatures err on the side of too-tight controls, they usually loosen them over time, and after the initial problems have been solved, to facilitate better management.

Sometimes, in moments of pique, legislatures may set up rigid oversight of implementation but then gradually lose interest. The initial issues that seemed such an affront to legislative power may recede, or the amount of detailed work involved may not be paying much in the way of political dividends, and other issues will press to the fore. Under these circumstances, the laws are likely to remain on the books, but the level of surveillance is likely to ease. An understanding may emerge that the agencies need no longer conform to the letter of the law.

Discretion and Control: The Politics of Finding Waste, Fraud, and Abuse

Efforts to control waste, fraud, and abuse illustrate a second strategy for maintaining budgetary accountability. Here it is not policy divergence from the budget during implementation that threatens accountability, but accounting systems that do not work, programs that are poorly designed, and excessive claims for funding. Agencies usually receive great leeway initially in how to manage money, but if flaws are found in their systems of controls, or if they are caught in wasteful or corrupt practices, they are likely to suffer additional controls and increased supervision.

Efforts to eliminate waste, fraud, and abuse may seem technical, to be managed by accountants who work out improved techniques for financial control, but as we have seen elsewhere in this book, what is technical may also be highly political. First, whoever is chosen to be the auditor must have enough independence to be credible but enough cooperation from agency heads to obtain reliable information and to facilitate implementation of recommended improvements. Gaining and maintaining that independence and negotiating for cooperation are themselves political efforts. Second, the effort to reduce waste, fraud, and abuse may become a highly visible political campaign, one with many pitfalls. Criticizing past administrations may be welcome, but describing the current administration as not well managed is likely to create unwanted tumult.

Inspectors general are program and financial auditors who work with a team within specific departments or agencies. They not only examine financial reports but also look for, and call attention to, instances of fraud, waste, and abuse; they work to identify the sources of these problems and make recommendations to attack their structural sources.

The federal government has two separate systems of inspectors general, one set created by statute, appointed by the president, and confirmed by the Senate; the other set appointed by the heads of the smaller and regulatory agencies. Many state governments also have inspectors general, and a handful of cities have them as well.

Inspectors general can help save hundreds of millions or even billions of dollars, a priority when the budget is tight and politicians want to grant tax reductions. On the other hand, they may reveal and publicize corruption and abuse of power, as well as wasteful practices, so that controlling them—and the bad publicity they may create—may be a priority for politicians and department

---

Minicase: Homeland Security Inspector General Not Renewed

The inspector general for the Homeland Security Department had a direct and somewhat abrasive manner, which may have contributed to his short tenure in office. Observers readily concluded, however, that it was his outspoken criticism of the agency he worked with that stimulated the Bush administration to let him go rather than renew his appointment.

The inspector general, Clark Irvin, argued that millions of dollars were missing and unaccounted for and that security programs were not working. " 'I think this was a voice that was a little too critical and made the administration a little too uncomfortable,' said Danielle Brian, executive director of the Project on Government Oversight, a nonprofit government watchdog group." [1]

1. Brian Ross and Rhonda Schwartz, "Official Who Criticized Homeland Security Is Out of a Job: Inspector General Had Reported Mismanagement, Security Flaws," ABC News, December 10, 2004, http://abcnews.go.com/WNT /Investigation/story?id=316582&page=1 (accessed April 1, 2005).

---

heads. The IGs can be effective in their complex role only if they are independent of direct political control, but their independence may make it difficult for them to function cooperatively to bring about managerial changes within their agencies.

Federal Inspectors General: "Straddling a Barbed Wire Fence"

Like the other forms of financial control described in this chapter, the federal inspector general system was created in response to perceived abuses. "It was a series of scandals and abuses within government as well as a renewed emphasis on prevention and detection that led to congressional realization of the need for an I.G. concept within the federal government and subsequent passage of the act." [24]

The first inspector general was appointed in the Department of Agriculture in 1961, in response to the Billie Sol Estes scandal. "Estes had been revealed to have parlayed fraudulent warehouse receipts, mortgages, and financial statements into a fortune from the Department of Agriculture, despite the fact that his activities were suspected by three different audit units within the Department." [25]

Widespread reports of cheating in Medicare and student loans in the Department of Health, Education, and Welfare, as well as overbilling and overtesting of Medicaid patients, prompted Congress to create an IG for that department in 1976. In 1978 the IG model was extended to other departments in the Inspector General Act, which installed IGs in twelve federal department and agencies. The law specified that the inspectors general would be appointed by the president and would report to both agency heads and Congress. Congressional intent was to create a powerful instrument to root out fraud, waste, and abuse in government by creating a semi-independent, centralized auditing and investigatory team for each major department.

The inspector general system gradually spread to other departments and agencies, and the scope of authority of inspectors general has increased over time. Nevertheless, over the last decade there has been some shrinkage. In 1993, there were sixty Offices of the Inspector General, employing 15,000,[26] by 2003, there were fifty-seven offices, employing 11,000.[27]

The reduction of the IG workforce reflected some reorganization and elimination of agencies, as well as the downsizing of the federal bureaucracy. One needs fewer overseers in a smaller bureaucracy, and reportedly many IGs felt they needed to take cuts proportional to their agencies'. However, all of the reductions may not have been voluntary. If a department or agency head is displeased with the expressed point of view of its inspector general, the head may cut the budget and staffing of the office. Also, the National Performance Review, during the Clinton-Gore administration, took aim at bureaucracies whose role was detailed oversight in budget and accounting, legal, and personnel offices, arguing that these overseers intimidated front-line managers, making them risk averse, and preventing them from innovating. As a result, IG offices were among those targeted for particularly deep personnel reductions.

The IG offices were cut at about twice the rate of the civilian federal workforce in the years between 1993 and 2003. The federal civilian workforce was reduced about 13 percent,[28] while the reduction of the IG staff from 15,000 to 11,000 represents about a 26 percent reduction. It was widely rumored in the IG world that the disproportionate reductions represented a kind of revenge for unfriendly or critical studies and bad publicity.[29]

This reduction in staffing occurred simultaneously with an expansion of the role of the IGs. The Chief Financial Officers Act required federal agencies to prepare financial reports and have them audited; the IGs were enrolled in the effort to examine those new financial reports. In addition, IGs have taken on more responsibility for criminal investigations and computer security. As the agencies that the IGs worked for cut back staffing, they often increased their contracting out, sometimes without sufficient staff remaining in house to supervise those contracts, creating more work for IGs. The budget cuts and staffing reductions therefore understate the degree to which the IGs were being pressed.

Although Congress designed the inspector general system to improve control over implementation of the budget when signs of waste, fraud, or abuse were observed, the system's ability to work as planned was questionable because of its odd structure and its need for independence to function. The inspectors general need to be independent to carry out investigations, but their independence is compromised by political appointment, by budget subordination of the IG offices to the department heads, and by their responsibility to both Congress and the departmental secretaries. The IGs continually struggle to gain and maintain sufficient independence to do their work. One longtime observer of the IG system characterizes it as having become increasingly political over the past 20 years,[30] but even in the beginning there was some question about how political the IGs were to be. For example, the early inspectors general in the Department of Agriculture were politicized because the two top positions were presidential appointees subject to Senate confirmation, and two assistant inspectors general were presidential appointees not subject to Senate confirmation, in an office that never exceeded forty-seven employees.[31] That is a very high proportion of political appointees in one office.

If inspectors general become caught between departments and Congress they can be rendered useless. The GAO evaluated the first inspector general, in the Department of Agriculture, negatively. There was "limited use of the office as a management tool, partly because of concern over external disclosure of inspection findings through routine distribution of reports to congressional committees and others."[32] Reported one observer of the inspector general system, "In my opinion, the IG's independence will not be any better defined than it has been and will always be a subject of dispute. IGs are 'straddling a barbed wire fence.' "[33]

The issue of independence of the inspectors general became salient when President Reagan fired all sitting inspectors general in 1981 and began to replace them with his own appointees.[34] Presumably the president wanted to make sure the inspectors general were not going to embarrass the administration, but in doing so he harmed the appearance of neutrality necessary for any kind of waste or fraud investigator. Some members of Congress were upset by the action:

> The Reagan massacre established for all time in the minds of many on the hill ... when a position is created as a presidential appointment, a president is going to appoint the kind of people he wants. ... Congress can add all the provisos it wants about being notified for reasons for removal—the fact remains that appointed incumbents serve at the president's pleasure. The

unnecessary rubbing of people's faces in this fact was the costly aspect of the massacre.[35]

The political will of department secretaries has clashed with the autonomy of the inspectors general. In 1988 Congress expanded the inspector general system to include several more cabinet departments, one of which was the Department of Justice. Like many other departments, the Department of Justice firmly opposed having an inspector general. The major reason given was that the attorney general (the political appointee of the president who heads the Department of Justice) would be unable to direct or stop investigations. That was indeed part of the intent of establishing the program—that inspectors general could carry out investigations without departmental obstruction. Nevertheless, Congress, in recognition of the sensitive matters the Department of Justice deals with, gave the attorney general permission to halt some cases if he or she gave Congress warning that he or she was about to do so.

A different kind of tension arises between loyalty to the president's policy goals and open revelation of financial and managerial problems. This tension has been reflected in efforts by the Department of Justice to curtail some types of investigation or some kinds of IG powers.

When the solicitor at the Department of Labor tried to stop an investigation by the inspector general at that department, the matter came to the Department of Justice for resolution. Did the inspectors general have authority for the kind of investigation they were making? The Department of Justice not only said no, they did not, but made a general statement applying to all inspectors general, limiting the scope of their investigations.

The crux of the matter seemed to lie in the kind of investigation, which the Office of Legal Counsel of the Department of Justice called "regulatory." What it specifically opposed was a case in which the inspectors general, finding that a department had not deployed resources to investigate some regulatory compliance issue, took it upon themselves to do it. The inspectors general claimed that they had the authority to investigate fraud in federal programs; the Office of Legal Counsel said they had the authority to investigate only if the matter involved fraud or corruption of public officials and the expenditure of federal funds.[36]

The legal counsel opinion was based on a selective reading of the history of the inspectors general law and ignored other specific delegations of authority in laws after 1978.[37] Still more disturbing, individual inspectors general stated that the Department of Justice was threatening that it would not defend them in case of lawsuit, if they pursued cases beyond the Department of Justice's judgment of appropriate scope. Said Sen. John Glenn, of Ohio, chairman of the Committee on Governmental Affairs, "As I understand it, your people have been told that if they

---

Minicase: Tension at the CIA

Congress created an Office of the Inspector General at the Central Intelligence Agency in 1989; the first inspector general took office in 1990. As might be expected, the CIA did not want an inspector general looking over its shoulder, and the agency's displeasure was frequently expressed in criticism of Fred Hitz, the IG. As Sen. Bob Kerrey put it, "The CIA has a proud but insular culture which tends to resist the scrutiny of an independent examiner." [1] But precisely because of the agency's secret missions, Congress felt the need for an independent inspector general.

Not only was the IG thrust between an agency that did not want him and Congress, which wanted good audit information in a secret environment, but he also had to wrestle with the possible consequences of overcontrol. Kerrey described the dilemma of the IG at the CIA:

> [A]n independent IG must not contribute to a climate in which the CIA is afraid to take risks when vital U.S. interests are at stake. An independent IG must not create an internal empire of inspectors which has the same chilling effect on creative action in Government that excessive regulation has on business. Like the congressional oversight committees, a good IG must ensure that the Agency acts in accordance with U.S. law and U.S. values without inhibiting the Agency's ability to act boldly.[2]

Successfully negotiating this kind of environment with these kinds of constraints requires more than good accounting and auditing skills. The difficulty of getting information and the sensitivity of each possible report make political skills essential.

1. *Congressional Record*, December 21, 1995, S.19138.
2. Ibid.

---

don't get prior approval in particular areas, you were told by the head of the DOJ Office of Consumer Litigation that continued investigation of FDA cases by Inspector General employees would place your special agents in jeopardy of personal tort liability. In other words, if there is a suit filed against you, they would not defend you, as would be the normal case; is that correct?" Richard P. Kusserow, inspector general of the Department of Health and Human Services, answered, "That's correct, sir." [38] The message was that the inspectors general had better clear every dubious case with the Department of Justice. This would give the Department of Justice enormous power to cut off any investigation of regulatory matters.

The reason for the Department of Justice's position in this case became clear when the name and policy position of Rep. Elliott Levitas of Georgia were taken as evidence of the intent of Congress in passing the inspectors general legislation. Levitas in a brief congressional career made a name for himself as a defender of the regulated against the regulators.[39] He argued on the floor of Congress that the inspectors general should be engaged in watching government officials, not in finding noncompliance and fraud in businesspeople subject to government regulations.[40]

After the Department of Justice memo limiting the scope of their investigations, inspectors general from various departments found that the subjects of some of their investigations were claiming the inspectors had no authority. The inspectors were forced in a number of instances to drop investigations in progress. They reported difficulty in interpreting what they were obliged to do under the law and what they were forbidden from doing. Collectively they tried to negotiate the matter with the Department of Justice but reported no progress. They then came to the Senate Governmental Affairs Committee to suggest that Congress strengthen and clarify the law to make their jurisdiction clearer. The committee called a hearing, with both sides present.

During the hearings Senator Glenn managed to get Department of Justice spokesmen to back down verbally from the threat to force inspectors to hire their own attorneys if sued over an investigation that the Department of Justice disapproved of. The Department of Justice spokesmen were somewhat conciliatory: They would meet with the inspectors general at any time; many of the investigations questioned by inspectors after the Justice Department policy statement were judged to be legitimate. But the department spokesmen did not budge on the issue of preventing inspectors general from investigating regulatory matters that the agencies were supposed to investigate themselves, even when the agencies lacked the resources, skills, or determination to do the investigations. The Governmental Affairs Committee recommended additional time to work out a negotiated settlement.

The proper scope of inspector general investigations was ultimately determined in favor of the IGs and a broad scope. Symbolic of this resolution was the public call of President Clinton for a crackdown on Medicaid and Medicare fraud in May 1995. The major sources of fraud in these programs are unscrupulous doctors and nursing homes that prescribe unnecessary tests or overbill. The campaign was spearheaded by the inspector general of Health and Human Services and clearly established the principle that inspectors general could and should investigate fraud perpetrated on the government.

As IGs got deeper into fraud cases, they began to press for broader authority to engage in criminal investigations. Years earlier there had been considerable opposition to IGs' engaging in criminal investigations—supporters of the business community and representatives of those being investigated wanted to curtail the power of the IGs to investigate their activities. The FBI and the Department of Justice were concerned about losing control of their investigations. Part of that concern may have been based on protection of turf, but it may also have been related to the attorney general's desire to be able to put a stop to particular investigations. Opposition to the IGs as criminal investigators gradually diminished, however, as they demonstrated that they could save a lot of money by investigating cases of fraud against the government.

A procedure grew up in which each investigator in an Office of the Inspector General had to ask the permission of the Justice Department (the U.S. Marshal Service) to engage in a criminal investigation, and the permission applied only to that case. The case-by-case approach was so clumsy that it was gradually replaced by an annual blanket grant of criminal investigation powers to particular IG offices, enforced by a memorandum of understanding that included requirements for training. The permission could be revoked for cause, such as abuse of power. IGs feared administrative delays in the granting of such blanket approvals, which could threaten or terminate ongoing investigations, so they asked for a statutory grant of power to do criminal investigations under the general oversight of the Department of Justice. Rather than assuming that they could not engage in such investigations unless the Justice Department gave approval, the IGs wished to assume they had the ability unless the Justice Department said otherwise.

The FBI and the Justice department initially opposed granting this authority to the IGs. By 2000, however, the Department of Justice had relinquished its objections, saying that the marshal service was swamped with work as a result of the deputations and a legislative deputation would eliminate that extra work.[41] After 2001 the criminal justice agencies were so absorbed in antiterrorist activities that overseeing each OIG's criminal investigations may have seemed a much lower priority. By 2002 the proposal had passed as part of the legislation creating the Department of Homeland Security. (The presidentially appointed IGs received statutory authority, but the agency-appointed IGs still operated on a permission basis.)

Although the IGs were pleased with this grant of independence, it was a marginal change. As the price for his support, the attorney general required a provision in the legislation allowing him to cancel any investigation without revoking the permission of an entire office.[42] Otherwise, to stop a particular investigation that might have security implications, that contradicted an existing law enforcement case, or that was politically threatening, the attorney general would have had to shut down a whole office's investigations, with possible negative publicity. What he asked for and got was more surgical precision in the level of his control. The IGs got more independence but did not gain much in the way of freedom from control of the administration in these criminal cases. The permission of a whole office could still be revoked for systemic reasons, such as failure to train staff adequately for dangerous situations or in the use of firearms, or for abuse of power.

Early in the Bush administration several highly questionable firings and appointments of politically connected IGs stirred the fears of the IG community. In one incident, a highly accomplished and respected IG in NASA was forced to resign, and the president immediately appointed a replacement who had spent a year on the White House staff. The director of NASA was considered to be close to the president, so this replacement was considered particularly political. The fired IG was known for her work on computer security but had also been critical of the deep budget cuts in the agency and the extent and manner of contracting out.[43] Whether or not the apparently forced resignation was due to the IG's forceful and critical positions, other IGs felt pressured and threatened. Another incident, at HHS, further roiled the IG community.[44]

The inspectors general began to press for the rest of their legislative agenda, which included a legislative basis for the council of inspectors general and some funding for it, and fixed terms of office, rather than service at the pleasure of the president. They also worked for clarification of the grounds for firing a sitting inspector general. A fixed and relatively long term of office gives public officials some independence of the political sphere; the longest term of office in Washington (fifteen years) is that of the comptroller general, who heads the Government Accountability Office (formerly the General Accounting Office) and whose role is not very different from that of the IGs. A number of state-level inspectors general also have fixed terms. With fixed terms IGs could only be fired for stated cause.

The Office of Management and Budget, as the representative of the Executive Office of the President and the executive office that works most closely with the IGs to see that they are implementing administration policies and proposals and not their own preferences, opposed fixed terms. The OMB representative argued that the IGs did not need any more independence. The following dialogue between Rep. Jim Cooper, D-Tenn., and Clay Johnson, deputy director for management at OMB, is instructive:

Mr. Johnson. I am not sure that anybody has indicated that there's not already sufficient independence. My understanding is that the independence level that exists now in the IG community is more than adequate. I can understand there's potential—that we are addressing potential here, but I think the way it's set up now creates a significant amount of independence. I personally would be opposed to a term. There were four, five IG changes that we made at the beginning of this administration that had nothing to do with malfeasance. We thought the person had the wrong set of skills for what the nature of the job was at that point in time. And having terms would have prevented us from getting somebody better suited for the job at that time.

The reasons you gave for just cause don't include matters such as that. Wonderful people, they have all the right statutory and education and experience requirements; they are just investigative rather than financial, or vice versa; and I think the administration's ability to deal with that is limited if you put a term on it.

Mr. Cooper. Mr. Johnson, it strikes me that your concern is not with the term, but the definition of "dismissal for cause." And if we define that to include a wrong fit for the agency, that might alleviate your concerns.

Mr. Johnson. But that is so broad. We could do that, but in effect, I think you have no term.

Mr. Cooper. My concern now, having talked to a wide number of IGs, is that they feel considerable pressure as individuals when they support sensitive areas and a more regular, private-sector-like situation might be helpful. Most people in the private sector kind of know what "for cause" is, and maybe we can adjust that slightly for government contacts because we do want the right fit and we need an appropriate balance between prevention and "gotcha."

Mr. Johnson. Of course, maybe the pressure they feel is the pressure to get it right, which is a good pressure to have.

Mr. Cooper. Well, we live in a political world, and there are a lot of folks who know that there are certain things that they will be in trouble if they investigate. And wouldn't it be wonderful if we lived in world when they could investigate wherever waste, fraud or abuse occurred? So let's work on a way and see if we can't do that.[45]

Johnson first argues that no one has charged that the IGs do not have enough independence. Given the general tact with which elected officials in Washington normally communicate, no one had charged anyone with anything, so Johnson was technically correct, but wrong in spirit. He certainly knew of and referred to the episodes that generated the hearings in 2003, the firings or involuntary removals of respected inspectors general and their replacement with political appointees close to the White House. The OMB spokesman tried to explain these episodes away. He claimed that the reasons for those personnel changes was a skills mismatch; if the president could only fire an IG for misfeasance, he argued, the president would be unable to make the necessary personnel changes to match the skills of the IG with the problems of the agency.

Because Johnson was denying that there was any problem, Representative Cooper spelled out the IGs' feeling of being pressed not to engage in certain investigations. Cooper maintained that it would be good for the public if IGs could begin an investigation on *any* topic to root out waste, fraud, or abuse and not be steered away from some issues that were perceived as sensitive.

Cooper tried to accommodate to the argument that the administration needs flexibility to choose staff with the right skills for the job at the moment by offering to include a skills mismatch as a legitimate reason for firing an IG. Johnson responded by arguing against that proposal, though it met the objection he had expressed; he seemed to switch sides at this point, arguing that if such an exception were made it would be the same as not having a term. He seemed to be arguing to Cooper that using such a broad reason for firing someone would destroy Cooper's plan. In arguing this way, Johnson perhaps inadvertently expressed the idea that a mismatch between skills and job was so broad that it could be used to fire anyone at nearly any time—and that was the prerogative that OMB was insisting on maintaining.

Johnson had begun his own testimony with a statement that his role was to work with the IGs to implement the president's policies. Speculating only a little, one can conclude that his opposition to terms for IGs stemmed from a belief that it would be more difficult for him to get IG cooperation if the president could not fire IGs pretty much at will (claiming a skills mismatch; impossible to disprove) and appoint administration loyalists.

Shortly after the twenty-fifth anniversary hearing on the IGs, quoted above, Representatives Cooper and Christopher Shays, R-Conn., put forth a legislative proposal to increase the independence of the IGs. The Subcommittee on Government Efficiency and Financial Management held one hearing on the bill in 2004, but the measure did not make it out of committee. The issue of IG independence did not go away, however. Democrats on the House Government Reform Committee released a report dated October 21, 2004, documenting the extent of politicization of the IG system under the Bush administration. Among the report's findings:

- More than one-third of the inspectors general appointed by President Bush worked in Republican administrations prior to their appointments as IGs.

- 64 percent of the IGs had held a Republican political job.
- Only 18 percent of Bush's appointments had previous audit experience, compared to 66 percent of Clinton's appointments.[46]

Despite the publicity, Congress took no immediate steps to remedy the situation. IGs are still straddling a barbed wire fence. The degree of their independence is questionable.

State and Local Inspectors General

Twenty states have at least one inspector general in a major agency or department (Table 8.1). Some of the offices are created by statute and hence are permanent; some by executive order, which can be revoked or continued by the next executive; and some only by fiat of an agency or department head. In some states, only one or a few agencies have IGs, but nearly half (nine)of the states that have an inspector general have a system that is statewide or nearly statewide in coverage. Some IGs have broad powers, including subpoena and criminal investigation powers, and others much more limited scope and powers. Equally important, the offices vary considerably in how independent the IGs are from department heads or the governor. To some extent these variables interact; for example some states grant IGs broad powers, but keep them leashed by making the IGs responsible only to the department head.[47]

The creation or expansion of an IG office or an increase in its powers or scope of inquiry has nearly always been precipitated by widespread and publicly acknowledged corruption. That was certainly the case in New Jersey.

In New Jersey, an inspector general office was created in 2000 to examine contractors for school construction projects and bar those who had records of corruption or shoddy work from bidding on school projects. The office was given subpoena powers and could pursue civil or criminal penalties, as appropriate, but its reach was limited. Banned companies were not prohibited from bidding on other state projects, and the IG was not allowed to examine companies that bid on nonschool projects or to look into cases where public officials had accepted bribes from contractors.[48]

With many corruption cases falling outside the scope of the existing IG, acting governor Richard Codey created a statewide IG position by executive order on November 29, 2004. "Codey said he created the post as part of an effort to restore integrity and trust in a state where corruption has flourished and the last governor was driven from office by scandal." Codey chose an IG with legal and prosecutorial experience, rather than a political background, arguing that the position needed to be nonpolitical and the IG needed to be able to follow cases

Table 8.1 State Inspector General Systems

State	Date created	E/S/A	Departments	Appointed by/Report to	Independence
California	1899	NA	Corrections	Exec. director corrections hires and fires.	Low
	1994	S	Youth and Adult Corrections as of 1998 but public reports start in 2005	Governor appoints, Senate confirms.	Moderate; no fixed term
Colorado	1995	S	Corrections	Dept. of Corrections head appoints and removes.	Low
Florida	1994	S	Govt wide	Agency head hires, fires.	Low
Georgia	2003	E	Govt wide	Governor hires and fires.	Low
Illinois	2003	S	Govt wide, several older ones rolled in its own	Agency head hires; legislature appoints; removal for cause.	High 5-year term
Kentucky	1977	S	Health	Secretary hires and fires.	Low
	1999	S	Environmental	Governor appoints/fires.	Low
	2002	E	Transportation	Governor appoints/fires.	Low
Louisiana	1988	E	Govt wide	Reports to governor, who can choose to make reports public.	Structurally low; no term of office but first IG stayed thru 3 govs.
Maryland	1990	A	Human Resource	Reports to secretary.	Low
	1994	A	Public Safety	Reports to secretary.	Low
	1998	A	Mental health	Reports to secretary.	Low

State	Year	Type	Scope	Appointment/Removal	Level
Mass.	1981	S	Govt wide	Governor, AG, state auditor choose; majority can remove.	High 5-year term
Michigan	1972	S	Family Independence Agency	Agency director appoints.	Low
New Jersey	2004	E	Statewide	Reports to governor.	In process; Senate passed 5-year term in 2005. Office may get statutory basis and dual reporting structure.
New Mexico	1989	A	Human Services	Dept. secretary hires.	Low
	1991	A	Transportation	Dept. secretary oversees.	Low
New York	1996	E	Govt wide	Governor hires, fires.	Low
	1999	S	Welfare	Governor hires.	Low
	2002	S	Workers Comp.	Governor hires.	Low
Ohio	1990	S	Gubernatorial agencies	Governor appoints, with advice of Senate.	Moderate; same term as governor.
Oklahoma	1979	A	Human Services	Dept. head appoints.	Low
Pennsylvania	1979	E	Gubernatorial agencies	Governor appoints, fires.	Low
South Carolina	NA	NA	Corrections	Dept head?	Unknown
Texas	1994	NA	Criminal Justice	Governor appoints, reports to board.	Low
	2003	S	Human Services	Governor appoints.	Low

Table 8.1 *Continued*

State	Date created	E/S/A	Departments	Appointed by/Report to	Independence
Virginia	1984	S	Corrections	Reports to Dept. of Corrections, secondarily to Secretary of Public Safety and Board of Corrections.	Moderate
	1999	S	Mental Health	Reports to governor; confirmed by legislature.	Moderate; term not concurrent with governor
W. Va.	1979	A	Human Services	Dept. head hires; direct reporting to dept. head.	Low

Note: Data are for the most recent incarnation; if office was created by a governor but later re-created by statute, the date and statutory status are given here. Level of information available is uneven from office to office. Degree of independence is a composite variable, using available data, including, where known, term of office (term is more independent than lack of term; term not coterminous with governor's is more independent than if coterminous); firing for cause only is more independent than fire at will; statutory authority more independent than executive order, executive order more independent than administrative creation; department-wide but reports to the governor gives some independence; governor controls report release is less independent than if office of inspector general controls release. Not all information was available for each IG office; more information might change the evaluation of the degree of independence.

E = Executive order (of governor); must be renewed by each governor or office ceases.

S = Statutory; permanent

A = Administrative order (of department head); exists at the pleasure of the department head.

NA = Information is not available.

wherever they led. There was considerable support in the state legislature for making the office statutory, so that future governors could not dissolve it, and there was also some interest in making the IG report to both the governor and the legislature, rather than just the governor, as in the IG office that Codey had created by executive order. The state senate easily passed the measure to make the office permanent, giving the IG a five-year term and including investigations of state and local governments and commissions in the office's scope. The lower house of the state legislature did not immediately follow suit.[49]

The issue of how much autonomy to give the IGs has been as difficult to manage at the state level as it has at the national level. To have high credibility that the state is rooting out corruption, IGs need broad powers, nonpolitical appointments based on a list of professional qualifications, and either a fixed term in office or a requirement that they can only be fired for specified cause. If department heads can hire and fire IGs at will, the IGs no longer look independent, and the public may suspect that the IGs are being fired to prevent them from investigating particular issues or releasing damaging reports. Along the same lines, if the IGs do not have subpoena powers and cannot force agencies to provide documents necessary for an investigation, even if they otherwise seem independent, they will not be able to carry out investigations in depth.

Florida has a statewide IG system in which the IGs have a broad mandate; they are even required to follow up on their recommendations to see that they have been implemented. The agency heads are explicitly forbidden from preventing an IG from carrying out an investigation or blocking a report that has been done. At the same time, however, the IG in each department or agency is hired by, and may be fired by, the department head. One wonders if a department head would hire an IG whom he or she didn't trust to be tactful about an investigation, or whether the threat of being fired might not create self-censorship, even if the agency head didn't directly interfere with an investigation.

Having an IG report to a department head facilitates constructive action. If the IG finds some financial problem or corruption, he or she reports it to the department head, who presumably takes corrective action without fear of negative publicity. However, this reporting structure may limit the scope of investigations, as well as public access to information about whether problems were or were not addressed. It is possible to create a structure that gives the IGs more protection.

Dade County, Florida, has an IG system with a different structure that gives the IGs more independence. There, the IG is appointed by an ethics board composed of five members, and he or she may only be fired by a two-thirds majority of the board (though one wonders what 3.3 votes might look like). The board itself is not controlled or appointed by the county board of commissioners or the county executive, mayor, or manager; its members are chosen by judges, law school deans, labor studies centers, and the Dade County League of Cities. The ethics board members have staggered, four-year terms. This structure would seem to provide the best possible buffering of the IG from political pressure. The IG's office notes that this independence was intentional, for the purpose of regaining public trust in the honesty of county government:

> The County Commissioners took great lengths to ensure that the Inspector General can carry out these goals while autonomous, independent and insulated from political influences. It is one of a few OIGs in the country that has jurisdiction to investigate officials at any level, including elected officials.[50]

The trend has been toward IGs in more states, broader coverage of state agencies within each state, and more integrated IG systems like that of the federal government. The degree of autonomy and independence granted to the IGs has been a more difficult issue, but it seems that the worse the corruption and the greater the public demand to clean it up, the more autonomy—as well as teeth—the IGs will be given. The irony is that honest governments that have nothing to fear from independent IGs do not in fact need them.

For students of budgeting it is important to watch not only the development and expansion of IG systems, but also their actual structure and independence. In the 1990s, at the federal level, the concern of reformers was that IGs would intimidate public managers and make them risk averse, playing a game of "gotcha" that is punishment oriented rather than prevention and improvement oriented. In recent years the danger has probably been the reverse, of public managers' intimidating and controlling their IGs. Politicians want to give the impression of cleaning up corruption and waste without making themselves vulnerable to the investigations of the IG offices and the bad publicity resulting from negative findings.

Campaigns to Reduce Waste, Fraud, and Abuse

The tension between appointed officials' policy control over investigations and the independence of the inspectors general is endemic to the system and adds a political dimension to budget implementation. A second source of political content in a technical process is political campaigns to reduce waste, fraud, and abuse. During his first term President Reagan, as had his immediate predecessors, launched a national campaign to reduce waste, fraud, and abuse in the federal government. Not only did his campaign make headlines, but examples of fraud and waste kept hitting the newspapers, making the issue particularly salient. Military purchases of $2,000 toilet seats, $600 hammers, and $7,600 coffeepots became public; military procurement became the subject of congressional hearings. During Reagan's second term, military procurement became a widely publicized scandal.

Reducing waste, fraud, and abuse seems like an ideal political campaign issue because it fits the public conception that there is waste in government, promises to clean it up, and offers to reduce tax burdens by cutting fat and leaving services alone. If done properly, it also helps cover over currently occurring scandals or abuses. On closer examination, however, such campaigns are fraught with difficulties both political and technical.

Campaigns against waste, fraud, and abuse often make the naïve assumption that there is fat in the public budget and that the fat is easily recognizable and surgically removable. In fact, the amount of fat is not easily determined, and it is almost always attached to something of value. For example, trying to get able-bodied people off the handicapped rolls requires tightening eligibility requirements. Inevitably, some people who are both eligible and needy will also be taken off the rolls. Should their plight become public knowledge, the result is likely to be worse publicity than if some undeserving person got public aid. There is a very real trade-off between denying some people aid who need it and preventing the undeserving from getting it.

Second, waste, fraud, and abuse keep recurring, no matter how much is reported eliminated, because a small number of mistakes are inevitable in any large and complex operation.[51] Thus a campaign to eliminate waste, fraud, and abuse can be embarrassing because the more you "save" the more you demonstrate how much more waste, fraud, and abuse exist. "No matter which administration is blamed, constant harping on fraud and abuse goes beyond its necessity as a deterrent to the point of further weakening an already dangerously tottering image of the governmental process."[52]

Moreover, much of the source of waste is systemic, which means that really getting to the basis of the problem may mean major revelations of structural problems and major reorganizations. To eliminate wasteful purchasing in the military would require a drastic overhaul of the military. Such a change is a long-term proposition, not something that can be accomplished by a short-term political campaign with highly publicized results and then silence.

Campaigns against waste, fraud, and abuse are useful political tools to bring down an opponent or discredit a predecessor, but they can boomerang and be used against one's own administration. Hence such campaigns are inherently political, regardless of their technical components.

Summary and Conclusions

Periodically the flexibility in the budget is abused, and legislative will is thwarted. Legislators may become angry and increase controls over an agency or program. Such controls may accumulate over time and remain in place long after they are needed. A morass of controls invites efforts to evade them, and even the legislature may gradually lose interest in enforcing outdated overcontrols.

Legislative bodies tend to become angry when they think their will has been thwarted. They do not tend to get as excited about poor financial management, but the Government Accountability Office and the inspectors general at the national level and inspectors general and auditors at the state level get upset about poor financial management, especially when it leads to major losses of money. Unlike the legislatures, auditors do not have line authority to make improvements. At the national level, the inspectors general have to persuade the management of their agencies to make improvements. They have to develop a working relationship with the managers they are observing, while maintaining their independence and reporting to Congress.

Improving financial management is not a neutral and technical topic, even when it is handled quietly, but when mismanagement involves millions or billions of dollars and makes government look bad, those who report it become unwelcome presences. Efforts to control the auditors or put a particular spin on their findings have sometimes marred the independence of the inspectors general.

The National Performance Review put some of the blame on auditors for creating an atmosphere of fear and overcontrol, but generally all they do is call attention to violations of rules and in some cases suggest new ones. The source of overcontrol is occasional intentional abuses of discretion that generate greater controls. Not enough attention is paid to moderating and eliminating the controls when they are no longer needed. This is not to argue that legislators are always on the moral high ground in what they want the agencies to do—they may insist that a contract go to a specific company, for example. Rather, it appears clear that agencies should be extremely careful to avoid abusing grants of discretion, and legislatures should impose the minimum amount of control necessary to regain compliance should they detect such abuse.

9. Budgetary Decision Making and Politics

Budgetary decision making includes five distinct but linked clusters: revenues, process, expenditures, balance, and implementation. Describing each decision stream separately tends to emphasize their independence. This chapter is about how they fit together into one decision-making process. Looking at the decision strands together also illuminates their differences and common themes.

Real-Time Budgeting

I call the pattern that results from the integration of the five streams of decision making *real-time budgeting*. "Real time" refers to the continual adjustment of decisions in each stream to decisions and information coming from other streams and from the environment. Budgeting, like the complex computer programs aboard spaceships, continually readjusts, in real time, for changing information.

Budgeting is characterized by semi-independent, overlapping streams of decision making that depend on one another for key pieces of information. What makes this process complex and interesting is that the clusters are not timed sequentially to feed into one another. The clusters occur at different intervals and last for different lengths of time. To make the key decisions in any one stream, actors may have to look backward, to the last time the decision was made in another stream, or forward, to anticipated decisions, or even sideways,

281

to decisions being made at the same time. Much of this information is tentative; it can and does change as the budget moves toward implementation.

Budgetary decision making takes the shape it does because of the characteristics of public budgeting described in chapter 1. First and foremost, budgets are open to the environment—to the economy, to the weather, to a variety of emergencies, and to changes in public preferences and political leadership. Openness to the economy means that estimates of revenues, and to some extent estimates of expenditures, may have to be revised several times during the budget process as better information becomes known. Budgeters cannot make one estimate at the beginning of the budget process and stick to it. Openness to changes in political leadership and public opinion means that budgets that were generally agreed to may need to be redone. The federal system of government means that changes at one level of government may affect budgeting at another level of government.

A second characteristic of public budgets is that a variety of actors with different goals compete for limited resources. Budgets have to be able to deal with policy conflict among these actors and with competition between them. When budget actors disagree, they may hold up whatever decisions they are in the process of making. Budgeting has to accommodate this kind of conflict and the resulting delays because, unlike many other political decisions, budgets have real deadlines. The later they are, the less use they are, so the problem of late decisions has to be handled in some way.

The solution to the problems of changing information and late decisions is a budget process that features fragmentation, with semi-independent decision streams, and interruptibility. Parts of the decision making may proceed without the rest, so as to complete the budget in a timely manner. The different strands of decision making proceed as if they were independent, referring to one another, bargaining when necessary to reach accommodation. If one decision-making strand gets stuck—as, for example, when a tax increase is being considered but has not yet been decided on—other decision streams can proceed by making assumptions about what will occur and adjusting their own work when the final outcome is known in the revenue stream.

The decision clusters are mostly independent, but they need information from one another to complete their work. The revenue cluster cannot proceed without some knowledge of spending requirements and balance constraints. Decisions about how to reduce a deficit are dependent on revenue estimates and spending estimates. Spending estimates depend on revenue estimates and balance constraints. Implementation depends on decisions throughout the process to that point, especially on the degree of underestimates of revenues or overestimates of expenditures, and the constraints of balance. Revenues, expenditures, balance, and implementation all depend on the process stream to organize them and allocate power to them.

Information coming from other decision streams may appear as a constraint, but one that is flexible rather than rigid. Thus a figure for estimated revenues already fed into the expenditure stream may change if the prediction on the economy changes. Or it may change if a decision is made in the expenditure stream that requires more revenue.

Constraints from other decision streams are flexible not only because the environment changes but also because actors in one stream can sometimes force a change in another stream. Actors who want to spend more money may be able to force a change in the tax structure, or even in revenue estimates; they may also be able to force a change in the definition of balance. Actors who want to reduce revenues may act to cut expenditures and define balance to suit their purposes.

Budgetary decision making is not linear and sequential, in the sense that some decisions are made first and form the frame for the other decisions. A simple model of decision making would argue that the definition of balance, the budget process, and the revenue estimates should be in place before the beginning of the decision making about expenditures and that the decision making should begin with targets for spending that keep within revenue estimates. Real budgeting does not look like this model for three by-now-familiar reasons. First, the budget is open to the environment, so new information becomes available at intervals. Second, decisions in each stream take different amounts of time to make and are remade at intervals that may be impossible to predict or schedule. Third, actors in one decision stream can jump over into other decision streams and force a change there in the middle of the decision making.

Consider, for example, some changes in the environment that affected revenue decisions at the local level in Illinois. In one case, the legislature passed a change in the law for tax increment districts—a form of project funding that uses the increased tax yield from property that results from public development efforts to pay off the initial project costs. The state had agreed to help share the costs of redevelopment by offering increments from the state sales tax to the cities that had sales tax increment districts, but then it found that some cities drew up their districts not to maximize development but to maximize the state funding offer. The size of the local demand on state funds was larger than anticipated. The state balked; it was no longer clear what proportion of the promised funds the state would provide. In the middle of a budget year, the state announced its revised guidelines and reduced funding levels. Spending decisions that had already been made had to be remade, and projects had to be reprioritized in the light of the changed law.

A second example occurred when the state changed the sales tax law to merge locally raised sales taxes with the state-collected sales tax, requiring a uniform set of exemptions but giving cities a little over two years to prepare for the change. The result for some cities would be a loss of revenues because they would have to conform to the state exemptions. They would have two years to decide how to adapt and to design alternatives and implement them. They might or might not accomplish the decision making in the revenue stream in time. In any case, the decision began two years ahead of the event and was thrust on the cities by the state at an unpredictable moment.

An example of decisions in one cluster that influence decisions in a second cluster occurs when actors try to define or redefine balance during the budget process. If it appears that there is a conflict between the amount of revenue available and the amount of spending desired, and the conflict cannot be easily reconciled, one option is to attack the definition of balance and loosen it. For example, underspending now for pensions that will have to be paid out later may be excluded from a consideration of deficits, or future borrowing that will be necessary to cover today's budget gaps may not be considered an expenditure.

Efforts to redefine balance were continuous at the national level for most of the 1980s. Gramm-Rudman-Hollings made this effort explicit by defining balance as a moving target of deficits of smaller and smaller size. Each year, then, the target for balance was to change. Unfortunately for the linear model of decision making, it was not clear that Gramm-Rudman-Hollings was constitutional, which made its targets somewhat dubious; and the response to its limits was to make the deficits appear to be of appropriate size, rather than to make them of the appropriate size. The result was a shifting definition of balance that was clarified every year as part of the budget process.

Budgetary decision making is not, and cannot be made, sequential. The solution is to make the key decisions in five parallel sequences and link them to one another for necessary information. The system of decision making by linking clusters in real time is wonderfully adaptive. Real-time decision making allows the streams to be disrupted, or interrupted, and repeated. Decisions can be adjusted or remade.

Budgeters have to have contingency plans to deal with missing information or late decisions. To respond to missing information, they may rely instead on the most recent decision. If individual policy decisions are coming along too slowly, they may simplify and speed up the decision making by grouping many decisions together. They may push up the urgency of decisions that are causing roadblocks by linking them to other urgent matters. The overlap of decision clusters allows solutions in one stream to resolve roadblocks in another stream. A solution in the revenue stream may unlock a problem in the expenditure stream; a change in process may solve problems of linkage between the streams.

A Comparison of the Decision-Making Streams

The focus of this book is to make clearer the nature of politics in public budgeting. After examining each of the five decision streams, one would have to say that what politics looks like depends on where you look. In some areas of budgetary decision making, narrowly conceived interest groups compete with one another for tax breaks or spending increases; in others, coalitions of interest groups that approach class interests compete for control of the scope of government services; in still others, interest groups have little role. Some areas of the budget are policy laden, while others appear policy neutral and technical. To get anything like a realistic view of politics in the budget requires a look at each strand of budgetary decision making.

Revenue politics is characterized by both a policy orientation and active interest group participation. The policy issues include who will be taxed and what the level of taxation will be. Narrowly defined interest groups try to deflect taxes from their constituents; broader coalitions of interest groups get involved in efforts to determine the distribution of taxation among income groups and the overall level of taxation.

The politics of process revolves around two policy issues and bargaining among the actors. The first cluster of policy issues includes, ironically, how much of a policy focus the budget should have, how clearly policy issues should be articulated, and concomitantly, how much conflict should be expressed and resolved during budget decision making. The second, related policy issue is how much articulation of citizen and interest group preferences the budget process should engage in. How much access should individuals, interest groups, agency heads, and the press have to budgetary decision making, and how much secrecy should there be? The result of these policy choices influences not only the level of accountability in the budget process but also, presumably, the level and nature of public expenditures and the amount of discipline in the budget process. The politics of process also revolves around the bargaining between budget actors for more power over budgetary choices. The bargaining over the distribution of power and the choices on key policy issues are often intertwined.

The politics of expenditures reflects several different aspects of politics. There is active interest group involvement, as well as extensive bargaining and competition. The competition among interest groups generally prevents one interest group from controlling budgetary decisions. At times, an emphasis on policy trumps the interplay of interest groups. The choices of which programs to fund and at what level may be carefully analyzed and considered against some characterization of the public good. Legislators can resist even powerful interest groups when they choose; to do so, they use the budget process to insulate themselves.

The politics of budget balance is primarily about policy. Three key issues are the role of the budget in managing the economy, the scope of government programs, and which level of government will balance its budget at the expense of which other level of government. These issues are often defined in terms of the target level of unemployment; the level of social services the public sector provides and the programs or services it provides that could be provided by the private sector; and the degree of progressivity of the taxes that pay for governmental services. The outcome of each of these policy decisions is far reaching. As a result, coalitions of interest groups representing wide segments of society take different stands on the politics of balance; liberals and conservatives, Democrats and Republicans, take opposing stances. The politics of balance is often partisan.

The politics of implementation is a contest between the goal of maintaining accountability by implementing the budget almost exactly as passed, and the goal of reshaping the budget during the budget year to accomplish some policy goal that was not agreed to during budget deliberations. Generally, the technical accountability model is triumphant, but at the cost of considerable effort in monitoring potentially policy-laden budget adaptations. Maintaining the neutrality of oversight can be difficult and problematic.

In short, no one view of politics in the budget stands alone. There is bargaining among actors in budget decision making, but it is framed by policy concerns expressed through the budget process; interest groups are active in budgetary decision making, but they are controlled, or can be controlled, both by competition among themselves and by the budget process that gives or denies them access to decision making. There is a contest between more technical and more policy-oriented approaches to budgeting, but in most areas there is some kind of balance between them. There are policy issues in the budget, but they may be played up or toned down by the budget process and format.

Common Themes

Though the politics of each strand of budgetary decision making varies, three somewhat related themes run throughout the chapters. One is the tension between openness and secrecy; another is the tension between pendulum swings of change and some kind of balance or stability; and a third is a pattern of deterioration and reform.

Openness versus Secrecy

One theme that cuts across the decision clusters is the tension between keeping decision making open and reporting accurate and meaningful information, on the one hand, and on the other hand, limiting public participation and either not reporting information or showering the public with loads of disaggregated data that are difficult to interpret.

The question of how open budget decision making should be is not simple. One cannot realistically argue that complete openness is good and all secrecy is bad. Open processes, with lots of public participation, not only take longer but are sometimes contentious. They may raise expectations to unrealistic levels, causing disappointment and frustration all around. Public and interest group demands may make it difficult or impossible to reduce public benefits, even in the face of a consensus that taxes need to be lowered. The decision making behind the design and passage of federal tax reforms in 1986 was closed to the public and interest groups. If the process had been more open, lobby groups would have insisted on maintaining their own tax breaks, and reform probably would not have been achieved.

Moreover, no budget can be inclusive and still readable. A budget that presented all relevant information, even for a small government, would be thousands of pages long and would quickly overwhelm the reader with detail. Every budget necessarily involves some selection about what information to present. The question is to what extent the selection process is guided by desire to evade accountability, protect cronyism, hide waste or corruption, and avoid blame. Analyzing what is not in the budget is often as revealing as examining what is included.

Although no budget can be fully open, budgetary secrecy, even well-intentioned secrecy, is a serious problem in a democracy. Secrecy can sever the relationship between the elected officials and the taxpayers, where taxpayers ask for or demand particular outcomes and the officials do something different, without explaining their choices or reporting what they did. The budget and the audit reports that go with it are major tools of accountability. A redacted audit report on a government contract, essentially edited by the contractor, raises suspicions about the purposes and success of the contract and the willingness of the government to hold the contractor accountable. Such actions make it look as if the government is working for the contractor, rather than looking after the public's interest.

While there may be some minimum necessary amount of secrecy in budgeting, when the level of secrecy increases, alarm bells should go off, Klaxons should sound, and warning lights should flash. For many years, the overall trend in budgeting was increasing openness and accountability. In recent years, however, this trend may have been reversed, particularly at the national level, but also, to a lesser extent, at other levels of government.

It is now more difficult to examine public sector contracts at the national level to see and monitor sole source (noncompetitive) contract awards, the ones most likely to be excessively expensive and based on cronyism. It is nearly impossible to see how many people are working for government, because only the civil service and public officials are counted, not the contractual staff. Contracting has increased at all levels of government, but there is seldom any reporting on large contracts in the budget document. Contracts are typically lumped together in one budget line called "contractual services." Citizens are unable to see what was contracted for, how much it cost, or whether the government got its money's worth. Contracting is opaque, compared to government provision of services, and contracting is an increasingly large proportion of public spending.

At the federal level, the watchdog inspectors general have been politicized, chosen much more than in the past for their loyalty to the party in power and the president. As described in chapter 8 (in box on page 263), an IG for the newly formed Department of Homeland Security was not renewed in his position, reportedly because he was critical of the effectiveness of the department and his openness was embarrassing to an administration that was arguing it was protecting people from terrorism. Although the states are increasingly developing inspector general offices of their own, the independence of these offices is often questionable as well. Political control over IGs makes it look as if there are some issues they are being steered away from, some potentially important things that the public is not being allowed to see.

At the national level, the size of the black, or secret, budget has jumped up in recent years. Many tens of billions of dollars of spending cannot be named or discussed and debated, or compared with other spending priorities. While there is nothing like the black budget at the state or local level, legislators do sometimes withhold budget information or release it in such disaggregated form that it takes months of teamwork by the press and many dollars to use the information.

The passage of omnibus legislation—bundling many important decisions together in huge packages and passing them quickly, without giving legislators a chance to read the bill, evaluate it, or object to parts of it—has also created a kind of secrecy at the national level. At the state level, New York State's may be the exemplar for a budget process that is formally open, while the real decisions are made behind closed doors.

While most public budgeting remains open and accountable, the direction of change is no longer clearly toward more openness. This turnaround requires some explanation. It suggests that there is no higher evolutionary end toward which budgeting is evolving. Furthermore, this change suggests that the openness of public budgets is not a given, determined by the degree of democracy in the society, but rather the reverse; the degree of openness and accountability in the budget frames the amount of democracy. The amount of openness and account-ability in the budget can erode; there are few who can see what is happening and complain, and hence few who can start the pendulum swinging back in a more open—and democratic—direction.

The tenuousness of the openness of the budget and its ability to function as a major tool of accountability suggests the importance of isolating those factors that seem to increase or decrease the level of secrecy. Based on the observations reported in this book, the following are some hypotheses researchers might want to investigate:

1. The greater the amount of corruption, the greater the amount of secrecy. Highly publicized corruption creates a need to appear to eliminate or reduce corruption—which stimulates the creation or expansion of over-sight bodies such as the IGs—while at the same time controlling the overseers and watchdogs so that they do not embarrass elected officials by revealing inefficiencies, fraud, or remaining corruption.

2. The waging of war and the experience of terrorism make it easier to sell secrecy as necessary for national defense. The more freedom and flexi-bility granted to defense agencies to carry out wars, the less the public knows about how money is being spent. Secrecy for convenience and political expedience may be hidden within the folds of the apparently necessary secrecy of war.

3. The New York State model suggests that a budget process that radically disempowers one of the key actors is going to generate informal ways of getting around that process, creating a second, less-visible process that distributes power more fairly. Thus budget processes that shift too much power to the executive branch may end up generating considerable secrecy or budget processes that occur behind closed doors.

4. When people or interest groups demand not only different but contra-dictory spending and taxing priorities, the amount of secrecy, or at least the amount of obfuscation, is likely to rise. In recent years there has been major pressure to reduce taxation, while program recipients still demand benefits and taxpayers insist on their services at the same level as before. When elected officials give in to these contradictory demands, deficits

result. Those same officials then often try to obscure the resulting deficits and their consequences. Deficits in general tend to result in more budget games and budget manipulation.

5. Fragmentation of the budget and the various tools used to take programs out of the competitive parts of the budget facilitate secrecy. Programs that supposedly fund themselves may be insulated from public scrutiny, and transfers into or out of them may be obscured. Off-budget entities are necessarily less visible than on-budget entities. They go off-budget not only to get out of the competition, but also to get out from under the rules, to gain freedom, which includes freedom from oversight and reporting.

6. Spending through tax breaks, rather than direct spending, contributes to secrecy because money that is never collected is less visible than money that is collected and then spent. At the local level, this problem is exacerbated by a lack of tax expenditure reporting. The more a state or local government focuses on taxation through exception, rather than reforming the tax structure more broadly, the more complex and less easily seen and understood this spending program becomes. Because the tendency to increase these breaks increases when the economy deteriorates, a failing economy is likely to reduce the information content of the budget.

7. The more the emphasis on contracting out, even with the most careful attention to achieving greater efficiency, the less information there is likely to be on crucial financial decisions. Only a few governments have made information available on contractors, and then the information is usually too disaggregated to interpret. Although reporting on contracts could be vastly improved, the very nature of contracting assumes a black box—that how the contractor does the work is not considered relevant, so long as the work is done as specified in the contract and for the agreed-on price. This perspective suggests the government has no right to knowledge about the number of employees, the costs of production, source of savings, or anything else other than the price and the description of the delivered product or project. From this viewpoint, which was maintained by the federal Office of Management and Budget, the more contracting out, the less information will be provided.

Fortunately, although the sources of secrecy in budgeting are increasing, there are also continuing pressures for maintaining or restoring openness and accountability. One powerful argument for maintaining openness is to enforce the budget agreements that were arrived at in public. Budget implementation is generally very close to the budget that passes in full public view; there is very little behind-the-scenes redoing of the policy choices in the budget. Actors who need to come to agreement on the next budget do not wish to see the last set of agreements come undone or be remade by someone else during the budget year. To keep the whole decision-making process going, the budget actors need to believe that their previous agreements will be implemented without change. Environmental changes sometimes reduce the causes of secrecy. The end of the cold war helped to reduce secrecy in the Defense Department, just as the wars in Afghanistan and Iraq have increased it. Pressure from the deficit to find and reduce waste and shrink the scope of programs has also contributed to congressional pressure to expand the authority of the IGs. Improved economic conditions reduce pressure to grant tax breaks to businesses, making spending programs more visible.

While these counterpressures help maintain a level of openness in budgeting, at times they may not be sufficient. In the worst case, the budget loses much of its utility as a tool of accountability.

Dynamics of Budgeting over Time

A second theme that plays out across the decision streams is a pattern of long-term change, in which processes or outcomes swing between extremes, or patterns reoccur in cycles. In the balance decision stream, a seriously constrained process is at one extreme, and ad hoc budgeting is at the other. Depending in part on the process in place at the time, outcomes have alternated between huge deficits and balance. In taxation, broad revenue sources were eroded by tax expenditures until the amounts of lost revenue were enormous, precipitating a reform that eliminated many tax breaks and reduced the dollar value of others. Then the process of erosion began again. In budget implementation, the discretion-abuse-control cycle has often resulted in controls that were too tight, which were evaded or not enforced. Sometimes a pattern of exceptions to the rules has grown up. A new grant of broad discretion might be made, if circumstances seemed to warrant it. In the budget process stream, there has been alternation between executive and legislative dominance. When one became too extreme, there was pressure to restore some level of balance. The process of locking and unlocking both revenue and expenditure decisions further highlights the pendulum swing model.

In some cases, the mechanism that generates the swing one way or the other is clear and nearly automatic. In other situations, the process seems sticky; it is unclear what would be necessary to turn the process around, to reverse the pendulum swing before its full arc, or to create some stability or equilibrium.

The tendency to use protection from taxation as a distributive benefit is inherent in the political system. Protection from taxes is a resource through which politicians gain electoral support. Moreover, tax breaks seem free, as they never appear in the budget as an expenditure. But when they accumulate over time, they can cause fiscal stress, generating the desire to put some controls on the giving away of tax breaks.

The controls may take many forms. One is the requirement for an offset to any tax reduction, making its cost apparent at the time it is offered. Another is to make tax expenditures more visible by requiring periodic reporting of the estimated costs of tax breaks. The third approach, when the aggregate costs of tax breaks are sufficiently high, is to reform the tax structure, lowering taxes for nearly everyone, using the lost revenue from tax breaks to fund across-the-board tax reductions.

Which strategy is used has implications for cyclicality or stable processes over time. Strategies that make the costs of tax breaks more visible or more painful may well reduce new or expanded tax breaks, creating a kind of stability in the system. By contrast, the model that allows taxes to be lowered for all, wiping out many of the tax breaks, clears the slate for a repeat cycle, even if the motivation to do so is temporarily reduced by the lower tax rates. Because it is not just the degree to which the tax is burdensome that creates pressure to grant tax breaks, but also the desire of politicians to give constituents and supporters something of value, reducing the number of tax breaks without increasing their visibility and political costs is not likely to interrupt the cycle. Nearly the same forces are in place at the end of the cycle as at the beginning, starting the process anew.

Budget processes that create unintended and unfair results generate sufficient pressure to either cause their evasion or bring the process to a halt. Thus Gramm-Rudman-Hollings (GRH) forced cuts in expenditures for a few major programs that were not major contributors to the deficit. This unfair outcome occurred because many programs were exempted from the so-called across-the-board cuts, so the remaining programs had to be disproportionately reduced to make up the difference. Not surprisingly, GRH was widely evaded, creating a much less open and understandable process and budget. Since evasion of the process did not solve the deficit problem, a new round of budget rules followed that intentionally minimized the unintended effects of GRH. The second round, the Budget Enforcement Act, was not evaded and contributed to the restoration of budget balance. But the very fact that the line held helped to create sufficient pressure to bring this process, too, to an end. Legislators found they had little pork to trade, to build coalitions of support; they had to offset any additional tax breaks with revenue increases or spending decreases, and they also had to offset any mandated expansion of entitlements. After balance was achieved, and even before the Budget Enforcement Act expired, pent up desire to increase political resources forced an explosion of increased expenditures, and shortly thereafter the president and Congress passed huge and popular tax reductions, without offsets.

It seems likely that the size of the resulting deficits and the consequences of borrowing to pay for them will at some point require Congress to come up with a third pass at a budget process that will help eliminate deficits and (one hopes) help prevent their return.

In the expenditure cluster, there has been a long-term tendency toward reducing competition, locking in revenue sources for particular expenditures. Trust funds (or what pass for trust funds in the public sector), entitlements, public enterprises, and a small handful of performance-based organizations have come to take up an increasing portion of the budget. But even the strongest locks on spending can be eroded or weakened over time. Competition does not cease once particular programs or expenditures have achieved some privileged status; others find a way to latch onto the successful program's resources. Thus mass transit managed to horn in on the Highway Trust Fund for a number of years. Spending is marked by long-term processes of locking and unlocking spending priorities.

Some locks are stickier than others. For example, putting prohibitions on certain forms of taxation into the constitution is a particularly strong lock; it may take decades or even a century or more to reverse. Writing tax and expenditure limitations into constitutions tends to lock in low-spending, small-government policies for generations. By contrast, legislatively mandated spending earmarks are much easier to reverse or alter when the dominant coalition in the legislature chooses to do so.

Shifting power back and forth between the legislative and executive branches also seems to have a sticky element to it. When debts or expenditures have gotten out of hand, there has been a tendency to blame the legislatures for lack of discipline and give increased budget power to the chief executives. If and when that power was used to thwart the policy intentions of legislators, the legislators often have taken back some of the delegated budget authority. However, when the executive and legislature are dominated by the same political party, the legislature may be happy to give the executive more budgetary power; when the two branches are dominated by opposing parties, the legislature may be more active in scrutinizing the executive budget, but it does not typically take back all the power that it has granted. The overall trend over time has been to give the executive more power over the budget, but to maintain sufficient legislative budget power to operate as a check on the executive when there is a difference in party or policy preferences.

Reconceptualizing Reform

This description of real-time budgeting and the patterns of change over time is intended to contribute to a descriptive theory of public budgeting. The theory is suggestive of how the politics of budgeting works and what kinds of reforms are likely to be desirable or effective.

The description of budgeting offered here suggests that there are multiple actors, with differential power over time, and that the actors' motivations are multiple and variable. Legislators are interested not only in constituency benefits but also in maintaining their own power and the power of the legislature. Equally important, at times they are interested in providing for the public good. When their personal or constituent interests clash with the public good, legislators sometimes opt for the public good. Sometimes they do not see a problem coming, or they underestimate the severity of the public consequences of their individual actions, but they learn from disasters and are often able to restructure their processes to increase discipline or delegate decision making to a location that is better buffered from interest groups. Restructuring can be successful when there is a consensus that it is necessary to avoid a disaster.

This observation-based conclusion suggests a model for reform. Those who want to improve budget decision making, strengthen the norms of balance, reduce, relatively speaking, the roles of narrow interests, or open up the budget process and document to more public scrutiny might appropriately work at making clearer the consequences of similar actions taken in the past or documenting the likely outcomes for the future. There is much turnover of decision makers and among their staffs; one ought not to assume that past experience is known or likely consequences understood.

The swings in budgetary decision making suggest that there are some internal mechanisms for balance, but they are not well regulated. They depend on knowledge of outcomes that often is not there, and the responses to problems may be inflexible over time. When constraints are devised, they usually address a major problem but pay little attention to possible long-term side effects. For example, when cities ran up huge debts, the state response was to limit cities' ability to borrow long term. Since there were also taxing limits, cities had no way to legitimately respond to the problems of growth. The consequence was a buildup in short-term debt, that was rolled over from year to year, for operating purposes, and deterioration of both cities' financial condition and the quality of information in the budget. The rigidity of some solutions does not match with future changed conditions. As a result, some states have lived with outmoded restrictions in their constitutions for decades or even centuries.

When the initial problem is extreme, the response may be extreme and lead to unacceptable long-term problems. Then the pressure to change the rules, or allow them to lapse, may take over, setting the stage for a new round of abuses and controls. If the original set of solutions could better envision the potential consequences over the long term, they might be more moderately phrased, solving the original problem without the kind of side effects that result in the deterioration or elimination of the rules.

The historical pattern suggests that research and reform should concentrate on identifying the places and times, the mechanisms, that allow balances to swing too widely and the turning points or mechanisms that historically have brought situations back from dangerous extremes. It may be that the size of the swings can be narrowed.

For example, a more careful monitoring of deficits, and intense publicity about early warning signs, may be helpful in averting the huge accumulation of deficits that sometimes occurs when small deficits are hidden or overlooked. If deficits are not allowed to grow too large, then pressure for rigid and enduring constraints will be less, and the cycle of control and evasion might be alleviated. A belief that all budgets should balance has left the public sector without a series of fallback positions and triggers for correction. Building a consensus about what kinds of deficits will be acceptable and for how long may be helpful; devising a measure of deficits and monitoring the effects on the economy of deficits of different sizes may also be helpful. This may help avert the argument that deficits are not harmful, so we can allow them or ignore them. It may be that we are willing to accept deficits from some sources but not others, for some periods of time but not longer than a certain number of years. If the conceptual murk can be cleared by a series of definitions, each acceptable to major groups of decision makers, then the level and degree of deficits may be plainer, and the efforts to eliminate them more effective.

A second issue where better warning signs might be helpful is budgetary secrecy. Perhaps warning bells should go off if secrecy in the budget begins to increase, say, if nonsecret matters are slipped into the black budget, if the IGs are politicized, or if the scope of their investigations is curbed. Maybe an alarm should be raised if budget deliberations are intentionally so rushed that legislators do not have time to read proposals before voting on them. Some violations of process represent serious threats to democracy and should be flagged and publicized, and possibly checked by congressional rules allowing a point of order to stop them.

Some such measures are in place, but there are holes in the safety net. For example, at the federal level and in some states, there are laws prohibiting unfunded mandates that are triggered when the costs being passed along are of a particular magnitude. However, that law does not prohibit underfunding of programs and is otherwise limited in scope. At the state level as well, there are many loopholes in the law. Similarly, there are controls and triggers on reprogramming, but they also may need some fine tuning.

A reconceptualization of budget problems needs to precede reform, from simple dichotomies—balanced-unbalanced, funded-unfunded—to more nuanced definitions that include continua and that focus on serious violations that have major policy consequences. If budget problems can be flagged earlier, they may not grow so large that the temptation to handcuff government results in poor management, public mistrust, or inability to collectively address public problems.

A second theme for reform that emerges from this book has to do with the interchangeability of budget roles. Reforms that simply have given the executive more power have not proved to be long-term solutions to budget discipline or balance. Governors have sometimes played restrictive roles and sometimes played expansionary ones; similarly, legislatures are sometimes restrictive and sometimes expansionary. History does not support the position that increased power to the executive will solve deficits or other budgetary problems.

Reform that changes budget processes to shift the location of budget power changes outcomes in the short run by shifting power to actors who have a particular point of view. If a state has a reform governor and an unreformed legislature riddled with corruption and eager for pork, then shifting power to the governor may bring about short-term improvement. But endless reinforcement of the governor's powers does not bring continuous budget improvement. Illinois may have the strongest governorship in terms of budget powers, but years ago, Gov. Jim Thompson shifted from more- to less-fiscally conservative accounting; he routinely hid deficits; and he was oriented to patronage spending for capital projects. Under his leadership the state ran deficits despite the strong executive budget. More recently, Gov. Rod Blagojevich has brought the state to a new level of financial mismanagement and deficit financing.

A balance of power between the executive and the legislature, so one actor can catch the other at bad practice, is probably more sound over the long run than the weakening of one and the continual strengthening of the other. The arrangements of the mid-1800s, when distrust of government drastically curtailed the powers of both governors and legislatures, were not particularly successful; it is not weak government that is required, but fairly balanced powers. This conclusion has echoes of the debate over the founding of the nation. Over the past decade, supporters of increased presidential power have argued that the president needs more budgetary power to control the deficit. They argue that Congress is profligate and only the president can exercise discipline. The experience of the states, however, suggests that shifting more power to the president is no long-term improvement.

Overall this book suggests that there is a relationship between budget process and outcomes, but that there is no single ideal process that will guarantee balance and limit taxation over time. Budgetary reform that emphasizes fiscal discipline has to have the serious support of key actors if it is to work; if recognition of the need for discipline erodes, or if the case is never well made, the process will not create the desired outcome. Process does not sit out there by itself, exerting discipline on unruly and unwilling actors. The actors create the process and try to abide by it once it exists, but if it is not working, they change the process, formally or informally.

A third theme of reform has to do with the ability of budgeting to help articulate to government what the public wants. At times budgets have been obscure documents, and audit reports have gathered dust. The public has no interest in them because they do not address public issues. Budget hearings are typically held after decisions have been already made. Officials sometimes fear citizen participation in budgeting, lest the process encourage the public to make demands that cannot be met or that violate what the officials feel are priorities, technical or political. Public participation complicates what is already a complicated process. At the same time, if the budget process does not allow for the articulation of citizen interests, at what point and in what manner can citizens express their approval or disapproval? Citizens may increasingly take policymaking into their own hands through binding and nonbinding referendums, which often result in simplistic and too-rigid constraints. A better-managed process that allows for dissent and also the articulation of interests is needed in many jurisdictions. Public officials need to solicit public advice in a form that they can act on, and then demonstrate that they have heard and followed the advice.

It may be better public policy to allow a controversy to be stated, than to use the power of budgeting to prevent an issue from being discussed and possibly resolved. Budgeting handles controversy all the time; it is designed to cope with the interruptions resulting from unresolved and controversial policy matters.

Avenues for Research

This book suggests many avenues for productive research, for students as well as scholars. It also suggests some lines of inquiry that probably will not be productive. Studies that compare last year's total appropriations to this year's total appropriations are unlikely to contribute much to the understanding of budget processes; they examine too small a portion of the budget and over too short a period. Studies of budgetary trade-offs may well produce major insights, if they adopt a realistic view of the way budgeting works. That is, they must assume that revenue constraints are variable, not fixed; that most routine trade-offs occur within departments and within the capital budget, rather than across sections of the budget; that major changes in spending priorities occur only over fairly long periods of time; and that budgets are structured so that some expenditures are much more flexible than others. The kind of expenditure makes a difference, since much of the politics of budgeting revolves specifically around the degree of flexibility and the attempt to lock in some expenditures.

The descriptive outline of budgeting presented here needs to be documented, elaborated on, and filled in. Much more research is needed on state and local budgeting and on the links between the decision clusters. One issue glossed over in this book for lack of information is the relationship between microbudgeting and macrobudgeting. Given a particular set of budget processes, what strategies do budget actors use, under what circumstances? How effective are those strategies? Once it becomes clear that the strategies are highly variable, not fixed, the way is opened for exploring the variations and the strategies' success. How do budget actors anticipate or measure the environment, and how do those estimates affect their strategies? To what extent does the allocation of power implicit in the budget process determine the outcomes, independent of strategies or the environment?

Another issue only lightly touched on is the tension between discretion and control. This book describes a discretion-and-control cycle for budget implementation but does not deal in any detail with the ways in which administrators re-create discretion within a control budget. More needs to be described about these internal dynamics and the different political value of different resources, depending on the degree of discretion they entail. New money, unencumbered money, money without strings, has a special value in a tightly controlled budget, so that there may in fact be two budgets, one with less and one with more discretion. Administrators may strive to get more money into the budget with greater discretion. When circumstances reduce the discretionary money, the impact on the politics of budgeting may be very different from a reduction in the more tightly controlled or earmarked portion of the budget.

A third theme that warrants future investigation is the process of locking and unlocking decisions. Budgeting involves a number of decisions that budget actors at the peak of their power try to make permanent. There are often attempts to unlock decisions, to reverse them, once they are made. Under what circumstances do locking or unlocking strategies work? More study needs to be made of these processes, such as the efforts to put bans on certain forms of taxation into state and national constitutions, or the establishment of trust funds or public enterprises. Efforts to create right-based entitlements need more explicit study. In each of these cases, more attention should be focused on the processes and circumstances for undoing them or reversing them.

A fourth theme of the book that needs further exploration is the relationship between the technical and political aspects of budgeting. The technical concerns of the budget include accurate estimates of expenditures and revenues, realistic evaluations of the economy, compliance with balance requirements (no matter how formulated), timely completion of decisions, prevention of overspending by agencies, and the creation of a plan that puts enough resources in the right places to get mandated work accomplished. The political concerns of budgeters include establishing and enforcing priorities, getting sufficient support for taxation to allow expenditures to occur and balance to be achieved without being thrown out of office, the creation of a workable budget process, the design and implementation of rules of balance, and the satisfaction of perceived needs for constituency benefits. These functions are not neatly divided into those performed by elected officials and those performed by career bureaucrats. Who performs which functions? How do they balance? When does political distortion of projections on the economy become so severe as to force the creation of an alternative, more neutral projection system; when do technical efforts to achieve balance cause major policy changes? Whose responsibility is it to maintain the informational integrity of the budget and its usefulness as a tool of accountability to the public? How far can that integrity be eroded before counterpressures are exerted?

More broadly, this book has characterized budgeting changes over time as pendulum swings. Changes in one direction begin to garner support for the opposite, or flaws in the current system make it obvious that a new system is needed. But more research has to be done on turning points, on the dynamics and timing of shifting from one policy extreme back toward the center or toward the other extreme. In some cases there may be equilibrium points, at which the forces in one direction offset those pushing the other way, resulting in at least temporary stability. When does such stability occur, and with what effect?

These suggested topics are only a preliminary list; there are many more possibilities. Such research could meaningfully be quantitative or qualitative, as long as it has a sufficiently long time span, views budget constraints as flexible, and is sensitive to the different kinds of resources in a budget and the different streams of budget decision making.

Summary and Conclusions

Public budgeting is highly political, but it is not the same thing as politics in general. It represents a special corner of politics, with many of its own characteristics. The peculiar politics of extraction called taxation may illustrate broader political desires to avoid unpopular decisions, but the process of turning taxation into distributive politics through the award of tax breaks and the eventual need for reform, the tension between spending and taxing, and the occasional passage of new or increased taxes are unique to the politics of budgeting. Real-time decision making is peculiar to budget decision making, with its intense sensitivity to the environment, its interruptibility, its nested options, and its time constraints. Budgeting has a bottom line and a due date, which distinguish it from many other political decisions. Budgeting carries in itself a way of measuring failure that creates pressures for action and reaction over time.

Budgeting is a particularly important arena of politics because many policy decisions are meaningless unless they can be implemented through the budget process. When political actors want to enhance their power, they often focus on power over budgeting as a way to do it. Consequently, battles over budgeting processes, which might otherwise seem dry, technical, internal matters, turn out to be lively contests. Individuals try to get into positions of budgetary power and then try to enhance the power of the positions they hold. Budgeting is the setting for major contests over the separation of powers and the balance between the legislature and the executive. Legislative committees battle with one another for jurisdiction, budget power becomes fragmented, and coordination becomes a major issue.

The budget document itself plays a unique role in the political system. It is a management document designed to help plan expenditures and maintain financial control; it may reflect important policy decisions made during the budget process and thus represent a summary of major government actions; and it presents to taxpayers an explanation of how their money is being spent. The role of the budget in providing public accountability is a crucial one in a democracy. Yet budgets do not always play this role well. Budgets sometimes change during implementation; the figures in the budget are not always accurate; and the information may be displayed in such a way as to obscure rather than elucidate key decisions. Budgets have to remain somewhat flexible, which may reduce their usefulness as tools of public accountability. Secrecy in making decisions may be necessary to buffer decision makers from the pleadings of special interests; and secrecy may be used to do something desired but formally prohibited.

The level of secrecy in budgeting needs to be carefully monitored. At present, the level of secrecy is relatively low but rising. When the level of secrecy increases and budget decisions are made out of public view, when audits can be edited of politically damaging judgments and inspectors general can be selected based on loyalty to the president, democracy receives a body blow. When secrecy is low, citizens can use the budget process and documents to hold government accountable. Citizens may be forced by the coercive power of government to pay taxes for programs they do not want, but this is a democracy, and citizens can and do rebel.

Notes

Chapter 1

1. Faculty Senate minutes, Northern Illinois University, November 4, 1998, 6.
2. Patricia Ingraham and Charles Barrilleaux, "Motivating Government Managers for Retrenchment: Some Possible Lessons from the Senior Executive Service," *Public Administration Review* 43, no. 3 (1983): 393–402. They cite the Office of Personnel Management Federal Employee Attitude Surveys of 1979 and 1980, extracting responses from those in the Senior Executive Service, the upper ranks of the civil service, and appointed administrators. In 1979, 99 percent of the senior executives said that they considered accomplishing something worthwhile very important; 97 percent said the same in 1980. By contrast, in response to the question, How much would you be motivated by a cash award? only 45 percent said either to a great extent or to a very great extent.
3. Lance LeLoup and William Moreland, "Agency Strategies and Executive Review: The Hidden Politics of Budgeting," *Public Administration Review* 38, no. 3 (1978): 232–239; 12 percent of LeLoup and Moreland's Department of Agriculture requests between 1946 and 1971 were for decreases. See Lance LeLoup, *Budgetary Politics*, 3d ed. (Brunswick, Ohio: King's Court, 1986), 83. For a more recent case study of an agency requesting decreases, see the case study of the Office of Personnel Management, in Irene Rubin, *Shrinking the Federal Government* (New York: Longman, 1985). See Irene Rubin, *Running in the Red: The Political Dynamics of Urban Fiscal Stress* (Albany: State University of New York Press, 1982), for an example of a department's refusing additional employees.
4. For a good discussion of this phenomenon, see Frank Thompson, *The Politics of Personnel in the City* (Berkeley: University of California Press, 1975).

5. See Rubin, *Shrinking the Federal Government*, for examples during the Reagan administration.

6. U.S. Senate, Committee on Governmental Affairs, *Office of Management and Budget: Evolving Roles and Future Issues,* Committee Print 99-134, 99th Cong., 2d sess., prepared by the Congressional Research Service of the Library of Congress, February 1986. OMB's role changed some in the 1990s, as it was engaged in helping implement the Government Performance and Results Act (GPRA) and various efforts at downsizing to help balance the budget. But it still remains a more top-down agency, implementing presidential policy, doing analysis, and making recommendations to the president. See Shelley Lynn Tomkin, *Inside OMB: Politics and Process in the President's Budget Office* (Armonk, N.Y.: M. E. Sharpe, 1998), for both the history of OMB and its recent roles.

7. See, for example, Kenneth Shepsle and Barry Weingast, "Legislative Politics and Budget Outcomes," in *Federal Budget Policy in the 1980s,* ed. Gregory Mills and John Palmer (Washington, D.C.: Urban Institute Press, 1984), 343–367.

8. Rubin, *Running in the Red*, 56.

9. For a vivid account of the relationship between pork barrel spending and building political coalitions, see Martin Shefter, "New York City's Fiscal Crisis: The Politics of Inflation and Retrenchment," *Public Interest* 48 (Summer 1977): 99–127.

10. See John Ellwood, "Comments," in *Federal Budget Policy in the 1980s,* ed. Mills and Palmer, 368–378.

11. Douglas Arnold, "The Local Roots of Domestic Policy," in *The New Congress,* ed. Thomas Mann and Norman Ornstein (Washington, D.C.: AEI Press [American Enterprise Institute], 1980), 252, quoted in Ellwood, "Comments."

12. Arnold, "Local Roots," 282.

13. Linda Harriman and Jeffrey Straussman, "Do Judges Determine Budget Decisions? Federal Court Decisions in Prison Reform and State Spending for Corrections," *Public Administration Review* 43, no. 4 (1983): 343–351.

14. Irene Rubin, *Class, Tax, and Power: Municipal Budgeting in the United States* (Chatham, N.J.: Chatham House, 1998).

15. See H. L. Platt, *City Building in the New South: The Growth of Public Services in Houston, Texas* (Philadelphia: Temple University Press, 1983).

16. On the symbolic aspects of mandates, see Paul Posner, *The Politics of Unfunded Mandates: Whither Federalism?* (Washington, D.C.: Georgetown University Press, 1998).

17. For more on contemporary budget strategies, see Irene Rubin, "Strategies for the New Budgeting," in *Handbook of Public Administration,* 2d ed., ed. James Perry (San Francisco: Jossey-Bass, 1996), 279–296.

Chapter 2

1. Catherine Rudder, "Tax Policy: Structure and Choice," in *Making Economic Policy in Congress,* ed. Allen Schick (Washington, D.C.: AEI Press [American Enterprise Institute], 1983), 196–220.

2. Ibid., 197. Rudder argues that committee members tended to be party regulars "with relatively high scores on party unity."

3. Ibid., 212. The reader should note that any attempt to add up the value of tax breaks is approximate. Nevertheless, this description of trends is probably fairly accurate.

4. Ibid., 211.

5. Randall Strahan, "Committee Politics and Tax Reform" (paper prepared for the 1987 meetings of the American Political Science Association, 3–6 September 1987). See also Randall Strahan and R. Kent Weaver, "Subcommittee Government and the House Ways and Means Committee" (paper presented at the Southern Political Science Association meetings, Memphis, Tennessee, 2–4 November 1989). Randall Strahan's book *The New Ways and Means: Reform and Change in a Congressional Committee* (Chapel Hill: University of North Carolina Press, 1990) deals with these themes at length.

6. Calculated from the *Budget of the United States, 1991*.

7. Martha A. Fabricius and Ronald K. Snell, *Earmarking State Taxes*, 2d ed. (Denver: National Council of State Legislatures, September 1990), tables 4, 5, and 7.

8. John F. Witte, *The Politics and Development of the Federal Income Tax* (Madison: University of Wisconsin Press, 1985), 68.

9. Timothy Clark, "Taking a Regional Stand," *National Journal*, March 22, 1986, 700.

10. Susan Hansen, "Extraction: The Politics of State Taxation," in *Politics in the American States: A Comparative Analysis*, 4th ed., ed Virginia Gray, Herbert Jacobs, and Kenneth Vines (Boston: Little, Brown, 1983), 429.

11. C. K. Yearley, *The Money Machines: The Breakdown and Reform of Governmental and Party Finance in the North, 1860–1920* (Albany: State University of New York Press, 1970), 39.

12. Hansen, "Extraction," 428.

13. Allen Schick, *Capacity to Budget* (Washington, D.C.: Urban Institute, 1990), 144.

14. David Osborne, *Laboratories of Democracy* (Boston: Harvard Business School Press, 1988), 27.

15. See Bryan Jones and Lynn Bachelor, with Carter Wilson, *The Sustaining Hand: Community Leadership and Corporate Power* (Lawrence: University Press of Kansas, 1986), for the relationship between economic decline and tax breaks for General Motors in Detroit; see Daniel Mandelker, Gary Feder, and Margaret R. Collins, *Reviving Cities with Tax Abatements* (New Brunswick, N.J.: Rutgers University, Center for Urban Policy Research, 1980), for the connection between economic decline and property tax abatements in St. Louis. For the relationship between declining economy and tax breaks in Cook County, where Chicago is located, see Arthur Lyons, Spenser Staton, Greg Wass, and Mari Zurek, "Reducing Property Taxes to Promote Economic Development: Does It Work?" Report prepared for the Comptroller of the City of Chicago, January 1988.

16. Witte, *Politics and Development of the Federal Income Tax*, 214.

17. Data on federal tax expenditures were put together by Brian Frederick, a PhD student at Northern Illinois University. The reason for using Joint Committee on Taxation data for the most recent years, despite the different methodology used by OMB and

the Joint Committee, is that OMB in 2003, decided to count long term capital gains tax reductions differently, making recent years' tax reductions look as if they were less than in prior years. Frederick explains, "In FY 2002 the OMB estimated the lower rate on capital gains to cost about $50 billion. In 2003 it only estimated the cost about $20 billion because it excluded all long-term capital gains that had previously been taxed at the corporate level. This new calculation makes it seem as if the cost of tax expenditures dropped in 2003 when that may not be the case. OMB is more accurate than the Joint Tax Committee in general because it uses look-back estimates rather than projections. However, for capital gains and dividends the JTC may be more accurate. My calculations use the JTC numbers for 2003 and 2004 just for this provision."

18. Paul R. McDaniel, "Overview of Tax Expenditures in the Budget," *Hearing Before the Committee on the Budget, Concurrent Resolution on the Budget for Fiscal Year 1994*, U.S. Senate, 103d Cong., 1st sess., February 3, 1993, 362.

19. Leonard E. Burman, "Is the Tax Expenditure Concept Still Relevant?" *National Tax Journal* 56, no. 3 (September 2003): 613–627, www.urban.org/UploadedPDF /410813_NTA_Tax_Expenditure.pdf.

20. NewStandard staff, "Analysts Say Dems Caved to Electoral Pressures in Extending Tax Cuts," September 29, 2004, http://newstandardnews.net/content/?action=show _item&itemid=1053 (accessed October 1, 2004).

21. Based on an analysis of information presented in *A Layman's Guide to Illinois Taxes*, Illinois Department of Revenue, September 1989, 23–25.

22 "Washington State Department of Revenues Tax Exemptions—2004," Table 4; Chris McGann, "Study Looks at Income versus Taxes," *Seattle Post Intelligencer*, August 21, 2004; Angela Galloway, "Lawmakers Use Public Office to Help Private Interest," *Seattle Post Intelligencer*, January 9, 2004.

23 "California Tax Expenditure Report, 2003–2004," www.dof.ca.gov/HTML/FS_DATA /TAX/TER_2003-04.pdf (accessed March 23, 2005).

24. Commonwealth of Massachusetts, "Tax Expenditure Budget, FY 2004," www.massdor .com/stats/teb/TEB2004.pdf (accessed March 23, 2005).

25. Texas Comptroller of Public Accounts, "Tax Exemptions and Tax Incidence," January 2005, www.window.state.tx.us/taxinfo/incidence05/incidence05.pdf (accessed March 23, 2005).

26. Lee Walker, *The Changing Arena: State Strategic Economic Development* (Lexington, Ky.: Council of State Governments, 1989); and Paul Peretz, "The Market for Industry: Where Angels Fear to Tread?" *Policy Studies Review* 5, no. 3 (February 1996): 624–633.

27. Illinois Economic and Fiscal Commission, report, "Corporate Incentives in the State of Illinois," Springfield, Illinois, August 2001.

28. Quoted in ibid., from "State Business Incentive Trends," in *The Book of the States, 2000–2001*, vol. 33 (Lexington, Ky.: Council on State Governments).

29. Charles Spindler, "Winners and Losers in Industrial Recruitment: Mercedes Benz and Alabama," *State and Local Government Review* 26, no. 3 (Fall 1994): 192–204.

30. Ibid., 202.

31. Jeff McCourt and Greg LeRoy with Philip Mattera, "A Better Deal for Illinois: Improving Economic Development Policy," Good Jobs First, January 2003, www. goodjobsfirst.org (accessed September 14, 2004); the $10,000 dollar subsidy cap per job created in Illinois was mentioned by Marc Breslow, in "Connecticut's Development Subsidies: Job Growth Far Short of Projections, High Cost per Job," Northeast Action, February 28, 2002, online at the Institute on Taxation and Economic Policy Web site, www.ctj.org/itep/ (accessed September 2004).

32. Jennifer Bott, "Two Big Tax Breaks Aim to Keep Jobs: At Stake: 868 Posts at GM, Parts Supplier," *Detroit Free Press*, March 18, 2004.

33. Spindler, "Winners and Losers," 198.

34. Breslow, "Connecticut's Development Subsidies."

35. McCourt and LeRoy with Mattera, "A Better Deal for Illinois."

36. Opinion letter 04-15, August 30, 2004, Disclosure of forecasts prepared by staff, State of Hawaii, Office of the Lieutenant Governor, Office of Information Practices, www .state.hi.us/oip/opinionletters/opinion%2004-15.pdf (accessed September 15, 2004).

37. Data were provided by M. Mazerov from the Center for Budget and Policy Priorities and posted as a report entitled "State Tax Expenditure Report" on the State Asset Development Report Card Web site, http://sadrc.cfed.org. CFED is the Corporation of Enterprise Development, Washington, D.C., which is responsible for the Web site. See also John Mikesell, "Tax Expenditure Budgets, Budget Policy, and Tax Policy: Confusion in the States," *Public Budgeting and Finance* 22, no. 4 (Winter 2002): 34–51.

38. Nebraska's 1998 Tax Expenditure Report, available at www.revenue.state.ne.us /tax_exp/1998/contents.htm.

39. Texas Comptroller of Public Accounts, "Tax Exemptions and Tax Incidence, School Property Tax," table 1, www.window.state.tx.us/taxinfo/incidence/ptoptax.html.

40. Department of Revenue, Washington State, "Property Tax Statistics 1998, Senior Citizens Property Tax Relief," http://dor.wa.gov/reports/te98/taxstats98/sencitizen.htm.

41. Illinois Economic and Fiscal Commission, "Senior Citizens Tax Relief Programs, 2002 Update," Springfield, Illinois, September 2002, available at www.ilga.gov/commission /cgfa/cgfa_home.html.

42. Ken Gordon newsletter to constituents, April 4, 2003, www.kengordon.com/pdf/ 03apr/April%204-TheBudgetandtheSeniorHomesteadExemption.

43. The description of the state's program is on its Web site, www.orps.state.ny .us/star/star_ref.cfm.

44. Jesse Hughes and Janne Moteket, "Tax Expenditures for Local Government," *Public Budgeting and Finance* 8, no. 4 (Winter 1988): 68–73.

45. The report is titled "Payments in Lieu of Taxes: Impact on Public Education," available at www.state.tn.us/tacir/PDF_FILES/Taxes/prop_tax_abate.pdf.

46. City of New York, Department of Finance, Office of Tax Policy, *Annual Report on Tax Expenditures, Fiscal Year 2004*, www.nyc.gov/html/dof/pdf/03pdf/taxpol_expenditures _04.pdf (accessed March 24, 2005).

47. City of Baltimore, *FY 2003 Executive Summary Tax Expenditures—City Real Property Tax Credits* and *Required Report to the Board of Estimates and Mayor and City Coun-*

cil, April 24, 2002, www.baltimorecity.gov/government/finance/ExecSum/pages /rev_tax_exp.htm.

48. Dave Flessner, "Incentive Breaks," *Chattanooga Times Free Press,* April 11, 2004.

49. "Local Tax Exemptions Drying Up," *Business News of Dayton,* December 2, 1996, www.amcity.com/dayton/stories/1996/12/02/story1.html.

50. For an account of the federal government's efforts to control this tax break, see Dennis Zimmerman, *The Private Use of Tax Exempt Bonds: Controlling Public Subsidy of Private Activity* (Washington, D.C.: Urban Institute Press, 1991).

51. State Comptroller's Office, "Annual Property Tax Report, Focus on School Taxes, 2003," Table 13, www.window.state.tx.us/taxinfo/proptax/annual03/focus.html.

52. Tennessee Advisory Commission on Intergovernmental Relations, "Payments in Lieu of Taxes: Impact on Public Education," available at www.state.tn.us/tacir/PDF_FILES /Taxes/prop_tax_abate.pdf.

53. National Education Association, "Protecting Public Education from Tax Giveaways to Corporations: Property Tax Abatements, Tax Increment Financing, and Funding for Schools," research working paper, January 2003, www.nea.org/esea/images /taxreport.pdf.

54. One example of the relative inefficiency of tax expenditures as a means of achieving program goals occurred in housing. In 1975 Congress passed a tax credit for the purchase of new homes, purportedly to encourage building and sales of new homes, at a cost of $600 million. Housing was increased by fewer than 105,000 units, which amounted to a subsidy of $5,700 per unit. More efficient subsidies could have been used, according to Thomas Reese, *The Politics of Taxation* (Westport, Conn.: Quorum Books, 1980), xvi.

55. Ibid., xix.

56. Timothy Clark, "How to Succeed against Business," *National Journal,* May 3,1986, 1059.

57. Ibid.

58. For an account of the lobbying to protect tax breaks, see Jeffrey Birnbaum and Alan Murray, *Showdown at Gucci Gulch: Lawmakers, Lobbyists, and the Unlikely Triumph of Tax Reform* (New York: Random House, 1987).

59. Eileen Shanahan, "Congress Expected to OK Tax Overhaul Bill," *National Journal,* April 23, 1986, 1951.

60. Karen Benker, "Tax Expenditure Reporting: Closing the Loophole in State Budget Oversight," *National Tax Journal* 39, no.4 (December 1986), 412.

61. John F. Witte, "Wisconsin Income Tax Reform," in *State Policy Choices: The Wisconsin Experience,* ed. Sheldon Danzinger and John F. Witte (Madison: University of Wisconsin Press, 1988), 108–129.

Chapter 3

1. Thomas Anton, *The Politics of State Expenditure in Illinois* (Urbana: University of Illinois Press, 1966), 73.

2. See Gloria Grizzle, "Does Budget Format Really Govern the Actions of Budget Makers?" *Public Budgeting and Finance* 6, no. 1 (Spring 1986): 64.

3. Jennifer Grooters and Corina Eckl, *Legislative Budget Procedures: A Guide to Appropriation and Budget Processes in the States, Commonwealths and Territories* (Denver: National Conference of State Legislatures, 1998). See also National Association of State Budget Officers, *Budget Processes in the States, January 2002*, Table I, p. 26, www.nasbo.org/Publications/PDFs/budpro2002.pdf (accessed October 2, 2004). The more recent study paints a more nuanced picture: In 35 states, the governor can give the departments targets or maximums for spending requests, in 24 states, the governor can reorganize departments without the legislature's approval, and in 37 states, the governor can make reductions in the budget without legislative agreement. However, in 32 states, the departments' budget requests appear in the governor's budget proposal, giving the legislature the opportunity to see what the departments asked for, and what the governor approved or disapproved, and hence the possibility of disagreeing with the governor's recommendation and substituting their own.

4. Grooters and Eckl, *Legislative Budget Procedures*, Table 6-3. See also National Association of State Budget Officers, *Budget Processes in the States, January 2002*, Table J, p. 30.

5. Robert Bland and Wes Clarke, "Performance Budgeting in Texas State Government" (paper delivered at the meetings of the Association for Budgeting and Financial Management, Chicago, Illinois, October 7, 2004).

6. Glenn Abney and Thomas B. Lauth, *The Politics of State and City Administration* (Albany: State University of New York Press, 1986), esp. chap. 9.

7. Marisol Bello, "Detroit City Council's Changes to Budget Get Mayor Veto," *Detroit Free Press*, June 3, 2004.

8. Allen Schick, *The Capacity to Budget* (Washington, D.C.: Urban Institute Press, 1990), chap. 6. See also Shelley Tomkin, *Inside OMB* (New York: M. E. Sharpe, 1998).

9. Grooters and Eckl, *Legislative Budget Procedures*, Table 6-4.

10. National Conference of State Legislatures, *Legislative Budget Procedures, 1997*, www.ncsl.org (accessed October 21, 2004).

11. Robert Bland and Wes Clarke, "Performance Budgeting in Texas State Government," in *Budgeting in the States, Ten Years Later*, ed. Edward Clynch and Thomas Lauth (Westport, Conn.: Greenwood Press, forthcoming 2005); and "Budget 101: A Guide to the Budget Process in Texas" (Austin: Senate Research Center, 2005), available at www.senate.state.tx.us/SRC/pdf/Budget101_2005.pdf (accessed March 26, 2005).

12. Carolyn Bourdeaux, "Legislative Barriers to Budget Reform" (paper presented to the Association for Budgeting and Financial Management meeting, Chicago, October 9, 2004), and personal communication.

13. Georgia Legislative Budget Office, "Georgia State Legislative Process,Updated 2001," www.legis.state.ga.us/legis/budget/process.htm (accessed October 22, 2004).

14. Grooters and Eckl, *Legislative Budget Procedures*.

15. Nelson C. Dometrius and Deil S. Wright, "Governors, Legislatures, Partisanship, and State Budget Processes" (paper prepared for delivery at the annual meeting of the State Politics and Policy Conference, Kent, Ohio, April 30–May 1, 2004).

Chapter 4

1. Howard Shuman, *Politics and the Budget: The Struggle between the President and the Congress* (Englewood Cliffs, N.J.: Prentice Hall, 1984), 27.
2. Ibid., 28.
3. Frederick Mosher, *A Tale of Two Agencies: A Comparative Analysis of the GAO and OMB* (Baton Rouge: Louisiana State University Press, 1984), 27.
4. Allen Schick, *Congress and Money* (Washington, D.C.: Urban Institute Press, 1980), chap. 2.
5. Congressional Budget Office, *The Economic and Fiscal Outlook: Fiscal Years, 1992-1996* (Washington, D.C.: Government Printing Office, January 1991), chap. 2.
6. Ibid., 57.
7. Allen Schick, *The Federal Budget: Politics, Policy and Process* (Washington, D.C.: Brookings Institution Press, 1995), 41.
8. Allen Schick, "The Deficit That Didn't Just Happen: A Sober Perspective on the Budget," *Brookings Review* 20, no. 2 (Spring 2002): 45-48.
9. Philip Joyce, "Federal Budgeting after September 11th: A Whole New Ballgame, or Is It Déjà Vu All over Again?" *Public Budgeting and Finance* 25, no. 1 (Winter 2005): 15-31.
10. Ibid.
11. Alexander Bolton and Jonathan E. Kaplan, "Congress Veils Appropriations Spending Totals," TheHill.com, May 28, 2003.
12. Peter Cohn, "Senate Spending Process to Go Forward Even without Budget Deal," www.govexec.com (*Government Executive Magazine*), June 8, 2004.
13. Ken Nakamura, "AFSANET Legislative Up-Date: The FY 05 Omnibus and State and Commerce Funding," December 10, 2004 (circulating e-mail from AFSA, the union for the employees of the State Department). Ken Nakamura is the American Foreign Service Association director of congressional relations.
14. Dan Morgan and Helen Dewar, "Tax-Return Provision in Spending Bill Dropped," www.washingtonpost.com, December 7, 2004.
15. Editorial, "The Cost of Congressional Caprice," *New York Times*, December 3, 2004.
16. Amy Klamper, "Pentagon Increases Reliance on Supplemental Budget Requests," www.govexec.com (*Government Executive Magazine*), December 6, 2004.
17. "Improvisational" and "ad hoc budgeting" are terms used by Allen Schick, in his book *The Capacity to Budget* (Washington, D.C.: Urban Institute Press, 1990). He meant by these terms making up or adjusting budget procedures as you go along, instead of using budget rules or routines that are known in advance, agreed to by all parties, and repeated from year to year. He argues that improvisational budgeting is a sign of reduced capacity to budget, which involves reasoned comparisons between possible items of expenditure.
18. Maryland is sometimes counted in this list and sometimes not. Because the legislature cannot raise the governor's proposal or add items to it, the governor cannot veto the appropriation, as it is his own proposal. But the legislature can add items if it provides new dedicated revenues to pay for them, and these the governor can veto.

19. National Association of State Budget Officers (NASBO), *Budget Processes in the States* (Washington, D.C.: National Association of State Budget Officers, 2002), 30. My figures here differ slightly from the text in the NASBO report, as the figures in the text and the tables do not match exactly. I follow the NASBO report in including Maryland.

20. James Gosling, *Budgetary Politics in American Governments*, 2d ed. (New York: Garland, 1997), 158.

21. These data are taken primarily from salary surveys done by NCSL in 1991, 1998, and 2003. Not all state legislatures participated in the study, and some provided data in one or two of these years rather than all three. I created panel data by looking only at the states that had provided data in 1991, taking the figures from the 2003 survey where provided, and looking up the remainder by counting staff who had "fiscal analyst" in their title. Since there had been considerable reorganization since the earlier date, and some fiscal staff were now combined with other policy analysts in one office, the search for titles gave me an idea how many people were actually doing fiscal analysis. While the averages are stable for this period for the twenty-five states for which I could put together panel data, some states expanded staff considerably during this period, while others contracted staff. Expanders slightly outnumbered contractors. I thank NCSL for providing the raw data.

22. Personal correspondence, Arturo Pérez, NCSL Fiscal Affairs Program, December 19, 2004.

23. Data come from the NCSL, *Legislative Budget Procedures in the 50 States*, 1983; *Legislative Budget Procedures in the 50 States*, 1988; and Grooters and Eckl, *Legislative Budget Procedures: A Guide to Appropriations and Budget Procedures in the States, Commonwealths, and Territories,* 1999 (chap. 3, n. 6). The data in this study had not been updated as of the end of 2004.

24. Nelson C. Dometrius and Deil S. Wright, "Governors, Legislatures, Partisanship, and State Budget Processes" (paper prepared for delivery at the Fourth Annual Meeting of the State Politics and Policy Conference, Kent, Ohio, April 30-May 1, 2004).

25. *Local Budgeting Manual,* Oregon Department of Revenue, Property Tax Division, revised February 2002.

26. Interview with deputy county attorney, July 20, 1995. The example is taken from Irene Rubin, *Class, Tax, and Power: Municipal Budgeting in the United States* (Chatham, N.J.: Chatham House, 1998).

27. Ibid.

28. Claude Tharp, *Control of Local Finance through Taxpayers Associations and Centralized Administration* (Indianapolis: M. Ford Publishing, 1933), 16; quoted in Rubin, *Class, Tax, and Power,* 190.

29. Rubin, *Class, Tax, and Power,* 214.

30. *City and Town Budget Manual,* a state-prepared manual prepared by the state of Indiana for local budgeting, 2005, www.in.gov/dlgf/pubs/manuals/cities/Chp2.pdf.

31. The federal government also passes on unfunded mandates to both the state and local levels. In 1995, Congress passed a law prohibiting unfunded mandates, but there were

many loopholes in the law and the problem persists and may be worsening in the last few years. However because local governments are legally subordinate to the states, the potential scope of mandates is much greater from the states to the local level. The states could, if they wished, completely preempt local decision making.

32. The source for this information is the Web site www.mass.gov/sao/mandatepage.htm.
33. David Barron, Gerald Frug, and Rick Su, *Dispelling the Myth of Home Rule: Local Power in Greater Boston* (Cambridge, Mass.: Rappaport Institute for Greater Boston, Kennedy School of Government, Harvard University, 2004), available at www.ksg .harvard.edu/rappaport/research/homerule/chaptertwofinance.pdf (accessed January 8, 2005).
34. Ibid.
35. Ibid.
36. Ibid., 91.
37. Ibid., 92.
38. Charles Glaab and A. Theodore Brown, *A History of Urban America,* 3d ed. (New York: Macmillan, 1983), 200.
39. Caitlin Rother, "Is Shift in Structure of Power Ahead? Strong Mayor Model Getting Another Look," *San Diego Union Tribune,* March 21, 2004, http://pqasb.pqarchiver .com/sandiego/.

Chapter 5

1. See Richard Stubbing, "The Defense Budget," in *Federal Budget Policy in the 1980s,* ed. G. Mills and J. Palmer (Washington, D.C.: Urban Institute Press, 1984), 81–110.
2. Office of Management and Budget, "Major Policy Initiatives," *FY 1987 Budget,* 12, quoted in Roy T. Meyers, "Microbudgetary Strategies and Competition" (PhD diss., University of Michigan, 1988), 305.
3. On the Export-Import Bank, see Jordan Jay Hillman, *The Export-Import Bank at Work: Promotional Financing in the Public Sector* (Westport, Conn.: Quorum Books, 1982), xiv–xv. See also *Congressional Record,* House of Representatives, H6361, July 30, 1997.
4. Ann Veneman, Secretary of Agriculture, testimony before the Subcommittee on Agriculture, Rural Development, Food and Drug Administration, and Related Agencies, Committee on Appropriations, U.S. House of Representatives, 107th Cong., 2d sess., February 13, 2002.
5. Meyers, "Microbudgetary Strategies," 284.
6. Roy T. Meyers, *Strategic Budgeting* (Ann Arbor: University of Michigan Press, 1994), 85ff.
7. Veneman, testimony before the Subcommittee on Agriculture.
8. Kathryn Foster, *The Political Economy of Special Purpose Government* (Washington, D.C.: Georgetown University Press, 1997).
9. Jeffrey Straussman, "Rights-Based Budgeting," in *New Directions in Budget Theory,* ed. Irene Rubin (Albany: State University of New York Press, 1988).

10. Mike Ramsey, "Pension Suggestions OK'd: State Task Force Skittish about Cuts It Offers for Consideration," *Springfield State Journal Register,* January 29, 2005, and online at the State Universities Annuitants Association Web site, www.suaa.org.

11. "Aid to Elderly Divides Young, Old and Politicians," *New York Times,* June 23, 1988.

12. Ibid.

13. U.S. House of Representatives, Committee on the Budget, *Hearing before the Task Force on Urgent Fiscal Issues, U.S. Farm Policy: Proposals for Budget Savings,* 101st Cong., 2d sess., June 28, 1990, 11.

14. Ibid., 16.

15. Mr. Smith of Michigan, "Agriculture Subsidy Concerns," House of Representatives, 107th Cong., 2d sess., June 25, 2002, *Congressional Record,* H3862.

16. E. J. McMahon, "Albany's 'Debt'-End," *New York Post,* May 19, 2004, www .manhattan-institute.org/html/_nypost-albanys_debt_end.htm; see also the city of New York controller's report for 2004, www.comptroller.nyc.gov/press/2004_releases /pr04-11-063.shtm.

17. The source is interviews with involved participants who chose to remain anonymous.

18. Tim Weiner, *Blank Check* (New York: Warner Books, 1990), 10.

19. Ibid.

20. Ibid., summarized from chap. 4.

21. Ibid., 5.

22. "Spy Satellite Unit Facing a New Life in Daylight," *New York Times,* November 3, 1992.

23. "House Approves Intelligence Funds," *Chicago Tribune,* December 22, 1995.

24. "Classified Funding in the FY 2005 Defense Budget Request," July 27, 2004, Center for Strategic and Budgetary Assessments, Washington, D.C., www.CSBAONLINE .org.

25. Richard Benedetto, "Data Sought on Secret Spending," *USA Today,* usatoday.com, February 2, 2004.

26. Brad Bumsted, "Lawmakers' Spending Kept Secret from Public," *Pittsburgh Tribune Review,* August 12, 2001.

27. Steven Walters, "Elections Board Voter-List Deal Draws Lawsuit, Official Lacked Authority to Sign," *Milwaukee Journal Sentinel,* December 23, 2004, www.jsonline .com/news/state/dec04/286914.asp (accessed February 9, 2005); see also, OMBWatch, "Wisconsin Speaker Pushing for New Sunshine Law," January 10, 2005, www .ombwatch.org/article/articleview/2601/1/1?TopicID=1.

28. Meyers, *Strategic Budgeting,* 70, 71.

Chapter 6

1. John F. Harris, "Deficit Worries Threaten Bush Agenda; GOP Lawmakers, Others Say War and Recession No Longer Justify Mounting Debt," *Washington Post,* February 7, 2005; A5.

2. See the National Council of State Legislatures, *State Balanced Budget Requirements: Provisions and Practice,* by Ronald K. Snell, www.ncsl.org/programs/fiscal

/balbuda.htm, originally posted 1996, revised 2004; and National Association of State Budget Officers, *Budget Process in the States, 2002,* Table K, www.nasbo.org/Publications/PDFs/budpro2002.pdf. Also useful is the study by the U.S. General Accounting Office, *Balanced Budget Requirements: State Experiences and Implications for the Federal Government* (Washington, D.C.: GAO, 1995). For the California referendum on measure 58, 2004, see the League of Women Voters educational Web site, http://ca.lwv.org/lwvc/edfund/elections/2004mar/id/prop58.html.

3. *Historical Tables of the United States Budget* (Washington, D.C.: Government Printing Office, January 1996), table 1.1.

4. David Stockman, "The Crisis in Federal Budgeting," in *Crisis in the Budget Process: Exercising Political Choice,* ed. Allen Schick (Washington, D.C.: AEI Press, 1986).

5. Ibid., 65.

6. Allen Schick, "The Evolution of Congressional Budgeting," in *Crisis in the Budget Process,* ed. Allen Schick (Washington, D.C.: AEI Press, 1986), 53.

7. Norman Ornstein, "The Politics of the Deficit," in *Essays in Contemporary Economic Problems,* ed. Phillip Cagan (Washington, D.C.: AEI Press, 1985), 311.

8. "Stockman Book Offers an inside View," *New York Times,* April 13, 1986, sect. 1.

9. David Stockman, *Triumph of Politics* (New York: Harper and Row, 1986), 124.

10. U.S. Congress, House, *Hearings before the Ways and Means Committee, Administration's Views on the Deficit and Possible Revenue Increases for the Next Three Fiscal Years,* 98th Cong., 1st sess., June 14, 1983, 15.

11. U.S. Congress, House, Subcommittee on Monopolies and Commercial Law of the Judiciary Committee, *Hearings, Constitutional Amendments Seeking to Balance the Budget and Limit Federal Spending,* 97th Cong., August 1982, 351–364.

12. U.S. Senate, *Balanced Budget—Tax Limitation Constitutional Amendment,* Senate Report 98-628, 1984, 13.

13. From a speech to the Association for Budgeting and Financial Management, Washington, D.C., October 15, 1993.

14. Jeffrey Birnbaum, "House Rejects Bid to Require Balanced Budget," *Wall Street Journal,* June 12, 1992, A2.

15. U.S. Congress, Senate, *Budget Reform Proposals, Joint Hearings before the Committee on Governmental Affairs and the Committee on the Budget,* 101st Cong., 1st sess., October 16 and 26, 1989, 167. Roy Meyers, *Strategic Budgeting* (Ann Arbor: University of Michigan Press, 1994), 75, lists the government-sponsored enterprises that were proposed in 1986–1987 including: the Corporation for Small Business Investments, the Airways Corporation, the National Public Works Corporation, the National Long-Term Care Corporation, and several similar corporations to carry out uranium enrichment.

16. U.S. Congress, Senate, *Budget Reform Proposals,* 147.

17. "Unfunded Mandate Report," National Conference of State Legislatures, press release, March 10, 2004.

18. National Conference of State Legislatures, *FY '06 Budget Analysis: Export of the Federal Deficit Begins,* February 9, 2005, updated February 15, 2005, www.ncsl.org/statefed/statefed.htm (accessed June 13, 2005).

19. Iris J. Lav and Andrew Brecher, *Passing Down the Deficit: Federal Policies Contribute to the Severity of the State Fiscal Crisis,* Center for Budget and Policy Priorities, revised August 18, 2004, www.cbpp.org/5-12-04sfp.htm (accessed March 28, 2005).

20. Tony Hutchison and Kathy James, *Legislative Budget Procedures in the Fifty States: A Guide to Appropriations and Budget Processes* (Denver, Colo.: National Conference of State Legislatures, 1988), 92–93; Jennifer Grooters and Corrina Eckl, *Legislative Budget Procedures: A Guide to Appropriations and Budget Processes in the States, Commonwealths, and Territories* (Denver, Colo.: National Conference of State Legislatures, 1998), table 7-2.

21. National Association of State Budget Officers, *Budget Process in the States, 2002,* www.nasbo.org/Publications/PDFs/budpro2002.pdf.

22. These results might reflect an upsurge in partisanship. Where the governor and legislature are of the same party, the legislature may be eager to grant the governor a freer hand to cut what he thinks best because there is underlying policy agreement. Where the governor and legislature are of opposite parties, the legislature may require more intense scrutiny of midyear cuts, with the goal of blocking cuts that contradict the legislature's priorities. More research is required to check out this hypothesis.

23. Dale Russakoff, "States Use Gimmicks to Tackle Deficits," *Washington Post,* June 1, 2003.

24. Ibid.

25. U.S. Congress, House, *Hearings before the Committee on the Budget,* 102d Cong., 2d sess., May 12, 1992, 8.

26. Example modified from ibid., 14.

27. Robert Albritton and Ellen Dran, "Balanced Budgets and State Surpluses: The Politics of Budgeting in Illinois," *Public Administration Review* 47, no. 2 (March–April 1987): 135–142.

28. Illinois Economic and Fiscal Commission, *Revenue Estimate and Economic Outlook for FY 1978,* Springfield, Ill., June 1977, 17; cited in Albritton and Dran, "Balanced Budgets," 144.

29. Naomi Caiden and Jeffrey Chapman, "Constraint and Uncertainty: Budgeting in California," *Public Budgeting and Finance* 2, no. 4 (Winter 1982): 114–115.

30. Albritton and Dran, "Balanced Budgets," 145.

31. Steven Gold, "Preparing for the Next Recession: Rainy Day Funds and Other Tools for States," Legislative Finance Paper no. 41, National Conference of State Legislatures, Denver, Colo., December 30, 1983, 2; Advisory Council on Intergovernmental Relations, *Significant Features of Fiscal Federalism, 1989* (Washington, D.C.: U.S. Government Printing Office, 1989), table 74.

32. Advisory Council on Intergovernmental Relations, *Significant Features of Fiscal Federalism, 1994* (Washington, D.C.: U.S. Government Printing Office, 1994), vol. 1, table 4.

33. Iris Lav and Alan Berube, *When It Rains, It Pours,* Center on Budget and Policy Priorities, 1999, www.cbpp.org/3-11-99sfp.pdf.

34. Bob Zahradnik and Nick Johnson, *State Rainy Day Funds: What to Do When It Rains?* Center for Budget and Policy Priorities, January 2002, www.cbpp.org/1-31-02sfp2 .htm.

35. Robert Zahradnik, *Rainy Day Funds: Opportunities for Reform*, Center for Budget and Policy Priorities, March 2005, www.cbpp.org/3-9-05sfp.htm.

36. Gold, "Preparing for the Next Recession," 7–8.

37. "Learning to Live in an Age of Strict Limits," *New York Times*, April 13, 1986, Week in Review, 5.

38. *Review of Legislative Mandates Imposed on King County, 1995–2000*, King County [Washington] Budget Office, October 11, 2000.

39. Ken McLaughlin, "Bid to Halt State's Tax Grab Has Wide Push; Little Opposition to Proposition 1A," *San Jose Mercury News*, October 23, 2004, www.mercurynews .com/mld/mercurynews/.

40. "City of Champaign, Proposed 2004 Property Tax Levy SS 2004 - 059, Report to City Council, from Steven C. Carter, City Manager," October 8, 2004; this memo is posted on the Champaign Web site, in its archives, at http://archive.ci.champaign.il .us/archive/dscgi/ds.py/Get/File-2170/SS_2004-059.pdf#xml=http://archive .ci.champaign.il.us/scripts/texis.exe/webinator/search/xml.txt?query=unfunded+man date&pr=default&prox=page&rorder=500&rprox=500&rdfreq=500&rwfreq=500 &rlead=500&sufs=0&order=r&cq=&id=4249eed41 (accessed March 29, 2005).

41. Advisory Council on Intergovernmental Relations, *Significant Features of Fiscal Federalism, 1985–1986* (Washington, D.C.: U.S. Government Printing Office, 1986), 163. See also Janet Kelly, *State Mandated Local Government Expenditures and Revenue Limitations in South Carolina* (Columbia: South Carolina ACIR, June 1988).

42. "Funding Federal and State Mandates," Legislative Reference Bureau Informational Bulletin 96-3, April 1996, page 11, www.legis.state.wi.us/lrb/pubs/ib/96ib3.pdf (accessed March 29, 2005).

43. Advisory Council on Intergovernmental Relations, *Significant Features of Fiscal Federalism, 1988*, 48–59. Later years calculated by the author directly from the Census of Governments, U.S. Census.

44. Charles Levine, Irene Rubin, and George Wolohojian, *The Politics of Retrenchment* (Beverly Hills, Calif.: Sage, 1981).

Chapter 7

1. A fund in governmental accounting is a self-balancing set of accounts. It is a way of segregating money for different purposes. Metaphorically, a fund is a bucket that receives money from specified taxes or fees and from which money can be taken only for specified purposes, which may be broad or very narrow. Money from different funds cannot be commingled without losing the benefits of this tracking system. Hence, interfund transfers are treated as a form of rebudgeting, which must come back to the legislative body to be approved, in public. There needs to be a good, logical reason for the transfer that justifies the spending of money from fund one in fund two. Such transfers are governed by rules.

2. Tom Cronin, "Board Requests 7.61 Percent Operating Budget Increase," *The Journal* (University of Illinois Springfield, student newspaper), March 9, 2005, www.uis.edu /journal/2k4sep15/frontpage.html.

3. Figures are taken from Allen Schick, *Capacity to Budget* (Washington, D.C.: Urban Institute Press, 1990), 112, Table 4.4, based on OMB data.

4. For a fascinating discussion of this case, see Barbara Hinkson Craig, *Chadha: The Story of An Epic Constitutional Struggle* (Berkeley: University of California Press, 1990).

5. Schick, *Capacity to Budget,* 113.

6. U.S. Congress, Senate Report 100-48, *On the 1987 Supplementals, to Accompany H.R. 1827,* 100th Cong., 1st sess., 4–5.

7. *City of New Haven, Connecticut v. United States of America,* slip opinion 86-5319, D.C. Circuit (1987). See also Walter Oleszek, *Congressional Procedures and the Policy Process,* 3d ed. (Washington, D.C.: CQ Press, 1989), 65.

8. General Accounting Office, *Forest Service Management: Little Has Changed as a Result of the Fiscal Year 1995 Budget Reforms,* A Report to the Subcommittee on Interior and Related Agencies, Committee on Appropriations, House of Representatives, GAO /RCED-99-2 (Washington, D.C.: Government Printing Office, December 1998).

9. Charles Levine, Irene Rubin, and George Wolohojian, "Resource Scarcity and the Reform Model: The Management of Reform in Cincinnati and Oakland," *Public Administration Review* 41, no. 6 (November/December 1981): 619–628.

10. See Irene Rubin, *Running in the Red* (Albany: State University of New York Press, 1982), for an example of a general fund borrowing from the water fund and causing deficits in the water fund.

Chapter 8

1. U.S. Congress, Senate, *Joint Hearings before Committees on Government Operations and on the Judiciary, Impoundment of Appropriated Funds by the President,* 93d Cong., 1st sess., 1973, 411; quoted in Louis Fisher, "The Effect of the Budget Act on Agency Operations," in *The Congressional Budget Process after Five Years,* ed. Rudolph Penner (Washington, D.C.: AEI Press [American Enterprise Institute], 1981), 173.

2. Frank Draper and Bernard Pitsvada, "Limitations in Federal Budget Execution," *Government Accountants Journal* 30, no. 3 (Fall 1981): 23.

3. Fisher, "Effect of the Budget Act," 156.

4. Ibid., 157.

5. U.S. Congress, House, *Hearings before a Subcommittee of the Committee on Appropriations, Department of Defense Appropriations 1981,* 96th Cong., 2d sess., 1980, pt. 4, 308.

6. Ibid., 246.

7. Ibid., 309.

8. U.S. Congress, House, *Hearings before Subcommittees of the House Appropriations Committee, Supplemental Appropriation and Rescission Bill,* 1981, 97th Cong., 1st sess., 1981, pt. 4, 31.

9. Ibid., 119.

10. See the Defense Appropriation for 1996, P.L. 104-61, sec. 8070, and the Intelligence Authorization Act, H.R. 1655, the authorization of the secret portion of the budget. Amendments 2881, 2882, 2883, and 2884 were discussed en bloc in the Senate, as reported in the *Congressional Record*, September 29, 1995.

11. Fisher, "Effect of the Budget Act," 150.

12. Ibid., 170.

13. Ibid.

14. Cited in ibid., from U.S. Congress, House, *Hearings before the Committee on Appropriations, Departments of Labor and Health, Education, and Welfare and Related Agencies Appropriations for Fiscal Year 1980*, 96th Cong., 1st sess., 1979, 175–176.

15. Fisher, "Effect of the Budget Act," 171.

16. George E. Hale, "State Budget Execution: The Legislature's Role," *National Civic Review* 66, no.6 (June 1977): 284.

17. Ibid., 285.

18. *The State Legislative Appropriations Process* (Lexington, Ky.: Council of State Governments, 1975), 36.

19. American Conference on Intergovernmental Relations,*The Question of State Government Capability* (Washington, D.C.: U.S. Government Printing Office, 1985), 116.

20. Ibid., 117.

21. Tony Hutchison and Kathy James, *Legislative Budget Procedures in the Fifty States: A Guide to Appropriations and Budget Processes* (Denver: National Conference of State Legislatures, 1988), 108.

22. Jennifer Grooters and Corrina Eckl, *Legislative Budget Procedures: A Guide to Appropriations and Budget Processes in the States, Commonwealths, and Territories* (Denver: National Conference of State Legislatures, 1998).

23. California Department of Finance, *California's Budget Process*, www.dof.ca.gov /fisa/bag/process.htm (accessed April 1, 2005).

24. Charles Dempsey, "The Inspector General Concept: Where It's Been, Where It's Going," *Public Budgeting and Finance* 5, no. 2 (Summer 1985): 39.

25. Mark H. Moore and Margaret Jane Gates, *Inspectors General: Junkyard Dogs or Man's Best Friend?* (New York: Russell Sage, 1986), 11.

26. *The National Performance Review: From Red Tape to Results, Creating a Government that Works Better and Costs Less* (Washington, D.C.: U.S. Government Printing Office, 1993), chap. 1.

27. U.S. Congress, House, *Hearing before the House Government Reform Committee, Subcommittee on Government Efficiency and Financial Management, 25th Anniversary of the Inspector General Act—Where Do We Go from Here?* 108th Cong., 1st sess., October 8, 2003.

28. The historical tables of the *2005 U.S. Budget* (table 17.1), www.gpoaccess.gov /usbudget/.

29. *Hearing, 25th Anniversary of the Inspector General Act.*

30. K. Daniel Glover, quoting Paul Light, in "Agency Watchdogs Need to Be Watched, Critics Say," www.govexec.com (*Government Executive Magazine*), October 31, 2003.

31. Thomas Novotny, "The IG's—A Random Walk," *Bureaucrat* 12, no. 3 (Fall 1983): 35.
32. Ibid., 39.
33. Ibid.
34. For accounts of these events, see Chester Newland, "A Midterm Appraisal—The Reagan Presidency: Limited Government and Political Administration," *Public Administration Review* 43, no. 1 (January/February 1983): 1–21; and Novotny, "The IG's."
35. Novotny, "The IG's," 38.
36. See testimony of William Barr, Assistant Attorney General, Office of Legal Counsel, Hearing before the Committee on Governmental Affairs, U.S. Senate, 101st Cong., 2d sess., *Oversight Hearings of the Operations of the Inspector General Offices*, April 25, 1990, 267–285; and Office of Legal Counsel, "Authority of the Inspector General to Conduct Regulatory Investigations," policy memo, March 9, 1989.
37. James Naughton, "Authority of Inspectors General to Conduct Criminal Investigations Relating to Regulatory Programs," *Oversight Hearings of the Inspector General Offices*, 147–200.
38. *Oversight Hearings of the Inspector General Offices*, 10.
39. See Barbara Hinkson Craig, *Chadha: The Story of an Epic Constitutional Struggle* (Berkeley: University of California Press, 1990), 40–46.
40. *Oversight Hearings of the Inspector General Offices*, 103.
41. There are many sources for this information. See, for example, the statement of Gaston L. Gianni Jr., July 19, 2000, in *Legislative Proposals and Issues Relevant to the Operations of the Inspectors General, Hearing before the Committee on Governmental Affairs*, U.S. Senate, 106th Cong., 2d sess.; and Senate Report 106-470, *Amending the Inspector General Act of 1978 (5 U.S.C. App.) to Establish Police Powers for Certain Inspector General Agents Engaged in Official Duties and Provide an Oversight Mechanism for the Exercise of Those Powers*, 106th Cong., 2d Session, 2000, the report of the Committee on Governmental Affairs, to accompany S. 3144.
42. Amendment 4893 to bill S. 2530 in the Senate reflected this change in 2002.
43. Jason Peckenpaugh, "IG Raps NASA's Use of Service Contractors," February 20, 2001, www.govexec.com (*Government Executive Magazine*); Paul Light, "Off With Their Heads," reprinted in *Governance*, April 3, 2005 (Brookings Institution publication; originally in *Government Executive*, May 2002).
44. Tanya N. Ballard, "Credibility, Fairness of Former HHS Inspector General Questioned," www.govexec.com (*Government Executive Magazine*), June 11, 2003.
45. *Hearing, 25th Anniversary of the Inspector General Act*.
46. Aliya Sternstein, "Democrats Charge Bush Politicized IG Posts," *Federal Computer Week*, November 22, 2004, www.fcw.com/fcw/articles/2004/1122/mgt-ig-11-22-04.asp; the report itself, *The Politicization of Inspectors General*, dated October 21, 2004, revised January 7, 2005, is available online at http://reform.democrats.house.gov/Documents/20050111164847-37108.pdf.
47. Information on state IG offices was compiled with research assistance by Brian Frederick, a PhD student in political science at Northern Illinois University.

48. "Corruption: Give the Inspector General Broad New Powers," editorial reprinted at www.nj.com (orig. *Newark Star Ledger*), January 13, 2003; news release, Office of [New Jersey] Attorney General John J. Farmer, Jr., "Attorney General Creates Office of Inspector General to Ensure Public Confidence in Government," May 9, 2000.

49. Tom Bell, "Codey Names Attorney as State's First Inspector General," www.nj.com, January 20, 2005; Josh Margolin, "Codey Applauds Votes Backing Watchdog Posts," *Newark Star Ledger,* March 15, 2005, reprinted by nj.com and available at www.nj .com/statehouse/ledger/index.ssf?/base/news-9/1110867259266050.xml; news release, "Senate Approves Kenny's Bipartisan Inspector General Bill," posted by New Jersey Senate Democrats on March 14, 2005, at www.getnj.com/onlygameintown /messages0305/171.shtml.

50. The quote is from the IG Web site, www.miamidadeig.org/ (accessed April 12, 2005).

51. The complexity of federal programs and the inevitability of some waste, fraud, and abuse are the central points made by John Young, "Reflections on the Root Causes of Fraud, Abuse, and Waste in Federal Social Programs," *Public Administration Review* 43, no. 4 (July/August 1983): 362–369.

52. Novotny, "The IG's," 37.

Name Index

This index lists the names of scholars from the notes starting on p. 302.

Abney, Glenn, 308
Albritton, Robert, 314
Anton, Thomas, 307
Arnold, Douglas, 303

Bachelor, Lynn, 304
Ballard, Tanya N., 318
Barrilleaux, Charles, 302
Barron, David, 311
Benker, Karen, 307
Berube, Alan, 314
Birnbaum, Jeffrey, 307
Bland, Robert, 308
Bolton, Alexander, 309
Bourdeaux, Carolyn, 308
Brecher, Andrew, 314
Breslow, Marc, 306
Brown, A. Theodore, 311
Burman, Leonard E., 305

Caiden, Naomi, 314
Chapman, Jeffrey, 314
Clark, Timothy, 304, 307
Clarke, Wes, 308
Cohn, Peter, 309
Collins, Margaret R., 304
Craig, Barbara Hinkson, 316, 318

Dempsey, Charles, 317
Dometrius, Nelson C., 308, 310
Dran, Ellen, 314
Draper, Frank, 316

Eckl, Corina, 308, 310, 314, 317
Ellwood, John, 303

Fabricius, Martha A., 304
Feder, Gary, 304
Fisher, Louis, 316, 317
Foster, Kathryn, 311

Frug, Gerald, 311

Gates, Margaret Jane, 317
Gianni, Gaston L., Jr., 318
Glaab, Charles, 311
Glover, K. Daniel, 317
Gold, Steven, 314, 315
Gosling, James, 310
Grizzle, Gloria, 308
Grooters, Jennifer, 308, 310, 314, 317

Hale, George E., 317
Hansen, Susan, 304
Harriman, Linda, 303
Hillman, Jordan Jay, 311
Hughes, Jesse, 306
Hutchison, Tony, 314, 317

Ingraham, Patricia, 302

James, Kathy, 314, 317
Johnson, Nick, 314
Jones, Bryan, 304
Joyce, Philip, 309

Kaplan, Jonathan E., 309
Kelly, Janet, 315
Klamper, Amy, 309

Lauth, Thomas B., 308
Lav, Iris J., 314
LeLoup, Lance, 302
LeRoy, Greg, 306
Levine, Charles, 315, 316
Light, Paul, 318
Lyons, Arthur, 304

Mandelker, Daniel, 304
Mattera, Philip, 306
McCourt, Jeff, 306
McDaniel, Paul R., 305
McGann, Chris, 305

Meyers, Roy T., 311, 312, 313
Mikesell, John, 306
Moore, Mark H., 317
Moreland, William, 302
Mosher, Frederick, 309
Moteket, Janne, 306
Murray, Alan, 307

Nakamura, Ken, 309
Naughton, James, 318
Newland, Chester, 318
Novotny, Thomas, 318, 319

Oleszek, Walter, 316
Ornstein, Norman, 313
Osborne, David, 304

Peckenpaugh, Jason, 318
Peretz, Paul, 305
Pitsvada, Bernard, 316
Platt, H.L., 303
Posner, Paul, 303

Reese, Thomas, 307
Rubin, Irene, 302, 303, 310, 315, 316
Rudder, Catherine, 303, 304

Schick, Allen, 304, 308, 309, 313, 316
Shanahan, Eileen, 307
Shefter, Martin, 303
Shepsle, Kenneth, 303
Shuman, Howard, 309
Snell, Ronald K., 304, 312
Spindler, Charles, 305, 306
Staton, Spenser, 304
Sternstein, Aliya, 318
Stockman, David, 313
Strahan, Randall, 304
Straussman, Jeffrey, 303, 311
Stubbing, Richard, 311
Su, Rick, 311

Tharp, Claude, 310
Thompson, Frank, 302
Tomkin, Shelley Lynn, 303, 308

Walker, Lee, 305
Wass, Greg, 304

Weaver, R. Kent, 304
Weiner, Tim, 312
Weingast, Barry, 303
Wilson, Carter, 304
Witte, John F., 304, 307
Wolohojian, George, 315, 316

Wright, Deil S., 308, 310

Yearley, C.K., 304

Zahradnik, Robert, 314, 315
Zimmerman, Dennis, 307
Zurek, Mari, 304

Subject Index

Page numbers followed by "t" indicate tables.

AARP, 205
Abney, Glenn, 90
Accountability
    acceptability and, 19,
        183–184, 186
    agencies and, 254
    in budget document,
        19–20
    budget execution and,
        230–231
    city manager government
        and, 142
    costs and, 20
    discretion, abuse, control
        cycle and, 249–263, 281,
        291
    doctoring audit reports
        and, 24
    hiding wrongdoing and
        mistakes and, 20, 24
    Inspector General system
        and, 263–273, 280
    openness vs. secrecy and,
        287–291, 295
    public, 231, 232, 242, 247
    in public budgeting, 2, 6,
        23
    spending decisions and,
        183–184
    taxation and, 44, 45
Accreditation model, 157, 159
Accrual accounting, 216
ACIR (Advisory Commission
    on Intergovernmental Rela-
    tions), 218
Actors
    balancing budget and, 190,
        192
    in budget process, 75, 76,
        85, 86, 88, 92, 96, 101
    centralization of budget
        processes and, 92
    change in budget process
        and, 102, 104
    environment and,
        181–182, 184

political, 76, 78, 85
    in public budgeting, 6, 7,
        12–17, 285, 286, 294
    in revenue decisions, 74
    secrecy in budgeting and,
        291
Addabbo, Joseph (D-N.Y.),
    251–252
Ad hoc budgeting, 102, 107,
    113–120
Ad hoc scoring rules, 117,
    118–119
Advisory Commission on
    Intergovernmental Relations
    (ACIR), 66, 218
Afghanistan, war in
    costs of, 188
    deficit and, 209
    supplemental appropria-
        tions and, 116, 234, 236,
        248
Agencies
    accountability and, 254
    autonomy of, 13
    budget cuts and, 193, 198
    climbing priority list of
        budget and, 147–150
    continuing resolutions
        and, 231
    discretion, abuse, control
        cycle and, 250–255, 257,
        291
    environment and spending
        priorities and,
        181–182
    head of agencies competi-
        tive strategies, 147–155
    Inspector General system
        and, 263–273, 280
    making programs look
        cheap, cost effective,
        150–152
    mobilizing support,
        152–155
    reprogramming and,
        240–242

restrictions on appropria-
        tions and, 250
    strategies for budget pro-
        posals, 147–159
    strategies to reduce compe-
        tition, 155–159
Agriculture, Department of,
    150, 153–154, 263–264, 265.
    See also Subsidies
Agriculture Committee
    (House), 168
Airport Trust Funds, 207
Alabama
    tax breaks, 60, 62
    tax case history in, 38,
        39–40, 44, 53
Alternative Minimum Tax,
    58
Amendatory vetoes, 240
Amendment 23 (Colorado), 8
American Farm Bureau Feder-
    ation, 204
American Medical Association,
    16
Amtrak, 161
Antiterrorist activities,
    234–235. *See also* Terrorist
    attacks
Appropriations bills, 79,
    81–82, 83, 94, 99
Appropriations Committee
    (House), 82, 96, 242, 244,
    245, 252
Appropriations Committee
    (Senate), 96, 241–242, 252
Appropriations Committee
    (state), 96, 97, 99
Arizona, local budget process
    in, 134
Arkansas, parimutuel betting,
    earmarking revenues, 44
Armed Services Committee
    (House), 174, 253–254
Armed Services Committee
    (Senate), 253–254
Aspin, Les (D-Wis.), 174

Association of State Budget
Officers, 214
Audit reports, doctoring, 24
Automatic cuts, 86
Available cash balance, 217
Aviation Trust Fund, 181

Balance
as constraint, 189–190
defined, 4, 189
Highway Trust Fund and,
190, 191, 207
Balance cluster, 32, 281, 282
Balanced Budget Act of 1997,
79
Balanced Budget and Emer-
gency Deficit Control Act of
1985. *See* Gramm-Rudman-
Hollings
Baltimore, Md., tax breaks in,
68
Baseline budgeting, 80, 169,
170
BEA. *See* Budget Enforcement
Act of 1990
Black budget projects,
173–177, 184, 288, 295
Blagojevich, Rod, 238, 296
Block grants, 81, 186
Board of Estimates, 140, 141
Borrowing
defined, 4
internal, 197, 198, 217, 226
for present expenditures,
165
state governments and, 215
Bottom-up budgeting, 87, 89,
92, 96
Boutique programs of HUD,
155
Brown, Jerry, 142
Budget and Accounting Act of
1921, 108, 112
Budgetary change
fiscal control, violations of,
232
policy control, violations
of, 232–233
politics of adaptation and,
230–248
tools for changing budget,
233–247
Budgetary independence, 157
Budget balancing, 187–229,
286. *See also* Deficits
actors in, 190, 192
choice of outcomes, 193,
297

cities and, 223–228
constitutional amendment
and, 120, 202, 203–206
environment, unpre-
dictability, and deficits
and, 194–196
federal level, 120, 200–209,
201*t*
local governments and,
219–223
payer/decider and,
196–200
role of each level of government and, 193
state level, 209–223
statutory approach to,
206–209
tax breaks and, 53–54
Budget Enforcement Act of
1990 (BEA)
deficit and, 204, 208–209
enactment of, 111
evaluation of, 112, 113,
292–293
federal budget process and,
107, 112, 113
mandates and, 160
offsets and, 113
Social Security and, 84
spending caps and pay-as-
you-go requirements of,
57–58, 113
spending decreases and,
115
temporary revenue
increases under, 112
use of supplementals and,
234
Budget execution and politics
of adaptation, 230–248
contingency funds, 243,
245–246
interfund transfers, 233,
247, 248
reprogramming, 233–234,
240–243, 244–245, 247,
248
supplemental appropria-
tions, rescissions, and
deferrals, 233, 234–240,
235*t*, 236*t*, 248
tools for changing budget,
233–247
Budget implementation
change in budget and, 232
characteristics of, 286
control and, 249–280
decision making and, 32

discretion, abuse, control
cycle and, 291
need for flexibility in, 232
rules and formulas for, 230
secrecy in budgeting and,
291
waste, fraud, and abuse,
politics of control and,
249–279, 291
Budget process, 5–6
ad hoc budgeting, 102, 107,
113–120
centralized, 103
citizens and, 297
committees in, 96–97
constraints in, 77–78, 86,
283
decision making and, 86
dynamics of changing,
102–144
elements of, 92
expenditures, determining,
145–186
federal, 94, 96, 97–98,
107–120
formula allocations and,
164
fragmentation of, 107, 109,
282, 290
goals in, 77, 78, 86, 101
information in, 97
local level, 93–94, 95,
97–98, 100, 131–143
locking in priorities and,
163–165, 185–186, 199,
293
outcomes and, 193, 297
policy and, 85–88, 232
political nature of,
75–101
power and, 88–93, 96–97,
104–106
prior rankings and, 164
public budgeting and,
76–78
public's access to, 92
relation of federal and state
governments and, 26–27
slow-growing economy
and, 117
spending decisions and,
145–186
spending in, 97
state level, 14, 26–27,
94–100, 120–140
strategies for, 35–36, 38
types of budget formats
and, 86–88

variation between federal, state, and local governments, 93–100
Budgets and budgeting
accountability and, 19–20, 231, 232, 242, 247
choices in, 3–4
constraints to, 7, 8–9, 12, 25–28, 283
defined, 3
interchangeability of roles in, 296
over time, 291–294
public scrutiny of, 23–24
reforms, 79–82, 104–107, 208, 227, 294–297
resources of, 4
role in economy, 192–193
scope of, 1–2
technical vs. political aspects of, 232, 297, 299
Buffer/contingency fund, 195, 199, 213, 243, 245–246. *See also* Rainy-day funds
Bureau chief, 12–13
Bureaucracy, 12–13
Bureau of the Budget (federal), 108, 109
Burman, Leonard, 57
Bush, Jeb, 127–128
Bush administration (George W.)
budget of 2005, 180, 209
budget of 2006, 205
deficit and, 118, 188
inspectors general and, 270, 272–273
tax breaks and, 58
tax cuts and, 53, 58, 114, 115, 118, 209, 236
Byrd amendment, 191

Cabinet government, 126
California. *See also* Proposition 13
balanced budget and, 189
circuit breakers in, 66
homestead exemptions in, 67
legislative oversight in, 258–259
local government funding in, 220–221
tax breaks in, 49
tax expenditures in, 59
Campaigns to reduce waste, fraud, and abuse, 278–279
Capital budget, 97

competition and, 151, 184
Capital gains tax, 52*t*, 53*t*, 55
Carry-forward funds, 254
Carter administration, 52, 110, 200, 202
Cash-flow accounting, 216–217
Ceilings for appropriations subcommittee, 114
Census Bureau, 222, 234
Center for Budget and Policy Priorities, 81, 218
Central Intelligence Agency (CIA), 173, 174, 252, 254, 267
Centralization
in budget process, 89, 92
effect of, 92
efforts of Congress toward, 108, 109–110
increase in, 103, 107
Chain of command, belief in, 13
Chamber of Commerce, 205
Champaign, Ill., state mandates and, 221–222
Charter, city, 131
Chicago, Ill., contracts in, 178–179
Chief executive officers, 14. *See also* Executive
Chief Financial Officers Act of 1990, 264
Children's Defense Fund, 150
Chiles, Lawton, 129, 256
CIA. *See* Central Intelligence Agency
Cincinnati, Ohio, and contingency funds, 245–246
Circuit breaker, 65–67, 66*t*
Cities
budget balancing and, 223–228
budgeting in, 100, 131–143
charters, 131
contingency funds and, 243, 245
debt and, 294–295
forms of government and, 140–143
interfund transfers and, 247
recessions and, 223, 246
state control over local budget process and, 132–140
Citizens for Tax Justice, 72
Clinton administration, 27–28, 264, 268, 273

Closed rule, 41–42, 92
Coalitions
budget balancing and, 190
of interest groups, 16, 28–29, 32, 185, 186, 285
Codey, Richard, 273, 277
Cold War, 148, 174, 291
Colorado
budget cuts and, 215
highly constrained budgeting in, 8–9
homestead exemption in, 67
local government revenue and, 219
Commerce, Department of, 157
Committee on Energy and Commerce (House), 174
Committees in budget process, 96–97
Competition
agencies' strategies to reduce, 155–159
agency heads' strategies and, 147–150
effect of, 184–185, 282, 293
elected officials' budget strategies and, 159–180
Complexity and obfuscation in budgeting, 168–173, 289–290
Comprehensive Budget Process Reform Act of 1999, 81–82
Congress
ad hoc budgeting, 113–120
breakdown in budget process and, 117, 119–120
budgetary control and, 109–110
budgeting after 1998, 113–120
on budget responsibility, 96
deferrals and, 238–239, 255
discretion, abuse, control cycle and, 250–257
failure to pass budget resolutions, 114–115
fragmentation of, 109
history of budget process and, 108–120
on impoundments, 255
lobbying, 156
1970s reforms of, 42
omnibus legislation of, 94, 96

reprogramming and, 233–234, 239–242, 250–254

supplemental appropriations and, 234, 247

2005 budget, 114–117, 180

veto power of, 239–240, 255

Congressional Budget and Impoundment Control Act of 1974, 109–110, 112, 113–114, 255

Congressional Budget Office, 110, 118, 124, 204

Congressional Budget Reform Act of 1974, 56, 84, 107, 238–239

Constitutional amendments for budget balancing, 120, 202, 203–206

on local government funding, 222

requirements for spending programs in, 164–165

Constitutions, and taxation, 48, 131, 138–139

Contingency funds, 195, 199, 243, 245–246. *See also* Rainy-day funds

Continuing resolution, 79, 82, 94, 96, 231

Continuing services, 169

Contracting out, 177–179, 290

Contracts

failures of, 178

no-bid, 178

noncompetitive, 24

for services, 177–179

Control, pattern of dynamics of, 249–250

"Controllables," 208

Cooper, Jim (D-Tenn.), 270–272

Corruption, 289

Cost-effectiveness and budget programs, 150–152

Cost shifting, 138

Council (city), and budgets, 93–94, 95, 140, 224

Council-manager government, 100, 131, 141–143

Courts, role of, 16–17, 48

Cox, Christopher (R-Calif.), 79–80

Cruise missiles, 174

"Current services" estimate, 80

Dade County, Fla., 277–278

Dauster, Bill, 83–85, 94

Dayton, Ohio, tax case history in, 38, 41, 43, 44

Decision clusters. *See also specific types*

interaction between, 282–286

interruptibility and, 30, 282, 300

openness and secrecy and, 287

real-time budgeting and, 281–285

state and local governments and, 298

types, 281

Decision making

avenues for research, 289–290, 297–299

balance cluster and, 32, 281

budgetary, 23–24, 30–36, 33*f*, 281–301

budget formats and, 86–88

common themes, 286–294

comparison of decision-making streams, 285–286

constraints on, 77–78, 86

dynamics of budgeting over time, 291–294

expenditures and, 145–186

information and, 86, 97, 282, 284

openness vs. secrecy, 287–291, 295

as process, figure, 33*f*

public scrutiny of, 23–24

raising taxes and, 40–43

reconceptualizing reform, 294–297

Defense and Homeland Security Appropriations Bill (2005), 115

Defense Department

abuse and controls at, 253–254, 279

black budget of, 173–177, 184

contracts, 24

EDA and, 158

increasing priority of projects and, 147–148

mobilizing support for programs of, 154

reprogramming and, 244–245, 250–254

secrecy and, 291

supplemental appropriations and, 236

2005 budget and, 116–117

Deferrals, 233, 238–240, 248, 255

Deficits. *See also* Budget balancing; Recessions

ad hoc budgeting and, 117

budget process and, 119–120

budget reform and, 293

causes of, 187–189, 194–195

cities and, 223–224

controls in 1986 & 1990, 110–113

cuts in response to, 198–199

eliminating deficits, 197–198

increase in, 53, 57

obscuring, 216–217, 224, 225, 227, 289–290

size of, 199–203, 201*t*

tax cuts and, 118

Deficit spending, 199, 200, 234

DeKalb, Ill.

case history of, 7–12

cost-effective programs in, 151–152

Democratic Party, and tax breaks, 54, 58, 61, 72

Detroit, Mich., 95

Dingell, John (D-Mich.), 174

Direct service delivery, 222

Discretion, abuse, control cycle, 249–263, 291

local level, 259–261

national level, 250–257

state level, 257–259

District of Columbia, 63, 65, 67*t*

Domenici, Pete (R-N.M.), 84

Drivers' licenses, mandated improvements to, 209

Dynamic scoring, 118

Earmarks and earmarking, 43–44

agencies and, 254–255

in Alabama, 39–40, 43

budget priorities and, 163–164

disadvantages of, 44

legislatively mandated, 40

local budgets and, 133

revenue politics and, 74

tax increases and, 40

Economic development
  as acceptable goal, 149, 173
  land writedowns and, 174
  positive spillovers, 166
  recapture of outlays and, 152
Economic Development Administration (EDA), 151, 158
Education. *See* Schools
Elected officials' budget strategies, 159–180
Electoral districts, redrawing, 123
Employment, federal, 27–28
Entitlements, 97–98
  attempts to eliminate, 80–81
  choosing program structures to reduce competition and, 159–160
  deficit and, 110, 111, 112
  defined, 77, 80
  local budgets and, 97–98
  from 1930s to 1970s, 109
  pay-as-you-go rules and, 81
  state budgets and, 97, 214
Environment
  budget balancing and, 196
  budget processes and, 33–35
  factors in openness, 23–25, 231
  revenue and, 38, 283
  secrecy in budgeting and, 291
  spending priorities and, 180–183
  tax increases and, 38, 42, 43, 45
Environmental Protection Agency (EPA), 250
Estes, Billie Sol, 263–264
Evergreen Freedom Foundation, 61–62
Executive Budget Office, 14
Executive budgets
  balancing, 114
  budget process and, 88, 103, 106, 140, 141
  federal level, 107, 108–109, 114, 116
  local government level, 141
  New York (state), 104
  state level, 99–100, 120, 123, 124–126, 128
Executive Office of the President, 21, 109, 270

Executive
  budget implementation and, 232
  budget process and, 83–84
  discretion of, 27–28
  legislative vs., 76, 88–89, 92, 93–96, 106–107, 293–296
  president, 94
  veto power of, 88, 89, 93–95
Expenditure cluster, 31–32, 281, 293
Expenditures, 145–186, 285–286
  accountability and acceptability, 183–184
  balancing benefits to varied groups and, 166–168
  borrowing for present expenditures and, 165
  broadening base of support, 165–168
  climbing priority list for, 147–150
  delay of, 216
  demand-driven, 195
  earmarking and, 163–164
  environment and spending priorities, 180–183
  formula allocations and, 164
  geographic dispersion, 166
  locking in priorities, 163–165, 185–186, 199, 293
  mobilizing support for, 152–155
  obfuscation, invisible decision making, and secrecy, 168–180, 184, 289–290, 295
  positive spillovers, 166
  prior rankings and, 164
  referendums and constitutional amendments and, 164–165
  revenue-driven, 194–195
  strategies of agency heads or program directors, 147–159
  top-down strategies, 159–180
Expense reports of legislators, 175, 177
Export-Import Bank, 149, 180

Farm subsidies, 149–150, 153–154, 167–168, 171, 186

FBI (Federal Bureau of Investigation), 269
FDA (Food and Drug Administration), 267
Federal Accounting Standards, 162
Federal-Aid Highway Act of 1956, 191
Federal Bureau of Investigation (FBI), 269
Federal credit reform, 179
Federal Express, 83
Federal Reserve System, 180
Federal trust funds, 162
Florida
  budget process in, 124, 126–131
  homestead exemptions in, 66, 67t
  inspectors general and, 277–278
  school referendum in, 164–165
  unfunded mandates in, 138–139
Food and Drug Administration (FDA), 267
Food stamps, 153, 154
Forest Service (federal), 241–242
Formula allocations and budget process, 164
Fragmentation, in public budgeting, 107, 109, 282, 290
Fund structure, 25
Furlough, 256
Future research, 289–290, 297–299

"Game the system," 111, 207
General Accounting Office (GAO), 173, 242, 253, 255, 256, 265. *See also* Government Accountability Office (GAO)
Georgia, budget process in, 98, 99
Glenn, John (D-Ohio), 266–267, 268
Glickman, Dan (D-Kan.), 168
GNP (Gross national product), 200
Gosling, James, 90
Government. *See also specific types*
  budget variations and, 93–100

forms of, 140–143
size and role of, 192–193, 202
special-purpose, 156–157
Government Accountability Office (GAO), 151, 244, 270, 280
Governmental Affairs Committee (Senate), 268
Governmental budgeting, 6–7, 199. *See also* Public budgeting
Government Performance and Results Act of 1993 (GPRA), 20, 21–23, 56–57
Government Reform Committee, 272–273
Governors
　budget cuts and, 214, 218
　role in state budgets, 120–131
　veto power of. *See* Veto power
GPRA. *See* Government Performance and Results Act of 1993
Graham, Bob, 126
Gramm-Rudman-Hollings
　constitutionality of, 284
　as constraint on budget process, 77–78, 113
　deficit and, 107, 111–112, 143, 206–208, 209, 219, 284
　defining balance and, 284
　exemption of programs from cuts by, 164
　taking items off-budget and, 180
　unfair outcome of cuts and, 292
Grants, 151–152, 194
Great Depression
　and cost controls, 133
　debt in Massachusetts and, 261
　deficit spending in, 200
　and entitlements, 109
　and property taxes, 135
　and tax increases in states, 135–136
Gross national product (GNP), 200

Halliburton, 24
"Handcuffing," 250, 252
Health, Education, and Welfare, Department of, 264

Health and Human Services, Department of, 268, 270
Health insurance, tax break on, 56
Health Planning Program, 16
Hearings, public, 136
Help America Vote Act of 2002, 209
Highway exit, paying for, 172–173
Highway Trust Fund, 161, 190, 191, 207, 293
Holdbacks, 243, 245
Home healthcare bill, 167
Homeland Security, Department of, 263, 269, 288
Homeland Security Inspector General, 263, 288
Home rule, 131
Homestead exemption, state losses from, 65–67, 66t, 67t
Hotel tax, 45
Housing and Urban Development, Department of (HUD), 155
Housing for the Elderly and Handicapped, 180
HUD (Housing and Urban Development, Department of), 155
Hutchinson, Kay Bailey (R-Texas), 83–84

Idaho, rescission in, 237–238
IDEA (Individuals with Disabilities Education Act), 209
Ideologies, and budget balancing, 190, 192
IGs. *See* Inspector General system
Illinois
　cash-flow accounting and, 216–217
　changes in environment and change in revenue in, 283
　creating of buffers in, 218
　earmarking in, 44
　income taxes in, 44
　line-item veto use in, 90, 91
　pensions in, 162
　rescission in, 238
　special purpose government in, 156
　state budgeting in, 120
　strong governorship in, 296

tax breaks in, 59–60, 62–63, 67, 67t
　trust fund use in, 162
Immigration and Naturalization Service, 195
Immigration and Naturalization Service v. Chadha (1974), 239, 255
Implementation cluster, 281, 283
Impoundments, 255, 259, 261
Income taxes, 44, 46–47, 48, 51, 53, 72. *See also* Tax breaks
Incrementalism, 182
Incrementalist bargaining, 28
Indiana, budget process in, 135–136
Indian Affairs, Bureau of, 241
Indian Trust Funds, 162
Individuals, in budget process, 6, 7, 16
Individuals with Disabilities Education Act (IDEA), 209
Industrial development revenue bonds, 70
Industry, state subsidies for, 49–50, 60, 69
Inflation, influence of, 80, 82, 86, 169
Infrastructure, revenues for, 50, 51, 55
Inspector General Act of 1978, 264
Inspector General system, 263–273, 280, 291, 295
Interest groups
　budgets and, 88, 89, 92, 101
　coalitions in, 16, 28–29, 32, 74
　decision making and, 285–286
　deficits and, 190
　determinism of, 28
　domination of budgets and, 185, 186
　"iron triangle" and, 154–155
　power levels and, 17
　raising taxes and, 40
　role of, 15–16
　state budgets and, 136
Interfund transfers, 233, 247, 248
Intergovernmental grant structure, 23, 34–35
Intergovernmental revenue system, 194–195. *See also* Grants

Interior Subcommittee of Appropriations Committee (Senate), 241–242
Internal service programs, 198
Interruptibility, 282, 284, 292, 297, 300
Interstate Highway System, 161, 167
Invisible decision making and secret budgets, 173–180, 184
Iowa, tax incentives in, 64–65
Iraq, war in
  costs of, 19, 188
  deficit and, 209
  noncompetitive contracts, auditing of, 24
  secrecy and, 291
  supplemental appropriations and, 107, 116, 236, 248
"Iron triangles," 154–155

Johnson, Clay, 270–272
Joyce, Phil, 114
Judiciary Committees, 254–255
Justice, Department of, 254–255, 266–268, 269

Kassenbaum, Nancy (R-Kan.), 207
Kellogg, Brown, and Root, 24
Keynesian theory, 200, 206
Kosiak, Steven, 174–175
Krog, James, 129–130
Kusserow, Richard P., 267

Labor, Department of, 266
Lamm, Richard, 219
Land Management, Bureau of, 241
Land writedown, 174
Lauth, Thomas, 90
Legislatures and legislators
  budget offices of, 123–124
  budget process and, 104–106
  discretion, abuse, control cycle and, 250–259
  executive budget powers vs., 76, 88–89, 92–96, 106–107, 293–296
  expense reports of, 175, 177
  motivation of, 14–15
  professional staff and, 123–124
  role of, 14–15, 120–131

state government and, 120–131
Levitas, Elliot (D-Ga.), 268
LGAC (Local Government Assistance Corporation), 172
Line-item budget, 86, 87–88, 125, 133
Line-item veto
  governors, 90–91, 95–96, 98–99, 100, 105, 123, 125, 128, 129
  mayors, 142
  president, 108, 109, 237
Line-Item Veto Act of 1996, 237
Loan guarantees, 97, 179–180
Loans from federal government, 97, 179–180, 264
Lobbying by interest groups, 16, 155
Local government
  budget balancing, 199, 219–223
  budget process, 131–143
  contingency funds, 243
  deficits, size of, 199–200
  deficit spending, 199
  discretion, abuse, control cycle, 259–263
  forms of government, 140–143
  inspectors general and, 273, 277–278
  off-budget process, 180
  relationship with state government, 132–140, 194–195, 218, 219–223, 294–295
  tax breaks and, 290
Local Government Assistance Corporation (LGAC), 172
Local Mandates Office (Massachusetts), 137
"Lock box" provisions, 81–82, 86
Long-term health care benefits, 167
"Look back" feature of Gramm-Rudman, 112
Lump-sum budgeting, 163

MAC (Municipal Assistance Corporation), 172
Macrobudgeting, 33–36, 33f, 298
Macropolitics, 78–85
Mandates, 158
  Budget Enforcement Act and, 160

intergovernmental system and, 23
minimizing competition and, 157
symbolic politics and, 19
unfunded. *See* Unfunded mandates
Mandates Monitor, 209
Maryland, budget process in, 120, 121–122
Massachusetts
  debt during Great Depression, 261
  overcontrol of cities and, 260–261
  schools in, 137, 138–139
  tax expenditures in, 59
  unfunded mandates in, 137–139
Matsui, Robert T. (D-Calif.), 72
Mayor-council form of government, 100, 141–142
Mayors
  abandonment of council-manager government and, 142
  budget process and, 132
  strong mayor form of government, 141
  veto power, 93–94, 95, 141, 142
McCallum, Scott, 210–211
McDaniel, Paul, 56
Medicaid, 268
Medicare, 81, 264, 268
"Member initiative grants," 91
Mentally ill and mentally handicapped patients, deinstitutionalization of, 17
Michigan
  circuit breaker in, 66
  local government funding in, 219
  tax breaks in, 50, 60
Microbudgeting, 33–36, 33f, 298
Micropolitics, 78–85
Mid-year budgets, 255
Military procurement, 279
Mills, Wilbur (D-Ark.), 41
MILSTAR, 174
Montgomery County, Ohio, 70
Moody's, 226
Municipal Assistance Corporation (MAC), 172
Municipal bonds, 55–56, 171–172

Municipal budget laws, 131, 133
Muskie, Edmund (D-Maine), 250, 252
Must-pass legislation, 79

NASA, 270
National Council of State Legislatures (NCSL), 124, 209, 215–216
National Performance Review (NPR), 242, 264, 280
National Reconnaissance Office, 173, 254
National Security Agency, 173
National Taxpayers Union, 204
NCSL. *See* National Council of State Legislatures
Nebraska, homestead exemption in, 66, 67*t*
Neutrality, states' lack of, 134–136
Nevada
    Legislative Council Bureau, 125
    state budget process in, 125
New Jersey, and inspectors general, 273, 277
New York (state), 67, 68
    balanced budget and, 189
    bonds for New York City, 171–172
    budget process in, 120, 289
    budget reform in, 104–106
    executive budget in, 104
    line-item veto use in, 105
    openness and, 288
New York City
    board of estimates in, 141
    bonds for, 171–172
    tax breaks in, 68
New York Times, 202–203
Nixon, Richard, 109, 255
No-bid contracts, 178
No Child Left Behind Act of 2001, 26–27
Noncompetitive contracts, 24
North Carolina, tax breaks in, 50
NPR. *See* National Performance Review
Nussle, Jim (R-Iowa), 117
Nussle-Cardin-Goss Budget Process Bill, 81–82

Oakland, Calif., form of government in, 142, 143
Obey, David (D-Wis.), 216

Obfuscation, invisible decision making, and secrecy, 168–180, 184, 289–290
"Off-budget"
    budget obfuscation and, 168
    Gramm-Rudman-Hollings and, 111
    purpose of, 180, 217
    Social Security and, 84, 188
    strategy of, 181
Office of Consumer Litigation (DOJ), 267
Office of Legal Counsel (DOJ), 266–268
Office of Management and Budget (OMB)
    agencies and, 118, 256
    budget process and, 14, 21, 23, 107
    inspectors general and, 270–272
    Reagan administration and, 200–201
    tax cuts and, 118
Office of Personnel Management (OPM), 22
Ohio, 70. *See also specific cities*
OMB. *See* Office of Management and Budget
Omnibus appropriation bill (2005), 107–108, 115–116
Omnibus legislation, 94, 96, 117, 119, 288
One-time revenues, 217
Open budget process, 92
Open rules, 40–43, 92
Operating budget, 151, 184
Operating expenses, 97
OPIC (Overseas Private Investment Corporation), 149
OPM (Office of Personnel Management), 22
Ordinance, budget, 95
Oregon
    local government budget law, 133–134, 219–220
    unfunded mandates, 219–220
Outcomes, of budget process, 193, 297
Outsiders, taxing, 45, 47
Overseas Private Investment Corporation (OPIC), 149

Packwood, Robert (R-Ore.), 72
PART process, 20
Pataki, George, 105

Patent and Trademark Office (PTO), 157
"Pay-as-you-go" provisions, 57–58, 81, 111–112, 208
Payer/spender separation in public budgeting, 17–23
Pay-go. *See* "Pay-as-you-go" provisions
Peck, Cheryl, 238
Pelosi, Nancy (D-Calif.), 116
Pennsylvania and balanced budget, 189
Pension trust funds, 161–163
Pérez, Arturo, 215–216
Performance budgeting. *See also* Government Performance and Results Act of 1993 (GPRA)
    accountability and, 20, 87
    defined, 86–88
    executive branch, 21
    state government, 98, 99
Persistence of state requirements, 132–134
Personalty, 49
Pew Research Center, 188
Policy control, violations of, 232–233
Political opponents, cuts to programs of, 198
Politics of adaptation, and budget execution, 230–248
Politics of balance. *See also* Budget balancing
    characteristics of, 286
    in cities, 223–228
    revenue estimation and, 218, 224, 229
Politics of choice. *See* Expenditures
Politics of deficits, 190, 192, 199, 200–209
Politics of expenditures, 145–186
Politics of implementation, 286. *See also* Budget implementation
Politics of process
    characteristics of public budgeting and, 28–29, 75–101, 285
    designing process to achieve policy and political goals, 85–93
    macro and micro politics, 78–85

variation between federal, state, and local governments, 93–100
Politics of protection, 46–71, 292
Politics of reform, 71–73
Politics of taxation, 74
Pork projects
earmarking and, 163–164
executives vs. legislators on, 107
legislators and, 14–15, 116
limitation of, 54
raising caps on discretionary spending and, 79
single-executive reforms and, 141
targeting, 154
veto power and, 90, 91, 237
Positive spillovers, 166, 167
Postal Service, 180
Power, levels of, 17
Predictability of tax increase, 45
President, 94. *See also specific administrations*
line-item veto, 108, 109, 237
veto power, 108, 109, 111
Priorities and public budgeting, 1
Prior rankings and budget process, 164
Prison overcrowding, 16–17
Process cluster, 31
Professional accreditation model and mandating, 157, 159
Professionalism, 13
Professional staff and legislatures, 123–124
Program budget, 86, 87–88
Program loyalty, 13
Progressive Era, 133, 141
Property taxes
abatement of, 70
choice of revenue and, 46, 47
constraints and, 77
Dayton, Ohio, case study, 41, 44
defining taxable wealth and, 48, 49
effect of increase in, 45
local budget process and, 135, 137
in Massachusetts, 137
private companies and, 61

schools and, 66–68, 70–71
tax breaks and, 65–67, 69
Proposition 21/2 (Massachusetts), 137
Proposition 13 (California), 59, 217, 220
PTO (Patent and Trademark Office), 157
Public budgeting, 1–36
accountability in, 2, 6, 19–20, 23
actors in, 12–17
advance planning of, 7
balancing and borrowing, 4–5
budget process and, 3–6, 76–78
characteristics of, 6–7, 76–78, 199, 281–282
choices in, 3–4
comparison with private budgets, 6–12
constraints in, 7, 8–9, 12, 25–28
decision-making process and, 5–6
environment and, 23–25
meaning of politics in, 28–29
payer/decider and, 17–23, 196–200
payer/spender separation and, 17–23
priorities in, 1
public scrutiny of, 19, 23–24
reforms in, 294–297
taxation and, 2, 7
Public enterprises, 160–161
Public hearings, 136
Public services
accreditation model and, 157, 159
balancing benefits of, 166–168, 186
cities balancing budgets and, 223–228
costs and, 150–152
cuts and, 198
geographic dispersion of, 166
highway exit, paying for, 172–173
pairing interests in, 154
positive spillovers and, 166, 167
structures for delivering, 156–157

Puerto Rico, line-item veto use in, 123

Rainy-day funds, 213, 215, 218–219
Reagan administration
budget deficits in, 110
campaign to reduce waste, fraud, and abuse and, 278–279
deferrals and, 239, 255
deficits and, 200, 202–203
increased defense spending and, 148, 173
inspectors general and, 265–266
tax reform and, 71–73
top-down budgeting and, 14
Real-time budgeting, 281–285
Realty, 49. *See also* Property taxes
Recessions
cities and, 223
deficits and, 188, 193, 195–196, 199, 200, 202, 207, 222, 223
recovery from, 204–205
spending during, 200
states and, 39, 209, 210, 213–219, 238
tax breaks and, 51, 59, 65
Reciprocity, norm of, 14
Reconciliation bill, 84, 94, 96
Redacting of audit reports, 24
Referendums and constitutional amendments, 164–165
Reform, reconceptualizing, 294–297
Reformism, 28
Regan, Donald, 203
Reischauer, Robert, 204
Reprogramming, 233–234, 240–245, 247, 248, 250–254, 296
Republican Party
as majority, 205
tax breaks of, 54, 72
in Wisconsin, 210–213
Rescissions, 233, 234, 235t, 236–238, 248, 255–256
Research, avenues for, 297–299
Resources, taxing, 45, 51, 57
Revenue
choices of, 46–48
one-time, 217
as sensitive to environment, 23–24, 38, 182–183

unexpected losses, 194
Revenue cluster, 30–31, 281, 282
Revenue politics, 37–74
    characteristics of, 38, 74, 285
    choices of revenue and, 46–48
    decision-making process and, 40–43
    politics of protection and, 46–71
    politics of reform and, 71–73
    raising taxes, 38–46
Richmond, Va., 142
Rose, Charles (D-N.C.), 167–168
Rostenkowski, Dan (D-Ill.), 42, 203
Roth, William (R-Del.), 84

Salary absorption, 256
Salary increases, federal level, 256–257
Sales Tax Asset Receivable Corp. (STARC), 172
Sales taxes, 45, 46, 47, 48, 284
San Diego, Calif., 142
Schick, Allen, 113, 117
Schools. *See also specific states*
    federally mandated programs for, 26–27
    property taxes and, 66–68, 70–71
    referendums and constitutional amendments and, 164–165
    tax breaks, effect on, 51
Scoring rules, 117, 118–119
Secrecy in budget, 20, 107–108, 173–180, 184, 287–291, 295
Segmentation, need for, 30
Senate. *See also specific committees*
    money bills and, 42
    tax breaks and, 58, 72–73
Senate Finance Committee, 72–73
Separation of payer and decider, 17–23, 196–200
Sequesters, 111, 207, 208
Shays, Christopher (R-Conn.), 272
Slow-growing economy and budget process, 117
Small Intercontinental Ballistic Missile program, 253–254

Smith, Nick (R-Mich.), 171
Social Security
    balanced budget and, 204, 205
    earmarking of taxes and, 44
    off-budget savings of, 84, 188
    private accounts for, 119, 161, 165
    surplus, 111, 188
    trust fund, 161, 165
Social Security Trust Fund, 161
Social Services Block Grant, 81
Soviet Union and Cold War, 148
Speaker's Task Force on Budget Reform (House), 79–81
Special-purpose governments, 156–157
Spending caps, 57–58, 86, 112, 180
Spending decisions. *See* Expenditures
Spending targets, 114
St. Louis, Mo., 165
St. Paul, Minn., calculating budget base in, 170
Staff, professional, and legislatures, 123–124
STARC (Sales Tax Asset Receivable Corp.), 172
State Criminal Alien Assistance Program, 209
State governments. *See also specific states*
    budget balancing, 199, 209–223
    budget cuts, 214–215, 218
    budget gimmicks, 215–216
    budget process, 120–131
    contingency funds, 243
    creating buffers, 217–219
    deficits in, 197–200, 209–223
    deficit spending and, 199
    democratic controls, 136–140
    discretion, abuse, control cycle, 257–259
    inspectors general and, 273–279, 274–276t, 280
    lack of neutrality, 134–136
    off-budget process and, 180
    pensions funds and, 161–163, 215
    persistence of requirements and, 132–134

recessions, 39, 209, 210, 213–219, 222, 223
    relationship with local government, 132–140, 194–195, 218, 219–223, 294–295
    rescission and, 237–238
    tax breaks, 290
    tax increases, 215–216
    unfunded mandates, 209, 213
Stealth bomber, 174, 176–177
Stenholm proposal, 204
Stevens, Ted (R-Alaska), 115
Stockman, David, 200, 202–203
Strategic Petroleum Reserve program, 180
Strong mayor form of government, 141
Student loans, 264
Subcommittee on Budget Process Reform (House), 79
Subcommittee on Government Efficiency and Financial Management (House), 272
Subcommittee on Oversight and Investigations (House), 174
Subcommittee on Tobacco and Peanuts (Agriculture), 167
Subsidies
    agricultural, 149–150, 153–154, 167–168, 171, 186
    secret, 179–180
Summit bargaining, 107
Supplemental appropriations, 234–237, 235t, 236t
    Defense Department and, 251–252
    deferrals and, 239
    department requests for, 229
    national level contingencies and, 243
    reprogramming and, 240
    use of, 248
    war spending and, 116, 234, 236, 248
Supplemental Security Income/State Supplemental Income, 217
Supreme Court
    on deferral requests, 239–240
    on one-house votes, 255

one-man, one-vote mandate of, 123
Surpluses, budget, 113, 189
Symbolic outputs, programs with, 149
Symbolic politics, 18

TABOR. *See* Taxpayers' Bill of Rights
Target budgeting, 86, 87
Tariffs, 46, 47, 48
Task Force on Budget Reform (House), 79–81
Taxable wealth, 48–49
Taxation. *See also* Property taxes
   acceptability of, 46
   increasing. *See* Tax increases
   payroll taxes, 161
   protection from, 292
   public budgeting and, 2, 7
   reduction of, 292
   temporary, 45
Tax breaks, 49–71. *See also* Tax expenditures
   as corporate welfare, 54
   costs of, 292
   economic performance and, 291
   as entitlements, 98
   features of, 49–50
   federal level, 50, 51, 52–58, 52t, 53t
   growth in, 42
   impact of, on school districts, 51, 66–68
   local level, 50, 51, 68–71
   as policy tool, 55
   secrecy and, 290
   state level, 50, 51, 58–67, 222
Tax collection, accelerating, 216
Tax cuts, 58, 114, 115, 118, 152, 209, 236
"Tax eaters," 18
Tax exceptions, 49, 71
Tax expenditures. *See also* specific states
   growth in, 42
   offsets of, 58, 113, 115, 152
   politics of choice and, 102–144
Tax holidays, 138
Tax increases, 38–46. *See also* specific types of taxes
   acceptability of, 45, 46, 73

accountability and, 45
decision-making process for, 40–43
defining taxable wealth and, 48–49
distributing benefits from, 44–45
earmarking, 43–44
environment and, 38, 42, 43, 45
politically weak and, 45–46
predictability of, 45
regional concerns and, 48
state governments and, 215–216
strategies for, 43–46
types of, 46–48
Tax incremental financing, 51, 62–63, 70
Tax increment districts, 283
Tax Increment Financing District (Illinois), 10
Taxpayers' Bill of Rights (TABOR), 8–9, 212, 215
Temporary taxes, 45
Tennessee, tax breaks in, 60, 68, 69, 70
Tennessee Valley Authority (TVA), 161
Terrorist attacks
   antiterrorist activities and, 234–235
   budget priorities and, 150
   spending for national defense and, 289
   supplemental appropriations and, 247
Texas
   budget process, 95, 98, 99
   homestead exemptions, 66, 67t
   Legislative Budget Board, 98, 99
   line-item veto use, 95, 99
   schools, 70
   tax expenditures, 59, 70
Thompson, Jim, 296
Tobacco settlement, 215
Top-down budgeting, 14, 89, 92, 96, 101, 159–180
Tradeoffs, 104, 157, 159, 160, 185
Transparency in budgeting, 178, 183, 184. *See also* Accountability
Treasury, U.S., 72, 74
Trust funds, 161–163, 185–186

TVA (Tennessee Valley Authority), 161

Underestimating costs of project, 152
Unemployment
   budget change and, 231
   deficits and, 188, 193, 194, 195–196
   target levels of, 286
   taxes and, 50, 60
Unfunded mandates, 26, 136–140, 209, 213, 219–220, 222
Unfunded Mandates Act of 1995, 209, 213
Universities, 157
U.S. Marshall Service, 269
User fees, 18, 46, 47–48, 152

Veneman, Ann, 153
Veto power
   executives, 88, 89, 93
   governors, 19, 90–91, 94–96, 98–99, 100, 105, 120, 121, 123, 125, 128, 129
   mayor, 93–94, 95, 141, 142
   nullification of Congress's, 239–240, 255
   president, 108, 109, 111
   sharing of executive and legislative budget power, 106
Vietnam War
   deficits and, 200
   DOD reprogramming and, 251–254
   spending priorities and, 109
Vilsack, Tom, 64

Wage taxes, 46
War, cost of, 236, 289. *See also* specific wars
Washington (state)
   homestead exemptions of, 66, 67t
   local government funding in, 219–220
   tax breaks in, 59, 61–62, 63
Waste, fraud, and abuse control, 262–279, 291
Waxman, Henry (D-Calif.), 24
Ways and Means Committee (House), 41–43, 72–73, 203
Weidenbaum, Murray, 203

WIC. *See* Women, Infants, and
  Children (WIC) program
Wider, Douglas, 142
Wisconsin
  balanced budget, 219
  budget processes, 90
  contract controversies, 178
  deficits, 210–213, 216

line-item veto use, 90
  tax breaks, 49–50, 73
Wisconsin Legislative Refer-
  ence Bureau, 222
Women, Infants, and Children
  (WIC) program, 153, 154
Workforce Restructuring Act
  of 1997, 27–28

World War I, 108, 133
World War II, 109

Year-end balance, 243,
  246

Zero-based budgeting, 86, 87,
  88